PALGRAVE STUDIES IN THEATRE AND PERFORMANCE HI
theatre/performance scholarship currently available, a
include a wide range of topics, from the more traditi
recent years have helped broaden the understanding
include (from variety forms as diverse as the circus and burlesque to street buskers, stage magic, and musical theatre, among many others). Although historical, critical, or analytical studies are of special interest, more theoretical projects, if not the dominant thrust of a study, but utilized as important underpinning or as a historiographical or analytical method of exploration, are also of interest. Textual studies of drama or other types of less traditional performance texts are also germane to the series if placed in their cultural, historical, social, or political and economic context. There is no geographical focus for this series and works of excellence of a diverse and international nature, including comparative studies, are sought.

The editor of the series is Don B. Wilmeth (EMERITUS, Brown University), Ph.D., University of Illinois, who brings to the series over a dozen years as editor of a book series on American theatre and drama, in addition to his own extensive experience as an editor of books and journals. He is the author of several award-winning books and has received numerous career achievement awards, including one for sustained excellence in editing from the Association for Theatre in Higher Education.

Also in the series:

Theatre, Performance, and the Historical Avant-garde

Günter Berghaus

First published in hardcover in 2005 by PALGRAVE MACMILLAN®
in the United States – a division of St. Martin's Press LLC, 175 Fifth Avenue,
New York, NY 10010.

Where this book is distributed in the UK, Europe and the rest of the world,
this is by Palgrave Macmillan, a division of Macmillan Publishers Limited,
registered in England, company number 785998, of Houndmills, Basingstoke,
Hampshire RG21 6XS.

Palgrave Macmillan is the global academic imprint of the above companies
and has companies and representatives throughout the world.

Palgrave® and Macmillan® are registered trademarks in the United States,
the United Kingdom, Europe and other countries.

ISBN: 978–0–230–61752–0

Library of Congress Cataloging-in-Publication Data

Berghaus, Günter, 1953–
    Theatre, performance, and the historical avant-garde / Günter Berghaus.
        p. cm.—(Palgrave studies in theatre and performance history)
    Includes bibliographical references and index.
    ISBN 1–4039–6955–8 (alk. paper)
        1. Experimental theater. 2. Avant-garde (Aesthetics) I. Title. II. Series.

PN2193.E86B475 2005
792.02′9—dc22   2005054609

A catalogue record for this book is available from the British Library.

Design by Newgen Imaging Systems (P) Ltd., Chennai, India.

First PALGRAVE MACMILLAN paperback edition: January 2010

10 9 8 7 6 5 4 3 2 1

Printed in the United States of America.

For Andreas

Contents ❧

List of Illustrations ·❧·

FIGURES

COVER: Lothar Schreyer, *Mann*, photograph of production in Düsseldorf, Kunstsammlung Nordrhein-Westfalen, 1986. Courtesy of Kunstsammlung NRW.

TABLES

TEXT BOXES

CHRONOLOGIES

Preface ❧

This study is largely the result of a lecture cycle, which I delivered at the University of Bristol in alternating years between 1989 and 1999. The recurrence of the series afforded me the opportunity to undertake further research and to teach related topics in the form of seminars and performance projects. The response I received from my students stimulated further investigations and, as a result, the form and content of my lectures changed significantly over the years. A first draft of this manuscript was completed in 2000 and served as a basis for a further set of lectures and seminars given at Brown University in Providence/RI in 2001–2002, which then developed into the form presented in this volume.

When, in 1988, I agreed to offer a course on the historical avant-garde in performance, I did not envisage my lectures to be disseminated in printed form. But when preparing reading lists for my students, I soon became aware that there was a distinct shortage of general, introductory texts on the subject. This lack stood in marked contrast to the wealth of publications dedicated to the avant-garde in the fine arts, to various Modernist schools, and their key representatives. The framing discourses of history, theory, and criticism in twentieth-century art have also been amply documented, but stage events and performative processes were, on the whole, only given scant consideration, presumably because they demand methodological tools that do not commonly form part of an art or a literary historian's training. Scholars from the discipline of theatre studies should, of course, be more attuned to these phenomena, but they, for the most part, have also been reluctant to extend their radius of attention to non-text-based performances of an experimental kind.

Initially, I felt inclined to offer in this volume a survey of all "major" movements of the historical avant-garde and to present a broad range of performances that exemplified their aesthetic aims. However, I soon came to realize that even generally recognized landmark performances could pose serious problems, as the documentary basis for assessing their aesthetic qualities was not always propitious. And when dealing with groundbreaking performances of artists, who never made it into the top ranks of the "Pioneers of Modernism" league, one is confronted with an even more arduous task. It has been my endeavor to base my investigation on as much documentary evidence as can reasonably be recovered from archives, libraries, museums, and private collections. These included, in the first instance, papers left behind by artists, such as texts, scores, scenarios, designs, essays, interviews, and so on. Needless to say, records of this kind require careful evaluation, as they tend to be highly selective and determined by the interests of the person who produces (or preserves) them, as well as by the characteristics and restrictions of the medium in which they were recorded. I have therefore complemented them with descriptions and interpretations published by eye-witnesses of the performances (audience members and critics) in the form of memoirs, letters, and reviews. A detailed, comparative analysis of these materials usually produced valuable insights into the performances, their shape, format, and the intentions behind them.

As theatre performances are not static objects but a web of interactions between stage and auditorium, they are subject to influences that needed to be considered in my analysis. Avant-garde performances aim to provoke personal responses rather than linear or uniform "readings," and every viewer experiences a performance differently. Spectators are usually active participants and coproducers of a performance; they arrive at the event with partial tastes and inclinations and react to the stage events according to these idiosyncratic predispositions. Many of the performances dealt with in this study were extremely challenging and could go far beyond the level of acceptance that audiences were able or willing to muster. This, of course, is the inherent obligation of the avant-garde. For an assessment of whether, how, and to what degree the artistic purpose of a performance had been fulfilled, these reactions needed to be carefully evaluated.

Similarly, scholars select their object of analysis according to preestablished attitudes and examine them in line with their socialization, ideological viewpoints, professional training, the established narratives in their academic discipline, and so on. Even if it had been my aim to produce an objective evaluation of a performance, I would have been unable to eliminate the factors of subjective receptiveness and personal appreciation. In fact, both have their rôle to play in a meaningful analysis of a performance event. For a theatre historian to describe and analyze a performance, the event has to come alive on his or her interior screen as a relived performance. This subjective experience will then have to be combined with objective analytical methods of evaluation, so that in the end a dynamic, evocative, and engaging study may result.

The issues noted above make it a difficult, if not unattainable task, to construct an "authoritative" account of the historical avant-garde in performance. In a complex terrain that is notoriously difficult to survey, I have chosen trends and events that were symptomatic of a given school or movement, stimulated discussions among contemporaries, and exercised considerable influence on later generations. The main focus of my investigations has always been directed toward stage events and the contribution made toward their success by actors, directors, designers, composers, and writers. Given the avant-garde's opposition to cultural institutions designed to purvey conventional artifacts and commodities, it is not astonishing that a large number of performances took place outside playhouses. Theatre as a social institution was usually shunned by avant-garde artists seeking to revolutionize the performance medium. This, of course, is not meant to say that theatre remained unaffected by avant-garde practices. Especially in the period of the historical avant-garde there existed a considerable overlap between the two. But the key rôle played by painters, poets, musicians, and the like in these performances shifted the emphasis away from conventional theatre practice toward alternative forms of production and presentation. Only in exceptional circumstances were the two worlds able, or willing, to enter into a productive relationship with each other.

It is well known that some of the great theatre practitioners of the time took an active interest in the avant-garde and learned some valuable lessons from the performances they were able to witness. For this reason, many avant-garde devices and techniques spread beyond the narrow circle of experimental artists and eventually entered the domain of modern theatre. Since all significant stage reformers have featured prominently in twentieth-century theatre historiography, I have chosen to omit most of these well-known figures from my discussion, even though in some respect they would have been relevant to this study. I have also excluded avant-garde drama not intended for stage performance. Although such works operate with notions of performativity and can therefore be considered performative texts (a kind of "theatre of the printed word"[1]), they consciously and often effectively resist realization on stage and should therefore be categorized as experimental literature rather than theatre (e.g., Gertrude Stein's *Saints and Singing*, Artaud's *Jet de Sang*, Raymond Roussel's *Poussière de soleils*, Wyndham Lewis's *Enemy of the Stars*).[2]

Readers of some early drafts of this volume felt that I was giving theatre history rather short shrift. They suggested that I reduce the art-historical introductions and instead make more detailed references to the drama and theatre of the period. In the end, I did not follow their advice as, in my view, the artists dealt with in this volume desired to overcome the limitations of theatre as a social institution and therefore they teamed up with painters, sculptors, or musicians, who shared their concerns. It was out of this collaboration that a genuine avant-garde approach to the performance medium arose, which went far beyond the established parameters of theatrical production, fostered the growth of a new aesthetics in the performing arts, and left a lasting mark on twentieth-century culture.

Throughout this book, I have attempted to recreate in the reader's mind a vivid picture of stage events as they were presented to their audiences at the time. In my opinion, too many writings on the avant-garde approach their subject from a theoretical angle rather than from the viewpoint of the spectator. All too often, the visceral experience of a live event gets submerged in the intellectual posturing of a critic, and creative works assume the status of a footnote to an artist's theoretical position. Of course, audiences take an interest in the creative aspirations of an artist and the aesthetic intentions behind a performance. But in the end, their appreciation of the work presented to them will be rooted in a personal response to the sensual and emotive force of the events on stage, rather than an essay or manifesto printed in the program.

The structure of this volume adheres to a conventional schema of art movements active in the early-twentieth century. This classification is used for convenience's sake only, as the various Modernist schools overlapped and influenced each other to a considerable degree.[3] Readers may miss chapters on Cubism and Surrealism, which indeed I had originally planned to incorporate into this publication. However, during the ten years of collecting material for this study, my files on Expressionism, Futurism, Constructivism, and Dadaism grew bigger and bigger, whereas little material related to an avant-garde performance practice in the Cubist or Surrealist movement could be found. Certainly, Picasso's *Parade* or Leger's *Création du Monde* were important expressions of the avant-garde spirit in the theatre, but whether they can be classified as Cubist remains doubtful. And in any case, they were works created for conventional playhouses and their frame of reference remained firmly attached to the institution of theatre. The same may be said about the poets and painters of the Surrealist movement, who possessed little knowledge and understanding of the practice of theatre and were therefore unable to develop valid alternatives to the established conventions of dramatic writing, design, acting, and performance. Antonin Artaud was the only member of the movement with actual stage experience: he had worked with Lugné-Poë, Dullin, and Pitoëff; he was an experienced actor in a variety of modern and classic rôles; he knew the conventions of contemporary theatre and was familiar with the aims of the stage reformers of his time. He was correspond to the main chapters of this book. Any studies included in the bibliography will be cited in the endnotes by short title only. When I quote or refer to a publication of a general nature not covered by the topic of this volume (e.g., B. R. Mitchell's *International Historical Statistics*, Lewis Mumford's *The City in History*, Max Planck's *Where is Science Going*), I give full bibliographic details the first time it is mentioned in the endnotes, and subsequently only by short title. These works will not be listed again in the bibliography.

Every reasonable effort has been undertaken to trace the owners of copyright materials in this book, but in some instances this has proven impossible. The author and publisher will be glad to receive information leading to more complete acknowledgments in subsequent printings of the book, and in the meantime extend their apologies for any omissions.

Acknowledgments ✆

This volume would have been unthinkable without the contributions made by students who engaged with me on performance projects and participated in the lively and extensive debates that formed part of my seminars and lectures at the University of Bristol in the years 1985 to 2000. The artistic talent and intellectual acumen of these collaborators enabled me to direct a number of key texts from the historical avant-garde, including, among others, Oskar Kokoschka's *Murder Hope of Women*, Lothar Schreyer's *Crucifixion*, some two dozen plays and mini-dramas from the Futurist repertoire, historical forms of literary cabaret (including those of Expressionists, Futurists, and Dadaists), Antonin Artaud's *Jet de Sang*, and Oskar Schlemmer's Bauhaus dances. These productions provided me with a research tool that was as significant as my investigations in libraries, archives, and museums, which accompanied the maturation of this study. The critical responses received from our audiences and, naturally, from the hundreds of students who participated in the lecture- and seminar discussions made me reexamine my views on the avant-garde, reflect on my attitude toward certain artists, and develop a deeper and keener appreciation of the productions discussed in this study.

Two grants from the British Academy and the Arts and Humanities Research Board of Great Britain enabled me to collect documents preserved in libraries and archives around the world. The writing of this manuscript has been made possible through a research leave granted by the University of Bristol and a generously low teaching load during my year as guest professor at Brown University in Providence, RI.

Ian Watson and Jean-Marie Pradier offered valuable support in the preparation phase of this project, and I received beneficial comments on my draft chapters from Ted Braun, George Brandt, Hubert van den Berg, John Emigh, Dietrich Scheunemann and, as usual, from my wife Kate Berghaus.

I also need to mention some book dealers and private collectors, such as Barbara Moore, Steve Clay, and Jan van der Donk in New York, who allowed me to copy material from their priceless possessions. In public institutions,

I found some extremely supportive librarians and archivists, who often provided an excellent service far beyond their call of duty. For this valuable support, I am particularly grateful to David Smith at the New York Public Library, Jennifer Tobias at the Museum of Modern Art Library, Jennifer Krivickas of the Widener Library of Harvard University, Mary Clare Altenhofen at the Fine Arts Library of Harvard University, Annette Fern at the Theatre Collection of Harvard University, Jean Rainwater at the John Hay Library, Nancy Jakubowski at the Music Library and Steven Thompson at the Rockefeller Library of Brown University, Vincent Giroud at Yale University Library, Ruth Dar at the Slade/Duveen Art Library of University College London, Giampiero Tintori at the Museo Teatrale all Scala, Alberto Rapomi Colombo at the Biblioteca Comunale in Milan, Alessandro Tinterri at the Biblioteca dell' Attore in Genoa, Manuela Sotti, Antonella Brogi, and Stefano Mecatti at the Centro di Documentazione e Ricerche sulle Avanguardie Storiche in Fiesole, Gabriella Belli at the Museo di Arte Moderna e Contemporanea di Trento e Rovereto, Gianfranco Maffini and Rossana Maggia at the Fondazione Russolo-Pratella, Jacqueline Munck at the Musée d'Art Moderne de la Ville de Paris, Angelika Ander at the Nationalbibliothek Wien, Barbara Wilk-Mincu at the Staatsbibliothek Berlin, Anita Kühnel at the Kunstbibliothek Berlin, Regine Herrmann and Renate Rätz at the Akademie der Künste in Berlin, Sabine Hartmann at the Bauhaus Archive in Berlin, Hedwig Müller, Monika Klocker, and Agnes Frey at the Theatermuseum Köln-Wahn, Elke Tausgraf at the Deutsche Bibliothek Frankfurt, and Galina Daruza at the State Central Theatrical Museum "A.A. Bakhrushin" in Moscow. Last, but not least, mention must be made of Walter Veltroni, who at the time of being in charge of the Italian Ministry of Cultural Heritage supported my research into Italian Futurism and facilitated my work in collections, which otherwise would have remained inaccessible to me.

A number of people and institutions supplied illustrative material and granted permission to have them reproduced in this volume. For this I should like to thank Michael Schreyer, Massimo Prampolini, Luce Marinetti, Mario Verdone, the Stadt- und Universitätsbibliothek Frankfurt/M., the Theaterwissenschaftliche Sammlung der Universität zu Köln, the Theatermuseum München, the Kunsthaus Zürich, the Bibliothèque Nationale in Paris, the Musée d'Art Moderne de la Ville de Paris, the University Library in Reading, and the Bakhrushin Theatre Museum in Moscow.

1. Introduction: The Genesis of Modernism and of the Avant-garde ᪥

MODERN, MODERNITY, MODERNISM

In our popular usage, "modern" is a term that designates a contemporary reality in contrast to the traditions of the past. A more precise philological examination reveals further layers of meaning: "modern" may function as a period designation (the present time as an age that is substantially different from the previous epoch), a factual term (describing new features not known before), and a value judgment (characterizing, e.g., the vagaries of fashion as opposed to the time-honored values of tradition; the great achievements, or deplorable degenerations, of the present time that stand in contrast to the attainments of the past). In "progressive" human societies every generation produces ideas, objects, or modes of operation that did not exist before. But for an innovation to be considered modern, it has to offer a substantial contrast to what was known before. What was modern yesterday becomes tradition today, and the cycle of eternal returns compels each generation into going beyond the achievements of their ancestors. However, what on the surface may look like a conflict known to the ancient Greeks just as much as it is to our contemporary society, reveals itself to be a far more complex matter in the history of ideas, where different concepts of time (cyclical, linear, or typological) and progress (abruptly, accumulative, dialectic, spiraling) have existed. Therefore, the term "modern" can characterize phenomena that went beyond the timeless battle of old versus new.

As the philologist and cultural historian E. R. Curtius informs us, the word "modernus" was originally coined in the early Middle Ages, as an adjective to *modo* (recently, now), analogous to *hodiernus/hodie* (of today) and as an antonym to *antiquus, vetus,* or *priscus* (old). It replaced the term *neotericus,* which Cicero had introduced when a need arose to distinguish the writers of his day from those of ancient Greece.[1] Thus, a period was considered "modern" when it contained a large number of innovative features that produced a substantial and far-reaching break with the past. For example, the Age of Charlemagne was considered a "saeculum modernum," and the twelfth-century Renaissance was experienced as "the dawn of a modern era." In the Italian Renaissance, it was hoped that the "rebirth" of antiquity would bring about a resplendent modern age following the long period of the Dark Ages. Thus the tripartite concept of Western history (Antiquity, Middle Ages, Modern Period) came into being, which still forms the basis of conventional periodization used today.

The Renaissance rang in the Early Modern period (1500–1789), which prepared the ground for the modern age through the opening of geographical horizons, the expansion of trade and commerce, the growth of towns, the foundation of an industrial economy, the scientific revolution, technological progress, and so on. However, in the cultural domain, the veneration of classical art and literature usually meant that the term "modern," when contrasted with "ancient," had a pejorative undertone. A positive valorization of modern works of art came to be introduced with the *Querelle des Anciens et Modernes,* when people such as Théophile de Viau berated the idolatry of the past and insisted: "One has to write in a modern manner" (Il faut écrire à la moderne).[2] In the course of the seventeenth century, the term "modern" was firmly established as a category of aesthetic criticism, sometimes with a ring of "iconoclasm" attached to it. The "Moderns" questioned the view that the present was only a figuration of the eternal and demanded that art and literature be firmly linked to contemporary society.

However, in a Neoclassical age this position was only acceptable to a minority of critics and artists. The mental revolution of the Age of Enlightenment—often referred to as "the invention of modern man"[3]—did not usually extend to a "modernization" of artistic styles and techniques. The ideal of a timeless beauty derived from ancient models continued to dominate aesthetic criticism. It was only with the Romantics that the age of steam engines, mechanized industries, and proletarian labor forces became a focus of attention among a wide range of artists and writers. Attitudes toward the Industrial Revolution may have been ambivalent, but after 1830, a consensus emerged that the great transformations of the past 50 years were to remain key features of a new civilization. From then on, the term "modern" came to qualify more than just some contemporary or recent innovation and was used to describe a new epoch, the "Age of Modernity."

THE EVOLUTION OF MODERNITY: PARIS IN THE NINETEENTH CENTURY

The "long nineteenth century," stretching from the French Revolution to World War I, was a period of great upheaval in the political world and of tumultuous changes in the social and economic fields. After a long process of maturation, the bourgeoisie became the dominant force in society and transformed the feudal economy into a capitalist system of production. Until the nineteenth century, the vast majority of the population lived and worked in the countryside. During the Industrial Revolution, factories gravitated toward the cities or prompted the growth of new towns near coalfields and iron deposits. They attracted impoverished peasants and farm laborers in search of work and concentrated people in compact urban agglomerations.[4] (See tables 1.1 and 1.2).

Table 1.1   **Mass migration from countryside to city, 1800–1910**

Country	1800		1850		1910	
France	12.5[a]	2.8[b]	19.5[a]	4.6[b]	38.5[a]	14.6[b]
Germany	10.3	1.5	15.5	3.1	48.8	21.3
England and Wales	6.7	8.2	50.0	21.8	74.8	40.7

[a] Urban population as percentage of total population in places numbering more than 5,000 inhabitants.
[b] Urban population as percentage of total population in places numbering more than 100,000 inhabitants.

(*Source*: Statistics for places numbering more than 5,000 inhabitants taken from D. B. Grigg, *Population Growth and Agrarian Change*, Cambridge: Cambridge University Press, 1980, p. 291; for places numbering more than 100,000 inhabitants taken from Andrew Lees, *Cities Perceived: Urban Society in European and American Thought, 1820–1940*, Manchester: Manchester University Press, 1985, p. 4.)

Table 1.2   **Population growth in some major European cities (in thousands)**

City	1800	1850	1870	1900	1920	1940
London	1,117	2,685	3,890	6,586	7,488	8,700
Paris	581	1,053	1,852	2,714	2,907	2,830
St Petersburg	336	485	667	1,267	722	3,191
Vienna	247	444	834	1,675	1,866	1,918
Moscow	250	365	612	989	1,050	4,137
Berlin	172	419	826	1,889	3,801	4,332
Milan	135	242	262	493	836	1,116

(*Source*: Statistics are taken from B.R. Mitchell, *International Historical Statistics: Europe 1750–1993*, 4th edn., London: Macmillan, 1998.)

These vast demographic changes in the course of the nineteenth century produced a new phenomenon: the Big City. The metropolis as a melting pot of immigrant populations functioned as an economic center, a colorful arena of pleasures and diversions, and a symbol of national glory. Typical features of modern life such as leisure and entertainment industries, printed and visual mass media, shopping malls and the rituals of consumerism, housing comforts and amenities (water, sewers, gas, electrical power, etc.) all made their first appearance in the nineteenth century, as well as many of the disturbing facets that still haunt the conurbations of the twenty-first century. Although similar developments could be observed across the industrialized world, Paris exhibited their most advanced and perspicuous forms and hence became the emblematic city of modernity and a model for many other capitals.[5] On the following pages, I shall describe some of these innovations, which transformed in Paris in the course of the nineteenth century, and indicate how these were experienced by contemporary observers. Subsequently, I shall discuss how these momentous changes were reflected in the arts and literature of the period, and how, toward the end of the century, modernity gave rise to a self-conscious concept of Modernism.

The combined effect of the French Revolution of 1789, the July Revolution of 1830, and the ongoing process of the Industrial Revolution put the middle-classes in a position of economic and political power, which caused Frances Trollope to observe in 1835: "The wide-spreading effect of this increasing wealth among the *bourgeoisie* is visible in many ways, but in none more than in the rapid increase of handsome dwellings, which are springing up, as white and bright as new-born mushrooms, in the north-western division of Paris."[6] Although a number of roadways had been opened up and lined with large apartment blocks, shops, restaurants, cafés, and theatres, the "building mania" of the restoration period did little to improve the quality of habitation in the old quarters of the city. Many visitors marveled at the fashionable new neighborhoods with their beautiful modern features and judged: "Paris is the city of the present, as Rome of the past."[7] Yet, they could not fail to notice that the rest of the city had been unable to cope with the dramatic increase of inhabitants. More than two-thirds of the Parisian population lived in primitive, overcrowded houses along narrow, winding streets, which collected garbage, industrial waste, and fecal matter, exuded a pestilential stench, and constituted a potentially deadly health hazard.

The resident population of the inner city was predominantly made up of workers and artisans, who lived and worked in buildings that could house up to 80 workshops.[8] Industrial laborers dwelled in the *banlieu*, usually in overcrowded conditions that gave them—as in the Arcis district—a living space of only seven square meters per person.[9] Seventy-five percent of this population was living in abject poverty.[10] Wages were so low that it was frequently impossible for a man to feed his family.[11] In the case of illness or loss of employment, people fell below the threshold of minimum existence. Eighty-three percent of families were so poor that in the case of death they were unable to pay the lowest tariff of 15 Francs for a burial.[12] The contrast could not be greater with regard to the fashionable streets and districts, where the bourgeoisie had erected their residences and squandered fortunes on the luxuries and exquisite diversions of life:

> Paris, more than any other capital, presents a strange picture that makes one feel as if different cities lay enclosed by one wall and joined together by streets that are lined by houses rather than ditches and trees. Indeed, each quarter is inhabited by people who seem to have nothing in common with those in the neighboring district. . . . An inhabitant of Chaillot or from Gros-Caillou remarks, when he crosses the Champs-Élysées or the Esplanade des Invalides: *"I'm going to Paris."*. . . One can find seven-storey blocks of houses here and two-story houses there; a superb colonnade stands next to a miserable hovel; the most beautiful street in the world, the rue de Rivoli, is surrounded by houses like those in rue Saint-Louis and the rue du Dauphin; there are shopping arcades paved with marble and galleries shining with gold and glass, which adjoin to malodorous and filthy squares: everything is contradictory in this bizarre city.[13]

By the mid-1800s, Paris reached a state of acute urban crisis. The density of population in the center amounted to 15,000 inhabitants per square kilometer.[14] Whereas many other European capitals had undergone a transformation, Paris had still remained basically "la petite ville de nos ancêtres," that is, a *pêle-mêle* of dwellings from all ages, sometimes picturesque, but more often in a state of terminal decay. The process of replacing the maze of narrow streets and overcrowded dwellings in the medieval quarters with a modern, rational, methodically planned infrastructure is often called "Haussmannization," after the Prefect of Paris, who between 1850 and 1870 was responsible for the systematic demolition of the old quarters in Paris and the building of some 85 miles of avenues and boulevards (see figure 1.1). His radical transformation of Paris was viewed by many contemporaries as a true sign of "Modernism"[15] and became the model of similar projects in other European cities.

Once the squalid roads, which previously had only allowed pedestrian access, had been turned into wide thoroughfares, people began to move freely across town by public transport.[16] In 1828, Paris had been furnished with a first public omnibus service. Horse-drawn vehicles were later replaced by streetcars, which circulated on 32 routes with evocative names such as

6

Figure 1.1 Haussmannization of the Montagne Sainte-Geniviève in Paris in an engraving by E. Roevens. Haussmann created large thoroughfares that facilitated cross-town traffic in Paris and laid the foundation for the modern features of Parisian town planning. The tenements of the traditional working population made way to large apartment blocks in the style of the Second Empire, which came to be emulated in many other European capitals.

Table 1.3   Growth of railway networks in selected European countries

Year	England (km)	Germany (km)	France (km)	Italy (km)
1840	2,390	469	410	20
1850	9,797	5,856	2,915	620
1875	23,365	27,970	19,357	8,018
1900	30,079	51,678	38,109	16,479

Source: Mitchell, *International Historical Statistics*, pp. 673–677.

Gazelle, Dove, White Ladies, or Dispatch. In 1850, there were ten companies running 400 buses across the city. The number of passengers rose from 11 million in 1829 to 40 million in 1855 and 110 million in 1870.[17] By the turn of the century, this had increased to some 450 million.[18] St. Lazare became the main railway station for traffic between Paris and the suburbs. In 1869, 13,254,000 passengers passed through its gates, of which some 11 million, or 83 percent, represented suburban traffic. The rapid growth of railway links (see table 1.3) gave rise to previously unknown mobility and ushered in "an age of movement,—an age of hurry and precipitation."[19] This new experience of time and space became another constituent feature of modernity with far-reaching consequences in the years to come.[20]

Haussmann's urban revolution eliminated, as Gautier observed, the "leprous quarters, malarial alleys and humid hovels" and gave Paris "a civilized attire."[21] Sanitary conditions were markedly improved with the building of some 350 miles of underground sewers and the replacement of public fountains with fresh springwater piped directly into houses.[22] The boulevards and squares of the city were fitted with gaslights,[23] and from 1859, houses were provided with private gas connections.[24] Such a magnificent illumination transformed the nightly aspects of the city and enhanced its reputation as Europe's foremost pleasure center.

> No city in the world offers a spectacle like Paris with its boulevards, especially . . . in the evening, when the gaslights come on, when theatres, café-concerts, department stores, bars of the glittering or simple variety light up their sign-boards and switch on their lamps, when the windows of the great circle are ablaze.[25]

Lemer enthused about "la capitale des lumières" in his description of Parisian nightlife:

> Everywhere you see brilliant stores, ostentatious displays, gilded cafés, permanent illumination: from rue Louis-le-Grand to rue Richelieu, the light flooding from

the shops allows you to read your newspaper. . . . People stroll through the streets where commerce keeps a radiant illumination going all night and makes it as bright as day.[26]

The new boulevards and avenues served as a vast open-air theatre where the prosperous middle-classes exhibited themselves in grand-opera style. Residents and tourists treated each other like characters in a play worthy to be stared at. "Paris is the principal city of loungers; it is laid out, built, arranged expressly for lounging. The broad quays, the monuments, the boulevards, the public places (. . . are) a sufficiently extensive theatre for lounging," judged Jules Janin in 1843.[27] Contemporary engravings show crowds of people sitting in cafés and staring at the traffic on the pavement. The poorer classes, who could not afford to frequent these places, still observed the spectacle from the sidelines. "The boulevards are now par excellence the social centre of Paris. Here the aristocrat comes to lounge, and the stranger to gaze," found Edward King on his visit to Paris in 1867.[28] The "lounger" or "flâneur"[29] was a new social phenomenon and a typical feature of the fashionable social life in Paris, centered on the boulevards.[30] An anonymous contributor to the *Livre des cent-et-un*, who regarded *flânerie* "the finest expression of modern civilization," linked this "characteristic feature of an advanced age" to the spectacle of the street, and judged: "This world is a vast theatre where thousands of actors of different temperament, habit and character . . . compete for the major parts, but hardly prove themselves worthy of the minor rôles. This, undoubtedly, makes the stage all the more animated and interesting to study."[31]

Migration from countryside to city was complemented by an analogous mobility *intra muros*, where it gave rise to a culture of restlessness and peripatetic existence. An American visitor to Paris in 1867 was struck by the instability of existence of the typical city tenant, who

> dwelled in a kind of metropolitan encampment, requiring no domicile except a bedroom for seven hours in the twenty-four, and passing the remainder of each day and night as nomadic cosmopolites: going to the café to breakfast, a restaurant to dine, an estaminet to smoke, a national library to study, a *cabinet de lecture* to read the gazettes, a public bath for ablution etc.[32]

Statistics show that the net increase of population was not due to new births, but to immigration, and that the majority of the newcomers were single men and women. Many adults never got married, and of those who did, many remained childless and experienced divorce rates ten times higher than in the countryside. Consequently, the traditional family network and the comfort of the domestic hearth were unknown to large sections of the urban citizenship. The result was isolation, autonomization, and alienation, which people sought to compensate for by throwing themselves into a cult of diversion. To the citizen or visitor with sufficient income, Paris offered a heady concentration of pleasures and entertainments, a rich and varied theatre and music culture, a public social life centered on some 4,000 cafés, bars, restaurants, clubs, and dance halls.[33] Many contemporary observers commented on the democratization of leisure activities, although statistics indicate that the lower classes were still largely excluded from the "city of pleasure."[34] Those who could afford it went to the circus, vaudeville, variété, or café-concert, where a whole range of new dramatic and theatrical genres found a mass following (see figure 1.2) "Serious" theatre became a speculative venture run by companies of shareholders. In the mid-nineteenth century, Paris had 41 theatres giving daily performances, and 67 others who only performed once or twice a week.[35] Together, they showed some 200 to 300 plays a year, generated an income of 16 million francs, and provided work for some 2,000 actors and singers.[36] It has been calculated that on an average night in 1867, Paris theatres had 30,000 visitors, while cafés-concerts, circuses, and similar venues tallied a further 24,000.[37] The pleasures and diversions of Paris were emulated in other European capitals and gave rise to a thoroughly commercialized theatre business served by dramatists, whose "play factories" churned out financially rewarding plays in conveyor-belt fashion.

Closely linked to the emergence of a distinctly modern leisure industry[38]—and feeding from the same social and cultural roots—was the development of a modern consumer society. The growth in commerce and real estate, supported by the thriving industry, filled the coffers of the bourgeoisie and turned them into big spenders.[39] The new public transport system allowed people to move freely between their residence and the fashionable quarters of the city, where the *magasins de nouveautés* could be found. These shops full of luxury goods invited the bourgeoisie to treat shopping no longer as a utilitarian act, but as a ritual of consumption. The Palais-Royal had demonstrated that a concentration of shops, cafés, restaurants, clubs, and entertainment venues could attract a steady flow of customers when it sheltered them from inclement weather and the dirt and dangers of the street. Private speculators seized upon the idea and created similar complexes, which were the precursors of the modern shopping mall: glass-covered and marble-paved passages that ran like "interior boulevards" through entire blocks of buildings.[40] These symbols of urban wealth, elegance and fashionableness were "constantly thronged with the superfluous population of loungers"[41] and

Figure 1.2 Theatrical-musical entertainment on the Parisian boulevards during the reign of Louis-Philippe, 1830–1848. Like the department stores, the café-concerts offered a profusion of entertainments at a low price to a mixed audience, who could come and go as they pleased.

seduced the population into unnecessary expenditure: "It was not enough for the arcades to deliver the passer-by from the perils of the streets; they had to hold him, to enslave him, body and soul. And as soon as he entered the corrupting arcades he felt so bewitched that he forgot everything: wife, children, office, and dinner."[42]

Based on cross-shaped church architecture, arcades were true temples of consumption, with boutique-like shops fitting into niches like chapels along the aisles, and opulent displays in showcases resembling magical icons (or fetishes) in a shrine. Here, the bourgeoisie could enter into the mythical dream world of commodity capitalism.

The arcades were among the first "streets" to be fitted with gaslights, which further increased their fairy-tale splendor:

> In the evening, a flood of gas light streams through the windows, casting a warm color on the pale faces of passing women, making the copper shine like gold, and transforming crystals into diamonds. It makes the rich array of manifold and multicolored trinkets, knick-knacks, and toys appear like luxuries radiating a magical and dazzling glow and imposing themselves on those, who are partial to their attractions.[43]

Out of the arcades developed the department stores, the *grands magasins*, which Zola rightly characterized as "cathédrales du commerce moderne."[44] Their most successful representative, the Bon Marché (1852; see figure 1.3), caused a revolution in retailing and became the model for many others: Le Louvre (1855); Bazar de l'Hôtel de Ville (1857/1866); Au Printemps (1865); La Belle Jardinère (1867); La Samaritaine (1869), and so on.[45] These huge stores not only offered the most amazing assembly of commodities ever seen under one roof, but also contained salons, restaurants, galleries, even reading rooms. As the "entrée libre" signs at the entrance doors emphasized, the visitors—and there were up to 100,000 a day[46]—could wander around by themselves, undisturbed by shop assistants, and were under no obligation to buy. Shopping developed into a pursuit that transcended needs, and visiting a department store became an equivalent to a stroll on the boulevards. With their "grand and magical splendour,"[47] the stores invited spectating practices that resembled those in the theatres fitted with gaslights.[48] And when the shops were closed, one could still engage in the popular pastime of window-shopping: "It is as good as a play to stand at the window of this shop and watch the people inside. . . . From morning to night it is surrounded by a starring, chattering crowd."[49]

Just as the earlier arcades had often taken their names from theatres and successful plays, stores such as the Magasin du Louvre indicated in their name

Figure 1.3 The spectacle of consumerism: The Great interior staircase in the Bon Marché department store in Paris, Ca. 1870. Engraving by Émile Lesaché. The wide, double-curving construction is reminiscent of the great staircase in the Palais Garnier, the Parisian Opera house, emphasizing the spectacle provided by the store's merchandize and profusion of buyers.

how much they were based on spectatorial practices in museums.[50] Although the merchandise was not necessarily affordable to all, the *vision* of this profusion of commodities had a lasting effect on the consciousness even of the lower strata of society. Walter Benjamin therefore compared the spectacle-like element of commerce ("schaustückhafte Element des Handels") to the Roman *ludi circenses*,[51] and Lefebvre called the displays "rhetorical happenings without clear boundaries between imaginary consumption, the consumption of make-belief, and real consumption."[52]

Nothing was to support this phenomenon more than the rise of another modern phenomenon: advertising. To find enough paying customers, shops had to attract large numbers of potential clients. Therefore, in the nineteenth century, publicity became a ubiquitous phenomenon. Big department stores spent between 500,000 and 1,000,000 Francs a year on advertising. Edward King judged it to be "a science in the gay city" and came across it at every turn, on shop fronts, on blank walls of houses, even on "little dogs run loose in the streets with their sides painted with some dealer's name."[53]

Similarly, the new mass media of tabloid newspapers[54] and illustrated magazines (e.g., *La Vie parisienne, Le Boulevard, La Vie moderne*) propagated fashionable lifestyles throughout the population. A multifaceted concoction of make-belief and commodity description insinuated pleasures and satisfactions through the consumption of signs of happiness, thereby displacing social dissatisfaction and projecting the desire for fulfillment and completeness onto the sphere of consumption. This mechanism not only applied to personal fashion items (hats, scarves, parasols, etc.) and spare-time activities such as visiting the café-chantant or racetrack, but also to symbolic furnishings and fittings in the parvenue household. Newly acquired riches needed to be shown off; bourgeois houses were therefore decorated in an opulent pastiche of various styles of the feudal past to signify "wealth" and "high social status." Also "art" formed part of this ritualized culture of conspicuous consumption. Although most people agreed that Grand Opéra was a heavy and boring fare, it, nevertheless, was a useful occasion to exhibit expensive jewelry and sartorial grandeur. To have "fashionable taste" stood entirely in the service of social functionality and had little to do with true connoisseurship. A large and highly profitable "culture industry" organized the intellectual market on principles that were basically the same as those that manipulated the consumer in the *grands magasins*. Monsieur Giraud in Dumas fils's play *The Question of Money* was a typical customer of such works of "culture" when he declared: "I have been told that a man in my position must have a taste for the arts. I am utterly ignorant in these matters, but I paid a lot of money for my paintings and statues."[55]

And it was not only the "man of the world" who had to be provided with prestige objects and élite diversions. Also middle-class women, whose lives had previously been restricted to a domestic existence, now entered the domain of public life—as consumers.[56] With money and time at their disposal, they treated shopping as an evasion from the boredom and restrictions of everyday existence. The times, when public spaces were dominated by men and respectable women avoided to be seen on the streets, had come to an end. Debans, for example, characterized the boulevards as: "It is a meeting place of the whole world. . . . Women play an elevated rôle here."[57] As if to warn visitors from less advanced countries, one of the Paris guides commented: "One thing that will strike the stranger is the immense proportion of women in the streets as compared with men."[58] Many of these undoubtedly engaged in purposeful activities, but others were *flâneuses*[59] attracted by the spectacle of modern life.

As these examples show, the nineteenth-century "spectatorial régime" was typical of the modern urban development. Some of the visual entertainments were driven by technology, others by social and ideological factors. The elevation of "spectating" to a mass phenomenon and the emergence of new social practices such as *flânerie* was not without political rationale. It has been suggested by Foucault and others that modern entertainments function as a regulatory device. However, as in all political interventions it is important to differentiate between social realities and the ideological-political interpretations of that reality. In the nineteenth century, the "Big City as spectacle" was as much a rhetorical trope as it was an objective phenomenon. Textual and visual representations in novels, guide books, illustrated magazines, and so on propagated an image of Paris as the paradigmatic modern city, where the spectacle of modern life could be observed from the sidewalks of the boulevards or the sofa-corners of the *grands hotels*. The roving eye of the tourist was increasingly "directed" by descriptions in popular guidebooks. The sensations and experiences resulting from this steered focus of attention were then communicated to following generations of travelers through publications belonging to the "My Year in Paris" variety. Thus, the myth of the modern Big City was born, and Paris as its first living representation became "the capital of the world, due to the splendor that increases daily everywhere: the asphalt-paved boulevards lit by brass-plated gas lamps, the growing luxury of stores at this endless, five-mile-long fair with ever-changing new buildings—all this offers a matchless spectacle."[60]

PREPARING THE GROUND FOR MODERNISM: ROMANTICISM, REALISM, SYMBOLISM

In the eighteenth century, the forces of modernization, which had matured in European social and economic life since the Reformation and Renaissance

---

TEXT BOX 1.1   SOME MODERNIST FEATURES IN NINETEENTH-CENTURY ART

- focus on contemporary subject matter
- search for new techniques of transposing objective reality into visual or literary media
- break with the aesthetics of preceding generations
- autonomy of artists and writers from traditional patrons and dependency on an anonymous market
- oppositional attitudes toward the new dominant middle classes, ranging from the bohemian desire to *épater le bourgeois* to socialist engagement and anarchist intransigence
- expansion of mediating agencies and the development of modern forms of mass communication
- increased awareness of the processes and means of artistic production
- skepticism toward the traditional forms of representation and emancipation from the dictates of mimeticism and narrativity
- fragmented representation of the object of artistic observation rather than pretending to reflect reality as an organic whole
- foregrounding of aesthetic means and techniques, self-conscious use of form, and presentation of art as artifice
- exploration of the subjective element in apprehending reality and transposing it into art
- a loss of faith in the ability of language to signify meaning

---

period, reached a strength and urgency that was increasingly at variance with the feudal order. When, in 1789, this conflict erupted in the French Revolution, the *ancient régime* was replaced with a political system more in tune with the necessities of the modern age. Less drastic, yet no less profound, were the transformations in the prevailing aesthetic conceptions of the time. The political and social developments of the years 1789–1810 and the great upheavals brought about by the Industrial Revolution fostered the growth of artistic movements, which advocated a break with the classical tradition that had dominated European culture since Renaissance times. They played a significant rôle in preparing the ground for Modernism and contained features, which we shall find again in the historical avant-gardes of the twentieth century (see text box 1.1).

Romanticism

Romanticism was the first pan-European movement to formulate a new aesthetic that was concerned with the Janus-faced aspect of modernity. People experienced a world transformed by steam engines and mechanized production lines as both frightening and fascinating. Although today Romanticism is often remembered for its antimodern tendencies and its retreat from contemporary realities into Gothic or exotic worlds, this was not how the movement as a whole responded to the challenges of the time. The Romantic project of recovering the authentic self from under the incrustations of the feudal order forced the artist into the social-political arena. Many Romantics, particularly in France, were involved in practical politics and often engaged in oppositional, if not revolutionary, activities. Their quest for spontaneity, creativity, and a "natural" way of living went hand in hand with a struggle against the restrictions imposed by religious tradition, social conventions, and the political authorities. And as feudalism and absolutism were successively replaced by capitalist structures, conflict with the new middle classes was unavoidable. Many artists reflected critically on the transformations brought about by capitalism and spoke out against the commercialism and materialism, egotism and greed that seemed to dominate bourgeois society. Consequently, artists changed their rôle from being a servant to the dominant social classes to becoming outsiders living in opposition to the established order.

Friedrich Schlegel was among the first to analyze the novel features of this epoch, which he experienced as frightening, amorphous, and chaotic,[61] and to equate the Romantic style with the modern world. In his notebooks of 1797–1803 he made no less than 150 entries on "the character of modernity," "modern aesthetics," "the absolute difference of antiquity and modernity," and so on.[62] His brother August Wilhelm Schlegel offered a similar equation of modernity with Romanticism in his lectures on dramatic art and literature, delivered in 1808, in which he declared: "The name 'Romantic' has been coined to characterize the specific spirit of modern art in contrast to antique or classical art."[63]

In France, it was Stendhal who offered a highly perceptive analysis of the revolutionary changes that had occurred in Europe since the French Revolution.[64] He expressed the view that "the ancient notion of beauty is incompatible with modern passions,"[65] that the arts needed to reflect these changes, and that the Romantic aesthetic had to be closely linked to "the present state of things," "the environment in which we live," and "the occurences of modern life" ("l'état actuel," "le milieu duquel nous vivons," and "les incidents de la vie des modernes"[66]). Similarly, Émile Deschamps, spokesman of the French Romantics, saw it as the writer's foremost task to be in tune with one's time: "Avant tout et en tout il faut être de son temps."[67]

In the 1820s, the literary journal *Le Globe* ran a number of articles on Romanticism, which on October 1, 1825 culminated in a fundamental essay on "Romanticism in a Historical Perspective," in which Deprès defined the movement as "the literature of modern nations, which voices best their civilization . . . and expresses in modern idioms the feelings that are typical of our times."[68] Baudelaire expressed a similar view in the essay, "What is Romanticism," in which he defined Romanticism as "the most recent, the most up-to-date expression of beauty. . . . Romanticism and modern art are one and the same thing."[69]

In the fine arts, it was Delacroix who, above all, came to be considered a champion of Romantic modernity.[70] But the style of painting he represented remained a minority position. Therefore, Maxime du Camp, when reviewing the artistic exhibitions at the Exposition Universelle of 1855, criticized the anachronistic attitudes of academic painters, who "do not participate in the movement of the age, do not put their finger on the artery of social life, do not listen to the echo of the common voice, do not know about the needs of their age, do not understand the people of their time, and do not respond to the trends of their contemporaries."[71] Instead, he praised the "Romantics, who have thrown themselves courageously into modern life," and have taken up new subject matters because they "wanted to be of their time."[72]

In artistic terms, Romanticism was the culmination of a revolt against the Neoclassical aesthetics and an attempt to create an art of and for the contemporary world. The Romantics rejected the classical concept of eternal beauty and sought to depict the changing world around them. The process of modernization, which they observed in the economic and social fields, was applied to aesthetic theory and became a fundamental principle of their artistic production. Instead of the rationalism of the Enlightenment, which had formed the philosophical basis of Neoclassical aesthetics, the Romantics made a sensualist subjectivism the foundation of their art. In their view, artistic genius could not be squared with preestablished rules and normative precepts. Instead of learning conventional formula, they encouraged the artist to follow his or her inspiration and intuition, to experiment and search for absolute originality. The Romantic "genius" as a reflective subject made himself the center of a work of art. Instead of copying exterior realities, he created a new and autonomous reality from a *Bewußtseinsakt* or *prise de conscience*. This shift of emphasis introduced many formal innovations in a highly self-conscious way and has caused many critics to comment on Romanticism as a precursor of Modernism.[73]

Jauss, Martini, Gumbrecht, et al. in their detailed examination of the semantic developments of the term "modern" have shown that in the 1830s a widely shared awareness of living in a new epoch brought about an understanding of modernity as a qualitatively new condition of the world, and not just an aesthetic trend. The Romantic ambivalence toward the modern predicament gave way to an acceptance of the fact that modernity as a new civilization would remain and that the old belief in a redemptive Nature had to be jettisoned. This did not mean that the Moderns discontinued their search for some regenerative possibilities, but in principle they accepted the urban environment and the social structures emerging within it as an inescapable reality.

Realism and Naturalism

In a different yet related manner, the Realists of the mid-nineteenth century offered a penetrating and wide-ranging analysis of contemporary society. They rejected the idealistic, affected, and pretentious works of previous generations and directed, with increasing scientific objectivity, their attention to the novel phenomena of the modern era: capitalist trade and industry, urban growth, new means of transport and communication, the abject poverty of the proletariat, and the ostentatious life style of the middle-classes. The Realists argued that a new epoch had dawned caused by science and technology. The aesthetic values of the Neoclassical and Historicist schools could no longer be brought into agreement with the changes triggered by the Industrial Revolution and the way people related to the world. Calinescu has demonstrated how during the first half of the nineteenth century two modernities came into existence: a socioeconomic modernity linked to capitalist industry, and an aesthetic modernity. Intellectuals who supported the latter often assumed a complex and contradictory attitude toward the former. They did not want to cut themselves off from the modern realities of urban civilization, but at the same time they despised the commonplace, prosaic, and utilitarian understanding of modernity by the middle classes.[74] The oppositional attitude that had already characterized the Romantics was now firmly targeted against the bourgeois class and developed into a radical stance of *épater le bourgeois*. This could either take the form of an intellectual contempt for the philistine's vulgar materialism, a bohemian disdain of the petty bourgeois' counting-house mentality, or a politically motivated, class-conscious opposition to the capitalist's greed.

Baudelaire is generally accredited with having been the first to reflect in a sophisticated manner the new phenomenon of modernity.[75] His poetry described the great transformations of his age and the novel features of urban culture with both concern and elation, and in his theoretical essays, he showed an acute awareness of the dynamic changes taking place in the society around him. He marveled at "the spectacle of elegant life and of the thousands of souls floating adrift in the underworld of a big city"[76] and saw it as the artist's duty to capture this flux of life in the historical present. He conceived of art as having two components: a universal part with the accumulated qualities of the past, and a modern part that reflects the many transitive, fugitive, and contingent features of the contemporary epoch.[77] In his view, every age has its beauty, which therefore contains both modern and eternal features. It is the artist's task to discover both of them in the contemporary world and to create from them an aesthetic experience that helps the viewer or reader to endure the shortcomings and negative aspects of the modern world.

A much more emphatic endorsement of modernity was given by the poet and critic Maxime du Camp, whose writings in many ways prefigure Marinetti's Futurism. In the preface to his collection of poems, *Les Chants modernes* (1855),[78] he described contemporary art and literature as being in a state of decadence and totally out of touch with the great advances made by science and technology:

> Science produces wonders and industry accomplishes miracles. Yet we remain impassive, indifferent or contemptuous, and go on plucking the strained cords of our lyres. . . . One discovers the force of steam, and we sing in praise of Venus rising from the foam of the sea. One discovers electricity, and we sing our songs to Bacchus, friend of the ruby grapes. This is absurd! . . . The cult of the old in this country is a lunacy, an illness, an epidemic.[79]

Du Camp attacked the Académie Française for being "not only useless, but in fact harmful" (23) and accuses the "official" culture of his age as being "envious of the young, of being antagonistic to those who are alive, of opposing everything that has a future. They are a curse of death against life; they are an exaltation of everything that is mediocre, mean, colorless, ordinary, well-known, repetitive, poor and on the verge of collapse"(17). These men belong to "a crusty old world" (28) and produce writings that are devoid of any modern ideas. At best, they aim at formalistic innovation, but produce little more than well-sounding phrases. They "certainly have not yet dared to arrive at works that can be considered modern and truly alive" (25). But now the time has come for an art of the future, which will reflect the splendid achievements of science and industry. Du Camp exhorts the young generation: "Let's leave the intellectual invalids grinding themselves to a halt with their useless regrets and naïve attempts of finding paradise in the past, when in reality it is waiting for us in the future. So let us love, work towards and fecundate the eternally young forces of progress" (35). In order to reach "the golden age ahead of us," he suggests that the pioneers join forces and "claim new ground on which to build the road into the beautiful lands of the future. This is not only our duty; it is our mission!" (54).

In his book on the Exposition Universelle of 1855, Du Camp made a number of suggestions for new subjects and decorative schemes that could be adopted by artists. As churches and palaces were, in his view, already crammed with paintings, modern artists had to find new outlets for their creativity, such as railway stations, these "modern cathedrals of industry and science."[80] Under the hands of intelligent artists, their ugly walls could be transformed and made to depict scenes that transport the traveler into foreign lands, describe modern inventions and discoveries, illustrate the history of scientific progress, and so on. Du Camp enlarged on this idea in an essay published two years later in the *Revue de Paris*, in which he called for a new order of architecture "that is in tune with the new industry."[81] He suggested that railway stations, and not churches, symbolize the modern museum of the people. These superb monuments, if given an appropriate décor, could make travelers feel like "being in a palace rather than a hangar" and transform the artistic tastes of the nation.

Théophile Gautier,[82] who had a quasi-Futuristic vision of a mechanical art of the future, expressed a similar idea in an essay on railways, originally published in 1837, in which he described an imaginary décor for a railway station depicting technological progress from the times of Archimedes to the age of steam engines.[83] In 1848, he demanded that "a whole new vast system of symbols must be invented, answering the needs of our times . . . . The formulas of the *ancient régime* are totally unsuited to our new Republic, and to make use of them would be to misunderstand or falsify our modern tendencies."[84] And in 1855 he wrote: "Initially one might have thought that the mechanical inventions would deal a mortal blow to the arts. But on the contrary, they have rendered them invaluable service. A new era of poetry has arisen from the discovery of steam power. . . . The locomotive shall be the pegasus of our time."[85] A few years later, the painter Gustave Courbet was reported to having taken up these suggestions. Sainte-Beuve and Champfleury both mention that he was working on a vast frieze with modern subjects to decorate railway stations.[86] However, railway companies were more concerned with recouping their investments than spending money on decorative schemes, and so these plans remained Utopian dreams of artists who followed the rallying cry of "one has to be in tune with the times" ("Il faut être de son temps.")

The period between 1830 and 1860 was the heyday of Realism. Artists belonging to this school not only discovered new subject matters, but also developed new methods of transposing objective reality into visual or literary media.

They sought to create an art and literature that was drawn from close observation and immediate experience of reality. In their approach, they were
fiercely anti-subjectivist and opposed to the aesthetic canons of previous
generations. The Realists were committed to representing significant and
characteristic aspects of the empirical, objective world, with a view of understanding the causal factors and revealing essential truths about human life
and society as an organic whole. In this undertaking, they were greatly
inspired by positivist philosophy and the new science of sociology. Auguste
Comte analyzed the laws that regulate the conditions and structures of social
life and attempted to "discover, by means of reasoning and observation, their
effective laws."[87] Hippolyte Taine applied Comte's scientific approach to cultural manifestations, and arrived at three principal factors that determine
their specific character: *race* (the national character or accumulated mental
characteristics of a people), *milieu* (the social, political, and geographical
environment), and *moment* (the historical situation or *Zeitgeist*).[88] Equipped
with these and various other scientific instruments of analysis, the Realist
novelists, painters, and dramatists were able to register the great changes and
upheavals of the nineteenth-century and describe how they affected different
strata of society.

In the 1860s and 1870s, a second generation of Realists came to the fore,
usually referred to as Naturalists or Impressionists. Inspired by new scientific
discoveries and aided by novel instruments of analysis, they expanded the
repertoire of forms used for conveying the new quality of life in an industrial
and urban environment. Although there is no agreement as to when
Naturalism superseded Realism (contemporary usage makes no clear distinction between the two terms), it is generally understood to be a more detailed,
painstaking reproduction of selected slices of reality with the aim of achieving
quasi-photographic verisimilitude. The Naturalists shared with the Realists
the general belief that art ought to be a faithful, objective representation of
contemporary life. Their method of "reproducing reality"[89] had a strong
affinity with the natural sciences, as it employed painstaking attention to
detail and aspired to absolute fidelity in the portrayal of facts observed. In
order to do so, a narrower focus was required, and this was directed, more so
than in previous generations, toward the harsh and unpleasant realities of life.
Art was largely divested of aesthetic ideals and became a quasi-scientific
analysis of social and physical realities.[90]

In the last phase of Naturalism, artists discovered that reality could never
be objectively reflected by art, but only be registered and processed by a
sensing and reasoning artist. For this reason, the formulaic conventions of
Realism and minutely detailed renderings of observed reality in Naturalism

were jettisoned in favor of

> a kind of skepticism, or at least unsureness, as to the nature of representation in art. . . . This shift of attention led, on the one hand, to their putting a stress on the material means by which illusions and likeness were made . . .; on the other, to a new set of proposals as to the form representation should take, insofar as it was still possible at all without bad faith. . . . Doubts about vision became doubts about almost everything involved in the act of painting; and in time the uncertainty became a value in its own right; we could almost say it became an aesthetic.[91]

The observing subject became a constituent feature of late-Naturalist theory. Part of this skepticism was fired by new scientific discoveries, for example, in the field of optics, which were of paramount importance for the development of Impressionism, and partly it had to do with a disbandment of the intimate link between positivism, materialism, and capitalism. Out of this skepticism grew a new school, which focused attention on the subjective component of the creative process and sought to overcome mimetic imitation by symbolic representation.

Symbolism

In the 1880s, the Naturalist–Impressionist impulse began to exhaust itself, and a number of counter-movements came into existence,[92] some of them only of passing and local significance, while others, such as Symbolism, operating on a pan-European scale and exercising a major influence on the fine arts, literature, music, theatre, and so on. Officially baptized in a manifesto by Jean Moréas (*Le Figaro*, September 18, 1886), Symbolism undertook a radical break not only with the artistic, but also with the political establishment. Many of the artists and intellectuals who joined the movement had a radical, anti-bourgeois outlook. In 1893, *L'Ermitage* asked a representative sample of them about their political allegiances and found that anarchism was their favored position.[93] In 1907, Poinsot judged that most Symbolists still tended politically toward anarchism, although many of the new recruits, and the "sober ones" of the earlier generation, embraced the doctrines of socialism.[94] However, there was also an a-political counter-trend among the Symbolists, linked to the Aesthetic Movement and the Parnassian school, who professed an attitude of *l'art pour l'art* (art for art's sake). They claimed absolute independency of the work of art from social reality and demanded total integrity of aesthetic expression. They treated art as an autonomous reality fashioned and controlled by the artist, and thereby anticipated the Modernist concept of art as an alternative to the alienated existence in capitalist-bourgeois society.

Members of the Symbolist movement revolted against the positivism and materialism of their age and rejected the exclusive equation of reality with scientifically observable data. Their desire to apprehend the mysteries of Being behind the flux of appearances made them relinquish scientific approaches in favor of intuitive methods stemming from occult and spiritualist domains. They continued the Naturalists' experiments with new formal languages capable of expressing the elusive and mysterious qualities of existence and developed further what had already been explored in the later phase of Naturalism: the subjective component in our perception of the world (Zola's "temperament" and Holz's "means of reproduction and the artist's handling of these"[95]).

The Symbolists sought to penetrate the world of appearances and to apprehend essential truths underneath the material surface of reality, especially in the spiritual and psychic realms. They wanted to open the doors of perception to the mystical and sublime, to fathom the divine essence of Being, and to invigorate the spiritual faculties that had withered in the aftermath of the industrial and scientific revolutions. But how were they to communicate the enigmatic experiences in the deeper recesses of the subconscious mind, or the equally perplexing processes in the higher reaches of consciousness?

The Symbolists' loss of faith in the ability of rational language to signify meaning made them question the whole process of communication and representation. They rejected the Realists' attachment to verisimilitude, narrative, singular perspective, closed form, and so on and argued that neither traditional artistic languages nor the "experimental" techniques of the Naturalists were capable of expressing the divine essence of Being. In their view, important aspects of the world were inaccessible and unintelligible to the rational mind and could not be conveyed by the prevailing tools and conventions of visual or verbal communication. To represent the full spectrum of human experience (which included the realms of fantasy, dreams, and visions), one had to take recourse to imaginative methods rather than the instrumental rationality of science. Consequently, they made use of suggestive rather than descriptive language. They expressed the inexpressible though symbolic signifiers. They communicated ideas, experiences, and emotions indirectly through metaphoric rather than mimetic imagery, and they used their associative and evocative power to reveal what conventional means of representation could not divulge.

In their latter phase, the Symbolists went a stage further. The epistemological crisis brought about by the breakdown of positivism caused a crisis of the

---

TEXT BOX 1.2   MODERNITY AND MODERNISM

Modernity

A historical and social condition that emerged in the sixteenth century and reached a peak with the Industrial Revolution and the establishment of capitalism as the determining force in society. The formation of modernity brought about radical changes that affected all spheres of social life: mass-migration, urban growth, new means of transport and communication, break-up of social ties, secularization, commodification, and so on. The rapid transformation of society and everyday life in nineteenth-century Europe produced a historical conscious-ness of a new epoch and gave rise to a cultural attitude that valorized present over past. It rejected traditions and customary conventions as anachronistic remnants of the past and took a positive stance toward the narratives of techno-logical progress, prosperity, individualism, and universal liberation.

Modernism

An artistic response to the crisis of modernity around 1900 and an attempt to break away from Realist methods of representing the modern age. The Modernists made use of the changed forms of communication in advanced industrial societies, incorporated the break-up of the conventional time–space nexus in their works, and sought to express the spirit of modernity and the novel experiences in the contemporary world by entirely new and experimental methods. As a generic term, Modernism includes a multitude of distinct, yet closely related schools and movements, such as Expressionism, Cubism, Futurism, Dadaism, Surrealism, and so on. Many of these artists and writers not only loved and admired the exhilarating aspects of modernity, but they also expressed their disquiet about the alienating aspects of mass society and technological civilization.

---

subject, language, and representation. This is precisely the moment when Modernism came in to existence. It brought to a conclusion the critical work undertaken by the Symbolists: questioning the historical paradigms of knowl-edge, deconstructing language as an instrumentalized vehicle of "epistemes," and undermining the fixed signifiers in a supposedly stable framework of representation (see text box 1.2).

In this respect, Symbolism was an important precursor of Modernism. What is more difficult is to attach a precise date to this turning point. Some critics favor the date 1886, as it signals the formal inception of the Symbolist movement. However, artists responded to the fundamental changes in the social and cultural domains in their own personal manner, often over an extended period of time. It may therefore be wiser to treat the years 1890 to 1914 as a transitional phase, and the years 1909 to 1912 as the period when Modernism materialized itself as a clearly recognizable artistic force.

Whatever periodization we may choose, there is no doubt that by the turn of the century many artists and writers had heeded Rimbaud's rallying call of 1873: "Il faut être absolument moderne" ("One has to be absolutely modern").[96] To be "modern" became the slogan of the day and, judging by the large number of publications that used it in their titles, the term appears to have had a considerable drawing power.[97] In fact, it became so fashionable to declare oneself "modern" that the Berlin cabaret author Leo Wulff published a satirical anthology on the follies of modernity, in which the "super-moderns" were lampooned and taunted[98](see figure 1.4).

By the turn of the century, the terms "modern" and "modernity" had become so pervasive that many felt that they had outlived their usefulness and could no longer be used to describe the character of their age. However, it was not only the term, but also the whole concept of modernity that had reached a point of crisis. For several decades, artists had operated with rather naïve assumptions about their ability to reflect and describe, in an objective manner, the vast transformation of the world around them. This is not to underestimate the attempts at exploring the subjective factor in the creative process; but the majority of "modern" works dealing with contemporary subject matter created a general impression that Realism and modernity were

Die Ganz-Modernen auf der Suche nach neuen Motiven.

Der alten Meister Schaffenskraft   Heut, da die echte Kunst erschlaffte,
Erscheint uns jetzt noch fabelhaft.   Liegt nur im Stoff das Fabelhafte.

Figure 1.4 "The Super-Moderns in search of new motifs." German caricature of "the follies of modernity" to be found on the "Island of Madmen," 1901.

two phenomena that inextricably belonged together. It was only with the end of the Industrial Revolution that the age of Positivism came to an end and a significant chapter in the history of modernity with it. Consequently, it was possible for Michael Georg Conrad to dedicate a volume to "the history of modernity" (1902)[99] and for Samuel Lublinski to draw up a "balance sheet of modernity" (1904),[100] followed by an analysis of "the exit of modernity" (1909).[101]

THE CRISIS OF MODERNITY AND THE ADVENT OF MODERNISM

In the first sections of this chapter I have discussed how in the nineteenth century—and in some respect even earlier than that—the foundations were lain for modernity establishing itself as a socioeconomic reality in most European countries, and how artists from a variety of disciplines sought to find ways of representing the physical and mental upheavals that shook European societies in the wake of the Industrial Revolution. On the following pages, I shall outline how around the turn of the century the process of modernization entered into a state of crisis, how a new consciousness evolved out of this experience, and how Modernism became an artistic expression of this mental state.

In the course of the nineteenth century, the everyday life of most citizens in industrialized Europe underwent a profound transformation. People had to adopt new lifestyles in the large urban centers; they had to get accustomed to new forms of habitation, new diets, new ways of earning a living; they were confronted with novel inventions and technologies (see chronology 1.1); they had to cope with the breakdown of family ties and traditional social networks, and so on. In short: the face of Europe came to be modified, mentally and physically, beyond recognition and, consequently, a "paradigm shift" took place in the popular mind, an awareness of living in a new era, whose new features far outweighed the ones persisting from the past.

But it was not only social change that affected people's view of the world, it was also the speed of the change. In previous centuries, renewal had always been experienced as something happening gradually and over a long period of time; toward the end of the nineteenth century, a feeling of cataclysmic commotion gained ground and had profound and wide-ranging consequences on the ways an individual related to the world and to his or her position within it. The new means of transportation and communication shook up people's conception of a linear time and space continuum and altered a person's cognitive mapping of the world. In the field of biology, there were new

CHRONOLOGY 1.1:   SOME MAJOR INVENTIONS AND DISCOVERIES IN THE AGE OF MODERNITY, 1769–1869

1769 James Watt patents a steam engine, with other patents to follow between 1781 and 1784

1800 John McAdam introduces new road-making technique in Britain

1801 Richard Trevithick builds a self-propelled steam carriage, which led to his London Carriage of 1803 and the first steam locomotive to run successfully on rails (1804)

1807 The first efficient steam boat built by Robert Fulton

1807 First public street lighting with gas in Pall Mall, London

1808 Humphrey Davy invents the arc light

1809 Samuel Thomas von Soemmering develops an electrochemical telegraph

1816 Karl Drais von Sauerbronn builds his first bicycle, the draisine, which is propelled by the rider's feet. The front wheel is pivoted on a frame and can be maneuvred by a handlebar.

1819 First transatlantic steamboat journey by the *Savannah*

1822 Joseph Nicéphore Niépce makes the first permanent heliograph

1823 Microscope with achromatic lenses provide a resolution of 1 micron or 1/1000 mm

1825 Opening of the world's first public steam railway, the Stockton & Darlington in northeast England, engineered by George Stephenson.

1827 Joseph Nicéphore Niépce makes the first photograph with a camera

1829 George Stephenson adapts the steam engine to power a locomotive for use on a railway line between Manchester and London, carrying both passengers and freight and running at 39 km/h (24 mph)

1830 Long-distance (1 mile) electromagnetic telegraph line by Joseph Henry

1830 Electromagnetic induction discovered by Michael Faraday, leading to the development of a disc dynamo in 1831

1832 William Sturgeon builds an electric motor

1833 Karl Friedrich Gauss and Wilhelm Weber build an electric telegraph

1834 Analytical Engine, the first automatic general-purpose calculating machine, by Charles Babbage

1835 Louis Jacques Mandé Daguerre invents Daguerréotype photography

1835 William Henry Fox Talbot develops a chemical process for recording negative images on paper

1837 First practical telegraph system by Charles Wheatstone and William F. Cooke

1837 Samuel F. B. Morse's electrical telegraph, patented in 1843, transmits signals on a distance of 32 km (20 mi)

1839	First pedal bicycle by Kirkpatrick Macmillan
1848	Construction of the first electrical long-distance telegraph line in Europe, from Berlin to Frankfurt/Main (500 km, 310 mi)
1849	Andreas Merian revolutionizes the construction of streets by covering them with asphalt. In 1854, he uses a steamroller to build an asphalt road from Travers to Pontarlier
1849	Antonio Meucci invents the *teletrofono*, or electric telephone
1854	Ignatio Porro patents a modern prism binocular
1857	Johann Carl Fuhlrott discovers the Neanderthal man near Düsseldorf
1860	Johann Philipp Reis invents a diaphragm microphone that transmits musical tones, and in 1861 coins the word *Telephon*
1860	Construction begins on the London underground railway system
1860	Étienne Lenior builds a first gas motor
1861	Coleman Sellers patents the Kinematoscope, which crudely projects series of photographs mounted on a paddle wheel
1861	Nikolaus August Otto builds the a two-stroke gas engine and in 1876, the four-stroke engine, which became almost universally employed for all internal combustion engines
1862	First practical arc lamp installed in a lighthouse at Dungeness, England
1866	Cyrus W. Field lays a first telegraph cable connecting the North American and European continents
1866	Werner Siemens discovers the dynamo-electric principle, making the economic generation of electrical energy in large quantities possible
1867	Pierre and Ernest Michaux present their *vélocipède*, an improved type of bicycle with cranks and pedals directly on the front wheel, at the Exposition Internationale de Paris
1867	William E. Lincoln patents the Zoetrope, an animated picture machine with photographs spinning round in a metal cylinder
1869	Solid rubber tires mounted on steel rims introduced to a new two-wheeled vehicle, which was the first to be patented under the modern name "bicycle"
1869	Union Pacific and Central Pacific Railroads complete the first trans-continental line in America

discoveries that reassessed the place of the human species in the animal world (Fuhlrott's discovery of the Neanderthal man in 1857; Darwin's *On the Origin of Species* of 1859; Huxley's *Man's Place in Nature* of 1863, etc.). Freud's papers on hysteria, sexuality, dreams, and the unconscious (published 1893 ff.) dissolved the concept of the "old stable ego"[102] and opened up unknown perspectives on the human soul. Even more momentous, if not traumatic, was the disintegration of the materialist–positivist understanding of the world, due to new scientific revelations that destroyed the classical understanding of the physical universe and provoked new philosophical explanations of an unstable and indeterminate state of existence. Becquerel's and the Curies' discovery of radioactivity (1896 and 1898 respectively), Planck's quantum mechanics (1900), Rutherford's and Bohr's atomic models (1911 and 1913 respectively) and finally Einstein's Special and General Theory of Relativity (1905 and 1915 respectively) shattered the traditional concept of an objective reality apprehensible through the human sense apparatus. The atom, which for a long time had been considered the smallest building block of matter, was shown to be no compact, stable entity, but to be made up of transitory, indeterminate electrons orbiting around a tiny nucleus, which in 1913 was discovered to be composed of even smaller particles. When Rutherford calculated that only a ten-thousandth part of an atom was made up of mass, the nonscientific community was also profoundly shocked and had to accept that the material world largely comprised of empty space (for these and some other major inventions and discoveries see chronologies 1.1 and 1.2).

CHRONOLOGY 1.2: SOME MAJOR INVENTIONS AND DISCOVERIES IN THE AGE OF MODERNITY, 1872–1913

1872 William Henry Ward files for a U.S. patent on a transmission system using a telegraph tower "broadcasting" to a number of receiving antennae

1873 James Clerk Maxwell, *Treatise on Electricity and Magnetism*, first theory of electromagnetic waves

1876 Alexander Graham Bell patents the telephone and gives the first demonstration of an electronic voice transmission system

1877 Thomas Alva Edison makes the first recording of a human voice and in 1878 patents a phonograph with a wax cylinder as recording medium

1877 Emile Berliner invents a "loose-contact" microphone, which increases the volume of the transmitted voice

1878 David Edward Hughes's first carbon microphone

1878 Teletroscope by Constantin Senlecq for the projection of pictures

1878 William Crookes confirms the existence of cathode rays and develops the Crookes Tube, a crude prototype for all future cathode ray tubes

1878 Charles Francis Brush produces the first commercially successful arc lamp

1879 Thomas Alva Edison invents an incandescent light bulb with carbon-filament

1881 First electrical streetcar in Berlin

1881 At the Paris Electrical Exhibition, musical performances are relayed from the Opéra and the Comédie Française

1882   Nikola Tesla conceives of an AC induction motor, first built in 1887

1883   Gottlieb Daimler constructs the first petrol motor, and in 1886 the first four-wheel motorcar running on petrol. It has a maximum speed of 16 Km/h (10 mph)

1884   Paul Gottlieb Nipkow invents a mechanical scanning device, an early version of a mechanical television

1886   Karl Benz presents the first successful gas-engine motorcar

1886   Ernst Abbe develops a microscope with apochromat objectives, which reaches the limit of resolution for visible light microscopes

1887   Heinrich Rudolph Hertz proves the existence of electromagnetic waves, thus laying the technical foundation for wireless telegraphy

1887   Emile Berliner invents the gramophone, an improved phonograph using flat-discs engraved with lateral grooves as a recording medium

1887   Oberlin Smith invents a magnetic recorder

1888   Nikola Tesla designs the first practical system of generating and transmitting alternating current for electric power systems

1888   Heinrich Rudolph Hertz produces long waves, now known as radio waves

1889   Eifel Tower built in Paris, the world's tallest structure until 1930

1891   Otto Lilienthal's first successful experiment with a gliding, bird-like aircraft

1891   Thomas Alva Edison patents the Kinetograph, a camera that records images on a 35 mm wide transparent celluloid strip coated with Eastman Kodak photographic emulsion

1891   Tesla coil, a transformer with important applications in the field of radio communications was invented

1891   George Johnstone coins the word "electron" as the indivisible unit of charge in electrochemistry

1891   Peugeot begins serial production of motorcars

1892   Rudolf Diesel patents his heavy-oil combustion engine, first manufactured successfully in 1897

1893   Thomas Alva Edison patents the Kinetoscope, a machine for projecting moving pictures

1894   Charles Francis Jenkins' Phantascope for the projection of pictures

1894   Wilhelm Conrad Röntgen discovers the X-rays

1895   Louis Jean Lumière and Auguste Marie Lumière present the Cinématograph for the projection of moving pictures

1895   Sigmund Freud and Joseph Breuer publish their *Studies on Hysteria*

1896   Guglielmo Marchese Marconi invents wireless telegraphy

1896   Samuel Pierpont Langley produces a steam-powered aeroplane that flies 900 to 1,200m (3,000 to 4,000 ft) for about 1 1/2 minutes

1896   Discovery of radioactivity by Antoine Henri Becquerel

1897   Karl Ferdinand Braun invents the oscilloscope, a cathode ray tube scanning device that developed into today's television and radar tubes

1897   Nikola Tesla files the basic radio patent

1897 Joseph John Thompson discovers the electron

1898 Valdemar Poulsen builds and patents the first working magnetic recorder, called the Telegraphone, and demonstrates it at the 1900 Paris Exhibition

1898 Marie and Pierre Curie discover in a uranium-containing mineral the naturally occurring radioactive elements polonium and radium, and coin word "radioactivity"

1900 Rigid dirigible airship by Graf Ferdinand von Zeppelin

1900 The largest European car manufacturer, Benz, claims to have built 2,500 motorcars

1900 Constantin Persky uses the term "television" in the catalog for the Exposition Universelle Internationale of 1900

1900 Max Planck's quantum theory

1901 Guglielmo Marconi transmits the first radio signal across the Atlantic Ocean, from Cornwall to Newfoundland

1902 Radio-telephone by Valdemar Poulsen and Reginald Aubrey Fessenden

1902 Gustave-Auguste Ferrié builds a radio receiver, called "electrolytic detector"

1902 Christian Hülsmeyer builds the Telemobiloscope, a precursor of radar

1903 Henry Ford founds the Ford Motor Company

1903 Orville and Wilbur Wright make the first flight in a heavier-than-air craft

1903 Samuel Pierpont Langley's Aerodrome, the first petrol-engine-powered aeroplane

1904 Guglielmo Marconi is awarded a patent for his radio apparatus

1905 Albert Einstein's special theory of relativity

1906 The first radio broadcast made in the United States by R. A. Fessenden

1911 Neon lamp by Georges Claude French

1911 Ernest Rutherford's theory of atomic structure describes the atom as a dense nucleus surrounded by a cloud of electrons

1913 Niels Bohr's atomic model shows electrons moving in fixed orbits around a nucleus

When the long-established foundations of the physical and psychological world began to crumble, an epistemic crisis befell Western society, which Max Planck summed up as: "We are living in a very singular moment of history. It is a moment of crisis . . . Many people say that these symptoms mark the beginnings of a great renaissance, but there are others who see in them the tidings of a downfall to which our civilization is fatally destined."[103] There were clear signs that the scientific revolution of the late-nineteenth / early-twentieth century repeated what had previously been experienced in the sixteenth century: Yeats's poem "Things fall apart; the centre cannot hold; / mere anarchy is loosed upon the world"[104] resembled John Donne's 1611 depiction of a world that is "crumbled out again to his Atoms. 'Tis all in pieces, all coherence gone."[105]

In the nineteenth century, many intellectuals took an ambivalent attitude to the changing environment around them, but they principally adhered to a materialist–positivist understanding of the world and, overtly or covertly, believed in the possibility of ameliorating the ills of society. After the turn of the century, to many of them this seemed no longer possible. A vanishing concept of reality combined with a profound feeling that the negative aspects of modernity were to persevere, if not get worse, provoked a profound disillusionment and caused a crisis in the intellectual world. Rationalism as an imbedded social practice of the modern age gave way to irrational dynamics. The artist, caught in the maelstrom of uncertainty, anxiety, and disquiet experienced the world as a chaotic, impenetrable labyrinth, and focused on the irrational, unconscious, primitive aspects of life rather than offering measured, rational, realistic depictions of human existence. Karl Pinthus expressed this clearly in the introduction to his anthology *The Twilight of Humanity* when he wrote: "The poetry of this generation reveals the chaotic character of the modern age, the disintegration of traditional social forms, despair and yearning, but also the fanatical craving for new potentials of human life, and it does so with just the same noisiness and wildness as one can encounter in reality."[106]

The artistic response to this situation we are now wont to refer to as the birth of Modernism. A whole catalog of works—now widely regarded as masterpieces of twentieth-century art—described the standardized, rationalized, secularized existence of the big-city dweller and the threatening void of a dysfunctional society. This is not to say that the positive features of modernity were entirely disregarded. In fact, in some countries that were still in the process of catching up with the advancements of science and technology, such as Italy and Russia, the view of modernity as something desirable rather than threatening still prevailed (giving rise, respectively, to Futurism and Constructivism). But such optimistic assessments of the wonders of a technological civilization were counterbalanced by works that fostered an awareness of the flipside of modernity and focused on the hazards and pitfalls of life in the modern era.

This mixture of critical, positive, and ambivalent attitudes toward modernity could also be found in works of the preceding century. But whereas in the nineteenth century, artists belonging to the "Modern" school tended to adopt a positive attitude toward the new realities, mixed in, maybe, with a healthy dose of skepticism and social critique, many artists of the early twentieth century focused their attention on the destructive forces of industrialization, presented a dystopic vision of an urban wasteland, and offered a fundamental critique of the "grand narratives" of progress, emancipation, perfectability of the world, which since the Enlightenment had dominated European thinking.

Furthermore, *Modernist* works of art differed from *modern* ones because they presented reality not as a given phenomenon, but as something processed by the human mind (see text box 1.2). If in the artist's psyche a shattered, incoherent, and absurd world conjured up images of chaos, energy, noisiness, and so on, then the forms employed to express this experience had to be similarly dissonant, disjointed, and fragmentary. The Modernist artist did not passively reflect but critically appropriated the radically changed world. In this sense, Modernist works were still "realistic," but in a manner that transcended mere imitation. Modernist art modified the categories of representation and enriched them with new techniques that went beyond the traditional "art holding a mirror to nature" concepts of Realism. Some of the formal elements of Modernism—such as the use of incongruous and contradictory ingredients, collage of components taken from a variety of contexts, simultaneity and fragmentation of elements—could produce in the reader/viewer a heightened awareness of reality. Defamiliarization, *Verfremdung, ostranenie* were some of the terms used for the method of "making things look strange" in order to direct attention to significant features of reality that otherwise would go unnoticed. Much of the emphasis on experimentation with form was not, as Lukács et al. intimated, pure aestheticism and formalism, but an attempt to find more adequate forms for an artistic rendering of the "modern" realities of the twentieth century. The fact that *some* Modernists believed that form equals content should not detract us from the fact that in most works the new forms were derived from new contents and gave expression to a subjective experience of a truly novel kind.

The Modernists' effort of finding new artistic languages for conjuring up the modern experience caused the artists to be highly self-conscious in the use of their medium of expression. This problematization of language is rightly considered to be a fundamental and constitutive aspect of Modernism (see text box 1.1). The subject of modernity, which had inspired many key works of art and literature in the second half of the nineteenth century, increasingly became a focus of theoretical reflections. Such a theoretically grounded artistic practice was different from that of the early nineteenth century, when critical reflections tended to be a by-product of creative production. Of course, there was no lack of theoretical statements issued by nineteenth-century artists and writers, but the early twentieth century introduced something substantially new and different. Between 1890 and 1930 a plethora of groups, schools, and movements propagated their artistic doctrines by means of short, theoretical statements printed in journals, newspapers, magazines or as broadsheets, flyers, and pamphlets. This manifesto mania resulted from a desire not only to be new, modern, and innovative, but also to establish clear boundaries and distinctions from what had gone on before and what coexisted on the contemporary scene. Unstated, yet from today's perspective obvious, was another key motive: to register one's claim of originality in a patent-like fashion so that one could beat the competition in the intellectual marketplace.

By the late-nineteenth century, the shift from a patronage to a market system in the arts—which had begun in the eighteenth century—had been completed. A rapidly increasing class of professionals and intellectuals operated in an overcrowded market situation.[107] This surfeit of individuals and schools seeking to find their place in the art or publishing industries had to lay particular emphasis on originality and innovation. As discussed below, fetishization of novelty was a built-in feature of capitalist commodity economy, or to use Adorno's words: "The new in art is the aesthetic counterpart to the expanding reproduction of capital in society. Both hold out the promise of undiminished plenitude."[108] Just as capitalism depended for its development on the ability to replace old commodities with new ones (or at least with newly packaged ones), bourgeois art of the modern period generated dozens of schools and cenâcles in an attempt to renew itself. From the 1890s onwards, a rapid succession of new styles emerged from the bourgeois "art factory." Marinetti was probably the first, but certainly not the only one, to make conscious use of spectacular promotion campaigns and advertising strategies derived from the mass media for marketing his cultural products.[109] For him, as for other artists, writers, composers, and so on the manifesto took on the rôle of staking a claim in the market.

Such a formal presentation of a wide range of new concepts of art and literature justifies the use of the generic term "Modernism" as opposed to "modern" (although contemporary language gave preference to the latter and reserved "Modernism" to the meaning of "to be modern at all cost"). Modern*ism* stands for a highly developed consciousness of the modern features of society and of the new and innovative means employed to depict this reality. The emergence of so many -isms with organized schools and doctrines attached to them makes it useful to have an omnibus term to denote the underlying similarities between these groups and movements propagating their otherwise divergent artistic interpretations of the modern world. However, I would not go as far as some critics who use the term Modernism to cover under one heading nearly all post-Romantic developments. When Modernism is understood as the noun of "modern," it makes it a very wide-ranging portmanteau term and eliminates all differences between nineteenth-century descriptions of industrial society and the modern city, and an art and literature that radically broke with the Realist representation of the storm of innovation that had swept the social and economic world.

THE CONCEPT OF THE AVANT-GARDE

Related to the concept of Modernism, yet different in emphasis and intention, was that of the avant-garde, which emerged in the nineteenth century more or less in parallel with the development of modernity. In the context of this study, I consciously disregard the vague notion of a timeless avant-garde that is applicable to any artist who is "ahead of his time,"[110] as it belongs to colloquial language, not to aesthetic criticism. The term "avant-garde" dates back to the Middle Ages, where it was used in military language to designate the advance troops of an army. Its figurative meaning of an advanced position in arts or literature originated in the Renaissance. Étienne Pasquier was possibly the first author to characterize a number of writers as "the avant-garde; or, if you prefer, the forerunners of other poets."[111] Around the time of the French Revolution, the term came to be applied to Jacobin politics and Utopian, future-oriented philosophies. The metaphor certainly appealed to radical intellectuals who regarded themselves as an advance guard leading the rest of mankind into a liberated future.

The concept of an artistic avant-garde as a parallel development to the political avant-garde (see text box 1.3) was first introduced by the early Utopian socialists. Henri de Saint-Simon held that artists, scientists, and

---

TEXT BOX 1.3 AVANT-GARDE

Originally a military term, it came to be applied to political and aesthetic domains, where it denotes a practice of assaulting traditional authorities and cultural institutions. The avant-garde in the arts propagates a radical break with preceding formulae of artistic production and promotes creativity as part of a wider cultural-political revolution. This transgressive, subversive stance separates avant-garde artists from other Modernists, with whom they share an interest in experimentation with new artistic forms and techniques. Avant-garde artists oppose conventional concepts, values, and standards, and instead aim at absolute originality in their creations. They operate in uncharted terrain with genuinely novel means of expression, creating works of art that are substantially and significantly different from the average production of their time, and are initially appreciated by only a small number of connoisseurs.

craftsmen were the most useful members of society and should therefore be in charge of the State.[112] He also assigned a positive function to industrialists, but the leading rôle in the future society should be played by artists.[113] He enlarged on this a few years later, saying "In the great enterprise of establishing a system of common weal the artists as people endowed with fantasy will open the march and proclaim the future of the human species. They will wrest a golden age out of the past in order to enrich future generations."[114] The idea was further elaborated by his pupil Olinde Rodrigues, who propagated the idea of the artist as a leader, priest, and Messiah, who would "serve as the avant-garde" of a new society and use "as his weapon" the various arts at his disposal. An eminent position is accorded to the theatre, as it is a medium with "electric and triumphant influence" and unleashes "the most vivid and decisive kind of action."[115] Similarly, Gabriel-Désiré Laverdant in his essay "De la mission de l'art et du rôle des artistes" of 1845 attached the ideas of progress and social justice to art and arrived at the conclusion that if "art as an expression of society expresses in its most elevated forms the most advanced social tendencies and is a forerunner and discoverer . . . , then art is worthy of its rôle of initiator and the artist of belonging to the avant-garde."[116]

The saint-simonean conception of the artist as the vanguard of a better society exercised considerable influence in the years to come. The image of the avant-garde artist marching in a united front with the political revolutionary, and the notion of radical, engaged art as a complement to political radicalism gained ground in the second half of the nineteenth century. In Anarchist and Communist circles the term "avant-garde" continued to have a predominantly sociopolitical meaning,[117] and when a union of artistic and political vanguards was considered, it always presupposed a subordination of art under politics. This caused writers such as Baudelaire to criticize the concept of the avant-garde for being too militaristic and disciplinarian.[118] Nonetheless, the idea of radical art merging with revolutionary politics continued to hold sway among artists of various persuasion—in the following century, for example, among Italian and Russian Futurists, Surrealists, and Constructivists, all of which sought to ally themselves to political liberation movements. In the end, most of these coalitions proved unsuccessful and caused a break in the "diplomatic relations between two bohemian states, Aesthetika and Politika."[119] The parties of the radical Left had no place for artists who did not toe the line. The artists, on the other hand, insisted on their independence. The slogan, "art and the revolutionary artists to power,"[120] did not aim at turning artists into politicians, but at transforming politics into a creative occupation and thus instituting change both in the arts and in politics. Unfortunately, the strategies and methods employed to further these goals did not find any backing from political parties of the Left. So in the end the paradoxical situation arose that avant-garde artists were accepted, if not honored, by the bourgeoisie, against whom they had rebelled, and that these artists were rejected by the revolution-ary forces, with whom they had sought to form a coalition.

It was a characteristic trait of all avant-garde movements that their opposi-tion to the established canons of art went hand in hand with a battle against the guardians of tradition and social propriety. The Dadaists' all-out assault on the institutions of bourgeois society ("We were in no doubt that the world had to be overturned. We wanted to prepare an attack that went beyond anything the war-waging nations had ever seen."[121]) contained an echo of the military semantics mentioned above. These militant revolutionaries in the "culture wars" of the Modernist period took it upon themselves to scout the enemy territory, attack the barriers erected by the forces of tradition, force a breach, and then move into the uncharted terrain of the future. The "advance guard" would then be followed by the regular "army" of Modernist artists, who shared with the élite corps an oppositional, progressive stance, but were less reckless in their actions and did not expose themselves to the same risks.

The Futurists characterized the "fearful invasion" of "a great army of mad-men" into "the land of paralysis," where they "raze Goutville to the ground" and lay the "great military Railroad into the future," as a revolutionary war.[122] Marinetti, who was well versed in the theory and practice of Anarchism, viewed these interventions in the social and cultural fields as a form of insur-rection that emulated the "destructive gesture of freedom-bringers"[123] and produced an art that was "like the throwing of a well-primed grenade over the heads of our contemporaries."[124] He concluded: "Art can be nothing but vio-lence."[125] So let the artist be "a gay incendiary," who sets fire to the libraries or raises his pickaxe in order to demolish the museums and academies.

A similar range of military metaphors was used by Emilio Settimelli, when he described the Futurists as the vanguard in the battle against traditionalism and academism in the theatre. Their task was to open up a breach for the more moderate Modernists (such as Pirandello, Rosso di San Secondo, Bontempelli, Chiarelli, etc.) to follow. Therefore, "leaving behind a tradition and imagining a new road to the future has often more value than the work that results from this victory over tradition."[126]

Also Hans Arp had this idea of another life in mind when he spoke of Dada as "a crusade in order to win back the promised land of creativity."[127] Ball compared his position in Zurich with that of a fighter in the trenches,[128] and in the "Manifesto against the Weimar Spirit of Life," the Berlin Dadaists declared themselves to be "an international anti-bourgeois movement."[129]

In this revolutionary battle, art was transformed from a marketable commodity into a weapon: "We know that we have to be an expression of the revolutionary forces, an instrument of the masses and the necessities of our times. We deny any similarity with the aesthetic profiteers and academics of tomorrow."[130]

Another metaphor often encountered in this context was that of the avant-garde as a purgative that clears out the constipation of body and mind. The concept of hygiene occupied a central rôle in Marinetti's writings.[131] "Dr F. T. Marinetti," as he proudly signed many of his early essays and theoretical reflections, conducted his surgical strikes against the perceived illnesses of the body politic, and earned himself the reputation of being *il Poeta Pink*, named after a popular medicine believed to "restore the weak organism and provide the best cure against anemia, sclerosis and general fatigue."[132] In a similar manner, the Dadaists described their activities as "practical self-detoxification,"[133] which "fulfilled the useful function of a purgative."[134] Such medical metaphors and references continued to be used after World War II. For example, George Maciunas aspired for the Fluxus movement to have the effect of "a flowing or fluid discharge from the bowels" and for this reason planned to sell his *Fluxus* magazine in a "nice box of a disposable enema unit."[135]

Whether functioning like a bomb or a cleanser, avant-garde art was in the first instance conceived as an oppositional force, whose critical, subversive rôle could take three forms:

(a) analysis—the artist holds a critical mirror to society;
(b) engagement—the artist promotes active intervention and change;
(c) forward vision—the artist projects an image of an emancipated society.

From a position of critical distance, avant-garde artists attacked the dominant ideology of bourgeois society, analyzed the reconciliatory functions of the category of "art" in capitalist countries, and criticized the prevailing aesthetic conventions. They subverted the institutional framework of the production, distribution, and reception of cultural artifacts and showed art to be an ideological construct sanctioned by custom and tradition. They divested art of the aesthetic forms that could offer refuge from the ugly, deformed, and alienated realities of capitalism, and they destroyed the illusions of organic perfection, self-contained wholeness, inner harmony, and beauty. The avant-garde advocated rupture, revolution, and destruction as vehicles of liberation and innovation, and employed transgression and shock as means of criticizing (a) the functions of art and the rôle of the artist in bourgeois society and (b) the means of expression employed in the creation of works of art.

If necessary, it even prescribed the transitory death of art as a therapeutic measure.

AVANT-GARDE, MODERNISM, AND THE MAINSTREAM

The radical, intransigent an attitude of avant-garde artists was markedly different from that of nineteenth-century innovators, who sought to affect a gradual evolution of artistic forms and social constellations. Artists belonging to the Modernist schools placed themselves somewhere between these two positions. They were more forceful in their criticism and reformist zeal than nineteenth-century reformers, yet never displayed the same attitude of radical opposition as avant-garde artists did in their manifestos, political actions, and works of art. The Modernists struggled against entrenched rules and conventions, yet never challenged the guardians of established cultural institutions. This, in turn, has caused a widespread interpretation of Modernism as an invigorating social influence and of the avant-garde as a nihilistic and destructive force. However, avant-garde art was not only characterized by opposition, protest, negativity; it also experimented with new forms of expression and anticipated in its creations a liberated art practice. The fact that for avant-garde artists the revolution was a means toward an end could be shown by dozens of quotations, ranging form the early part of the twentieth century (e.g., Richard Huelsenbeck: "Where new values are to be created, the old ones have to be cleared away . . . Dada's demonstration of nothingness, of madness and destruction was a constructive task"[136]) to the postwar period (e.g., Fluxus artist Emmett Williams: "The revolution enables me to build new structures with words after tearing down old structures"[137]). Given this intimate bond of art and anti-art, destructive impulses and forward-looking visions, the relationship between artist and society can be described as falling into three categories:

(a) The conventional artist, who produces for the mass market and has an uncritical, affirmative attitude toward society.
(b) The Modernist artist, who seeks to capture those aspects of the contemporary world that are transforming traditional culture and society. As such, the Modernist artist is at odds with the conservative forces, who try to preserve the civilization of a by-gone era.
(c) The avant-garde artist, who has an intuitive perception of impending changes, expresses a vision of how these will affect society, and who seeks to open up a terrain for these innovations to take place. As such, the avant-garde artist attempts to provoke radical change before others see a

need for it. Here, art takes on a visionary rôle and acts as an instrument of social change.

The historical avant-garde was never a homogeneous phenomenon, but encompassed a wide range of artists who were opposed to the aesthetic and social conventions of their day. They formed an integral element of Modernist culture, but were far more radical and uncompromising than the average Modernist cohorts. Avant-garde art was produced by small, close-knit groups of nonconformist individualists, whereas Modernism was a "broad church" that included many hangers-on and undistinguished associates. The avant-garde formulated the most advanced and forward-looking concepts, and then left it to its followers to translate these visions into concrete reality. The Modernists were like the rank and file who follow the shock-troopers after they have occupied a new territory. To take the military metaphor a stage further: after the Modernists have explored the "virgin soils," the mainstream artists move in, exploit the land, and use it to cultivate staple products for mass consumption.

The avant-garde was the "cutting edge" of Modernism and produced genuinely novel and original works of art. Modernist artists assumed the task of translating the innovative achievements of the avant-garde into "a movement-idiolect or a period-idiolect,"[138] which would then become a characteristic feature of a given period and produce new norms accepted by society. The Modernists emphasized the need to go with the times, but they did not ignore the roots of the modern culture in older traditions. George Steiner has gone as far as claiming that Modernism was a deliberate attempt at salvaging a cultural past that was in danger of complete dissolution, and could therefore amount to "a strategy of conservation."[139] Other critics see Modernism as the "new tradition" of the modern era; it superseded the older, Realist tradition, but remained liable to academic institutionalization.

Modernist artists operated in close cooperation with the mediating agencies of museums, theatres, newspapers, and so on, whereas avant-garde artists refused to fulfill any subservient functions in bourgeois society. They established a critical distance to the reified and alienating life-praxis in middle-class society and confronted the bourgeoisie with a fragmented and distorted image of reality. Avant-garde art relied on its autonomous status in order to perform its critical, anticipatory functions, yet at the same time tried to escape this position by turning artistic creativity into an emancipatory social praxis. The possibility of the work of art fulfilling its progressive, transformational, and liberating function was thus predicated on the autonomy it tried to overcome.

As artistic autonomy was such an important issue in the aesthetic debates of the late nineteenth and early twentieth century, the dividing line between different types of autonomy needs to be clearly established:

(a) The *l'art pour l'art* concept of aestheticism: detachment of art from the functionalist, utilitarian life-praxis in bourgeois society provided a sacred realm, in which the human being could recover its lost wholeness. These sanctuaries of art isolated from the social sphere offered an escape from everyday routines and allowed an experience of a life in harmony with itself. It masked the contradictions of an alienated existence and promised to resolve them in an aesthetic refuge, pretending that real needs could be satisfied in an unreal world.

(b) The Modernist insistence on autonomy: artists could protect the independence of works of art from nonaesthetic functionality, concern themselves with the medium itself, and focus on its inherent aesthetic qualities. This led to formalist concerns with innovation and technical perfection. Content and social purpose were seen to be of minor significance. This self-reflexive (and often self-absorbed and self-sufficient) art stood for an aesthetic revolution without consequences in the social world.

(c) The avant-garde concept of autonomy: artists aimed at establishing a critical distance to social determinism and to the affirmative rôle of art in capitalist society. They offered a critique of the ideology of art in bourgeois society and demonstrated an awareness of the institutionalized conditions of artistic production. The avant-garde artist anticipated a society in which the instrumental rationality of the capitalist system would be eradicated. Art served as a model for a liberated future and anticipated a non-alienated existence to be accomplished through a creative art/life praxis.

As bourgeois society was not monolithic in terms of ideology and social practices, artists found a variety of ways of relating to the cultural bodies of their epoch. Yet, rejecting bourgeois society while at the same time operating within its artistic institutions caught the artist in a paradoxical situation that knew no easy solution. Although the avant-garde opposed the reactionary or traditionalist aspects of bourgeois art, this opposition also strengthened a structural feature of capitalist society: its constant drive to renew and advance itself. Market economies rely on internal competition in order to sustain growth. Both avant-garde and Modernist artists were caught up in this dilemma; the difference in their response to this problem was only a matter of degrees and was effectively annulled by their joint operational platform within the bourgeois art establishment. Both countercultures succumbed to the institutional embrace and ended up being yoked to the very system they tried to overcome. The concept of alterity they promoted came to be incorporated into the machinery of progress and was neutralized in just the same manner as the attempts to break up the institutionalized distance of art from life.

To illustrate the above-mentioned broad tendencies, I shall quote some selected examples taken from the "classic" phase of Modernism and the avant-garde. The Futurists were the first to undertake a systematic attack on the bourgeois institutions of art, and were also the first to experience how their protest actions, carried out *within* the institutions, came to entertain rather than shock their audiences. The first theatrical "evenings" (*serate*) in 1910 caused major scandals, disrupted the social peace, provoked police interventions and interdictions from political authorities, and so on (see chapter 3). However, after a while audiences came to these events "to find distraction and excitement . . . to see and experience something new and to feel stimulated and fortified."[140] Consequently, the Futurists relocated part of their artistic practice, moved out of the bourgeois institutions, and took their actions to the streets, to working men's clubs, and popular meeting halls. At the same time as bringing art into the public domain, they participated in elections, political demonstrations, and protest actions, and finally founded their own Party (1918) in order to promote their concept of an Italian Revolution.[141] One can say that during this period, Futurism had achieved a close union of aesthetic and social action and a fusion of art and life.[142] Looking ahead at the future, Marinetti sketched out a cultural set-up based on these experiences, where artistic creativity was no longer restricted to professional activities in bourgeois institutions, but invaded the popular living quarters, where "life will no longer be a simple matter of bread and labor, nor a life of idleness either, but *a work of art*."[143]

Marinetti's desire to take art out of the hands of the bourgeoisie and integrate it into a new, liberating life-praxis, gave rise to the idea of founding "cultural centers which function as places to organize 'Free Exhibitions of the Creative Genius,' "[144] and an all-encompassing project called "Futurist Reconstruction of the Universe." Originally a manifesto signed by Balla and Depero, it became a program, to which many artists contributed and gave rise to truly innovative creations in a broad spectrum of applied arts. However, as far as the Futurists' participation in the political life of the country was concerned, the erection of a Fascist State prevented them from fulfilling their sociopolitical-artistic program of action. The same can be said about the Russian Cubo-Futurists and Communist-Futurists. Although their coalition with the political revolutionary forces lasted longer, their impact on the life of ordinary citizens was negligible and they were the first victims of the conservative backlash under Lunacharsky and Zdanov. Also the Expressionist rôle in the Munich Revolution[145] and the failed alliance of the Surrealists with the French Communist Party[146] indicated that the union of artistic and revolutionary forces, which Saint-Simon and his followers dreamed of, was never more than an Utopian idea.

This is not to say that the avant-garde movements did not leave any lasting trace behind. Many of the items produced by Futurists and Constructivists for the everyday use of ordinary citizens affected the future history of production design. Through the Bauhaus, it changed the face of the modern city. However, it was not usually the *revolutionary* concepts of the avant-garde, but the *compromises*, undertaken by Modernists with business acumen, which achieved commercial success. In the first quarter of the twentieth century, many of the innovative traits and achievements of the avant-garde were adopted by the Modernist movements, presented in exhibitions, and popularized among the educated élite. And once Modernism had established itself as a dominant trend in the arts, its devices filtered through into the mainstream, where they were picked up by a novelty-hungry culture industry. The capitalist consumer market successfully colonized Modernist art and integrated it into its portfolio of commodities. By the mid-1920s, many ideas originally propagated by the avant-garde had become assimilated by the mainstream and could be encountered in watered-down form in popular movies, department stores, bars, cafés, and the like.

To see how much the "radical chic" of Modernism proved to be prey to capitalist interests one only needs to compare commercial products aimed at the middle-classes in, say, 1910 and 1930. An army of epigones in the fields of applied arts and fine arts, literature, and theatre turned previously radical and innovative ideas into marketable objects and offered these to a bourgeois clientele with "progressive" tastes. Once the concepts of the avant-garde had become absorbed by the wider community of artists and popularized among the modern-thinking public, they ceased to be in the forefront of aesthetic innovation and had to be replaced with new ideas. The avant-garde always conceived of itself as a highly ephemeral phenomenon and not as an institution. Already Jarry's predicted that when the former avant-garde had turned into "mayors in little towns and academicians, . . . a new generation of young people will appear, find us completely out of date, and hence abominate us in their pasquills. This is the way how things should be."[147] Similarly, Marinetti described Futurism as a short-lived affair, soon to be overtaken by "younger and stronger men, who will probably throw us into the waste paper bin like useless manuscripts—we want it to happen!"[148] And, in the same vein, Huelsenbeck proclaimed that "Dada has the right to dissolve itself and will exert this right when the time comes. With businesslike gesture, freshly pressed pants, a shave and a haircut, it will go down into the grave."[149]

This attitude also determined the form and function of many avant-garde creations. At the *Manifestation Dada* at the Grand Palais (February 5, 1920), Picabia challenged his spectators with the statement: "Dada works must not exist for any longer than six hours."[150] Yet, despite this intention of being a transitory phenomenon, the avant-garde took root, was copied, and eventually became part of the establishment. As early as 1917, a visitor to the Cabaret Voltaire could declare: "It is nearly like an academy. They are building their own tradition."[151] In 1920, Huelsenbeck foresaw the danger of Dada becoming commodified by the culture industry: "The mediocrities and the gentry in search of 'something mad' are beginning to conquer Dada."[152]

For this reason, avant-garde artists liked to employ the most ephemeral of all media, performance, to express their artistic concerns. A single, unrepeatable, and therefore unique stage event counted for much more than a poem printed in a magazine or a painting exhibited in a gallery. Furthermore, performance being a live event involved the artist in a direct confrontation with the audience, whose reactions could be responded to in a direct, improvised manner. Therefore, if avant-garde art was to be a militant practice, this battle could be fought most effectively in a theatrical setting.

TEXT BOX 1.4   SOME KEY FEATURES OF AVANT-GARDE ART

- Against the autonomous status of art in bourgeois society: art should not be a sanctuary separate from the everyday business of politics and economics and should not offer any illusion of wholesomeness, ideal beauty, redemption, contemplation, and edification.
- Merging of art and life: instead of being restricted to operate within the established cultural institutions, art should form the basis of a new life praxis and organize the environment and everyday existence according to creative principles.
- Negotiating a position between the paradoxes of art and anti-art, autonomy, and intervention. There exists a double bind between revolt against art and a creative engagement with art, between establishing a critical distance from society and overcoming the artist's detachment from society.
- Changing the established cultural and political order by means of shock, provocation, disturbance, intervention, and so on. Calling into question the habitual communication structures and discourses. Rejecting aesthetic canons, conventions, and precepts.

- Crisis of language: questioning the referential and communicative functions of art and revealing verbal and visual language to be a construction or artifice determined by social context and artistic intention. Form reflects on itself, its codes, referential status, and signifying power.
- Crisis of representation: against the concept of art as a mirror held up to nature; against the organic and closed concept of art. "An object has not one absolute form—it has many; it has as many as there are planes in the region of perception."[153] New techniques of fragmentation, collage, and montage; multi-focal perspective, simultaneity, discontinuity; juxtaposition of material; disjointed discourses rather than linear renderings.
- Self-reflexivity: the work of art is not a mimetic copy of an objective reality but an expression of the artist's consciousness of that reality. These mental filters are foregrounded in the portrayal and enhance the audience's awareness of the artificiality of the construction.
- Crisis of individuality: disintegration of the organic, coherent, integrated subject (Rimbaud's "Je est un autre"[154]). Not only reality has lost its coherent structure, but also the observing subject. Perception is a stream of sensations. Emphasis on subjectivity in the production and reception process.
- Placing the spectators at the center of the work and forcing them to take an active rôle in the creative act. The audience as coproducer: instead of existing in splendid isolation from the work of art and taking an objective, distanced stance toward its presentation, the spectator has to resynthesize the fragmented reality exhibited in the artwork through an active engagement with its form and content.
- New Utopianism. Futurist refashioning of the world on a changed basis. Constructivist ideal of a prosperous human and industrial future. Positive attitude toward the liberating potential of technology. The machine as a metaphor of creativity and progress.

TOWARD AN AVANT-GARDE CONCEPTION OF THE PERFORMING ARTS: ALFRED JARRY AND WASSILY KANDINSKY

In the nineteenth century, theatre was predominantly a sector of the entertainment industry and catered for bourgeois audiences with a taste for escapist, melodramatic, and sentimental drama. The art theatre of the period only occupied a small, albeit influential position in the cultural landscape. Its authors and directors made a conscious effort to address the pressing issues of the time and produced a steady stream of works categorized by their authors, audiences, and critics as "modern." This designation could refer either to a subject matter taken from contemporary life, or to the use of stylistic devices that defied the classic Aristotelian model. Büchner, Chekhov, Tolstoy, Ibsen, Strindberg, Hauptmann, and Granville-Barker were the best-known representatives of this trend, and they were supported in their undertaking by directors such as Laube, Brahm, Antoine, Stanislavsky, and Reinhardt, among others.

Toward the end of the nineteenth century, one can observe a distinct countertrend, both in dramatic writing and theatrical production. Several of the founding fathers of the modern stage sought to demolish the narrow confines of Realist aesthetics. Wedekind, Strindberg, Maeterlinck, and many other playwrights directed their attention to the subjective experience or spiritual dimension of reality. Craig, Appia, Fuchs, Fort, Lugné-Poë, and others stripped down the Naturalistic paraphernalia that cluttered the stage and instead worked with a stylized, symbolic, or abstract décor. Dramatists and directors discovered the scenic spectacle and the physical craft of the actor as art forms in their own right, and the work undertaken by these reformers prepared the stage for the acceptance of Modernism in the theatre.

The years 1890–1914 were a transitional period, which saw a theatrical avant-garde emerging out of a cultural climate of renewal and experimentation that had been prepared by Post-Impressionists, Symbolists, and *Art Nouveau* artists. Critics regularly refer to this generation as "the first avant-garde" or "the first wave of Modernism." I have no principal objection to this, but I would still classify these artists as innovative reformers rather than exemplary figures of Modernism or representatives of the avant-garde. The founding fathers of the modern stage pursued an artistic program that was certainly modern, in some ways even ahead of their time, but they still treated theatre as a handmaiden of dramatic literature. They retained the concept of theatre as a fixed and repeatable spectacle and never questioned the unspoken assumptions of what constitutes a theatrical production. It fell to the historical avant-garde to challenge the criteria of what constitutes a scenic work of art and to create performances that were not just interpretations of dramatic texts, but autonomous, transient events that attained power and impact from their temporal and physical immediacy. Of course, every performance is a unique and unrepeatable event; but the avant-garde in its most radical manifestations abolished the product-oriented working method of institutionalized theatre. Instead of mounting a well-rehearsed and tightly controlled production, fixed for cyclical reproduction, they created unpredictable fields of action that attained their unique quality through improvisation and an active participation of the audience.[155] As an illustration of this new principle, I should like to discuss two representative examples taken from the early period of the historical avant-garde.

Alfred Jarry

Alfred Jarry was a person who, more than anybody else in this transitional period, presented himself and his artistic œuvre as a model of avant-garde creativity. In 1894, he met the influential theatre director Lugné-Poë and decided to refashion a juvenile puppet play, *Les Polonais*, which he had occasionally performed to friends in his private marionette theatre and also recited, mimed, and acted out in various literary soirées and salons. On January 8, 1896, he proposed to Lugné-Poë a production of the play at the Théâtre de l'Œuvre and in April/May had it published in Paul Fort's review, *Livre d'art*. On June 11, 1896, a first book edition, issued by the *Mercure de France*, appeared and gained him an appointment as secretary and dramaturg at the Théâtre de l'Œuvre. As the critical response to the play text was predominantly negative,[156] Jarry felt badly hurt in his artistic sensibility and began to adopt in his private life a behavior that was extreme even by the standards of the Parisian bohème.

When, on December 9 and 10, 1896, *Ubu Roi* was given the only two performances during the author's lifetime, it caused one of the greatest scandals in French theatre history and became a benchmark against which future avant-garde events were to be measured. Jarry and his small circle of supporters at the Théâtre de l'Œuvre used the theatre as a means of setting themselves apart from the bourgeois patrons of the arts in France. The controversies surrounding *Ubu Roi* established a clear demarcation line between the avant-garde and the mainstream. The publication of the text was preparatory work for this undertaking; but its full oppositional force could only be experienced in a public performance. For this reason, the two nights of scandal that shook the Théâtre de l'Œuvre in 1896 were principally different in intention and effect from the publication of a book, however provocative the text may have been.

The outrage caused by the première of *Ubu Roi* should not make us forget that Jarry possessed a serious, albeit radical, conception of the theatre.[157] He felt that European theatre since the introduction of the Italianate system of scenery and stage architecture had exhausted itself in a meaningless duplication of life. In order to find a way out of the cul-de-sac created by the Realist/Naturalist tradition and its "slice-of-life" aesthetics, the stage needed to be re-theatricalized. Jarry sought to shatter the illusion of reality by means of extreme simplification. He argued for a theatre of artifice and demanded that the stage sets and properties be iconic, suggestive, and evocative. Schematic and highly stylized scenery with a deliberate crudeness and naïvety was to offer a visual manifestation of the substance of a play. Rather than being tied to narrative, psychology, and contemporary issues, Jarry's theatre was to present universal topics in a distinctly timeless and abstract manner, and convey its underlying themes by means of archetypal images. Jarry wanted to use theatre as a catalyst that stimulated the imagination and allowed the audience to conceive of new worlds rather than cling to the banalities of everyday existence. He sought to eliminate all that impedes the creative act in the mind of the audience. Thereby, the spectator would become an active participant and coproducer of the spectacle, rather than a passive consumer of a theatrical entertainment.

At a time when leading actors and actresses were fashionable High-Society figures, who used the stage for satisfying their egomania rather than further-ing the dramatic arts, Jarry wanted to submit the actor to the control of the playwright and theatre director.[158] He demanded a de-individualized, mechanical type of acting, with a monotonous delivery style, expressive ges-tures and movements, a heightened physicality, and an emphasis on nonver-bal forms of communication, primarily derived from the marionette theatre, the Elizabethan Dumb-Show, and medieval Mystery plays.

However, in the 1890s there was little opportunity for bringing such ideas to fruition. The two dominant types of theatre—the Boulevard stage with its unashamed commercialism, and the Realist/Naturalist tradition—were still unassailable institutions. Parisian theatre, and in effect, most European theatre at the time, was a commercial institution concerned with trivial histri-onic displays, bound by moribund conventions, and exploited by financial speculators. Jarry felt that if one wished to reinstitute theatre as a serious art, one had to destroy first of all the prevailing artistic and social conventions of this bastion of tradition. The Symbolist reformers, with Paul Fort and Lugné-Poë at the forefront, took a serious interest in Jarry's absurdist conceptions, but were unwilling to lend full support to his radical visions. Conversely, Jarry entertained a certain sympathy with the idealist bias of Symbolist the-atre, but also felt that its archetypal universality was rather vague in concep-tion and would benefit from a more radical approach. Jarry was serious about his innovative ideas and pursued them with great zeal. At the same time, he held the bourgeoisie in absolute contempt, as they possessed no understand-ing of and no interest in the artistic side of theatre. Therefore, *Ubu Roi* was designed to function as a dynamite thrown at an audience who visited play-houses only to parade their dresses and jewels and to seek superficial diversion in the merry company of stars and starlets.

Jarry's anarchist convictions, combined with his antagonistic and erratic personality, produced a rather explosive constellation that came to erupt in the first performances of *Ubu Roi*. His correspondence from the time of set-ting up the production indicates that he was consciously striving "to react against established traditions" and to introduce elements that would "incite the old ladies and make certain people shout 'Scandal!' "[159] He wanted the stage "to act like a mirror" that would make the audience "dumbfounded at the sight of its ignoble double."[160] And as he was effectively in charge of the show (Lugné-Poë was little more than nominal director), he was able to put these ideas into practice. The accounts of the première certainly show that his provocations and shock tactics bore fruit.[161]

As was the custom at the Théâtre de l'Œuvre, Jarry delivered a lecture before the performance; but he did so in a clownish outfit, with disheveled hair, and in an exaggerated enunciation. When the curtain went up, the stage set did not bear any resemblance to Poland or any of the locations King Ubu visits on his perambulations. In accordance with Jarry's writings, the décor looked like a naïve children's painting that mixed indoor with outdoor elements and resembled simultaneous scenography in the medieval manner. It cobbled together the arctic and temperate zones, showed an apple-tree in bloom, a palm tree with snow falling from the blue sky, and a bare tree growing at the foot of a bed. On one side of the backdrop a skeleton dangled from the gallows, on the other side was painted a bed, complete with chamber pot. A fireplace served for the characters' entrances and exits; scene changes were indicated by placards brought on by a black-suited "Father Time" figure; nobles, financiers, and magistrates consigned to the "mince grinder" in Act III were "acted" by marionettes, and the Horse of Phynance was a pantomime dummy. Many of the costumes were incongruous to the characters (e.g., Bordure attired like a Hungarian Gypsy musician; Bougrelas in a baby dress with bonnet; Ubu wearing a black suit with one trouser leg rolled up to his thigh). The actors wore masks, spoke with strange accents, and imitated the stiff and jerky gait of marionettes. The Gargantuan farce was accompanied by fairground music played on two pianos and various percussive instruments.

The public dress rehearsal on December 9, 1896 was attended mainly by an invited audience, who only began to voice their displeasure in Act III.5. The official première on December 10, 1896 found a more turbulent reception from the very beginning of the show. In order to pacify the rioting spectators, actors improvised a range of scenic actions not foreseen in the playtext. These were mainly routines taken from the popular stage, and in an odd manner fitted the style of Jarry's drama; however, the resulting chaos made it impossible for the audience to understand the plot of this savage and unsavory charade of a play. The actors' attempts at placating the audience were countermanded by several friends of the dramatist, who fanned the unrest by booing when the spectators clapped, and vice versa.[162] In the end, the exasperated actors observed from the stage an unscheduled performance unfolding in the auditorium.[163] The traditionalists and curiosity seekers, who objected to the play's scatological and obscene humor, reacted with indignation and, finally, paroxysms of rage. But as the press reviews made abundantly clear, the cultured élites of Paris felt insulted by the play and its presentation. The critics described the drama as a vulgar hoax devoid of artistic value, and they interpreted the production as an anarchist insurrection equivalent to the bombs that had recently shaken Paris (the Figaro called it a "literary form of terror" by "anarchists of art"[164]). Others surmised that Jarry had directed a political satire at the bourgeoisie and the present government. It is not astonishing, therefore, that Lugné-Poë drew the necessary conclusionse, cancelled subsequent performances, and severed his contact with the scandalous author.

Jarry's *Ubu Roi* was widely discussed in artistic circles, and not only by those who had actually seen the performance at the Œuvre. Reviews in literary journals were also read outside France, and copies of the play found their way into the hands of writers across Europe. In Italy, Jarry found an ardent admirer in F.T. Marinetti, who established an epistolary contact with the infamous writer and came to Paris to make his acquaintance. Subsequently, he chose Jarry as a rôle model, both for his dramatic writings and for the cultivation of scandal as a means of theatrical communication.[165] Other admirers included Apollinaire, Artaud, and the postwar founders of Absurd Theatre.

The Symbolist circle who had organized *Ubu Roi* and then found itself taken aback by Jarry's radicalism and anarchist fervor, supported a whole generation of theatre reformers and was instrumental in the development of an anti-Realist performance aesthetics. Some of them remained attached to the movement's principal tenets, others amalgamated them with conception stemming from other quarters. Among the designers, for example, one finds influences of Post-Impressionism, Art Nouveau, the Nabis and Fauves, or of Cubism. All of them shared Jarry's belief in an abstract décor, although their attempts at overcoming the Naturalist-illusionist stage could make them arrive at quite diverging theoretical formulations and practical solutions. The most important and influential of these was developed by Wassily Kandinsky, whose concept of abstraction unleashed one of the most profound revolutions in modern theatre.

Wassily Kandinsky

This Russian lecturer in law came to Germany in 1896, where he enrolled in the art school of Anton Azbé and then at the art academy in Munich. In 1911, he became a founding member of the artist association *Der Blaue Reiter* and worked on an almanac of the same name. This anthology of 1912 (reprinted in 1914) became one of the most influential publications of the period, as it set out a new program for a formal language of artistic expression based on spiritual experience. At the turn-of-the-century, speculation into the hidden dimension of reality was a widespread phenomenon and part of the crisis of modernity referred to on pp. 26ff. Kandinsky's notebooks and personal library show that the painter was heavily influenced by contemporary writings of a mystical, spiritual, and occult nature and that his study of these works was most intense during the years when he turned toward developing his theory of abstract art (ca. 1908–1910).[166] In his short memoirs of 1913, *Rückblicke*, Wassily Kandinsky recalled the impact the discovery of radio-activity had on him:

> In my soul, the disintegration of the atom equaled the disintegration of the whole world. Suddenly the stoutest walls came tumbling down. Everything became uncertain, unsteady, fragile. It seemed to me that science was shattered: its most important basis had turned out to be only a delusion, an error of the scholars.[167]

This dissolution of matter[168] devastated Kandinsky's belief in an objective, real world and a positivist, materialist science that could explain it. As a result of this, Kandinsky became interested in the work of scientists who were carrying out research into phenomena of the para-material world.[169]

Kandinsky's first experiments in abstract painting[170] were soon complemented by abstract theatre pieces. In 1909, he finished the draft of a play, called *Riesen* (*Giants*); in 1911, he wrote the essay "Über Bühnenkomposition" (On Stage Composition), which led to a revision of *Giants* and its publication in 1912 under the title *Der Gelbe Klang* (*The Yellow Sound*). This "stage-composition," as he characterized the play, combined color, sound, and motion in a highly intricate manner and aimed at giving expression to the spiritual essence of the world and of bringing the addressees into contact with the spiritual essence of their soul. It was not held together by a narrative structure and did not convey any concrete message in the traditional sense. Rather, it operated with highly symbolic and mysterious elements and an often elusive stage language, which betrayed the influence of Maeterlinck, an author Kandinsky greatly admired.[171]

During his first years in Munich (1896–1914), Kandinsky had the opportunity to acquaint himself with the latest developments in Symbolist theatre and the great reform program promoted by Peter Behrens and Georg Fuchs.[172] *The Yellow Sound* in its final version was written with the stage of the Munich Art Theatre in mind and would have been produced there, had the outbreak of World War I not prevented it (see pp. 138–139)[173] Kandinsky also came into contact with the ideas of Rudolf Steiner, who in

1907 began to produce plays by the French theosophist Edouard Schuré and as of 1910 directed his own mystery-dramas.[174] These experiences reinforced Kandinsky's belief that European theatre in its existing form had reached an all-time low that could only be reverted by a radical program of renewal. To achieve this aim, the "firm, cold crust formed over the inner essence of theatre [. . . which] has become so strong, thick and cold that the pulsating force appears to have been numbed for all time,"[175] needed to be cracked open. Once this had been achieved, the vital force that gave theatre such a magnetic pull could reassemble and fuse its now disparate elements. Thus, the spiritual dimension of the theatre would be able to "discharge the highest tension" and "transmit all the forces of the arts to the waiting rows."[176]

The term Kandinsky used at that time for the transmitting force operating between cosmos, artist, and viewer was *Klänge* (sounds or vibrations). His concept of *Klänge* was heavily influenced by the theosophist Annie Besant and the anthroposophist Rudolf Steiner, who had put forward in their writings an explanation of human communication with the material and spiritual world. Kandinsky adopted Besant's idea that thoughts produced radiant vibrations, which could affect other people and elicit corresponding vibrations in their souls. He applied this theory to the world of communication in the arts and arrived at the conclusion that the sensory stimuli of color, tone, touch and so on go beyond their physical effect and call forth psychic vibrations in the addressee. Especially the sensations stemming from music and pure art (i.e., abstract colors and forms) are able to penetrate directly, without cognitive interference, the soul of the receiver, where the irradiations of one sense create a resonance in others. The correspondence between different sense impressions can cause mutual reenforcement and reciprocal influence of the elicited sense reactions. The result is synaesthesia, that is: a sense impression triggering off an inner sensation that belongs to another sense (e.g., color audition).

Kandinsky had first experienced the effect of synaesthesia during his Moscow days in the 1890s, when he visited an exhibition of French Impressionist paintings and a performance of Wagner's *Lohengrin*.[177] His fascination with color impressions that evoke sound sensations, and of musical chords that bring color to life, led him to a more thorough investigation of the mechanisms of sensory perception and the causes for the innate affinity of tone, color, taste, smell, and touch.

He came to the conclusion that synaesthetic sensations are possible because they all emanate from the same source: "Behind the material world, inside the material world, the creative spirit is hidden."[178] This spiritual force is the common, unifying denominator behind the different artistic media: "In their most profound essence, these means are all alike: Their ultimate aim extinguishes their external dissimilarities and reveals their inner identity."[179] From these insights, Kandinsky proceeded to develop a new artistic language that could express and represent the spiritual essence of the world.

In his view, the artist had to abandon the goal of depicting the world of physical appearances and instead explore and unveil the inner harmony of things behind the material surface of reality. During the years 1908–1912, Kandinsky's works made the transition from being descriptions of an outer reality to capturing the inner, spiritual essence of Nature. During the same period, he developed the conviction that art was a realm that had to be separated from the phenomenological world and become established as an autonomous, organic domain on an equal footing with the first Nature created by God.[180] In his view, the constructive principles of Nature find an analogy in the compositions of an artist. Both are rooted in the divine forces of creation. It is the task of the artist to establish a connection to the spiritual essence of the world and to develop from its inner necessity the compositional rules for the work of art: "A composition is a work which overwhelmingly or exclusively develops 'out of the artist', as for centuries it has been the case in music . . . Both arts produce complete, objective works of art, which like works of nature are by necessity autonomous creations evolved out of themselves."[181]

Because of his creative disposition, the artist is able to divine the creative forces operative in the cosmic order. When the sounds or vibrations of the universe find a corresponding resonance in the soul of the artist, they elicit a sounding work of art. Its sensory stimuli generate corresponding vibrations in the soul of the receiver and produce a complex web of vibrations, which constitute the process called "reception of a work of art." The combination of different abstract media creates a Total Work of Art, which affects the viewer on various, yet interrelated levels, and brings about a spiritual refinement and enlightenment in the receiver's soul.

Kandinsky's enquiry into the spiritual forces behind the material surface of reality led him to a radical reevaluation of the psychological mechanisms and communicative structures operating in the world of the arts. In his theory, the "great synthesis" of poetry, music, scenery, dance, and acting would not affect each viewer in the same manner. The addressee's personal disposition determines whether he reacts more to the stimuli of music or dance or abstract colors. When the recipient is sensitive to the vibrations of the *Gesamtkunstwerk*, several of his senses will be touched and influence each other synaesthetically. Such a simultaneous, multifaceted response will create a heightened enjoyment and a more profound experience of the performance.

The synaesthetic Total Work of Art finds its completion when it is being taken in and responded to by the viewer. It is the spectator who synthesizes the vibrations radiating from the work of art. In Kandinsky's theory, the union of the arts does not take place on stage, but in the soul of the receiver. The viewer participates in the creative process and becomes a coproducer of the *Gesamtkunstwerk*.

This conception, which was widely disseminated in Europe through the *Blue Rider Almanac*, had a profound impact on artists from a variety of disciplines, schools and movements. It stimulated debates on many issues pertinent to the theatre and left a lasting mark on subsequent developments in the historical avant-garde.

2. Expressionism ✷

1917–1918	Theoretical statements outlining an Expressionist acting style by Wauer, Diebold, Kornfeld, Holländer, Sebrecht, Emmel, Blümner, and Lauckner
April 28, 1917	Kaiser, *Von Morgens bis Mitternacht*, dir. Otto Falckenberg, Munich: Kammerspiele
June 3, 1917	Kokoschka, *Hiob, Der brennende Dornbusch, Mörder Hoffnung der Frauen*, dir. Heinrich George, Dresden: Albert-Theater; repeated April 11, 1918 at Frankfurt/M: Neues Theater
June 18, 1917	Mary Wigman Dance Evening at Pfauen-Theater in Zurich
September 1917– April 1919	Sturmbühne in Berlin
November 2, 1917	Johst, *Der Einsame*, dir Gustav Lindemann, Düsseldorf: Schauspielhaus
November 10, 1917	Mary Wigman presents her *Ecstatic Dances* at the Laban School in Zurich, repeated in 1918 in Davos, Zurich, St. Gallen and Winterthur, and in 1919 in Berlin, Bremen, Hamburg, and Dresden
December 8, 1917	Kornfeld, *Die Verführung*, dir Gustav Hartung, Frankfurt/M: Schauspielhaus
January 18, 1918	Hasenclever, *Der Sohn*, dir. Richard Weichert, Mannheim: Nationaltheater (this was the first Expressionist production of the play)
March 30, 1918	Johst, *Der Einsame*, dir. Otto Falckenberg, Munich: Kammerspiele
June 16, 1918	Unruh, *Ein Geschlecht*, dir. Gustav Hartung, Frankfurt/M: Schauspielhaus
November 28, 1918	Kaiser, *Gas I*, dir. Arthur Hellmer, Frankfurt/M: Schauspielhaus; dir. Gustav Lindemann, Düsseldorf: Schauspielhaus
October 15, 1918	Stramm, *Sancta Susanna*, dir. Lothar Schreyer, Berlin: Sturmbühne
Spring 1919–Spring 1921	Lothar Schreyer at Kampfbühne in Hamburg, produces nine plays: August Stramm's *Haidebraut* and *Kräfte* (October 21, 1919); *Krippenspiel* (December 16, 23, 26, 1919, January 6 and 13, 1920); Hölderlin's *Empedokles* (February 24, 1920); Schreyer's *Kreuzigung* (April 12, 1920), *Mann* (May 16 and 25, June 1 and 8, 1920) and *Kindsterben* (November 9, 1920); Herwarth Walden's *Spiel der Liebe* and Sünde (March 1921)
March 13, 1919	Johst, *Der junge Mensch*, Hamburg: Thalia Theater
September 30, 1919	Toller, *Die Wandlung*, dir. Karlheinz Martin, Berlin: Die Tribüne

INTRODUCTION

"Expressionism" as a general aesthetic term is widely used in theatrical circles and can denote a whole range of acting styles that aim at an immediate expression of feeling. However, in a narrow sense, the term Expressionism—with a capital E—relates to a specific historic and predominantly German phenomenon. It can first be detected in paintings by the Dresden group of artists, "Die Brücke," founded in 1905. In 1910, the Berlin journalist Herwarth Walden published the first issues of the Expressionist journal, *Der Sturm*, and turned it into one of the most widely read periodicals in Europe. In 1911, the Munich circle of Expressionists, "Der Blaue Reiter," came into existence. The trend toward more direct representations of inner feelings was also taken up by poets, dramatists, and composers. In the 1910s, the generic term "Expressionism" was attached to any kind of creation that derived its inspiration from subjective rather than objective realities. However, contrary to other avant-garde movements of the period, the Expressionists never developed a unified group mentality or issued any programmatic foundation manifesto. There existed only loosely connected groups that published a plethora of proclamations and statements, none of which was ever considered binding by their members.

The first traces of an Expressionist style of drama can be found in the works of Strindberg and Wedekind. In 1909, Oskar Kokoschka, a painter, staged a drama, *Murderer Hope of Women*, that was Expressionist through and through. The event was followed by the first spate of Expressionist playscripts, but due to the outbreak of World War I none of these were actually staged at the time. Some authors reflected on how these unusual texts could be performed, and it was from these statements that a theory of Expressionist acting developed. Toward the end of the war, several Expressionist plays were tried out in the theatre—usually in front of very small audiences—and the first experiments with an Expressionist acting style took place. The heyday of Expressionist theatre followed in the immediate postwar years, and it continued to be a dominant factor in German theatre until about 1924.

Expressionism in its early phase was characterized by an attitude toward art and society that questioned many of the key tenets of conventional nineteenth-century culture. It continued the work undertaken by Naturalist writers and Impressionist painters, who had also condemned the idealized world of appearances beloved by the bourgeoisie and had directed their attention away from the realms of eternal beauty to the real world. When they discovered that straight transcripts of material reality were neither possible (because the interventions of the human mind could not be eliminated) nor desirable (because this method could only capture the surface appearance of reality), they concentrated their efforts on the inner side of human nature—either as an extension of the real world or as a spiritual counterbalance to material reality.

This gave rise to two dominant trends in the artistic world of the turn of the century, psychological realism and symbolism, both of which focused attention on the state of the human soul, the spiritual world, the essence of being underneath the superficial appearance of reality. The artists representing these schools prepared the way for the Expressionists, who also sought to reveal an inner vision, experience, or feeling of universal significance, but did so in an act of immediate rather than symbolic communication. Instead of regulating and channeling the flow of emotions and imposing an objective form on a subjective experience, the Expressionists took recourse to the subconscious mind and sought to compel the viewer to respond with *Einfühlung*, an empathetic emotional response, rather than *Verstehen*, a rational understanding.

In the years preceding World War I, German society—and in fact European society as a whole—was in a state of pervasive crisis (see pp. 29–32). Expressionism was a reaction to this situation, and at the same time, an indication of a young generation's vision of a better future. The Expressionist artist wanted to start afresh. He was a herald of a new humanity and detested a culture that functioned like "a scaffold for a collapsing building, or a corset for a decaying body," as Herwarth Walden put it in 1913.[1] Many Expressionists considered themselves to be revolutionaries—either in the sense that they acted in opposition to the prevailing order of society or that they rebelled against the traditional canons of art. Although a wide range of artists with different philosophical and political beliefs joined the Expressionist movement, they were all united by a common aim, formulated in negative rather than positive terms: opposition to bourgeois society, and more specifically to the tastes and values of Wilhelmine Germany. Most Expressionist artists came from a middle-class background and had undergone a conventional education at *Gymnasium* or university. When they entered the real world, they could not help but become aware of the gap that existed between the lofty ideals of humanist and classical culture which, supposedly, were the foundations of bourgeois society, and the depressing political and social reality of Wilhelmine Germany. Consequently, they aimed at a complete renewal of art and society. But where could they start, and how could they proceed?

The Expressionist artists took their inspiration from those parts of human nature that were untarnished by industrial civilization. It was the human soul in its virgin state, the life of primitive tribes in Africa or Oceania, or the artistic expressions of children. It could also be the deeper and darker layers of the unconscious mind. From these elements of the primitive, irrational world, they sought to create a new and pure art.

EXPRESSIONIST THEATRE—A GENERAL CHARACTERIZATION

Also, theatre artists of the Expressionist movement wanted to rediscover the essence of humanity underneath the crippling fetters of convention and good education. They believed that salvation of mankind was only possible when the incrustations of bourgeois society could be cracked open and the human soul set free. Therefore, strength of feeling and pathos of expression meant more to them than refined mastery of form. Expressionist theatre did not follow any established rules. It was irregular, eerie, and bizarre (see figures 2.1–2.4).

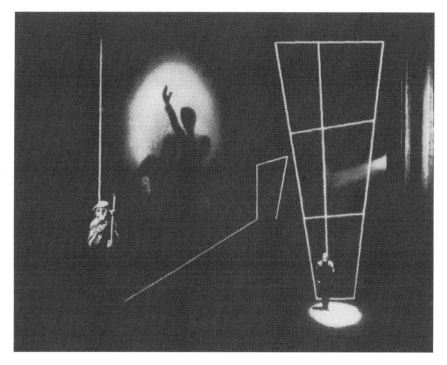

Figure 2.1   Andreyev, *Life of a Man*, directed by Gustav Lindemann, designed by Edvard Munch and Gustav Wunderwald. Düsseldorf Schauspielhaus, 1908. Expressionist stage designs translated the dramatic substance of a play into abstract visual patterns that never defined a realistic setting but presented an abbreviated image of the main character's interior life. The reality of the stage was constructed from an entirely subjective viewpoint.

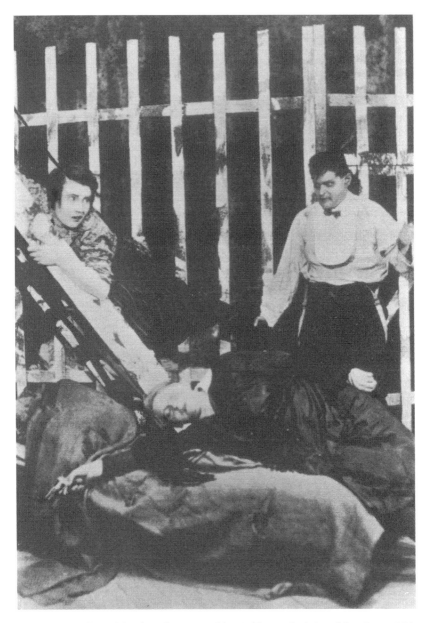

Figure 2.2 Frank Wedekind, *Lulu*. Directed by Erich Engel, designed by Caspar Neher, with Gerda Müller as Lulu, Lucie Höflich as Countess Geschwitz, and Fritz Kortner as Dr Schön/Jack the Ripper. Emil Faktor described the production as a "tragedy of desperation," a "whirlwind of action," an "explosion of drama," with Kortner playing his rôle "like a martyr and slave of his passions," with "an ice-cold energy, nurtured by the tremor of standing in front of the final abyss," and Müller portraying Lulu with a "natural female refinement and an animal-like, untamed sensuality?".

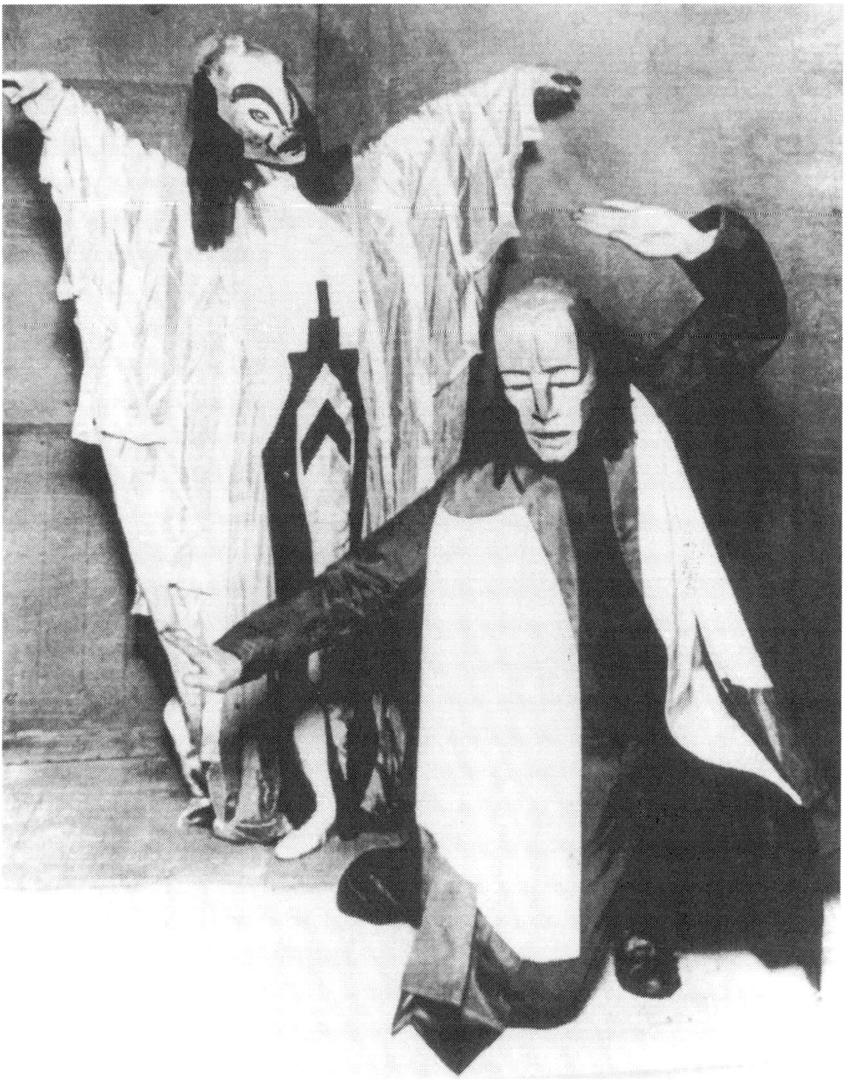

Figure 2.3 W. B. Yeats, *The Only Jealousy of Emer*, Amsterdam, 1926, directed by Albert van Dalsum, masks by Hildo Krop. Although the play itself was patterned after a Japanese Noh drama, the masks bear no relation to Japanese traditions. They reflect a primary world and the protagonist's mystical self, and comment on the nature of dreams and the deeper realities, in a typically Expressionist manner.

Figure 2.4   Walter Hasenclever, *Der Sohn*, Stadttheater Kiel, 1919, directed by Gerhard Ausleger, designed by Otto Reigbert. The abstract and distorted scenery externalized the feelings of the son, especially his oppressed existence. As in previous productions of the play, the sets reflected the psychic processes and the drama unfolding in the protagonist's soul.

The unrestrained outpourings of the Expressionist actor showed a human being in a state of delirium seeking to reach his or her audience with a liberating, primeval cry. No wonder these paroxystic outbursts appeared to the contemporary observer like an anarchical mutiny of a hysterical individual.

The success of Expressionist acting rested on the individual performer's ability to communicate a deeply felt inner truth. The critic Bernhard Diebold demanded from the Expressionist actor: "He must express himself immediately from his own soul, without tricks of transformation, without imitating a character—for what meaning can psychology have compared to spiritual expression?"[2] This, of course, ran counter to the whole tradition of European acting since the Renaissance period. The Expressionists rejected the artificial, declamatory style, then prevalent in the theatre, as well as the minute recreations of ordinary life in the Realist school. Instead, they placed the individual and his or her emotions center stage. They wanted to create, as Friedrich Kayssler wrote in 1915, a "theatre in which the soul will reign supreme."[3] Consequently, the actor had to base his performance on his own emotional experiences, and not imitate someone else's behavior. He had to explore his own soul and encounter himself in his darkest dreams and fears. The actor's whole body—voice, movement, gesture—exploded when he transmitted a profound feeling. His stage performances sent him into trance-like rapture, where he could reveal the deepest secrets of his unconscious mind and show his audience the viscera and entrails of his emotional constitution.

Expressionist theatre was brought to life through a physical style of acting, not through the quality of a dramatic text. The best Expressionist plays were little more than scenarios with plots sketched out only in rough outline. This compelled the actor to fill in the gaps from his own emotional reservoir and personal experience. He could not simply follow someone else's dramatic inventions or stage directions, but had to work as an original artist realizing *himself*. However, such uninhibited emotional explosions did not square too well with the need to perform a play that had been written by another person. The ecstatic Ego-performance somehow had to relate to a preestablished text. This is where the *art* of Expressionist acting came into play, which was demonstrated so masterfully by Fritz Kortner, Paul Wegener, Gustav Hartung, Heinrich George, Werner Krauss, and Alexander Granach.

Newspaper reviews, photographs, and some rare film documents give us a fair idea of what Expressionist acting looked like on stage.[4] The intense feelings portrayed demanded total involvement of the actor's mind and body, up to the point of physical exhaustion. Every part of his physique had to reflect and project an inner emotional state. The result was a jerky and convulsive style of acting, with jolting movements, quivering gestures, and sudden thrusts of the head. Rage or despair was expressed through grotesque poses, bulging eyes, and bared teeth; hope through the eyes and arms soaring up into the air (see figures 2.2 to 2.4). Similarly, the spoken word became a physical gesture. "The word was made flesh," Herbert Jhering judged when he saw Werner Krauss in Reinhard Goering's *The Sea Battle*.[5] Instead of phrases measured in a flowing style, the actor hammered out his text in an abbreviated, clipped enunciation, breathlessly speaking in a hasty and staccato rhythm, issuing noises from deep within his throat as one had never heard on stage before. It was a "Schrei" performance par excellence.

This exaggerated acting style was further heightened by make up. Faces had strong decorative lines drawn on them to create a woodcut effect and to make them look like masks. Bared parts of the body were painted with non-naturalistic colors and the hair was sculpted into bizarre shapes and patterns. To further increase the intensity of the performance, the Expressionist actor sought to bridge the gap between the stage and the auditorium by acting close to the footlights, by directly addressing the spectators and more than metaphorically stepping out of the confines of a play production. These "Ich" performances turned the actor into an object of identification and allowed the audience to experience in themselves the visions and pains of the character on stage, thereby turning the theatre into a unifying temple of emotions.

KOKOSCHKA'S *MURDERER HOPE OF WOMEN*

The first example of an Expressionist play, *Murderer Hope of Women*, came from Oskar Kokoschka, who also directed its first performance in 1909. Before discussing the production, which had the hallmark of an avant-garde event of the first order, I present some biographical information on the artist that will help our understanding of Kokoschka's unusual drama and his intentions behind the first production in Vienna in 1909.

The Austrian artist was born in 1886 in a small town by the river Danube. As a youth, he visited a magic lantern show that stimulated his imagination and made him ask: What is reality? Where are the frontiers of the real and the imagined? Is life a dream? And indeed, it seems that young Oskar lived more in a dream world than in the real world. Many events related in his autobiography were not, in fact, real-life occurrences, but experiences on his interior screen. But for Kokoschka these visions were just as significant as exterior reality.[6] From an early age, he gave expression to his mental pictures in the form of drawings. He also created stage designs for famous works of dramatic literature and tried his hand at playwriting.

In 1904, through the good offices of an art teacher, he was awarded a scholarship for the Academy of Applied Arts in Vienna. Kokoschka blossomed in this environment and produced his first illustrated book, *The Dreaming Youths*. Later, he described this publication as a "love letter" to a certain Lilith Lang, the sister of one of his fellow students. This girl had set him ablaze with passion. The name Lilith conjured up in his mind images of the Sumerian wind goddess and of the seductive power of Adam's first wife. When he asked the girl for her hand, she rejected him outright. Kokoschka not only suffered the pains of unrequited love, but he also discovered that art could appease the afflictions of the heart.

He offloaded his angst and despair in the play *Sphinx and Strawman* (which in its first version contained a beguiling character called Lilly), the first draft of *Murderer Hope of Women*, and some sketches for a *Pietà* painting. The latter was used in 1909 to advertise the first performance of *Murderer Hope of Women*, and the subject turned up again in various other forms when he experienced his second love affair, with Alma Mahler. As we shall see below, Kokoschka's treatment of the *pietà* theme may offer us some valuable clues as to the meaning of the play and its scenic realization. However, before the young painter could contemplate a stage production of *Murderer Hope of Women*, he had to gain in theatrical experience. This was afforded to him in October 1907 when the Wiener Werkstätte opened a cabaret and invited Kokoschka to contribute to its first season. Inspired by his early magic lantern experience and by a display of Javanese Wayang puppets in the Natural History Museum in Vienna, Kokoschka wrote a shadow play, *The Speckled Egg*, and had it performed on October 28, 1907.

A year later, Kokoschka was given an opportunity to present some of his paintings in a major collective exhibition, the Wiener Kunstschau. Gustav Klimt liked his works very much and called him "the greatest talent of the younger generation," but the general public reacted to his works with consternation and incomprehension. In response to this, Kokoschka began to adopt a new persona. His appearances in public gave a vivid demonstration of an avantgarde artist living in opposition to society and the artistic establishment. He distanced himself more and more from the tasteful Art Nouveau style that dominated Vienna at that time, joined the bohemian circle of Peter Altenberg, shaved his head and presented himself in Viennese cafés as a wild "punk" (or to use his own words, as a "bull in a china shop"[7]).

On March 29, 1909, *Sphinx and Strawman* was performed at the Cabaret Fledermaus, and Kokoschka discussed with his cast the production of his as yet unfinished play, *Murderer Hope of Women*. Aware of the attention he had received at the first Kunstschau, he planned a *succès de scandale* for the next edition of the show, approached the organizers of the exhibition, and received their permission to have both plays staged in the garden of the building.

Murderer Hope of Women was written, as Kokoschka stated in his autobiography, as a means "to express my attitude to the world" and as "an antidote to the torpor that, for the most part, one experiences in the theatre today."[8] Although rooted in deeply personal experiences, the play also reflected

Kokoschka's interest in prehistoric cultures and the civilizatory process. He admitted to having been deeply impressed by Bachofen's study on matriarchy, but one can also detect influences of Freud and Weininger, and of the playwrights Wedekind, Strindberg, and Claudel.

Kokoschka approached theatre with the attitude of a painter rather than a poet or a dramatist. Instead of using conventional dramatic language, he composed theatrical images that gave visual expression to his concepts and ideas. The 1907 draft of *Murderer Hope of Women* operated only with stage pictures, and in the later versions of the play, the stage directions take up more space than the dialogs. The text did not adhere to any rules of grammar or syntax. Just as a painter would arrange shapes and colors on a canvas, Kokoschka placed words next to each other. He was interested in their aural qualities and semantic associations rather than their literal meaning. He made rhythmic speech patterns clash with melodious flows of soft vowels and consonants, and set clusters of harsh sounds against ariose sentences. The characters' intense states of mind were meant to be given physical realization by means of body language and vocal production, and not through conventional acting techniques. None of this had ever been explored in the theatre before, but in the years to come, many of these characteristics were considered to be hallmarks of Expressionist theatre. The only inspiration Kokoschka may have received from the contemporary stage came through the dances of Grete Wiesenthal, a Viennese precursor of *Ausdruckstanz*. Like in her works, the movements, gestures and mimic expressions in *Murderer Hope of Women* oscillate between angular, aggressive and vigorous sequences, and soft, flowing, solemn or purely decorative poses.[9]

The text of the play focuses on the clash of the male and female principles and shows human beings in an existentialist situation, where libidinous and vitalist forces are battling with spiritual and cultural urges. The two protagonists are not only locked into a feud for predominance, but are also animated by an internal struggle of mind over matter, spirit over body, mystical endeavors over carnal desires. The theme of the battle of the sexes is conveyed by means of sense impressions rather than story line or character psychology. The archetypal figures are emanations from the unconscious mind and express the innate contradictions within the human soul. It is, therefore, appropriate for the play to be set in a timeless and undefined location.

In his autobiography, Kokoschka wrote that his play expressed his understanding of the Greek concept of Eros and Thanatos and that he "pondered day and night on the secret that lies beyond love and death."[10] The female protagonist has traits of Penthesilea, Queen of the Amazons, and her male counterpart appears as an Achilles-like warrior prince. The oppositional forces of male versus female receive symbolic representation in the images of sun and moon (the active, luminous principle versus the passive, mysterious powers of darkness), and the colors red and blue (vitalist instincts versus spiritual aspirations; white signifying the absence of both, i.e., death). The Man is linked to the symbol of the sun, of spiritual and civilizatory powers. His armor is blue, while the clothes of the Woman are red and her movements have strongly animalistic qualities.

This may offer a key to our understanding of the *pietà* painting and its relation to the play *Murderer Hope of Women*. In the poster of the 1909 production, the Woman is depicted as a chalk-white Virgin Mary, with the scarlet body of the dead Man draped over her knees. The *pietà* figuration links the Man with Christ (just as the gash in his side and the crowing of the cock do in the play), who has to undergo a Passion in order to achieve peace and redemption. Hence the color red, signifying life, on the corpse draped over the Woman who is characterized by the color white, signifying death, on her face. For the Woman to be resurrected into a spiritual life, she has to give up her material existence first. "One does not become human once and for all just by being born. One must be resurrected as a human being."[11] When the Man rises from his tomb (the womb-like cage), the Woman realizes that she has to undergo the same journey and experience material death in order to become a complete human being. She assents to death not as an end, but as a passing over into another existence. The murder becomes an act of spiritual liberation and the murderer "the only hope of womankind."

This seemingly traditional distribution of gender rôles may find some justification in the first printed version of the play, but is contradicted in the autobiographical text, "Vom Erleben," where Kokoschka described the theme of the play thus: "In my first play I had offended the thoughtlessness in our patriarchal civilization by advancing the idea that man is mortal and woman immortal, and that only a murderer could attempt to revert this basic fact in the modern world."[12] As Kokoschka was developing his art theory, he made the meaning of the play more ambiguous and refused to offer a clear-cut solution to the battle of the sexes. With each version (1909, 1913, 1916, and 1917) he increased the reader or viewer's responsibility for finding his/her own meaning of the play and for developing a personal response to the issues raised by the drama. The play no longer allows one interpretation, but suggests as many as there are viewers of the play.

On June 10, 1909, an advertisement for "A Kokoschka Evening" appeared in the Viennese press, announcing "a drama followed by a comedy, directed by Ernst Reinhold."[13] On June 18, the *Neue Freie Presse* gave the date for the

Figure 2.5   Oskar Kokoschka, *Murderer Hope of Women*, Albert-Theater Dresden, 1917. Directed and designed by O. Kokoschka. Kokoschka's set was highly symbolic and emphasized the play's archetypal images of the (phallic) prison tower and the (womb-like) cage. Merging both in one structure indicated the interdependency of the protagonists, called Man and Woman. The costumes aimed at a more "realistic" depiction of Bronze Age Greece.

"Kokoschka Evening" as June 26 and announced the engagement of Tini Senders from the Hofburgtheater, and Marianne Heller and Anton Fleischer from the Raimundtheater. Whether any of these actors had ever read the text of the two plays and whether they had given more than a general promise to appear in the show remains doubtful. But at least a production had been set up, rehearsals with friends and fellow students from the art academy and drama school were underway, and the stars from the legitimate theatre had probably penciled into their schedule a date for a rehearsal (which at that time meant little more than being shown moves and positions on stage).

Kokoschka fueled public expectation by distributing all over Vienna the now famous poster with the garish colors and repulsive treatment of the *pietà* subject. It confirmed to the wider public, who had not seen his paintings at the Kunstschau, what the newspapers had written about him: that he was a "ferocious savage" (*Oberwildling*) intent on shocking the bourgeoisie. Kokoschka was proud that the *pietà* image "sent the Viennese into paroxysms of rage. Thanks to the notoriety of my pictures, the tickets were sold out a week before the performance."[14] Undoubtedly, expectation was running high, but a sudden change in weather caused the première in the open-air theatre to be postponed until July 4, when the *Neue Wiener Journal* could announce: "The Kokoschka evening cancelled last Saturday due to unforeseen circumstances will now take place, good weather permitting, at nine o'clock tonight at the Kunstschau."[15]

The rescheduling of the performance meant that the star actress from the Hofburgtheater was unable to participate and that some last-minute alterations in the cast were required. This is probably why Kokoschka wrote in his autobiography: "I had simply improvised with my friends the play [*Murderer Hope of Women*] at a night-time rehearsal in the garden. I gave the principals and other players an outline of the action and wrote down each of their parts in short key phrases on slips of paper, after first acting out the essentials of the play for them, complete with all the variations of pitch, rhythm and expression."[16] However, the reports in the local press do not confirm Kokoschka's claim that the whole production was "simply improvised." Rather, they suggest that Kokoschka's planning went slightly awry, but that there was still enough time to engage a musician, Paul Zinner, to write a score with lots of brass and percussion for the play. A surviving photograph of Kokoschka, Reinhold, and another friend gives a clear impression of a group of young, self-consciously rebellious artists taking on the artistic establishment and delighting in *épater le bourgeois*. The performance on July 4, 1909 certainly established their reputation and served as a useful public relations exercise for their artistic ideas.

The Viennese newspapers inform us that "the exotic poster, which in recent days had been beckoning from every street corner"[17] attracted "a very distinguished audience, which awaited the Kokoschka evening with great anticipation." Apparently, they interjected some sarcastic comments, but otherwise reacted with "well-meaning hilarity" to "the manneristically constructed word excesses, the incomprehensible, ecstatic screaming, the staggering movements of human clusters on stage." The leading actress, Marianne Heller, interpreted her rôle with "Salome ardor" and "was able to grab the audience's attention with verve and style." The chorus of men and women shouted the text to the sound of drums and cymbals, ran around with torches in their hands, and made little attempt to link words to actions. At the end there was applause, mingled with a few boos, and when the audience demanded to see the author, a stagehand informed them that "Mr. Kokoschka had retired to avoid accepting the ovations."

The reviews confirm that "performers, most of them drama students, hurled themselves into their parts, as if acting for dear life." Although the critics did not describe the costumes, they are invoked in Kokoschka's statement: "As there was no money, I dressed [the actors] in makeshift costumes of rags and scraps of cloth and painted their faces and bodies . . . with nerve lines, muscles and tendons, just as they can be seen in my old drawings."[18] These "old drawings" are presumably the woodcuts that accompanied the text in its first published version in *Der Sturm* and are likely to reflect the style of the 1909 production (for a different realization of the text see figure 2.5). Kokoschka described the performance as having caused a riot in the audience, the intervention of a regiment of Bosnian soldiers, and his near arrest by the police. As nothing of the kind is reported in the Viennese press, we should handle this statement with a certain degree of skepticism. But there is no doubt that for weeks the event prompted major debates in coffee houses and at dinner tables on the rôle of art and theatre in modern society.

It is symptomatic that Kokoschka wrote no further plays after his recovery from love sickness (excepting a Comenius drama penned much later in his life). Playwriting appears to have been a therapeutic outlet for this young, overwrought artist torn between the oppositional forces of love and hate, attraction and repulsion, seduction and domination. Much of Kokoschka's feelings for the three significant women in his early life—his mother Romana, his muse Lilith, his mature lover Alma—was poured into the vessel of dramatic writing, or at least into the first drafts of his plays. Subsequent rewrites transformed the raw emotional material into highly stylized and deeply symbolic forms. The artistic quality of Kokoschka's plays rests exactly on this tension between form and content, refinement of allegoric style and immediacy of feeling.

LOTHAR SCHREYER'S STURMBÜHNE AND KAMPFBÜHNE

Kokoschka's brand of Expressionism was a typical example of theatre and drama becoming a means of expressing an artist's anguish and erotic feelings. Another, more mystical and spiritual motivation can be found in the work of Lothar Schreyer. Contrary to Kokoschka, Schreyer felt a great need for communal rituals. He grew up in a family rife with discord and violent conflict. As a student he confessed to feeling "cold right down to the deepest soul. What I need is you, friends, and your radiating sun. My soul is empty and full of expectation. I am so much longing for you. Where are you friends, now that I need you so much?"[19] When he got married to the sweetheart of his youth, he did not find in her a like-minded soul. In fact, she distinctly objected to his artistic and intellectual cravings. The theatre, therefore, became to Schreyer a substitute family, a circle of fellow searchers for spiritual enlightenment, who eventually formed an esoteric group pursuing the cultic mission of forming the New Man of the future.

Schreyer's theatre was not Expressionist in the common sense of the word and certainly very different from the productions of Expressionist plays in Weimar Germany. One can discern between three principal roots of his theatrical aesthetics: the cultic drama of the Christian Church and of so-called "primitive" people; the abstract theatre of Wassily Kandinsky; and the declamations of sound poetry at the literary soirées of Futurists, Dadaists, and Expressionists. Schreyer placed the word at the center of his creations, but he always treated the spoken text as a sound shape rather than a vehicle of precise meanings. In his pre-Expressionist period, he occupied himself predominantly with literary drama and saw in theatre only "the final purpose of dramatic poetry."[20] After 1915, his interest shifted increasingly from drama to theatre, from writing plays to becoming a *Bühnenkünstler* (stage artist). His purpose was no longer to bring a play to performance, but to act upon divine inspiration and materialize a deeply felt sacred principle by means of theatre. The resulting *Bühnenkunstwerk* (artwork of the stage) was an independent artistic medium on a par with drama, music, or painting.

For several years, Schreyer concerned himself, both theoretically and practically, with the investigation of the key elements and basic components of this *Bühnenkunstwerk* and discovered them in "the spatial media of form and color and the temporal media of sound and movement."[21] The resulting stage compositions went far beyond the traditional, naturalist–illusionist, or psychological theatre. The actor was no longer a servant to literature and the play did not in any way determine what happened on stage. Rather, the performer became a sound-producing body moving in a stylized scenic environment, and the play was seen as a "fragment"[22] (i.e., one of many, equivalent, components) of the stage work. Performances were powerful, nonintellectual, cultic events that united the viewers in a common experience, touched their souls, and affected their spiritual condition. In an essay of 1918, Schreyer made it absolutely clear that his work did not aim at reforming theatre but at overcoming theatre.[23] He rejected the theatre that had become a business and an entertainment, and instead looked for a ceremonious ritual that provided "spiritual gathering," "hours of devotion," "a way of spiritual elation," and immersion into the "ecstasy of universal harmony."[24]

Schreyer began his theatrical career at the Schauspielhaus Hamburg, where he worked from 1911 to 1918 as a dramaturg and assistant director. Being an avid reader of *Der Sturm*, he formed a small *Sturm* circle in Hamburg and participated in the Expressionist *Kräfte* group, named after the play by the *Sturm* dramatist August Stramm. When, in February 1916, he had a first personal encounter with Herwarth Walden, he offered him some of his playtexts for publication. *Nacht* appeared in the *Sturm* issue of July 1916, followed by 11 others over the next 6 years (as well as 13 critical essays on theatre). Between autumn 1916 and October 1918, he commuted weekly between Hamburg and Berlin, initially acting as an unofficial contributing editor of *Der Sturm*, becoming the journal's editor in chief and in August 1917.

During these years, Schreyer was active for *Der Sturm* on a number of levels. He organized several *Sturm* exhibitions, gave many public lectures on Expressionist drama and theatre, attempted to set up a *Sturm* circle in Lübeck, and organized five *Sturm* soirées in Hamburg. The local press described these as avant-garde events of the first order, bizarre to the extreme and incomprehensible to the normal citizen with a "healthy" taste in art and theatre. Beside many poetry recitations, they contained a performance of his play *Night* (October 22, 1917).[25] In Berlin, *Der Sturm* expanded from being a literary journal to developing into the center of a network of cultural activities. Following the establishment of a *Sturm* Gallery and *Sturm* publishing house, Schreyer was put in charge of setting up a program of theatrical activities, which began with a series of *Sturmabende*, or literary soirées, the first of which, on September 1, 1916, was dedicated to the Expressionist poet and dramatist August Stramm. They also opened an art school with courses in stage design, acting, painting, poetry, and music. Walden, a trained musician, headed the music section, and painting courses were staffed by a frequently changing faculty of avant-garde artists. Rudolf Blümner was in charge of acting and recitation, and Lothar Schreyer signed responsible for stage art.

The successful work undertaken with their students, who had not previously received any formal training in acting and were hence relatively untarnished by the conventions and techniques of conventional theatre, prompted Schreyer and his colleagues to found their own theatre. As they did not have the financial resources to staff and equip their own playhouse, they decided to operate as a club that would rent premises whenever a production had been put together. In September 1917, *Der Sturm* announced the founding of a Verein Sturmbühne as a "select circle of people" who were opposed to the existing theatre and wished to develop a *Bühnenkunstwerk* with a decidedly contemporary and spiritual orientation.[26] The personnel was to be drawn from the *Sturm* art school, and club members were encouraged to become active collaborators in the venture. To provide them and the wider public with information about the works to be performed by the Sturmbühne and to promote the organizers' artistic concepts, they also founded a journal, *Sturm-Bühne: Jahrbuch des Theaters der Expressionisten*, of which eight issues were released between January 1918 and October 1919.

Although the articles published in *Sturm-Bühne* contain some interesting critiques of existing theatre culture and a variety of essays on the new artwork of the stage, they did not indicate any further development from the program that Schreyer had already outlined in his essays for *Der Sturm*, and in fact provide next to nothing on the work of the Sturmbühne itself. Schreyer was a very prolific writer, but most of the articles published in 1916–1918 repeat in different form what he expressed in his most important essay, "Das Bühnenkunstwerk," of 1916.[27] The form of theatre he promoted in this manifesto of Expressionist theatre was visionary, spiritual, and cultic in orientation. It was centered on the word, but the dramatic text was not meant to represent or interpret an everyday reality, but rather to conjure up a new world complete in itself. Words were meant to be brought to life by the rhythmic sounds issued by an actor specially trained in the techniques of *Klangsprechen* and *Sprachtongestaltung* (see below). The abstract quality of the sounds gives the words a gestalt and turns a concept (the referent of the word) into an artistically formed material reality. The gestalt-shaping process is entirely governed by artistic necessity, and conventional grammar, syntax, and morphology are irrelevant for it. The resulting sounds convey a cosmic experience and through their concentrated form assume a stage presence of great evocative power. The gestalt of the sounds is related to the gestalts of color, form, and movement, and all four together form an organic unity. They are developed by the *Bühnenkünstler* (stage artist), who is often identical with the director. Each element is meticulously designed and brought into unison with the other components. Together they form a scored *Spielgang*, a mixture between a director's book and a stage manager's prompt copy. They possess highly symbolic forms that communicate by means of association and facilitate intuitive identification with the emotive and revelatory force of the composition.

Equipped with such an artistic program, Schreyer began rehearsals for his first production, *Sancta Susanna* by August Stramm. Performances were announced in the *Sturm-Bühne* issue of September 1918, together with the statutes of the club that encouraged readers to enroll for artistic training at the *Sturm* school and stipulated that performances of the Sturmbühne were exclusively open to club members (of which there were about 500 by 1919[28]). The only performance of *Sancta Susanna* on October 15, 1918 (a planned second performance on December 3 had to be cancelled because of the political unrest in Berlin) took place in the Künstlerhaus in der Bellevuestraße, was directed and designed by Schreyer, and had a musical accompaniment written by Walden. The actors were drawn from the *Sturm* school and had been trained by Schreyer in the art of recitation and movement. They were dedicated amateurs who never attempted a professional stage career. The information provided by the reviews[29] indicates that Schreyer performed the play on a simple trestle stage in front of a backdrop of four interlocking colored crescents. He undertook no attempt to follow Stramm's stage directions, eliminated the specifics of the location (the play was set in a monastery) and costumes (the two characters are nuns), and stylized the production to a degree where everything became timeless, abstract, and symbolic. The actors moved in an extremely stylized manner, and vocal production was entirely nonnaturalistic. This heightened artificiality reduced the individuality of human expression and turned the dramatic characters into scenic symbols. Jhering alluded in his review to verbal acrobatics of a religious or operatic nature and of movements that resembled those of marionettes and anatomical exercises: "One lady speaks, sings, whistles a litany. A second lady, crouched on the floor with her back to the audience, responds with piercing, hissing and vertiginously high sounds. The antiphony continues in shrill dissonances until the lady lying on the floor begins a coloratura aria. Her sighs and words wind themselves up to the top of the scales and then come down again." In a later memoir, Schreyer gave an interesting description of the costume used for Susanna: "I wanted her, being a run-away nun, to appear naked, so to speak. In the end, the costume consisted of skin-colored bandages wound around her breasts and hips. Her head was covered by an equally skin-colored hood, which only left her eyes, nose, mouth and chin free, thus also making her head appear naked."[30] Jhering mentioned that the actor playing the rôle of Klementia wore a face mask and that one of the minor figures walked on thick-soled buskins (i.e., the *kothurnoi* of tragic actors in late antiquity), which again contributed to the extreme stylization of the figures.

Possibly unhappy with the development of the Sturmbühne,[31] and possibly disturbed by the political chaos in Berlin before and after the November Revolution, Schreyer left for Hamburg, where he sought to set up an alternative venture. In spring 1919, he founded the Kampfbühne as an organization that was similar to the Sturmbühne club, but smaller in size and without propaganda organ. Nonetheless, it soon boasted of 200 members, rising to 300 in the following year.[32] The council of management assembled a rather heterogeneous mixture of people who were not all in agreement with Schreyer's artistic ideas. Differences of opinion and direction within the club led to heated debates and even physical altercations after the first performance.[33] It took nearly a year before Schreyer could silence the opposition to his theatrical concept. As a consequence, many club members stayed away from future presentations, and only a small circle of dedicated followers remained actively involved in the venture. These supporters came to form a homogeneous community, that displayed many features of an esoteric sect or mystic cult, with Schreyer and a handful of actors as artist–priests at its center. Most of their activities remained hidden from the wider community, and only on special occasions did they present the exoteric aspects of their work to an outside world.

Initially, Schreyer had also planned to show his productions at the Sturmbühne in Berlin. But apart from two guest performances at Max Reinhardt's Kammerspiele, the Kampfbühne performed only in Hamburg.[34] They received technical support from some professors and students of the School of Applied Arts who had joined the Expressionist Kräfte group. The assembly hall of the Kunstgewerbeschule am Lerchenfeld was fitted with a simple platform stage, reminiscent of medieval Mystery plays, measuring 1.5 m high, 5 m long, and 2.5 m deep.[35] The press was not admitted, excepting a few critics who had agreed to attend without reviewing the performances (and who adhered to their promise, as only one write-up has been located in the Hamburg newspapers of the period[36]). For this reason, critical assessment of the productions is virtually impossible, and only the surviving papers of Lothar Schreyer give us an insight into what he was aiming at in rehearsals and on stage.[37]

In line with the strongly cultic quality of Schreyer's theatre, the amateur performers—mainly teachers, white-collar workers, and office clerks—were led through a drawn-out rehearsal process (up to 100 for each play) that focused primarily on the technique of *Klangsprechen* and also included meditative and religious exercises. Schreyer saw in this activity much more than just a preparation for a performance: "Our work was less focused on a final product than on working together and achieving spiritual harmony in the group."[38] Not unlike some of Grotowski's experiments in the 1970s and 1980s, the therapeutic rituals conducted by Schreyer provided a means of self-discovery, of establishing a harmonious relationship within the group, and of connecting with the divine forces of life:

The human being, relieved of his self-determination, is able to hear his inner voice—his ground note—and pass through the gate that leads into the domain of superhuman forces, for which I cannot find a better name than cosmic forces. Before he can subordinate himself to the ground note, which I want to call divine human harmony, he has to fight with demonic forces. We experienced terrible things here, but also unforgettable happiness. Rehearsals provided us with the incredible gift of experiencing human growth and becoming one with the cosmic harmony of life. With the completion of each play we had moved a stage further towards the fullness of this unity. For this reason, only the rehearsals mattered to us, and the performances were nothing but an intermediary stage, which we immediately aspired to go beyond.[39]

Schreyer's *Klangsprechen* was more than just a means of vocal training for actors. It brought to life the sound quality of the playscript (or *Wortdichtung*, a highly compressed dramatic poetry, usually only a few pages long, using fragments of words that were placed in an order determined by rhythm rather than syntax). In order to achieve this aim, the actors had to engage in breathing and vocal exercises that had a meditative quality and led them into a state of deep introspection. Once they had reached their "inner soul," they could open up to the metaphysical cosmic forces and experience mystical ecstasy ("außer-sich-sein," *ek-stasis*: the moving beyond oneself as a precondition of transformation). As these trance exercises were carried out in a group of like-minded spirits, they created an *unio mystica* of individual, community, and cosmos.

Technically speaking, the *Klangsprechen* was an innovative feature similar to Schoenberg's *Sprechgesang*, but functionally it was much more than a vocal realization of a character's lines. The sounds of the words were chosen to express the "ground note" of a scene or of the whole play which the actor had to bring in line with his personal "ground note." Although the conventional pronunciation of a word determined a basic sound shape, actors had to modulate that sound, shape its pitch, volume, and rhythm.

Compared to this innovative vocal work, Schreyer's choreographic imagination fell far behind the achievements of early Expressionist dance (see below). His movement repertoire was extremely limited and further hindered by masks (particularly the full-body masks) that he had created on the basis of illustrations found in books and magazine articles dedicated to the theatrical cultures of Japan, China, Tibet, Cambodia, Samoa, and the like. Although Schreyer possessed no practical knowledge of the ancient techniques of masked dances and their use in trance or exorcism rituals, he speculated on the anthropological and religious significance of masks and intended to write a book about this, entitled *Man and Mask*.[40] For Schreyer, masks were a means of going beyond psychological realism, of detaching the actor from his individuality, and of achieving a visual concentration of a play's theme. The full-body masks (some were even more than life-size) transformed the bearer into a medium of higher cosmic forces (see figure 2.6 and cover illustration). As such they were a natural consequence of Schreyer's earlier attempts (see *Sancta Susanna*) to achieve de-individualization and instrumentalization of the actor's body. Even in his early productions when masks were not used, gestures, movements, and postures failed to attain a complexity that was comparable with the great inventiveness he showed in his treatment of the voice. His arrangements of scenic space did not give relief or plasticity to the moving bodies, and his costume design focused on shapes and colors

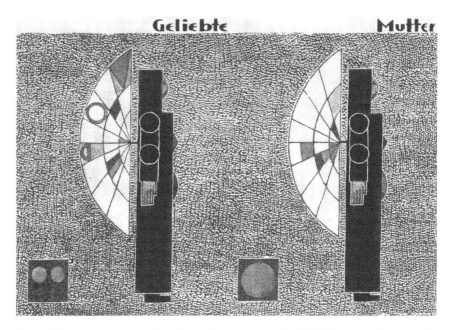

Figure 2.6   Lothar Schreyer, *Kreuzigung*, from *Spielgang Werk VII*, Hamburg: Werkstatt der Kampfbühne, 1920. Costume design for Lover and Mother. This play was to be performed on a simple platform stage, reminiscent of medieval Mystery plays, measuring 1.5 m high, 5 m long, and 2.5 m deep. Schreyer developed a notation system that fixed all relevant scenic processes in a score by means of normative symbols. *Kreuzigung* was the only Spielgang ever printed.

rather than on how they might enhance the actors' movements. With the incorporation of masks and, in the end, whole-body masks, the scope for complex movements decreased and his last production, *Moon Play*, was little more than a static oratory.

In his essay, "The Essence of Physicality,"[41] Schreyer examined the physical-material reality of the theatre in relation to time and space. He replaced the term "actor" with "physical shapes moving in space" and emphasized that this physical shape (*Körpergestalt*) was not an organic body, but an artificial creation. He regarded the actor's personality and individuality as an impediment in the process of shaping this *Kunstkörper*. Only a depersonalized, dehumanized actor could be a medium of art. In his chapter on movement in the book *Expressionistisches Theater*, Schreyer described the actor's body as a physical instrument and a medium for conveying psychic and spiritual realities. Choreographic patterns (*Bewegungsgestalt*) were determined by their symbolic meaning, which he reduced to simple correlations such as circularity revealing creativity, linearity revealing determination, angularity revealing changeability. Circular motions played a particularly important rôle in his productions of Stramm's *The Bride of the Moors* and *Forces*, where they were even inscribed on the floor cloth of the stage, and in his own play, *Man*, where the male dancer circled around the immobile earth mother throughout the play. But when compared with Laban's circle dances (*Reigen*), it becomes apparent that Schreyer was unable to translate his philosophical sources into an aesthetically convincing and intelligible stage language. He remained a poet with a good visual eye, but was much less talented in terms of developing the actors' physical expressiveness.

Schreyer was responsible for all aspects of his productions and developed them in accordance with his *Spielgänge*. The first plays the group worked on (autumn 1918 to spring 1920) employed highly stylized voice and movement, but no masks, whereas the productions of the second period (April 1920 to March 1921), written by Schreyer himself, were scenically composed down to the smallest detail and produced with the help of a costume designer, mask maker, and musician. Nine of the thirteen *Spielgänge* (twelve in manuscript form and one printed) were actually produced. To what degree the ideas fixed in the *Spielgänge* were actually realized on stage is impossible to determine. But due to the scenarios' profusion of detail—some of them are over 300 pages long—we do at least possess a solid basis for an assessment of Schreyer's and his group's aspirations. The basic principle of the *Spielgänge* was to subdivide a page into four bars of text and to score nine main instruments in a grid of horizontal and vertical lines. The nine score categories were (a) playtext, (b) form, (c) color, (d) movement of form and color, (e) movement of individuals, (f) movement of groups, (g) vocal sounds, (h) musical sounds, and (i) natural sounds. Some of these categories were further subdivided, for example: form was split into mass and outline; color into spread and brightness; movement of form and color, of individuals and groups were all further broken down into direction and speed; vocal sounds were classified according to timbre, pitch, volume and speed. In the only printed Spielgang, *Kreuzigung*, Schreyer attempted to develop from these a proper notation system and to translate verbal descriptions into normative symbols (for two characters from the play, see figure 2.6, which does not show the notation system, but the characters only).

The scores allowed the Schreyer to correlate all major aspects of his productions and to ensure that vocal delivery was in harmony with movements and gestures, that the color of the light fitted in with the music. The categories (b) and (c) were related to stage set, costumes, and lighting, but as there were hardly any furniture or props on stage, Schreyer focused on elaborate costume designs and careful consideration of the direction, intensity, and tint of the lights. In fact, because of the lack of scenery, the lighting became a particularly important medium of artistic expression, usually conveying the cosmic forces that propel the characters into dramatic action.

Schreyer's *Spielgänge* indicated that his artistic concepts were principally in agreement with those of the stage reformers Craig, Appia, Fuchs, Tairov, and the like, who also sought to deliver theatre from its subservient position to literature, liberate the stage from all decorative and naturalistic clutter, and elevate the art of scenic design to a position equal to that of actors and musicians. The standardization of scenic elements and their reduction to abstract symbols (e.g., red–blue, light–dark, circle–triangle, linear–spiraling) were an attempt to develop a universal language that could employ material signs in order to express metaphysical truths. Schreyer believed that the combination of signs in his *Spielgänge* worked with a morphology and syntax that was superior to those of conventional language (both scenic and verbal) and was able to express emotional and spiritual realities that no other form of communication could convey. The highly condensed mode of scenic expression, arrived at through a long process of reduction and abstraction, was most suited to the archetypal characters and conflicts in his plays. Schreyer's approach was largely based on Kandinsky's theory of abstraction and the spiritual in art, but his search for a universal, elementary language also brought him close to the Constuctivists. It is, therefore, not astonishing that, in summer 1920, Gropius invited him to become a teacher at the Bauhaus. When in Weimar, he kept in contact with the Kampfbühne; but once the group lost its leader, it folded. Schreyer tried to have his last major play, *Mondspiel*, produced by the Weimar stage workshop, but his Expressionist roots were by then too much in contradiction to the institution's new direction. After a trial performance on February 17, 1923, the production had to be canceled (see chapter 5, pp. 211–212) and Schreyer withdrew into a kind of religious exile.

LABAN, WIGMAN, AND EXPRESSIONIST DANCE THEATRE

Nineteenth-century dance fitted into a similar pattern of representational aesthetics as I have outlined above in the introduction to this chapter. After the turn of the century, the first dance reformers (Loïe Fuller, Isadora Duncan, Ruth Saint-Denis, the Wiesenthal Sisters, Émile Jaques-Dalcroze, to name but a few) opened up new possibilities for a modern form of dance and created an alternative to the French and Russian ballet which had hitherto reigned supreme. Expressionist dance came into existence, one can say, in 1913, when

Rudolf Laban and Mary Wigman presented their first original dances in Munich, which was at that time the center of Expressionist art in Germany.

Rudolf Laban[42] was born in Hungary in 1879 and followed in his father's footsteps by entering the military academy in Vienna. A visit to Mostar, where his father was military governor, afforded him the opportunity to see the dances of a Sufi brotherhood (the "Whirling Dervishes") that left a lasting impression on him and influenced his spiritual vision of dance. In Vienna, he started directing folk dances for his battalion, and in 1900 he decided to follow his artistic calling and move to Paris. He trained as a painter, worked as a theatre designer, and earned his livelihood as a book illustrator for various publishing houses.

At that time, dance was only a sideline of Laban's artistic interest. Not having undergone the long and gruesome training of a ballet dancer, he could only aspire to be an amateur choreographer. In Nice, he tried to form a group of dancers and have them perform his drama *The Earth*. But it was only after his return to Germany (in 1907) and his move to Munich (in 1910) that he began to dedicate himself seriously to questions of dance and movement. In the early part of the twentieth century, Munich was probably the most innovative and exciting art center in Europe after Paris. Its museums and theatres presented the most recent trends in European art, and in the bohemian quarter of Schwabing, an extraordinary phalanx of avant-garde artists lived and produced some of the most forward-looking artworks of the period.

Laban's move from Montparnasse to Schwabing caused a considerable change in his artistic orientation. Visitors to his studio reported that he gave up his Impressionist style of painting and converted wholeheartedly to Expressionism.[43] Through his friend Hermann Obrist he was introduced to the world of Wassily Kandinsky, Rudolph Steiner, and Georg Fuchs, founder of the Munich Arts Theatre (1908) and author of the influential book, *The Revolution in the Theatre* (1909). Furthermore, the *Körperkultur* movement with its eurhythmic and gymnastic exercises had a strong following in Munich, and the city possessed some of the best cabarets of the time, where highly original and unconventional dance creations could be seen.

In the early 1910s, Laban found himself in the midst of a theatrical culture that was more open and innovative than anything he had experienced before. He became fully engaged in this scene, devised dances and choreographed shows at various carnival festivities and artists' balls. In the summer of 1912, he founded his own performance group, and in 1913 opened his first dance school. He assembled around himself some of the most charismatic dancers of the period, such as Alexander Sakharov, Mary Wigman, and Suzanne Perrottet. Inspired by Kandinsky's theories and abstract paintings (see chapter 1), Laban set out to undertake a corresponding effort with the expressive means of the human body. What the painter Kandinsky had called composition, and the musician Schoenberg harmonics, Laban wanted to undertake with choreography. He sought to discover the inner laws of dance and to liberate it from its representational nexus. By developing the principles of abstract, or absolute, dance, he found ways of expressing the spiritual dimensions of human existence and the essence of Being underneath the surface of reality. Instead of dance visualizing music or presenting narratives, Laban's art of movement concentrated on the dancer's body as a vehicle for divine truths. However, contrary to the mystical thinking of many Expressionists, Laban had a very analytic mind and searched for *objective* principles behind *subjective* experiences. His Expressionism was not only concerned with giving direct expression to feelings, but also with discovering the laws and principles of movement within the dancer's body and in relation to the surrounding space. In Laban's view, movement develops into dance, when an inner motive force finds a clear form. His system of choreology[44] analyzed how the inner impulse translates itself into movement, how this flux takes on different qualities as it develops in space, and how this kinetic work of art can be used to express archetypal feelings, thoughts, character traits, attitudes, and so on. These concepts were first taught at his school in Munich and then through his treatises and essays. It was also demonstrated in the dances of his pupil, Mary Wigman.

Marie Wiegmann, as she was then called, was born in 1886 into a prosperous middle-class family in Hanover.[45] As part of her education, she was instructed in social dancing. During a visit to an aunt in Amsterdam, she witnessed a demonstration of Jaques-Dalcroze's "eurhythmic" dances, which fired her enthusiasm and made her decide to become a professional dancer. Soon afterward, in her hometown, she had a chance to see a performance of the Wiesenthal sisters. And when in 1910 she heard that Émile Jaques-Dalcroze was opening a school in Hellerau near Dresden, she was one of the first pupils to enroll.

Dalcroze's eurhythmics[46] was a kind of gymnastics that had been developed to enhance the rhythmic feeling of young musicians and singers. Over time, the rhythmic training of the body became an aim in itself and turned into a dance that trained the harmonic sensibility in a wider sense: harmony of body and soul, of human being and nature, of individual and society. Eurhythmics became a typical expression of the *Jugendbewegung*, the reformist youth movement that acted in defiance of the rational, materialist culture of the bourgeoisie and sought to escape from the industrialized cities into an idealized world of authenticity, individuality, and self-realization. Dance and music formed an essential part of their activities, together with new dietary habits and a reform of dress manners. The *Wandervögel*, as they were also called, roamed the countryside, lived in small communities or health farms, danced in free-floating robes, or even naked, in the midst of nature. Isadora Duncan popularized a return to the natural movement of the body. Dalcroze's schools of rhythmic gymnastics swelled to more than 120 with no less than 7,000 students enrolling each year. The new icons of "body culture" imbued "Rhythm" and "Harmony" with a mystical dimension and made them the catch phrases of the period.

Marie Wiegmann's initial enthusiasm for Dalcroze's concept of eurhythmics soon gave way to a critical examination of his didactic methods and to questioning the musical bias of his philosophy of movement. Wiegmann discovered in her own exercises a rhythmic principle that was independent of music. Her inner sense of rhythm gave her dances an organic quality that made music altogether superfluous. In fact, she felt that music restricted her inner impulse to move. The Expressionists inspired her to ecstatic dances that gave free reign to the flux of life, the pulse of the heart, the natural flow of her limbs. When she heard that Suzanne Perrottet, Dalcroze's assistant and then a demigod of eurhythmic dance, was abandoning Hellerau to join Rudolf Laban's school in Munich, her decision was made: she rejected the offer to run a Dalcroze project with the Werkbund in Cologne and another one to choreograph for Max Reinhardt at the Deutsches Theater. Instead she went to find Perrottet and Laban in Munich.

Laban was at that time teaching body culture in Monte Verità near the Lago Maggiore. During that memorable summer of 1913, he was joined by Wiegmann, ready to discover "free dance," that is, to rediscover herself and the world through the medium of dance. Three weeks of improvisations and exercises in the beautiful landscape of the Ticino proved to be a turning point in her life. When she received a telegram from Hellerau offering her to become the director of a Dalcroze school in Berlin, she showed it to Laban, who regretted losing such a talented dancer, but nonetheless congratulated her on the offer.[47] Wiegmann decided to reject the idea of becoming a eurthymics teacher and instead entered into a close working relationship with Laban. Between 1913 and 1917, they developed the principles of Expressionist stage dance, Laban in the first instance as theoretician and choreographer, Wigman—as she was now called—as a dancer (for one of her early stage words, see figure 2.7).

Initially, they did not abolish music altogether, but rather let the dance follow or interpret the rhythmic structure of a musical piece. They operated with natural body rhythms that could be accompanied by melodic singing

Figure 2.7   Mary Wigman, *Hexentanz* (Witch Dance), second version, 1926. Mask: Viktor Magito. This is a revised version of the solo dance in Wigman's debut performance in Munich (February, 11 1914).

and percussion, but the music was always subservient to the movement. In 1914, they gave several demonstrations of this "free stage dance" in Munich and Cologne. Laban continued to work with nonprofessional dancers and to develop his concepts of dance as a source of spiritual regeneration. He organized large-scale festivals and celebrations, which involved hundreds of amateur dancers and often lasted all night. These dance dramas dealt with archetypal situations of life and death, with ancient myths and the cosmic drama of humanity and nature. In this, he drew on the mystic philosophy of the Sufis, the Rosicrucians, the Theosophists, and the Pythagorean concept of dance as a primordial power reflected in the macrocosm of the universe and the microcosm of the human body.[48]

During World War I, Laban moved his dance school to Switzerland. The Swiss years were, as he later described them, a nightmare. He had financial problems and recurring trouble with the emigration authorities; he lived in a *ménage à trois* with his wife Maja and his lover Suzanne Perrottet, to which he added a second mistress in the person of Dussia Bereska. Despite his domestic upheavals, several serious illnesses, and bouts of clinical depression, he managed to write a substantial part of his first major theoretical study,

The Dancer's World, which was published in 1920. The book summed up the intensive research he had undertaken in the 1910s on the dynamic and spatial structures of pure dance, as well as the results of his philosophical and spiritual studies. Laban always combined the mystical dimensions of dance with precise observations of dancer's movements. From this he developed the key ingredients of his training system: eukinetics dealing with the temporal, dynamic, and expressive quality of movement; choreutics analyzing the spatial dimensions of dance; the scales that describe the relation between movement and space; the theory of effort that dealt with the inner impulse and how it affected the quality of movement.

Laban's interest in the harmonic laws of movement made him explore the anatomy of space—within the dancer's body, within his kinesphere, and in relation to the fixed architecture of the stage. He analyzed the rhythmic and dynamic qualities of dance, the ebb and flow of the movements between preparation, action, and recovery, the connections between tension and release, strength and resistance, lightness and weight. He examined the quality of time and duration as opposed to a mathematical measuring of time. He also investigated the crystalline structure of space and the organic quality of movement. Laban believed that dance would only be considered on a par with the other arts when a transient performance could be fixed and preserved in a precise graphic record. He, therefore, began to develop a notation system that eventually would make dance a literate art.

When, after World War I, Laban returned to Germany, Expressionism was in full swing and had become a major force in the theatre. The time seemed right for him to present to the general public the results of his research and experiments of the previous ten years. In 1920, he founded the Tanzbühne Laban in Stuttgart and moved it, in 1922, to Lake Pönitz in Holstein. The group had 50 members, lived an intense communal life on a dance farm and rehearsed, improvised, and experimented with Laban's concepts of "absolute" or free dance.

In 1924, they were given their own theatre in Hamburg and renamed themselves Kammertanzbühne Laban. Their performances, which also toured Germany, Austria, Italy, and Yugoslavia, consisted of both Expressionist dances and dance dramas and incorporated experiences made with absolute dance during the previous years. They not only created theatrical pieces centered on physical expression, but also re-admitted the spoken word, choral chanting, classical and modern music, costumes, and stage sets. This varied program was held together, as Laban said, by making dance a medium for the representation of inner attitudes and conflicts.[49] During the following years, Laban opened dozens of schools, where his concepts of dance were taught both to professionals and amateurs, to dancers and actors. The long-term effect of his training methods and aesthetics of Tanztheater was pervasive, even after the Second World War II, as can be seen in the work of Pina Bausch and German postwar dance theatre.

EXPRESSIONISM IN THE THEATRE OF THE WEIMAR REPUBLIC

In the first years after World War I, Expressionism, more than any other artistic movement of the time, provided German artists with a vehicle to reflect the chaos and anxiety of a nation emerging from a war, a revolution, and a dismantled monarchy. Suddenly, the plays written many years ago seemed painfully in tune with the new *zeitgeist*. Expressionism, which had already established itself as a major force in the fine arts and literature, conquered the theatre. The first tentative productions during the war had been hardly noticed by the general public. Hasenclever's *Son*, for example, was premièred in 1916 in a very low-key production in Prague, and a private performance a week later in Dresden was characterized by one critic: "Licho, the director, is still rooted in the school of Otto Brahm. *Sturm und Drang* is decelerated into Ibsen-tempo."[50] Also Gustav Hartung could not find the right idiom for Kornfeld's *The Seduction* in Frankfurt in 1917. The atmospheric production had more in common with Symbolism than Expressionism. Max Reinhardt's approach to Sorge's *The Beggar* (December 23, 1917) contributed to the confusion, as his detailed mannerism did not bring out any of the raw despair behind the play. The critic Julius Hart even pitied the actors for presenting "substrata of ideas" rather than "men of flesh and blood."[51]

The situation changed in 1918, when the unknown Richard Weichert produced *Der Sohn* at the National Theatre in Mannheim, in a design by Ludwig Sievert. The reviews indicate that both the acting and the visual presentation of the play summed up the main character's exclamation: "But one only lives through ecstasy!"[52] In a statement outlining the concept of his production, Weichert described Expressionism as "exteriorization of innermost feelings," as "volcanic eruption of the motions of the soul," and as "boundless ecstasy of heightened expression,"[53] Therefore, rather than illustrating the action of the play in a realistic manner, he opted for "depicting psychic processes . . . and for locating the actual site of the drama in the inner world, the son's soul." He placed the main character in a center stage position, cast him in a spotlight and had the other characters act around him in semidarkness: "The bright beam of the light symbolizes the son's soul . . . while the other figures have a shadow-like existence, half human, half vision." Hasenclever attended the première on January 18, 1918 and reported to his publisher: "Completely new, incredibly daring direction by Richard Weichert. It was my strongest ever experience in the theatre. The audience demanded eighteen curtain calls and the press was ecstatic."[54] From now on, people could not get enough of the plays of Hasenclever, Kaiser, Sorge, Johst, Goering, Unruh, Toller, and the like. Major plays were given dozens of productions, and major productions ran for more than a year. The "twilight of humanity" envisaged by the Expressionists[55] became a dominant theme in the new era of the Weimar Republic.

From the many innovative realizations of Expressionist aesthetics in the theatre, one stands out as particularly important and influential: Karlheinz Martin's staging of Toller's *Metamorphosis* at the Tribüne in Berlin. The small experimental theatre was founded in 1919 as an antidote to Reinhardt's half-hearted endeavor at the Deutsches Theater to give Modernism a home in Berlin. "Das junge Deutschland," as his series of innovative new plays was called, only proved to the young generation that the "big houses" were too much entrenched in the Brahm school of acting to replace their Realist pre-disposition with an Expressionist type of theatre. Karlheinz Martin and his dramaturg, Rudolf Leonhard, held the view that "a revolution in the theatre has become imperative" and that there was a need "to establish a style of pres-entation that corresponds to the changed consciousness of our times and is opposed to traditional theatre, which has deteriorated into a museum for the collection and exhibition of literary relics." [56] To achieve these aims, they set up their own theatre enterprise, with a repertoire of new plays that endeav-ored "to create a new way of thinking" and aspired toward "artistic purity" imbued with emotional impact. They sought to create a spiritual union of actors and spectators and to turn their theatre into an assembly of like-minded souls sharing a common experience. Therefore, they sought to abol-ish the proscenium arch, eliminate illusionistic décor, and bring the stage action closer to the audience. Such novel techniques would result, so the directors hoped, in an "activist theatre" that contained "truth rather than pre-tence," was "pathos-laden" and "ecstatic," and revealed "soul and conviction in an immediate fashion."

Toller's play *Metamorphosis* neatly fitted into this scheme as it responded to topical and widely debated issues and used a dramatic language that was Expressionist through and through. It showed five stations in the transforma-tion of a man who volunteered for front-line service and finally joined the revolution. Robert Neppach's stage design worked with spare scenic cyphers, atmospheric lighting, and just a handful of props. The Berlin star critic Alfred Kerr judged that Martin's direction "brought all the horrors of war onto the stage—not as a drawn-out lament, but with a powerful impact as no-one else has seen before."[57] Emil Faktor felt that after all the theorizing and statements of intention that had been published during the war, here for the first time one could experience a "thorough-going revolution" and "a fortunate advance into virgin territories of modern theatricality."[58] Kerr agreed with him that "Herr Martin has pushed theatre history a stage forward. In this he was particularly helped by Fritz Kortner, who welded together feeling and the power of the word. Here is a new man. Here is a new value." Emil Faktor dedicated a second review to a detailed examination of Kortner's acting. It included the following characterization: "His forms of expression vacillate between hot and flaming pathos and nervously quavering sensuality. He is an actor of great vivacity who feels more attracted to the interesting facets of his rôle than to mere exuberance. He even manages to breathe individuality into those feverish moments, when he whirls with his arms like a harvester and spins around his own axis. He creates gestures that go right to the bottom of the words' meaning."[59] Herbert Jhering praised Kortner in a similar vein: "Words coagulate and dissolve in a rhythmic fashion. Screams erupt and vanish again. Movements surge back and forth. There was no psychology and development, only aggregation and concentration. . . . Kortner's playing pushed himself beyond the limits of the stage and made him burst into the auditorium . . . with a rising, expanding, startling power that draws together all the forces of the theatre."[60]

The great achievements in German Expressionist theatre were no doubt helped by the recent advances in lighting technology and stage machinery. For example, Linnebach's Neues Schauspielhaus in Dresden, completed in 1914, possessed four hydraulic stage elevators, a revolving stage, mobile wagons with built-in electric motors, a mobile cyclorama, and a most sophisticated skydome with specially designed arc light, spotlight systems, and apparatus for the projection, refraction, and diffusion of colored light beams.[61] Also Max Reinhardt's wizardry as a director depended to a large extent on the ingenuity of his technical staff, who made use of new technologies in order to create stage effects one had never seen before.

Expressionist theatre artists availed themselves of these new inventions and combined them with new aesthetic concepts. The aim was to translate the dramatic substance of a play into abstract visual patterns that never defined a realistic setting but presented the main character's interior life (see figures 2.1 and 2.4). Stage sets were suggestive, atmospheric, and visionary. Reality was constructed from an entirely subjective viewpoint and defied the established laws of perspective and spatial dimensions. Distorted scenery and deformed stage objects had evocative, not descriptive, functions. They externalized the feelings of the main characters and visualized the dramatic leitmotifs of the play. Any realistic detail that did not pertain to the essence of the drama was omitted.

The two main principles of these settings were abstraction and distortion. Location was indicated through symbolic ciphers, such as a tree, a bed, a window, or a staircase. The scenery was placed in a fragmented, but rhythmically organized, spatial environment. Instead of balanced horizontal and vertical levels, the stage consisted of deformed and fragmented lines, tilting walls, slanting angles, and asymmetric planes. These angular and contorted constructions were meant to reflect the protagonist's anguished soul and the hostile world that he or she inhabited. This dramatic expressiveness was further emphasized by the lighting design. Instead of illuminating the stage evenly and using floodlights to give it a general cover, the stage was cast into semidarkness and selectively lit in certain areas by directional beams. The actor moved between corridors of light and darkness, here emerging into the limelight and having his facial expressions heightened by follow spots, there receding into the shadows of the stage.

Once the new technical devices and the complex scenic apparatuses had become common features of German playhouses, the new aesthetics were also applied to musical drama.[62] The problem with opera is that productions usually require an institutional apparatus that is not geared towards avant-garde experimentation. Furthermore, the very nature of musical drama demands a compositional approach that runs counter to the principles of Expressionism in an orthodox sense. Schoenberg started to compose in a distinctly Expressionist style from about 1908 onwards; however, it took until 1918 before the term "Expressionism" entered the music-critical debates.[63] Most of the compositions that deserve to be called Expressionist were written in a "stream-of-consciousness" manner, often expressing the composer's inner states of anxiety in periods of deep personal crisis. Such paroxystic outburst of emotions invariably disregarded established canons and accepted conventions. The aim was not formal perfection, but intensity of feeling. The composer did not seek to invent pleasing harmonies or beautiful melodies, but indulged in dissonances, extended chromatic scales, tonal freedom, irregular and frequently changing rhythms, and so on. The resulting work sounded more like a colorful collage of fragments than a well-crafted composition.

Not many musicians were willing to work in such a manner, and consequently only a handful of operas qualify to be categorized as Expressionist (and they were produced rather late in the history of the movement, e.g. Schoenberg's *Lucky Hand* and *Expectation* received their première only in 1924, Berg's *Wozzeck* in 1925). Hindemith's settings of *Murderer Hope of Women* and *Sancta Susanna* were based on Expressionist play scripts, but hardly qualify as Expressionist operas. Of course, once Expressionism had been established as a stylistic principle, it could be applied to any stage work. Just as there were Expressionist renderings of Shakespeare's or Schiller's dramas, there were productions of Beethoven's *Fidelio* or Handel's *Xerxes* that employed Expressionist principles, usually in stage and costume design. However, when compared with Karlheinz Martin's radical stagings at the Tribüne or the distinctly innovative concepts of Schreyer's Kampfbühne, the Expressionist *mise-en-scène* of an otherwise routine opera production hardly deserves to be called "Expressionist theatre." Nonetheless, contemporary audiences began to use the term "Expressionist" as a catch-all phrase for Modernism in the wider sense, and will have thought differently about this.

Between 1919 and 1921, Expressionism came to dominate German theatre and entered the mainstream. What had originally been a radical, avant-garde attitude and outlook on art and society became a fashionable style, increasingly mannerist, convoluted, and drained of its original "gutsiness." Of course, it would have been impossible to prolong the emotionality and sweeping intensity of the early Expressionist productions beyond an initial, feverish excitement, as it exhausted both performers and audiences alike. By 1922, many artists and theatregoers would have agreed with Kortner that Expressionism "is no more a form of theatre than a revolution is a form of State."[64] The international return to an ordered postwar society (usually referred to as *rappel à l'ordre*) also affected the artistic life in Germany and ushered in a "new sobriety," variously referred to as *Neue Sachlichkeit* or *Konstruktivismus*. I shall discuss this transition, which took place around 1922/23, in chapter 5.

3. Futurism ⌇

CHRONOLOGY 3.1:   FUTURIST THEATRE

January 15, 1909	F. T. Marinetti's *La donna è mobile* in Turin, Teatro Alfieri
February 20, 1909	*Foundation and Manifesto of Futurism* published in Le Figaro
April 3–5, 1909	F. T. Marinetti's *Roi Bombance* in Paris, Théâtre Marigny
1910	First Futurist *serate at* the Politeama Rossetti in Trieste (January 12, 1910), Teatro Lirico in Milan (February 15, 1910), Politeama Chiarella in Turin (March 8, 1910), Teatro Mercadante in Naples (April 20, 1910)
January 11, 1911	*Manifesto of Futurist Playwrights (The Pleasure of Being Booed)*
September 13, 1913–January 19, 1914	Tumiati's tour with Marinetti's *Elettricità*
September 29, 1913 **1913–1914**	*The Variety Theatre Manifesto* Futurist *serate* at the Teatro Costanzi in Rome (February 21, and March 9, 1913), Teatro Storchi in Modena (June 2, 1913), Teatro Verdi in Florence (December 12, 1913), Teatro dal Verme in Milan (April 21, 1914)
1913–1914	Futurist performances at the Galleria Sprovieri in Rome and Naples
1913–1916	Plastic Complexes by Balla and Depero
April 1914 **(publ. March 11, 1916)**	*Manifesto of Dynamic and Multichaneled Recitation*
January 11, 1915 **February 1–** **March 1, 1915**	*Manifesto of Futurist Synthetic Theatre* The first *Futurist Synthetic Theatre* tour of the Berti-Masi Company
January 30, 1915 **(publ. May 12, 1915)**	*Manifesto of Futurist Choreography and Scenography*
March 8–May 1916	The *Futurist Synthetic Theatre* tours of the Ninchi and Zoncada-Masi companies
1916–1918	Futurist collaborations with Variety stars Molinari, Petrolini, and Spadaro

April 12, 15, 27, 1917	Balla's *Feu d'artifice* at the Teatro Costanzi in Rome
April 14, 1918	Depero's *I balli plastici* premièred at the Teatro dei Piccoli in Rome
June 13–15, 1919	Prampolini's *Matoum e Tevibar* at the Teatro dei Piccoli in Rome
April 11, 1919	Azari's *Manifesto of Futurist Aerial Theatre*
March 21–31, 1920	*Teatro del Colore* season at the Teatro Argentina in Rome
September 30, 1921– February 4, and 1922	First Italian tour of the *Futurist Theatre of Surprise*
December 12, 13, and 17, 1921	*Futurist Synthetic Theatre* program in Prague
June 2, 1922	*Il ballo meccanico futurista* at Casa d'Arte Bragaglia in Rome
June 20, 1922 (revised March 1923)	*Manifesto of Futurist Mechanical Art*
April 19, 1922	Opening of the Cabaret Diavolo in Rome
April 1, 1923	Pocarini's *Teatro Semifuturista* premièred in Gorizia
January 11– February 8, 1924	Tour of *Il Nuovo Teatro Futurista*
April 1925	Prampolini's *Magnetic Theatre* exhibited in Paris
April 27, 1927	Vasari's *Angoscia delle macchine* in Paris, Salle Grenier Jaune
May 12, 1927– March 13, 1928	*Théâtre de la Pantomime Futuriste* in Paris, Turin, Bergamo, and Milan
1930–1931	Futurist Aerodances in Paris and Milan
January 11, 1933	Marinetti's *Total Theatre Manifesto*

MARINETTI'S SOCIOPOLITICAL CONCEPT OF "ART AS ACTION"

Futurism, launched in 1909 by the Italian poet and publicist Filippo Tommaso Marinetti, was the first radical expression of an avantgardist, Modernist spirit in the arts. It was responsible for creating, and consciously disseminating to the public at large, an image of the avant-garde assuming a position of principal contrariety to society, and of avant-garde theatre acting in opposition to its audiences.

In their manifestos, the Futurists proclaimed the bankruptcy of a country that clung to the past and ignored the great advances of the industrial era. In their works, they tried to capture the experience of a modern world transformed by steam engines, electricity, automobiles, locomotives, and aeroplanes (for a

Figure 3.1 The Futurist conception of remodeling traditionalist Venice. A caricature of André Warnot in *Comœdia*, June 17, 1910, showing Venice before and after the advent of Futurism.

constrasting depiction of these two words, see figure 3.1). Futurist art was an exaltation of modern, urban life and sought to obliterate the contemplative, intellectual culture of Belle-Epoque Italy. The Futurists ridiculed the ossified cultural and political institutions and the servile respect paid to Italy's glorious past. Instead, they sought nothing less than to revolutionize society in an all-encompassing manner: moral, artistic, cultural, social, economic, and political. Art was to be an active force in the Futurist battle for a liberating future and stood in marked contrast to the ivory-tower position that art had assumed in the preceding period.

Before founding the Futurist movement, Marinetti was a well-known writer, poet, and journalist, who had studied law at the Universities of Pavia and Genoa and had shown a lively interest in Left-wing politics and contemporary philosophy. Marinetti's *Weltanschauung* during this period was a mixture of beliefs derived from Nietzsche's radical individualism, Bergson's dynamic concept of the universe, Marx and Engels's analysis of capitalist society, and Bakunin and Sorel's philosophy of violence. Marinetti was far more serious in his political engagement than most of his bohemian friends. During the Milan uprising of May 1898, he followed with great interest the revolutionary actions on the barricades; he visited meetings held by the Socialist Party and the trade unions; he made the acquaintance of the socialist leaders Labriola, Turati, and Kuliscioff, and became friends with the revolutionary syndicalist Walter Mocchi. He also frequented the anarchist circles of Milan, recited his poetry in their meeting halls, and gave lectures on art and politics in their educational centers.[1]

As a result of these contacts and activities, Marinetti developed an ideological outlook that veered between anarchism, syndicalism, and ardent nationalism. In the cultural field, he engaged himself in the artistic debates of the period and favored a position of interventionism, iconoclasm, provocation, and radical opposition to the status quo. This revolutionary stance he proclaimed in a large number of articles and speeches, as well as in his literary works, which were often dedicated to anarchist friends. To take his writings to the people, he recited them in theatres and community halls up and down the peninsula. Out of these personal experiences with live performances as a means of galvanizing people into action he developed his concept of "Art as Action" (*art-action* was the French term Marinetti coined for it[2]). It formed the basis of the literary school, to be called Electricism or Dynamism, which he intended to establish in 1908. He developed, together with a small group of friends, an artistic program designed to stir up controversy and to aggravate a country steeped in traditionalism and festering with decaying institutions. When it was finally unveiled, in 1909, its name had changed to Futurism.

The launching of the *Foundation and Manifesto of Futurism* on February 20, 1909 came close to declaring war on the cultural establishment. Marinetti conceived of Futurism as a violent jolt that would set ablaze the somnolent and stultified cultural scene in Italy and ring in an "Italian Revolution." He described this battle as a "hygienic measure," modeled on the violent gestures of anarchists and libertarians. His iconoclastic actions were intended to stimulate a renewal in the arts and in society as a whole. The *Foundation and Manifesto of Futurism* made it clear that the one could only be realized in conjunction with the other. Hence Marinetti's exultation of the masses and the world of industrial labor, of political agitation, strikes and, especially, of the anarchists' violent actions. Futurism was conceived as a means of bridging the gap between art and life. Life was to be changed through art, and art was to become integrated into life. It was Marinetti's firm belief that artists with their superior creativity, intuition, and vitality had an important contribution to make to this process of renewal. From developing a program of change in art and life it was a natural and logical step to extend it to the political arena, to publish a series of political manifestos, and to become actively engaged in the political struggles of the era.[3] However, a mere handful of artists and intellectuals could not achieve the Futurist project of liberating mankind from the encumbering forces of the past and of leading humanity into a golden future. Marinetti and his companions realized that art alone, as a weapon wielded only by an intellectual élite, would not have the necessary force to overthrow the existing system. They had to seek allies and take their concept of Art as Action into the midst of the sociopolitical revolutionaries.

During the "Crisis of the Left," which emerged between the Socialist Party's acceptance into the established political system and the rise of the Communist Party as a new magnet for the revolutionary forces of the Left, there existed in Italy a plethora of subversive groups and associations in all major and most minor cities. It was within this amorphous pool of radicals and subversives of the extreme Left that Marinetti centered his political engagement. The artists who later formed the Futurist movement had already established close personal links with these groups long before Futurism saw the light of day as an organized movement. Inspired by the French Symbolists' contacts with the anarchist movement, several of Marinetti's friends— Boccioni, Russolo, Carrà, Notari, Buzzi, and Lucini—frequented the libertarian circles of Lombardy, contributed poems, designs, or illustrations to their journals, organized exhibitions in their clubs, gave poetry recitations and lectures in their adult-education institutes, and so on. This bore fruit in the following years. Anarchists, syndicalists, and revolutionary socialists of the industrial north followed with interest the growth of the Futurist movement and greeted its artistic and political program with qualified enthusiasm. One can assume that, by 1910, interest in Futurism was widespread in the organizations of the extreme Left. This, of course, is not to say that they all agreed with Marinetti or his political pronouncements. Marinetti probably caused more discussion than consent in anarchist and syndicalist circles. But nonetheless, a lively dialog ensued between the political subversives and artistic revolutionaries. The anarchist journals *La rivolta*, *Il viandante* and *Università Popolare* of Milan, *Il libertario* of La Spezia, and *La barricata* of Parma published fundamental articles on the Futurist movement.[4] Maria Rygier, one of the leading figures of the anarcho-syndicalist movement, confessed: "I have followed with great attention and not without a certain aesthetic sympathy the diverse manifestations of the young Futurist movement."[5] Leda Rafanelli, another a prominent anarchist, reported similarly: "All anarchists, despite their culpable ignorance about art and artists, felt the attraction of this rebellion."[6] Also the young Gramsci—soon to become the leader of the Italian Communist Party—engaged in the debates on the Futurists and defended them against their critics.[7]

FUTURIST POLITICAL ACTION THEATRE

As Marinetti made quite clear in his early manifestos, the Futurist movement not only had the aim to bring about an aesthetic revolution, but also to effect a total overhaul of society. His project of renewal encompassed all aspects of human existence, and was conceived as a total and permanent revolution. What was later called "Futurist Reconstruction of the Universe" was aimed at a transformation of life in the modern metropolis. However, as Marinetti emphasized in several interviews and articles of the period, the Futurists were not to become like professional politicians whom he disparagingly referred to as "litigation merchants, prostituted brains, emporia of subtle ideas and polished syllogisms."[8] Throughout the first years of the Futurist movement, its members were engaged revolutionaries active in both the artistic and political fields. They explored many ways of creating an emancipatory life praxis, where artistic and sociopolitical activities were integrated into a unified whole. It is not astonishing, therefore, to find artistic events to be shaped by their political function, and vice versa, primarily political events to be given an aesthetic appearance. This "aestheticization of politics" and "politicization of aesthetics" was probably best demonstrated in the performative genre, which I shall refer to as "political action theatre."

Marinetti deprecated the "sedentary nature" of books and other print media[9] and praised theatre as the only effective medium to influence the Italian spirit.[10] Therefore, from the inception of the movement, the Futurists made use of performative means in order to disseminate their political and artistic aims. Futurist politics were performative, just as Futurist performances were political. Politics came to be conducted like a theatrical enterprise, and vice versa, politics played a significant rôle in Futurist theatre. In fact, both merged to such an extent that it is impossible to separate the one from the other. Claudio Vicentini described this political aesthetics most aptly:

> The theatrical performance is the twin brother of the political demonstration. Both emerged from the *serate*; both have been constructed according to the same model of action; both develop in a discordant situation which involves all people

present; and both evoke each other in turn. The demonstration has the theatrical quality of a performance, and the performance has the political efficacy of a demonstration.[11]

One month after the publication of the *Foundation and Manifesto of Futurism*, Marinetti published a leaflet, *First Futurist Political Manifesto for the General Elections of 1909*, which was distributed in Milan and formed part of the street agitation in the run-up to the election. A year later, he planned to stand in the regional elections in Piedmont with an anarcho-syndicalist program of a nationalist bent and embarked on forming a Union of Revolutionary Forces. In order to promote this coalition of intellectual subversives and proletarian revolutionaries, he undertook a lecture tour centered on a speech, "The Necessity and Beauty of Violence."[12] At the same time he organized a political theatre event (*serata*) in Trieste and participated in irredentist demonstrations, which led to his arrest and the opening of a police file on him. These political street actions and theatrical performances, designed to propagate the Futurist political and artistic program, were complemented by spectacular stunts in public spaces and open-air arenas. One of them was carried out in February 1910, when in order to advertise their theatrical evening (*serata*) at the Teatro Lirico in Milan, the Futurists climbed onto the platform of the cathedral and amidst fluttering pigeons showered the tourists and passers-by with thousands of flyers.[13] A similar publicity event took place in July 1910, when they distributed their manifesto *Against Traditionalist Venice* from the Clock Tower of Piazza San Marco. Palazzeschi remembered the action:

> Armed with a trumpet, we climbed up the Watch Tower in Venice on a bright Sunday afternoon, at a time when the Piazza San Marco swarmed with a throng of festive and chattering people. After three blasts from the trumpet at carefully chosen intervals, all faces were directed upwards. With some bewilderment people wondered what, after such an unexpected and inexplicable announcement, could happen from above. Marinetti regarded Venice as the fortress and symbol of universal passéism, and using a megaphone he began to shout: "We reject the old Venice . . . etc."[14]

Far more radical in concept and execution were the disturbances during the performance of Richard Strauss's *Der Rosenkavalier* at La Scala in Milan, on February 27, 1911. The action still had a primarily artistic function: promulgating Futurist music and criticizing traditionalist opera and its bourgeois audiences. On February 27 the opera was given its Italian première at La Scala, and consequently there was a full house of typically upper-bourgeois and aristocratic extraction. At the end of the second act, the Futurists took up their positions in the upper gallery and showered the audience with flyers, which carried the statement:

> We Futurists demand that La Scala should cease to be the Pompeii of the Italian theatre and the showcase for the great publishers. Instead, every season it ought to present three experimental opera productions of young, unknown and audaciously innovatory Italian composers.[15]

At the next national elections in October 1913, the Futurists extended their canvassing methods from putting up posters and holding speeches to creating Futurist spectacles in the streets. In a letter to Guglielmo Jannelli, Marinetti instructed his young disciple in Messina on how the leaflets with the *Futurist Political Program* were to be distributed:

> Have immediately printed, with your usual ultra-Futurist energy, 15,000 flyers like the one enclosed or even half that size, but keep the same proportion of letters. Take paper of different colors, but they must be bright, otherwise the print will be illegible. Then, take a car and . . . make a tour through the principal streets of Messina, throwing the flyers with the verve that distinguishes you.[16]

The next time the Futurists invaded an opera house and performed their brand of action theatre, the event was more politically motivated than in 1911. On September 15, 1914, Puccini's *Fanciulla del West* had its première at the Teatro dal Verme in Milan. A few weeks earlier, World War I had broken out, and the Futurists decided to organize one of the first demonstrations for Italy's intervention in the war. Again, they chose the occasion of a prime event in the Italian cultural calendar to publicize their ideas. After the first act of the opera, Marinetti, from the upper gallery, unrolled a huge Italian flag, while Boccioni, on another gallery, tore an Austrian flag to pieces and threw the fragments into the auditorium. The next day they repeated the action in the city center. At the Galleria Vittorio Emanuele they displayed an Italian flag and shouted: "Long live France, long live war, down with Austria" and distributed flysheets with the *Futurist Résumé of War* printed on them.[17] When the police intervened, they marched to the square in front of the cathedral and burned eight Austrian flags on a funeral pyre. For hours, the whole gallery was in pandemonium with fights and brawls raging inside and outside the cafés. As a result of the action, Marinetti, Boccioni, Carrà, Mazza, Russolo, and two others were arrested, charged with "attack on relations with a foreign State and burning of a foreign flag,"[18] and had to spend six days in prison.

THE ENGINEERING OF THEATRE SCANDALS

As a young man, Marinetti was an ardent theatre goer. He published his views on contemporary Italian theatre in a large number of reviews and essays and criticized his country for being "absolutely unaffected by the modern spirit and contemptuous of the heaving research that animates the soul of our century."[19] This lack of a "modern spirit" was a cultural as well as a socio-economic fact. The Italian bourgeoisie was overwhelmingly conservative in their attitudes and forced Marinetti into an increasingly oppositional rôle against "this lugubrious *fin-de-siècle*."[20] He disapproved of the audiences who had been raised on a diet of *pièces-bien-faites* and, therefore, went to the theatre "only to laugh, digest . . . and look for an erotic *frisson*."[21] Marinetti acted as a champion of modern art, and not only in his critical writings. When, for example, d'Annunzio's *La città morta* was given a negative reception at the Teatro Lirico in 1901, Marinetti was enraged and organized a counterattack, invading the stalls of the theatre and "delivering boxes to the ears and blows to the bellies" of the conservative spectators.[22] He was a staunch supporter of Enrico Annibale Butti and admired his ability to shock spectators out of their contentment and conformity. He praised Butti's "audacious theses" and daring formal innovation, which whipped his spectators into "ferocious rage" and unleashed "a storm of controversy, of boos and frenetic applause."[23]

Marinetti clearly relished the scenes that Butti provoked in the theatre and sought to match them with a production of his own play, *Le Roi Bombance* (King Guzzle). The work was heavily influenced by Alfred Jarry's *Ubu Roi*, which had caused such a scandal at its Paris première in 1896 (see above, pp. 47–50). Although Marinetti had not been present at this memorable event, he had established contact with Jarry in 1903 and had sent him a copy of his drama (apparently, Jarry was very impressed with it [24]). The work was announced for the winter season 1905–1906, but had to be delayed for a variety of reasons.

In the meantime, Marinetti wrote *The Electric Puppets*, which included his proto-Futurist vision of a modern world and a critique of the forces of tradition and sentimentality. Its première in Turin, on January 15, 1909, offered a first impression of Marinetti's formula of *art-action*, of an art that invaded society and stimulated active responses from the spectators rather than serving as an object of contemplation or consumption. The performance went down in the chronicles of Italian theatre history as an event comparable to the Battle of *Hernani* and the scandal that surrounded *Ubu Roi*. Marinetti's later claim[25] to have read out the *Foundation and Manifesto of Futurism* from the stage indicates that he regarded the production as a practical demonstration of the ideas the Futurist movement sought to promote. The evidence we possess of the Turin performance indicates that nothing could have warned the spectators, or given them reason to suspect, what they were about to witness. The Modernist French title of the play had been changed to *La donna é mobile*, promising something amusing just like the popular aria from *Rigoletto*.[26] So when the unsuspecting audience arrived at the Teatro Alfieri, hoping for an evening of light, yet stimulating, entertainment, Marinetti detonated the bomb that was to signal the end of Italian theatre as he knew it. The reviews of the memorable event[27] indicate that he had organized a claque to ensure that the audience was going to be an active partner and not just a passive witness of the proceedings on stage.[28] Marinetti's desire to use the theatre as a tribune of agitation and an arena for public debate turned the mediocre performance of a weak play into a major scandal that was reported, as Marinetti later claimed,[29] in 418 newspaper articles. Provocation and scandal were his weapons in the battle he was to wage on the cultural establishment. They were tools with which to stir spectators out of their complacency. *Poupées électriques*, although outwardly disguised in the trappings of "digestive theatre," gave a first taste of Marinetti's vision of theatre that could play an activating rôle in society and offered a first impression of what the Futurist movement was going to promote with unabating determination over the next 20 years.

Another foretaste of the game which Marinetti, the Futurist, was going to play with his audiences was given at the première of *Le Roi Bombance* on April 3, 1909 at the Théâtre Marigny in Paris. The production was organized by the Théâtre de l'Œuvre and directed by Lugné-Poë, who had staged Jarry's *Ubu Roi* in 1896 for the same theatre (see pp. 47–50) The reception of Marinett's "intestinal epic" was such that *Le Vrai Mondain* could write: "Our Parisian audience will not forget this spectacle for some time."[30] Since all reviews mentioned Marinetti as the head of a new artistic movement called Futurism, it is likely that the majority of people who visited the production had read or at least heard of the *Foundation and Manifesto* published in *Le Figaro* six weeks prior to the opening night. Therefore, expectations ran high, and by the end of the evening everyone was certain that they had witnessed a theatre scandal of the first order. *Le Provençal de Paris* judged the "three nights of battle and fever . . . to have marked . . . a date in the history of riotous theatre evenings." Many papers drew parallels to the "Battle of *Hernani*," and most reviewers felt reminded of "the heroic days of *Ubu Roi*." The audience reactions, as described in the papers, were certainly very similar to those given to Jarry's play: "The Marigny theatre had more resemblance to a public meeting than a theatrical performance: people yell, shout, imitate animal sounds" (*Gil Blas*). "Raised arms, cries of rage, sounds of animals. Is this a meeting, a controversial gathering? No, it is the première of *Le Roi Bombance*" (*Le Vrai Mondain*).

Again, as in Turin before, Marinetti had organized a claque, which managed to create an atmosphere of general mayhem, which later became a hallmark of Futurist theatre performances: "The spectacle took place in the hall as well as on stage," *Le Provençal de Paris* wrote. A similar description was offered by *L'Intransigeant*: "They performed as much in the auditorium as on stage."[31] Marinetti enjoyed the glory of being "the most booed author of the century,"[32] adding—with a view to future productions he had in mind—"But the century is still young!" A year later, Marinetti would make "The Pleasure of Being Booed" a cornerstone in his aesthetics of Futurist theatre, conceived as insurrection or, as Mayakovsky put it, "A Slap in the Face of Public Taste."

THE FUTURIST SOIRÉES (*SERATE*) AS A NEW TYPE OF PERFORMANCE ART

Theatre was conceived by Marinetti as a means of "introducing the fist into the artistic battle"[33] and of enabling "the brutal entry of life into art."[34] Marinetti believed that theatre as a form of "cultural combat" would lead the artists out of their ivory tower and give them a chance "to participate, like workmen or soldiers, in the battle for world progress."[35] The Futurist performer became the advance guard of the Futurist revolution, employing fighting methods that were derived from the anarchists' *beaux gestes destructifs*.[36] Theatre, when imbued with such a bellicose spirit, would have the necessary force, Marinetti believed, "to snatch the soul of the audience away from base, day-to-day reality"[37] and have a liberating effect on society at large.

To some extent, the first *serate* continued what Marinetti had practiced for many years prior to the inception of the Futurist movement: poetry recitations and lectures on topics of a controversial artistic or political nature. As of 1910, the term "Futurist *serata*" meant: presenting the key ideas of the Futurist movement in a large theatre and offering the audience examples of how these principles could be translated into performative language. The first *serate* always contained a combination of (a) the reading of manifestos, and (b) the presentation of artistic creations that had arisen from these theories. This allowed Marinetti to introduce the Italian public, successively, to Futurist poetry, painting, and music.

For more than ten years, Marinetti had gathered experience as a reciter of Symbolist and anarchist poetry in various French and Italian theatres, often causing altercations and agitated audience reactions. He used this experience to launch a new, Futurist, type of recitation, characterized by visualization and gestural presentation of poetic and theoretical texts. However, from the first *serata* in Trieste onwards, another key element formed an integral part of the program: Futurist politics. The *serate* had the function of not only familiarizing the art world with the aesthetic principles of Futurism, but also of propagating their ideology of anti-traditionalism, patriotism, rebellion, and so on. Marinetti called events such as the Milan *serata* of February 15, 1910 a *comizio artistico*, that is, a political meeting with an artistic format.[38] In an essay of 1914 he tried to establish six key criteria that differentiate a Futurist *serata* from other events of a similarly noisy type and included among them, beside several artistic principles, the systematic demolition of traditional art and politics.[39]

In this respect, the recitation of a manifesto or of selected examples of Futurist poetry no longer aimed at interpreting a literary text with artistic finesse, as had been the case in the poetry recitations during Symbolist soirées. The Futurist reciter now served as an object the audience could react *against* (see figure 3.2). The reading set in motion a mechanism that went far beyond the appreciation of an artistic creation. The text functioned as a score, the reciter as a conductor, and the audience as the orchestra. The main task of the reciter was to challenge the spectators and to provoke them into reactions of an unpremeditated form.

The *serate* were a weapon in the political and artistic fight for a total renewal of Italian public life. They were an all-round attack on the cult of the past and the social forces that sustained it. Not only did they serve to glorify war and revolution, they *were* an act of insurrection, "like the throwing of a well-primed grenade over the heads of our contemporaries."[40] But they were also a medium of artistic expression, and it was in this combination of art and politics that the anarchist tradition of "generative violence" found its concrete application. The Futurist *serata* was a vehicle through which art and life could be joined together into a compact union. As such, it was different from demonstrations and other forms of action theatre, where the political rationale prevailed. Vicentini captured this very well when he wrote:

> Theatrical action and political action, although imbued with the same characteristics and setting the same process in motion . . . have diverging functions and obey different criteria of success. Or, to put it differently, the model of Futurist actionism is always the same, but its application in the two ambits is not. . . . In

Marinetti's conception, the political demonstration is not the same as the theatrical spectacle, even if it contains the same characteristics. The one can never assume
the functions of the other without rendering it superfluous.[41]

Marinetti's Art as Action was an artistic-political battle directed *against* an
audience he regarded as reactionary, passive, lazy, complacent, and so on. In
order to shake these spectators out of their stupor, the *serate* had to be
provocative. Depending on where the performances took place, a different
composition of the program ensured that nobody in the auditorium could
remain unaffected by what was presented on stage.

On the day of a performance, the Futurists usually carried out a publicity
action: cars painted in wild colors drove through the streets, Futurist slogans
were shouted through megaphones, leaflets were flung on passers-by, and so on.
More publicity material was distributed in shops, cafés, and restaurants, or to
groups of people chatting in the market square. Cangiullo mentions an example
where, on the evening before a *serata*, they entered the municipal theatre, disturbed the performance, and showered the audience with Futurist manifestos.[42]

In the beginning, the *serate* were major events for audiences ranging
between 2,000 and 5,000 spectators. The recitation of manifestos and the
display of Futurist paintings on stage introduced a wide array of people for
the first time to the ideas propagated by the Futurists. The seats in the upper
gallery were cheap (approximately 1 Lira), which explains the regular presence of Futurist supporters from the poorer sections of society—students,
artists, young workers—up in the gods. It was characteristic of the *serate* that
they attracted people who rarely went to the theatre and certainly never to the
traditional playhouses where the *serate* were staged ("people who have never
been seen before and who evidently only come to the theatre when a *serata* is
on," was the *Corriere della sera*'s description of these sections of the audience
on the occasion of the Milan *serata* in 1910). During the Futurist events,
however, they would rub shoulders with the *gente perbene*, who occupied the
5 to 10 Lire seats in the stalls, dress, circle, or boxes. This audience composition invariably proved to be explosive to a high degree.

As the Futurists gained experience with this loose format, they mastered
the art of provocation and learned how to retaliate the audience's counterat-
tacks. This aggressive stance turned every *serata* into a veritable battlefield.
(see figure 3.2) Initially, the Futurists had difficulty in handling the audience
reactions and controlling the progress of the performance. But after a while
they developed a certain virtuosity in the "martial art" of theatre. They learned
how to handle aggression (verbal or physical) and to channel audience
reactions as they saw fit.

Figure 3.2 A Futurist serata. A caricature by Filiberto Mateldi. Marinetti's Art as Action was an artistic-political battle directed against an audience he regarded as reactionary, passive, lazy, complacent, and so on. This aggressive and provocative stance turned every serata into a veritable battlefield.

The riots and scandals that surrounded the *serate* served as an excellent public-relations exercise for the Futurists and brought the movement to the attention of the wider public. They made Marinetti a household name all over Europe—more so than any of his previous activities had done. The *serate* gave the Futurists a bad name in some circles (which the artists did not mind, since they regarded these people as reactionaries and beyond redemption anyway), but others felt admiration for this small group of artists who, within the span of a few years, had captured the public imagination and exercised a growing influence on the cultural climate of the country.

Two examples may suffice here to give an impression of the atmosphere that reigned at a Futurist *serata*, of the performative strategies employed by Marinetti and his collaborators, and of the audience reactions they provoked.[43]

On Sunday March 9, 1913, a *Grande serata futurista* was to be held at the Teatro Costanzi in Rome. The daily newspaper *La Tribuna* announced a program that comprised of a Futurist symphony by Maestro Pratella; recitation of Futurist poetry by Buzzi, Palazzeschi, Folgore and Marinetti, Boccioni presenting his manifestos on Futurist painting and sculpture; and Marinetti giving a speech, *Advice to the Romans*. On the day of the performance, thousands of people flocked to the theatre, and the streets around the building were in such a hullabaloo that the police had to intervene to safeguard public order.

In the end, 4,000 people were admitted—more than Caruso ever attracted to this theatre. From the moment they arrived, the audience turned the whole building into an inferno, and for the next two-and-a-half hours they waged "a continuous battle of whistling, howling, rioting, fisticuffs, thrashings, assaulting the Futurists with potatoes, chestnuts, tomatoes, apples and other objects . . . They shouted abuse and obscenities, and behaved like real hooligans" (*Giornale d'Italia*). What astonished the reviewer most was that this type of behavior was not only displayed "by the plebeians on the balcony, but also by the aristocrats in the boxes." The audience consisted of a cross section of society: "In the boxes next to the proscenium we noted several exponents of the Roman aristocracy, known to be 'black' because of their attachment to the Vatican. Needless to say, the whole intellectual world of the city was present. And up in the gods nested the most unruly student population."[44]

The "Battle of Rome" began from the moment Pratella lifted his baton and intoned the first bars of his music. A shower of fruit and vegetables hailed down on him and broke a few instruments. From the royal box, Prince Altieri bombarded the musicians with anthracite coal, of which he had taken a whole sack load into the theatre. From the edge of the stage, Marinetti hurled invectives at him: "You syphilitic lout! Son of a priest!" The only effect this had was that the hailstorm increased in intensity. The next instrument to go to pieces was a flute. One after the other, the musicians retreated and brought their instruments into safety. In the end,

> Maestro Pratella remains on his own at the conductor's desk. He exhorted the musicians not to disperse. But Pratella's Futurism does not extend to the point where he can conduct a symphony without an orchestra! Melancholically, he abandons his platform. He retires to the stage amidst whistling and other high-frequency noises and joins the company assembled around the leading actor, F. T. Marinetti. (*Messaggero*)

Now Marinetti approached the footlights and began a lecture on the aims and fundamental principles of the Futurist movement. When he read out a particularly offensive passage that affronted the members and sympathizers of academic or ecclesiastical institutions, the noise level in the house reached such a high that he was forced to interrupt his speech for several minutes. An equally rowdy reception was given to the poetry recitations. At one point,

Marinetti had to stop. He looked at the audience and made what looked like a conciliatory offer: "Okay, I'll make you content now."—Pause—The spectators quieten down.—"I shall now recite *La vispa Teresa* [*Gay Theresa*, a most traditional and extremely stupid popular song, G. B.], the only poem that is suitable for Roman audiences." The turmoil that followed this announcement reached unprecedented heights. Marinetti, at the top of his voice, entered into an altercation with Prince Altieri, Prince Boncompagni, Prince Potenziani, Marquis Cappelli, Marquis Marignoli, and their companions in the Royal Box:

> You son of a priest!—Buffoon!
> Jesuit disciple!—Imbecile!
> Effeminate!—Charlatan!
> Parasite!

Boccioni supported him by shouting: "We despise you scabby dogs! You are the quintessence of human cowardice!" And Marinetti threatened Prince Altieri: "I'll wreck your mug when you leave the theatre!" How Boccioni managed to present his manifesto and Marinetti to read out Papini's *Speech Against Rome* after having fomented such an atmosphere was a miracle that caused the *Giornale d'Italia* to write, not without admiration: "The Futurists are, one by one, men of real genius, who know how to do, and to say, the most audacious things without losing their control in the general disorder, as so many spectators did last night." According to Walter Vaccari, Marinetti in the end gave up reading Papini's text, and with the words "I confirm all of Papini's insults and therefore will distribute my friend's discourse in printed form!" he threw a pile of leaflets containing the text of the speech into the stalls.[45]

This brought the *serata* officially to a close. However, in the corridors of the theatre, discussions continued and pitched philo- and anti-Futurists into another battle. Boccioni joined the crowds and began a violent quarrel with Prince Altieri. Also Marinetti attacked the Prince, who turned his back on him and walked away into the street. Marinetti kicked his unprotected backside and lost his shoe in the attack. (When it was returned to him later, he exclaimed: "And I thought it had disappeared in his rear!") The fight continued in the rain, and the aristocrats employed their umbrellas to defend themselves against their enemies. Boccioni and Marinetti received a good thrashing before the police arrived. To avoid arrest, they cut and ran.

On November 30, 1913, an important exhibition of Futurist paintings organized by the journal *Lacerba* opened at the Libreria Gonnelli in Florence.

To coincide with this major show, the local Futurist circle planned to hold a *serata*, and the publisher Vallecchi hired the Teatro Verdi for December 12. The performance went down in the chronicles of Futurist theatre as the "Battle of Florence." Hours before the performance, the playhouse was surrounded by a clambering crowd. Estimates of how many people managed to squeeze into the auditorium vary between 5,000 (*Lacerba*) and 7,000 (*Corriere della sera*). The general spirit of excitement and expectation created a tense atmosphere that needed only a tiny spark to set off an explosion. Soffici remarked that the spectacle had begun long before the curtain had gone up, and Viviani remembered that

> already before eight o'clock the Teatro Verdi—one of the largest in Florence—was overflowing with a restless and electrified public. In the stalls and boxes more than six thousand people were packed like anchovies in a tin. . . . From time to time one could hear the somewhat timid sounds of metallic sirens, whistling on keys, and even the hoarse honking of a car horn. Clearly, this crowd had not arrived in the theatre with the intention to listen, but only to raise hell and make a racket.[46]

When, finally, the performers appeared on stage, "an inferno broke out. Before any of us could open his mouth, the hall was boiling over, resounding with savage voices in the fever of excitement. There was an atmosphere like that of an execution field before the capital punishment is about to be carried out."[47] And Cangiullo remembered:

> When the curtain went up, a howling tribe of cannibals raised their thousands of arms and greeted our apparition with a volley of objects from the animal, vegetable and mineral world. . . . No one thought of taking the first word. We were totally overwhelmed by this reception. We looked at our audience and began to read the banners that were displayed from the dress circle: "Perverts! Pederasts! Pimps! Charlatans! Buffoons!"[48]

After about five minutes, the audience began to calm down. Marinetti approached the footlights and exclaimed: "I have the impression I am down below the Turkish Fortresses in the Dardanelles. I can see your munitions running out and they still have not hit us." And immediately he was given proof that his assumption was wrong. The spectators had still masses of missiles left, causing Viviani to ask himself why neither the management of the theatre nor the many policemen had prevented people from carrying sack loads of projectiles into the auditorium. But it was not only the ammunition that caused disturbances. People had also arrived with car horns, cow-bells, whistles, pipes, rattles, and so on. Those who could not command any such instrument, at least made use of their door keys. After a while, Marinetti managed to interject another couple of sentences:

> It seems to me that this game has been going on too long. We shall wait until there is at least an intermittent silence. We ask those who support us to get the upper hand over the crowd, if necessary with force. Listen to us first, and when you've heard our new ideas, then you may whistle. Your asphyxiating and stinking missiles only demonstrate that traditionalism seeks to defend itself as best it can.[49]

As was to be expected, the audience retaliated this invective with an ear-splitting noise. Marinetti was exhorted: "Get off and hide in a lunatic asylum!" To which he replied: "I prefer our loony bin to your Pantheon!" And immediately the fracas started again. Marinetti advised his fellow-players: "We have to attack at all cost."

Amidst a barrage of vegetables that covered their heads in a shroud of pulp, the performers tried their best to get through the program they had announced on the posters and in the newspapers: Soffici talking on Futurist painting, Carrà slating the art critics and explaining his theory of paintings of odors, Boccioni speaking on plastic dynamism, Marinetti and Cangiullo reciting poems, and as the "clou" of the evening, Papini giving a lecture against traditionalist Florence. Since hardly any of the words reached the ears of the spectators, the speeches were printed in the next issue of *Lacerba*. The paper *L'unità cattolica* wrote with amazement: "Not only the working-class audience perched on the balcony were throwing potatoes. No, the upper classes and the petty bourgeoisie too gave a nice demonstration of the civil education they had received in their colleges and grammar schools." There were a few dozen friends of the artists who made some attempt at cooling down the spectators. However, brandishing a club that had been broken out of the banister only produced the opposite effect. Brawls erupted between supporters and opponents of Futurism. Rosai describes how he and a few friends sought to pacify their opponents:

> Holding their arms we prevented them from throwing their projectiles down onto the heads of the calmer part of the audience. We did not always succeed in grabbing them on time. One of them hit Marinetti's eye with a light bulb, and other actors were struck by further missiles. Up in the gods, Zanini and I took a fanatic by his legs and let him dangle for a few minutes from the parapet. When we pulled him up again, he was the calmest and humblest person in this tide of frenetic beings.[50]

Police intervened to prevent worse incidents from happening, but the turmoil continued. Cangiullo and Papini watched the audience from the stage and smoked a cigarette. Marinetti took out some binoculars and had a closer look at the scenes unfolding on the balcony. After a while, the hail of vegetables turned the stage into a cesspit. "Throw an idea, not a potato, you idiot!" Carrà hissed at a spectator, whose neighbor answered by blowing a children's trumpet. Marinetti commented, to everybody's amusement: "That's the signal for the departure of his intelligence!" And Boccioni shouted: "The projectiles you are throwing with such profusion are the fruit of your cowardice multiplied by your ignorance." A spectator came up to the stage and offered Marinetti a pistol. "Go on, commit suicide," he suggested, to which Marinetti replied: "If I deserve a bullet of lead, you deserve a bullet of shit!" But it was not only the actors who had to suffer from the transgressive behavior of their enemies. Soffici remembered:

> Not everything that was destined to hit us actually reached its target. A cauliflower, an egg, a slice of maize cake, a chestnut pudding thrown from the upper balcony hit the bald heads and shoulders of gentlemen in dinner jackets or the elegant hats of the ladies down in the stalls, where they provoked violent protests and screams. . . . We could observe from the stage how here and there in the auditorium altercations of words developed into altercations of fists. Infuriated people in the dress circle leaned forward and disputed with those bending down from above. They may have been members of high society, but their vocabulary was that of hawkers and fishwives. Given the impossibility of developing an orderly argument, the whole thing degenerated into an exchange of heated phrases and a skirmish of invective and repartees between stage and auditorium.[51]

Toward the end of the performance, Marinetti tried to explain the *Futurist Political Program*, which had been published three months earlier in *Lacerba*. His attacks on "the cowardly pacifists and eunuchs" and "the miserable mire of Socialists and Republicans" finally brought the house down. The police came on stage and declared the performance to be over.

The *serate* were the Futurists' first attempt at revolutionizing the established forms of theatrical communication. And indeed, the *serate* represented a clear break with the conventions and traditions of theatrical culture. They were not "scandals" in the normal sense of the word, that is, spontaneous eruptions of public ire, like those after the first performance of *Hernani* or *Ubu Roi*. Marinetti had *planned* and *organized* the events in a systematic and logical manner in order to *provoke* such reactions. He had initiated the *serate* with a clear political aim in mind: to storm the citadels of bourgeois culture and turn them into a battleground of a new sociopolitical praxis. Or as Carrà put it: "Having issued our appeal to youth with a manifesto, we realized that this was still too indirect a way to rouse public opinion. We felt the need to enter into a more immediate contact with the people: thus were born the famous Futurist *serate*."[52]

Although the program of each *serata* contained items of an artistic nature, these were often only an excuse for political agitation or for propaganda for the Futurist movement. The Futurist artists slipped into the rôle of performers, but they eschewed all characteristics associated with the acting profession. They did not transform themselves into fictive characters. They wore neutral evening clothes (only Balla sported his colorful waistcoats or cravats), and instead of realistic settings, the stage was equipped with a few functional pieces of furniture (usually a table and a couple of chairs). At this early phase of the Futurist movement, Marinetti did not choose the theatre because of the artistic possibilities it offered, but rather because it was the most effective medium for polemics and propaganda in an evolving mass society. ("As only 10% of Italians read books and magazines but 90% go to the theatre, the only way to inculcate a warlike spirit in Italians is through the medium of theatre."[53]) Papini underlined this fact when he wrote that through the *serate* the Futurists could divulge their ideas to a large number of people, "who otherwise would not have taken notice of them, had they simply and quietly been issued in printed form. In many ways, the theatre has taken the place of the old church. Modern man, who wants to put himself into contact with the masses, can put this modern temple to good use."[54]

The *serate* broke down the conventional relationship between stage and auditorium. Scenes such as the one in Florence, in which the performers stood on stage and watched the main action unroll in the stalls could equally well have taken place in a Dadaist soirée ("Our theatre will entrust the stage direction to the subtle invention of the explosive wind and the scenario to the audience," Tzara would say in 1917;[55] and describing the soirée at the Salle Gaveau on May 26, 1920, he judged: "The spectacle took place in the auditorium. We were gathered on the stage watching the audience let loose."[56]) Like the Dada performances, the *serate* eliminated the "actor" and replaced him with an artist who did not *represent* a character, but rather *presented* himself and his ideas. Premeditated elements were combined in these "exhibitions" with a large amount of improvisation. Richter said about the Dada soirée at the Kaufleuten Hall on April 19, 1919: "Tzara had organized the whole thing with the magnificent precision of a ringmaster."[57] The same applied to Marinetti's manner of setting up each *serata*. But this in no way restricted the importance of the extempore. Within the framework of a well-organized and rehearsed program there was wide room for improvisation. In fact, the success of the later *serate* depended heavily on the improvisatory element, which, according to newspaper reports, had not yet been fully developed in the first *serate*. Some reviews dedicate nearly as much space to the improvised components as to the fixed items of the program (which shows how impressed spectators were with the performers' ability to handle interventions from the auditorium). However, the art of the extemporé largely depends on the performer having enough *lazzi* at hand and commanding over a well-stocked repertoire of quips and repartees. Comparing the reviews of many *serate*, it becomes apparent that the Futurists, like the *Commedia dell'arte* players before them, used the same stock of jokes and provocative remarks over and over again.

Between 1910 and 1914, the Futurists organized some 20 major *serate*. By the end of 1913, Marinetti began to realize that the format was becoming a restricting rather than liberating force in Futurism. Despite the introduction of new elements such as painting and music (see figure 3.3), the *serate* became repetitive and audiences began to react according to plan rather than impulse. The reputation of the Futurists and the notoriety of their *serate* had taken their toll. Clearly, a new direction was required.

This is where the small-scale events in art galleries, performances of a new type of Futurist drama, and a range of experiments with popular forms of theatre came into existence.

Figure 3.3 Luigi Russolo and Ugo Piatti with an orchestra of noise intoners. These mechanical instruments were first presented in the *serata* at the Teatro dal Verme in Milan on April 21, 1914.

FUTURIST EXPERIMENTS WITH NEW
THEATRICAL FORMATS

Much of this chapter so far has been dedicated to a discussion of the Futurists' political engagement and the provocative nature of the resulting performances. However, it would be misguided to suggest that the Futurists employed the theatrical medium only as part of their strategies of "art as a weapon" or "Art as Action." The Futurist were also engaged in artistic experiments that had little or no direct connection to the political battles they were waging. The *Variety Theatre Manifesto* of 1913 and the first tour of a professional theatre company with a Futurist repertoire in 1913–1914 indicated that the Futurists were serious in their attempt to reform literary theatre and that they undertook concrete steps to implement the concepts first outlined in the *Manifesto of Futurist Playwrights* of 1910. In 1915 followed the Futurist Synthetic Theatre, presented in the form of a manifesto, a theatre tour, and an anthology of plays, and in 1916 they undertook several collaborations with artists from music-hall, variety, and café-concert.

Futurist theatre of the early 1910s was provocative, activating, and dynamic. It tried to break down stultifying conventions in dramatic literature and theatrical institutions. It sought to activate the audience and to fuse the spheres of art and life. The Futurists questioned the traditional rôle of theatre in society, the function of the performances in the life of their spectators, and the communication structures employed by actors and playwrights (i.e., the artistic format of the dramatic texts, the acting styles used in their presentation, the relationship between stage and auditorium during the performance, the design and technical apparatus of the stage, etc.).

Marinetti and his followers despised the traditional theatre both as a social institution and as a marketplace for the presentation of mediocre and regurgitated wares. They fought the commercialism of the enterprise and the intellectual mediocrity of its representatives. They developed counterstrategies to demolish a repertoire that was offered to the spectators in the form of the well-made play, historical costume drama, or psychological realism. And, of course, they abhorred those audiences who went to the theatre merely to digest a heavy evening meal and to parade their intellectual vanities and latest wardrobe acquisitions.

The Futurists demanded that theatre offer "a synthesis of life in its most typical and its most significant aspects."[58] When "reality pulsates around us and assails us with barrages of unrelated facts, each one locked into the next, fused together, knotted together, utterly chaotic,"[59] theatre could not go on pressing the experience of the modern world into five-act verse dramas with "imposed conventions of crescendo, exposition and dénouement."[60] The traditional language of the stage no longer provided adequate means for giving expression to the modern experience of the world. Therefore, the Futurists sought to condense the diversity of life in "dynamic, fragmentary symphonies of gestures, words, noises and lights."[61] Their notion of simultaneity and compenetration opened up new concepts of multimedia spectacles and a novel use of color, sound, and dynamic movement in a multidimensional stage architecture.

Futurist theatre was a violent assault on the nerves of the spectators. By eliminating the barrier of the proscenium-arch ("the action develops simultaneously on the stage, in the boxes, and in the stalls"[62]) they invaded the auditorium, took the spectators by the collars and shook them out of their passivity and torpor. The Futurists created an atmosphere and environment that united actors and spectators in a common experience. This novel stage–audience relationship turned even traditional playhouses into spaces for modern and vibrant theatre. The Futurists abolished the "fourth-wall" conventions and offered their audiences an immediate sensation of a new and dynamic reality. The emphasis on the physical, sensory qualities of performance enhanced the nonrepresentational character of theatre. Futurist performances were anti-psychological, anti-naturalistic, "real" rather than "realistic." There was an emphasis on scenic spectacle rather then on literary texts. In this way, the Futurists rediscovered the "theatrical" nature of theatre.

It is not astonishing that these performances shocked and scandalized Italian audiences, who had grown up on *boulevard* plays, well-oiled comedies, romantic costume drama, or naturalistic problem plays. The Futurists ridiculed and parodied all traditional genres and challenged the ways in which these were presented on stage. They polemicized against "the Solemn, the Sacred, and Serious, the Sublime in Art with a capital A,"[63] against stage fare that was "mediocre, banal, re-vomited, too well-digested,"[64] and against a dramatic tradition that was "dogmatic, stupid, logical, meticulous, pedantic, strangling."[65] Comparing the spontaneity and improvisatory quality of most Futurist performances with the predictable conventions and facile theatricality of the "great" and admired comedians of the Italian stage, one can easily imagine the cleansing, purgative effect Futurism had on the Italian theatre system.

BALLA AND DEPERO'S PLASTIC COMPLEXES AND MECHANICAL BALLETS

Marinetti's attempt at reforming theatre made an important contribution toward redefining the theatrical event from an aesthetic and political viewpoint. However, as a writer and poet he tended to adhere to a literary conception of theatre, as were most of his friends and colleagues in the Futurist circles of

Milan and Florence. It fell to the painter Giacomo Balla and the Roman group of artists that had formed in his studio to introduce the concept of "art performances," that is, a time-based art that explored the boundaries of performative and object-centered art, to investigate new presentation formats of performative events, and to redefine the concepts of actor and scenic space. Since many of these ideas became major concerns of avant-garde artists throughout the twentieth century, I should like to present here at least some of the innovations first instigated by Balla and his Roman circle of Futurists.[66]

During the initial phase of his Futurist career, Balla moved further and further away from traditional painting. His works became increasingly abstract and extended beyond the canvas into the third dimension and finally into time-based art. In the manifesto, *Futurist Reconstruction of the Universe*,[67] he described how he sought to apply the Futurist principle of dynamism to painting and how this forced him to move beyond the flat surface of the canvas and create "the dynamic volume of speed in depth." The manifesto signaled a major turning point in the evolution of Futurist aesthetics. Here, Balla and Depero suggested that art should no longer be a mere reflection of the world, but rather a Futurist recreation of the world based on abstract, absolute, and universal principles. Their manifesto offered an integrated, unified theoretical perspective on how life could be transformed into the ultimate Total Work of Art. The manifesto also contains a detailed description of the resulting "Dynamic Plastic Complexes," three-dimensional kinetic objects that explored abstract "force-lines" in space. They were created from colored strands of wire or cotton thread, glass, tissue paper, fabrics, mirrors, sheets of metal, tinfoil, and various other brightly colored, luminous materials, with chemical liquids adding special olfactory qualities. They could be lit from inside, and springs, levers and other mechanical devices kept them in motion. As the elements rotated, expanded in different directions at different speeds and transformed themselves into cones, pyramids, spheres, and so on, they emitted mechanical sounds, which were further enhanced by means of built-in noise machines.[68] Cangiullo reported that Balla occasionally interacted with "this magical kaleidoscope of aggressive colors . . . and pyrotechnical environment by singing, dancing, accompanying himself like a man possessed, his chest crushed under his guitar."[69]

The kinetic and luminous quality of the objects created a magical atmosphere that "made art present" rather than focusing it on "the re-evocation of the lost object."[70] These "plastic-moto-rumoristic" constructions can hardly be classified any longer as "sculpture." Balla himself used the term "dramatic" for them and described them as "action developed in space." We are dealing here, no doubt, with a proto-theatrical phenomenon, and it is no wonder that

Figure 3.4   Giacomo Balla, *Feu d'Artifice*, produced by the Ballets Russes at the Teatro Costanzi in Rome, April 12, 1917. This choreography for moving and light emanating objects translated Stravinsky's music into the abstract language of the stage.

some of the elements and ideas resurfaced again in later avant-garde movements (see, for example, Moholy-Nagy's *Light-Space-Modulator*, chapter 5, pp. 220–221). Ball returned to the Plastic Complexes again later in his mechanical ballet *Feu d'artifice* (see figure 3.4) in which dancers were replaced by transparent conical and rectangular structures, brightly painted, and illuminated from within. They interpreted Stravinsky's music as a mobile electromechanical architecture and gave a visual representation of the "fireworks' state of mind."[71] Light as a source of energy was correlated to types of movement, forms, and colors. The 50 cues of the lighting plot foresaw bursting light beams for the transparent and mobile crowns, incandescent glowing under the opaque covers, projected rays from the side of the stage producing some five minutes of scintillating audiovisual spectacle.

Also Depero, who described his main artistic endeavor of this period as *superamento del quadro* (overcoming the confines of the picture frame),[72] experimented with Plastic Complexes (see figure 3.5), which led progressively from polymaterial sculpture to mobile, plastic architecture. His "colorful complexes in motion" sought to give expression to "mobility and the magic sense of transformation"[73] and to "our mechanical, electro-speedy, magically artificial and ultra-noisy sensibility."[74] In 1914, he theorized on his experiments in a manuscript, "Plastic Complex—Free Futurist Game—Artificial

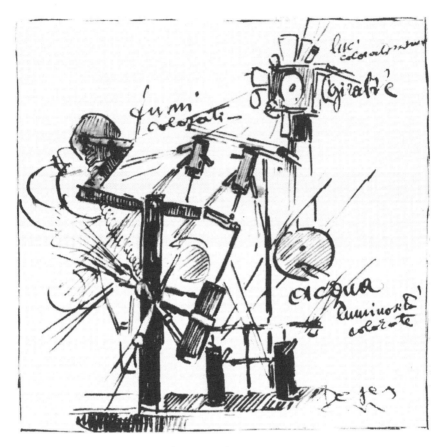

Figure 3.5   Fortunao Depero, *Plastic Complex* (1915). The indications on the drawing translate as: very colorful lights, rotating, colored smoke, water, colored luminosity.

Living Being."[75] Depero seemed to have been particularly interested in the noise equivalents to colors, shapes, and motions and envisaged his noisy, movable, polymaterial architecture to be inhabited by "Artificial Living Beings." Unfortunately, his drawings and photographs of 1914–1915 do not give a clear indication of how the complexes were to be employed in the theatre. But they were certainly not designed to function merely as kinetic sculptures. What Depero had in mind was ultimately "ballets constructed with applications of automatic contraptions which dance new and entertaining mimes."[76] They grew out of his desire to extend his paintings into the third dimension and to set them in motion; then, in the next stage, he sought to break down the corporeal boundaries of the moving object and to integrate it as a structural component into the environment. The additional elements of light and sound turned this entity—no longer painting, no longer sculpture, no longer architecture—into a non-ephemeral spectacle. There was only one step further he could go: to present the show to an invited audience for a limited period of time and to call it "theatre." This became Depero's program for his scenic projects of the years 1916–1918[77] (see figures 3.6 and 3.7), whose principal aims he summed up as:

- To progress from vague impressionist techniques of pictorial representation to precise three-dimensional constructions that form a unified and total work of Art, where the disparate elements retain their freedom of signification.
- To offer not a naturalistic imitation of nature, but constructions of a new artificial reality, an autonomous universe created according to artistic principles.
- To avoid psychology and to express emotions and sensations through the plastic drama and rhythmic dynamism of materials.
- Sculpture becomes architecture becomes environment becomes a multisensorial world, which incorporates all visual and aural forms of expression.[78]

Figure 3.6   Fortunao Depero, *I miei Balli Plastici*. Painting of 1918 depicting the dances performed by marionettes at the Teatro dei Piccoli in Rome in April 1918.

Figure 3.7 Fortunao Depero, *Balli Plastici*. Photograph of The Great Savage, one of the marionettes in the play, *I selvaggi (The Savages)*.

PRAMPOLINI'S VISION OF AN ACTORLESS, ELECTROMECHANICAL THEATRE

Enrico Prampolini was a young Roman artist who was greatly inspired by the experiments with an abstract, polymaterial art, which several Futurist artists were carrying out at that time. It led in 1913–1915 to several essays, of which one stands out as a major contribution to an avant-garde conception of theatre: *Futurist Scenography and Choreography*, published on May 12, 1915 in *La balza futurista*.[79] In this essay, Prampolini tried to arrive at a clarification of what constitutes the specific quality of the artwork of the stage, and how it differs from the other artistic media that contribute to the creation of a scenic spectacle. His first and most fundamental assumption was that "the stage is not a photographic enlargement of a slice of life." While other scenographers are craftsmen who do little more than imitate aspects of reality with the means of painting and sculpture, Prampolini wanted to establish a new *art* form: an abstract, autonomous scenic event, uncontaminated by other artistic conventions and constructed from the elements of pure form, color, light, and movement, liberated from any subservience to the written or spoken word. This total, abstract, and autonomous work of art would develop its force and lyrical beauty from the intrinsic material quality of its constituent elements and would no longer serve to illustrate a dramatic text or provide the background for the actors' performance.

Prampolini wanted "to attribute to the stage the essential values that belong to it." In order to achieve this objective, he analyzed systematically the individual components of scenic architecture and of the dramatic action that takes place within its frame. His aim was to overcome the dichotomy of actor and stage machinery and to create performances, in which "the abstract entity of the stage becomes one with the scenic action." But Prampolini not only addressed questions of stage production; he also pursued a rigorous investigation into the nature of theatrical perception and communication. The "dynamic synthesis" of his theatre would exude a powerful emotive quality through its own, material-specific lyricism, rouse the audience's emotions and intuitive capacities by incorporating them into the scenic spectacle, and seek their active collaboration rather than satisfy their desire to witness a replica of real life.

Prampolini envisaged a theatre where the single elements could be placed in a new order according to the logical rules of scenic construction. Each unit would be able to "speak" its own, media-specific language; but acting in unison with the others they would create a dynamic ensemble that offers unsurpassed sensual appeal to the audience. The temporal media of sound and motion would be integrated into the spatial media of color, form, and plasticity. The scenic architecture would become mobile and noise-producing, while the actor would take on chromatic and spatial qualities.

Once such a system of an integrated, total artwork of the stage had been firmly established, literary drama could be readmitted to the theatre. If the dramatic text was "suited to our sensibility and implies a highly synthetic and

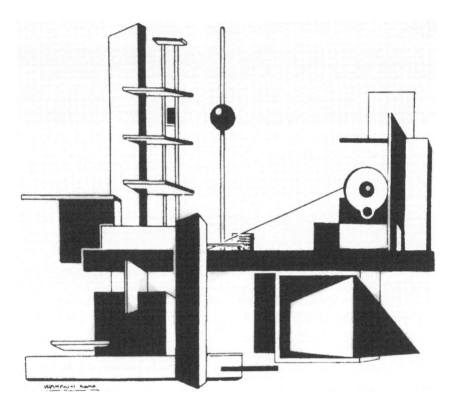

Figure 3.8   Enrico Prampolini, *Magnetic Theatre*, design exhibited at the Exposition des Arts Décoratifs in Paris in 1925, where it won him the Grand Prix d'Art Théâtrale. Prampolini described the theatre in the following manner: "It is made up of a mass of plastic constructions in action which rise from the centre of the theatrical hollow instead of the periphery of the 'scenic arc.' Auxiliary moving constructions rise, first on a square movable platform, standing on an elevator. On this in turn is erected a moving, rolling platform going in the opposite direction to the first, and likewise carrying other planes and auxiliary volumes. To these plastic constructions, ascending, rotating and shifting movements are given, in accordance with necessity. The scenic action of the chromatic light, an essential element of inter-action in creating the scenic personality of space unfolds parallel to the scenic development of these moving constructions. Its function is to give spiritual life to the environment or setting, while measuring time in scenic space."

intense conception of the scenic action and treatment of subjects," it could be employed as one beside many other elements in the theatre. Then the text would no longer occupy a privileged position, but rather complement the visual and aural elements and interact with them on equal terms. In short, it would serve as a performance script rather than striving to be a literary masterpiece.

In Prampolini's vision, the plastic dimension of the stage is the three-dimensional moving architecture that *encloses* the atmosphere (and does not *extend into* the atmosphere as is the case with free-standing sculpture). The chromatic element is enhanced by electric light sources and iridescent gases enclosed in glass tubes, which emanate powerful and dynamic irradiation into the stage atmosphere and strengthen the lyrical quality of color as a material force in space. The result is an "electro-mechanical architecture, powerfully vitalized by chromatic emanations from a luminous source . . . which will move, unleashing metallic arms, reversing planes and volumes amidst an essentially new modern noise." (see figure 3.8) In its final conse-quence, this "renovated stage" will give rise to the "illuminating stage," where the "actor gases" of a "luminous dynamic architecture" replace the human performer. This novel theatrical action will be created by a new type of stage artist, who subsumes in himself the rôles of playwright and stage designer. Prampolini not only wanted to abolish the traditional divisions between play and interpreter, set design and stage action, architecture and lighting; he also sought to overcome the gap between stage and auditorium and to replace these separate spheres with one interactive whole, so that "these exhilarating, explosive gases will fill the audience with joy or terror and turn them into actors themselves." The total artwork of the stage as envisaged by Prampolini in his first theatre manifesto was a Futurist reflection of the modern world. But rather than *describing* the synaesthetic experience of our dynamic exis-tence, he wanted to evoke the emotive qualities of simultaneous sense impres-sions by *recreating* the same experience, in abstract form, with the integrated means of a luminous-dynamic stage machinery.

THE GALLERY PERFORMANCES

The Futurists were among the first to move out of traditional theatre spaces and organize performances in a variety of venues not intended for theatrical use. These could be public buildings, meeting-halls, clubs, or galleries. This led to some site-specific performances, in which the physical environment determined the dramatic action; others were neutral spaces that were fitted out for the specific requirements of a performance. An example of the former was the *Futurist Mechanical Ballet* performed in 1922 in the American Bar of

Figure 3.9 Ivo Pannaggi, Costume design for the Mechanized Man in the *Mechanical Ballet*, performed on June 2, 1922 at the Casa d'Arte Bragaglia in Rome. This production inaugurated the second wave of Futurist experimentation with mechanical theatre. The performance served as a launching pad for the Manifesto of Futurist Mechanical Art.

the Casa d'Arte Bragaglia (see figure 3.9); typical examples of the latter were the performances in galleries, which can be regarded forerunners of the "time-based artist performances" or "live-art" events of the 1960s and 1970s.

It appears that in 1913–1914 a typology of afternoon performances in gallery spaces was developed and more or less adhered to on subsequent occasions. Most of these events were organized to open a new exhibition or to function as an accompaniment to it. Like the *serate*, they were announced to the public with spectacular street propaganda, distribution of manifestos, and so on.[80] Usually organized as Sunday matinée performances, they basically employed three different theatrical formats: simple recitations of poetry, semi-dramatic cabaret performances, and scenic spectacles. For the first type, the pictures that decorated the walls of the performance space were used as a colorful background against which an unrelated poetic text was given vocal and gestural presentation. For the second type, a musical accompaniment was added, and in the third, all these elements plus scenic and olfactory means were integrated into a unified whole.

The select audiences and the intimate space of a gallery allowed a more sophisticated and elaborate range of artistic experimentation than was possible with the *serate* performed in the vast spaces of municipal theatres. As with the *serate*, the gallery performances relied on audience participation but, on the whole, audience reactions were good-natured and amiable rather than confrontational and aggressive: "The performances were unpredictable and entertaining, and were created to a large extent by the spectators themselves. . . . The actions of the audience determined what happened on stage. . . . They had great fun echoing our actions, interrupting us with jokes, and following us round the hall."[81]

As an example of this kind of performance I should like to describe *Piedigrotta*, the first major theatrical offering in the permanent Futurist gallery in Rome on March 29, 1914. Cangiullo's scenario evoked the Neapolitan folk festival of the same name[82] and applied the Futurist principle of simultaneity to the theatrical medium, creating a *Gesamtkunstwerk*, whose unified effect relied on a combination of sound poetry for several voices, music played on traditional and specially made instruments, lighting effects, costumes, and the smell of firecrackers. If the idea of ambulant street vendors distributing freshly baked pizzas had been realized, the show would indeed have qualified as a Total Work of Art for all five senses!

The stage set consisted of a backdrop, painted by Balla, evoking the gay and dynamic atmosphere of the Neapolitan carnival. Around the walls hung the paintings of the Futurist exhibition, adding further "jerky forces, speed, intense light, colors, movement" to the scene, as a reviewer pointed out.

A number of red lanterns shed a light that resembled "diluted Chianti wine." While Marinetti recited Cangiullo's poem, a troupe of dwarfs entered the hall and moved around him in a strange procession. They wore fanciful costumes and grotesque hairstyles made out of vellum, and created a ferocious cacophony with their homemade instruments. Cangiullo produced an accompaniment on an untuned piano. According to *Lacerba*, there was a perfect fusion between Marinetti's delivery of the "words-in-freedom" and the onomatopoeic instruments of the dwarf chorus, complemented by the audience's voices and gestures. The atmosphere in the gallery is aptly evoked in a report of the *Giornale d'Italia* of March 31, 1914:

> Aural and visual sensations emanate from all parts of the room, especially from the paintings, and cluster around their concentric point, Marinetti. . . . The chaotic orchestration of sound, colors, forms, smells, tastes, contacts, convulsions of laughter, exploding and effervescent joy grows, grows, and finally erupts like a flaming volcano. . . . It created a lively impression of the Piedigrotta festival with its dancing, madness, drunkenness, recklessness, suffocation, and deafening noisiness.

The rendering of the Neapolitan festival in *Piedigrotta* in the form of a Dionysian carnival, an eruption of madness, *joie de vivre*, and orgiastic vitality, created an effect that closely resembled the Dada events, which Huelsenbeck described as "a rather violent indicator of the colorfulness of life."[83] Hugo Ball's characterization of the "Dada Circus" as "a mixture of buffoonery and a requiem mass"[84] could also be employed to describe the performance. Sgabelloni's account certainly gives the impression that the event was noisy and dynamic, with a multitude of artistic media employed to "evoke the sense of joy, merriment and madness that is so typical of the Neapolitan popular festival." As such, they resembled the recitations at the Cabaret Voltaire, which Huelsenbeck characterized as being "a direct reminder of life . . . and defying formulation, because they are a direct symbol of action. And so ultimately these simultaneous poems means nothing but 'Long live life!' (*Es lebe das Leben*!)"[85] This and other "Futurist Afternoons" developed poetry recitations into a fully fledged performance genre that anticipated the experiments with simultaneous poems and noise music at the Cabaret Voltaire (see below, pp. 145ff.).

ARTIST CABARETS AND BANQUETS

A further development from the gallery performances were the Futurist cabarets that opened in various Italian cities in the 1920s. They were a practical application of the concept of a "Futurist Recreation of the Universe," an attempt to merge art and life in a theatrical environment. In these venues, everything from the furniture to the wall paintings, from the lampshades to the colors of the cocktails was designed according to Futurist principles. To go to these night clubs came close to immersing oneself into a Total Work of Art, in which every component was integrated into an overall scheme. A careful balance of heterogeneous parts produced a vibrant and dynamic whole: from the dynamic interplay of colors, lines, and forms, which the eye perceives, to the noise, sounds or music the ear takes in; from the taste of the cocktails and food to the smells pervading the room. The cabaret was an all-embracing world, where the separations between performer and scenery, between décor and furniture, between stage and audience were overcome. For here there existed not only an interrelation and compenetration of the elements coexisting in a structured habitat, but also an interaction between organic and inorganic "actors" (i.e., the performer and the environment, the audience and the architectural shell, the performer and the audience). The architecture was not a static "container," but a mosaic of elements in constant flux. The "iridescent compenetration" of components, as Balla called this phenomenon, led to dynamic results that could be used as an instrument in the hand of the artist. The environment in its totality was designed in such a way as to exercise a pulsating, energetic, vitalistic influence on the audience. The unification of polarities in a total synthesis was meant to stimulate in the spectator a new sensibility and a playful, energetic approach to life. In a Futurist cabaret the boundaries between art and life, between aesthetic and everyday reality were broken down. The whole space became a field of dynamic emotions and created an atmosphere of unlimited expansion of creative energies.

The first cabaret of this kind was Balla's *Bal Tic Tac*, which opened in 1921.[86] The performances ranged from Arabian belly dancing to Spanish flamenco, from *Cotillon patriottico* to *Grande show alla sorpresa*, from *Thé danzante* to *Suono della Jazz-Band*. One week the whole club was turned into Viareggio beach and the audience had to dress up (or rather, down) in bathing suits and pajamas; another week the theme was decidedly patriotic and "ladies in *low-cut dresses* and gents in tails rubbed shoulders with the sober blackshirts of the Fascists and the blue uniforms of the Nationalists."[87] But whatever the theme of the evening, a large and heterogeneous audience frequented this extraordinary night club and made it a favorite nightspot in the capital.

In April 1922, Anton Giulio Bragaglia opened an art center in an old Roman bath, designed and decorated by Virgilio Marchi, Giacomo Balla, and Ivo Pannaggi. Visitors were struck by the unusual mixture of cozy and fantastic décor, modern and old design, the multilevel distribution of rooms, which forced visitors to move up and down through a labyrinth of corridors. One of them judged: "The rooms of the Circle, animated by a suggestive orchestra and mysterious lighting, constitute the most amazing and bizarre night club in Europe."[88] Aniante describes this *Cabaret notturno* as "good applied Futurism," where after midnight artists mixed with a bourgeois clientele, where an animated number by an American dancer gave way to more spiritual offerings by local poets, and where one could enjoy the atmosphere of an "irrational revolution. The most absurd and disparate motifs were reconciled without anyone batting an eyelid."[89]

Its popularity was even surpassed by Depero's *Cabaret Diavolo*, which opened on April 19, 1922 after six months of intense preparation and functioned until the end of 1924. To get down into the heart of the cabaret, the visitors had to descend in three stages, for the venue was arranged on three levels: the Paradise, the Purgatory, and the Inferno. The walls were covered with large paintings, the furniture was designed in Futurist style and had lights built into their structure. Apart from the wall paintings and furniture, each room contained ten wooden puppets depicting, in the Inferno: the damned souls cooking in an oven; in Purgatory: paradise on earth; in Paradise: the ascending angels on Jacob's Ladder. The Dantesque scenes in each room were brought to life by flickering lights in bizarrely fashioned lampshades. The critic Pietro Solari in *Il resto del Carlino* compared the illumination with Baroque dancing waters and gushing fountains, whose blazing colors and light and dark contrasts created a mysterious and fascinating, yet at the same time frightening atmosphere. Theatrical entertainments consisted of dances, poetry readings, songs, and Futurist music. In the Inferno room, Depero had installed a little marionette theatre, which was used for the *Devil's Newspaper* (*Gazzetta del Diavolo*), a weekly event where Camillo Mastrocinque presented a histrionic run-down of the latest news and Prampolini staged *I palombari notturni* (*The Night Divers*) by Folgore and Bontempelli. The restaurant was the venue of the *Soupers dei Diavolisti*, where Depero gave a foretaste of what later was to become Futurist cuisine.

Marinetti, Fillia, Depero, Dottori, Diulgheroff, and many other artists of the movement were involved in an attempt to revolutionize Italian gastronomic culture, heralded by a manifesto on *Culinaria futurista* in 1920, celebrated in the Taverna del Santopalato (inaugurated on March 8, 1931 in Turin) and substantiated in the Futurist cookbook *La cucina futurista* of 1932. The dinners and banquets held at the Santopalato were full-scale theatrical events and truly aspired to be Total Works of Art. The interior design and furniture were complemented by the shape, texture, color, and—naturally—the taste of the food. Futurist ceramics and special table scenery enhanced the enjoyment of the meal (see figure 3.10). For the "aerobanquets" held in Novarra, Chiavari, and

Figure 3.10   Table scenery for a Futurist banquet in 1932. In Futurist banquets, the dining table was designed like a stage set for a performance largely carried out by the dinner guests.

Bologna the Futurists decorated the walls and tables with aluminum sheets, and arranged the tables at sloping angles to give the impression of aeroplanes in mid-flight. Instead of flowers the table scenery made use of artistically carved and brightly colored potatoes; bread was replaced with rolls shaped like mono-planes and propellers; *vinum vulgaris* was served in oil cans by waiters wearing waistcoats and celluloid shirts painted by Depero, and multicolored cocktails enhanced the visual appearance and taste of the dishes. Eating futuristically meant that all five senses were fully engaged in the event. Unusual combina-tions of ingredients challenged the traditional training of taste buds; the aboli-tion of knives and forks enhanced the pre-labial tactile pleasures; measured doses of poetry and music accentuated the flavors of the dishes; and appetizing or suggestive perfumes were sprayed by waiters onto the napes of diners' necks.

But what made the dinners performative was (a) the narrative content of the courses, and (b) the theatrical offerings that accompanied them. For example, an entrée used olives stuffed with little rolls of paper, which the guests had to spit out, unroll, and read out to the great delight of the other revelers. For a dish called *Total Rice*, consisting of rice and beans garnished with frog legs and slices of salami, diners had to imitate the sound of croaking frogs. For the *Tactile Dinner Party*, guests had to wear pajamas made of, or covered with, a variety of tactile materials (e.g., silk, velvet, felt, aluminum, sponge, cork, bristles). When they had been led into a pitch-dark dining room, they had to select a partner according to the tactile sensations caused by the clothes. Then, together with their chosen companions, they explored with their fingers the three courses being served to them: Polyrhythmic Salad, Magic Food, and Tactile Vegetable Garden. The *Official Dinner* was a more loquacious event, where celebrants were encouraged to let their conversation be determined by the political institutions alluded to in each dish. Many banquets were accompanied by gramophone or live music, dance interludes, arias by opera stars, or jazz tunes by cabaret singers.

All in all, the Futurist banquets were a successful demonstration of Marinetti's formula "art = life" and probably the most complete realization of the "reconstructed universe" as a Total Work of Art. They extended the concept of performance into domains traditionally regarded as social life and enabled people from a nonartistic background to turn their everyday behavior into a creative activity. The attempt to fuse different aspects of human existence and to give them an artistic shape made these experiments historically significant. They can also be regarded as precursors of the much later avant-garde food art practiced by Daniel Spoerri, Bobby Baker, or Alicia Rios.

THE FUTURIST MARCH INTO THE MAINSTREAM

Most of what has been written above has been concerned with Futurist performance art developed outside the conventional framework of theatrical institutions. However, the Futurists were not only iconoclasts and radical innovators. Particularly in their second phase they also operated as reformers within the established system. This is not to say that the Futurists were reneging on their theories; rather, they were exploring them beyond the level of simplistic shock effects and "gestures," which had sometimes characterized the early performances.

The first years after World War I were a period of economic, political, and cultural upheaval. Futurism had declined to a state of near-insignificance, and the theatres offered little opportunity for avant-garde experimentation. The situation began to change in 1921, when Marinetti launched the Futurist Theatre of Surprise; in 1922, the Futurist Mechanical Theatre was inaugurated; in 1923, Pocarini's Teatro Semifuturista, and in 1924, the Nuovo Teatro Futurista went on tour. On a national level, the revival of an innovative theatre culture was signaled by the founding of Bragaglia's Teatro degli Indipendenti and Pirandello's Teatro d'Arte. For the first time, major theatres opened their doors to Futurist artists and put a relatively sophisticated technical apparatus at their disposal (see figure 3.11). Several of Marinetti dramas were performed in conventional playhouses, and a new generation of playwrights acknowledged their debt to the revolutionary concepts and techniques first introduced by the Futurist avant-garde. Also outside Italy, Futurism became a major force of innovation in the arts and in literature.[90] Theatres in Prague, Berlin, and Paris announced their first Futurist productions, and international theatre exhibitions offered showcases to Futurist scenographers and designers.

Probably the first "official" recognition of the Futurist achievements in the theatre was given in a study of 1921, when the critic Francesco Flora praised the Futurist battle against the "ridiculous imbecility, clumsy sentimentalism, wooden rhetorics, and irremediable histrionics" of the Italian acting profession, and the "necessary dissolution of the inert, stupid, bestial, pompous and melodramatic techniques that are employed by the insipid playwrights of today when they construct their cardboard figures and unforgivably primitive storylines."[91] The Futurists' attempt at educating their audiences and preparing them for a new style of drama was indeed bearing fruit. In the *Manifesto of the Theatre of Surprise* (1921) Marinetti could claim with some justification that the Theatre of the Grotesque owed its success to the Futurist Synthetic Theatre. In *After the Synthetic Theatre and the Theatre of Surprise We Invent the Anti-Psychological Abstract Theatre* (1924) he maintained, not without reason, that if audiences were now applauding Pirandello, they were also paying homage to this playwright's Futurist technique (although used in a watered-down form).

By the mid-1920s, Futurism had become recognized, if not respected, as a major cultural force. There now existed groups and representatives in all major and many minor cities of the peninsula. But as the First Futurist Congress of 1924 showed, the membership pursued diverse and wide-ranging interests, which could no longer be confined to the parameters of the early Futurist movement. The theatre aesthetics of *secondo futurismo* built on what had been developed by the first generation of Futurists. The execution of these ideas became more artistic, professional, sophisticated—and therefore

Figure 3.11 Lydia Wisiakova and Vaclav Veltchek in *Les Troi Moments* by Casavola and Folgore. It was performed as part of Enrico Prampolini's *Théâtre de la Pantomime Futuriste*, one of the most successful Futurist productions, staged in Paris, Turin, Bergamo and Milan. This photograph from the program booklet shows the metamorphosis of a faun and nymph into modern Big-City dwellers. It indicates that the Futurists knew how to transform myths of the past into myths for the future.

more acceptable—to the public. After years of testing and trying out ideas, a wealth of experience had been accumulated, which could now serve as a basis for a fully developed theatrical practice spanning a wide spectrum of presentational formats, ranging from small-scale cabaret and medium-size playhouse performances via open-air spectacles to sumptuous operas and large-cast dramas in leading theatres.

Numerous Futurist theatre productions of the 1920s and 1930s indicated that Futurism in its second phase was far from being a spent force. But although these performances were innovative events, they rarely moved into entirely new and unexplored terrains. Many of the shows fall under the category of Mechanical Theatre (e.g., *Ballo meccanico futurista* by Paladini and Pannaggi, featured in figure 3.9, Prampolini's *Psychology of the Machines* and *The Dance of the Propeller*, Depero's *Anihccam del 3000*, Vasari's *Anguish of Machines*) and explored in much more detail the ideas developed in the 1910s by Balla, Depero, and Prampolini. Other productions indicated that the Futurists were not only exercising influence abroad, but were also assimilating international trends into their own works. To indicate their openness to the avant-garde in other countries, a group of Neapolitan Futurists called themselves "Circumvisionisti"; the "Activist-Destructivists" were Dada influenced; echoes of Neue Sachlichkeit can be found in the Nuove Tendenze group (again, the name is emblematic for a non-stagnant Futurism); Masnata, Benedetta, and Paladini showed themselves to be particularly open to Surrealist aesthetics; and Depero adopted many elements of North-American urban culture following his sojourn in New York in 1928–1930.

As Futurism gained access to the theatre establishment and plans were undertaken to found a Futurist National Theatre, the danger of becoming part of "tradition" could not easily be circumvented. In fact, some of the older Futurist artists positively strove toward this aim and sought to turn Futurism into a publicly acknowledged, State-funded corporation. However, many second- and third-generation Futurists opposed this trend and ensured that Futurism continued to be a lively and controversial cultural force until the mid-1930s.

Most scholars nowadays would agree that the Futurists cleared the path for Italy's reentry into the league of major theatrical nations. Without Futurism, there would not have come into existence an Italian "art theatre" or a Theatre of the Grotesque. Also internationally, the influence of Futurist theatre was pervasive: it redefined the constitutive components of theatre and redrew the boundaries of the performance medium; it introduced new concepts of playwriting, stage design, and acting, its architectural projects redefined stage–audience relationships (see figure 3.12); it gave rise to a new culture of

Figure 3.12 Virgilo Marchi, Two designs for a Futurist theatre. For many years, Marinetti sought financial support from the Fascist government for an ultramodern Futurist theatre. Several Futurist architects developed grand schemes for this project, which never materialized.

experimentation and contributed to a general broadening of the theatrical horizon. How exactly Futurism affected other artists is not always easy to determine. Some spectators described how they experienced Futurism as a "fuel of liberty" (*benzina di libertà*) that gave them the incentive "to live their own life, a life that is intense and strong, without fear of tomorrow, . . . a life of true freedom, of courage, strength."[92] Contemporary critics certainly confirm that the experiments "again and again impressed the audience and made them think about the necessity to arrive . . . at a dismantling of the present theatre, at destroying the pedantic and boring theatrical techniques, in short: at progress in the theatre."[93] But translating this general intention into theatrical practice can be a complex and contradictory process. For example, in 1915, Diaghilev felt drawn toward the Futurists and sought to incorporate some of their innovative concepts into the next Italian season of his Ballets Russes. But admiration and enthusiasm soon turned into skepticism and finally disapproval. The commissioned works were either never performed or dropped from the repertoire after their première. Nevertheless, *Parade*, a ballet elaborated in Rome by artists who became distinctly hostile to Futurism, contained many Futurist traces when it was shown in Paris in May 1917.[94]

Influences often take a subliminal or osmotic route and are not always easily recognizable. It is not unusual for conventional theatre directors to become aware of and responsive to yesterday's avant-garde, without necessarily adopting its full spectrum of innovatory devices. When—as in the case of Futurism—the spectrum encompasses every aspect of theatrical production, it is not astonishing that even after many years some experiments can be rediscovered and serve as inspiration to a new generation of artists. A number of connecting lines can be drawn to Dada and Surrealism.[95] Other, more indirect links led to the Theatre of the Absurd, to Happenings, Poor Theatre, Environmental Theatre, Physical Theatre, and so on. This may explain why, for example, in the late 1920s, Kurt Schwitters suddenly tried to establish contacts with Depero, why in the 1930s, Artaud sought the acquaintance of Marinetti, or why in the 1960s, the New York avant-garde performer Michael Kirby felt compelled to write a book on Futurist theatre.

4. Dadaism ❧

Dada was, in chronological terms, the third avant-garde group that fulfilled all the main criteria of a radical, antibourgeois opposition movement as outlined in chapter 1. During its incubatory phase (1910–1914), the theatrical experiments undertaken by the Futurists were widely reported in newspapers and art magazines and exercised a pervasive influence on other, still nascent, avant-garde movements. Hugo Ball, founder of Dada, began his artistic career as an Expressionist, but gradually, after 1912, he assimilated the more radical tenets of Marinetti and his followers. The journals *Der Sturm* and *Die Aktion*, which had a predominantly Expressionist orientation, also published works by Italian Futurists, and Herwarth Walden, chief promoter of Expressionism, was a key figure in introducing Futurist art in Germany.[1] Hausmann, Mehring, Höch, Grosz, Ball, and possibly other artists who would later join the Dada movement saw these shows and derived great inspiration from them.[2] Ball had great admiration for Marinetti's innovative poetry and incendiary manifestos and intended to produce a Futurist theatre matinée in 1914. He planned a literary anthology for the Kurt Wolff Verlag with several Futurist contributions, and received, in July 1915, a parcel of visual poems (*parole in libertà*) by Marinetti, Cangiullo, Govoni, and Buzzi.[3]

Tristan Tzara, the Romanian poet who became the second leader of the Zurich group of Dadaists, was also, as Huelsenbeck recalled, "in contact with the Futurist movement and carried on a correspondence with Marinetti. By that time, Boccioni had been killed, but all of us knew his thick book, *Pittura scultura futuriste*. . . . From Marinetti we also borrowed bruitism or noise music, *le concert bruitiste*."[4] Friedrich Glauser remembered how "Tzara confessed to me his ambition to 'invent'—that's how he called it—a new art movement. The fame of the leader of Italian Futurism, Marinetti, did not give him any rest. He reveled in his memories of a visit by this aesthetic sect to Bucharest."[5] When Tzara took over the leadership of Zurich Dada, he acted, as Hausmann suggested in his memoirs, like a kind of super-Futurist "who wanted to exceed Futurism by his own length and marinate Marinetti in his own sauce."[6]

Given the widespread admiration that Italian Futurism commanded in Zurich, it is not astonishing that it acted as a model for the early Dadaist movement. As far as the theatre was concerned, an important intermediary between the two groups was Alberto Spaini, the only Italian national who played a significant rôle in the Cabaret Voltaire. Spaini was a friend of the Florentine Futurists and had experienced a number of Futurist *serate* in Italy. In 1912, he became correspondent of *Il resto del Carlino* and moved to Berlin, where he made the acquaintance of Hugo Ball, Emmy Hennings and Hans Richter. In 1914, he assisted in a soirée at the *Sturm* Gallery, in which he recited several poems by Marinetti. In 1916, he moved to Zurich and advised the Dadaists on how to turn their Cabaret, which had until that date been a rather lame undertaking, into the avant-garde venue it later became famous for. The Meierei, where it was housed, was given new décor that included Futurist paintings and *parole in libertà* on the walls.[7] When, on March 23, 1916, the group organized a carnival soirée at the Cabaret Voltaire, they advertised in two Zurich newspapers that they were going to perform "a Futurist comedy and some Futurist program-music."[8] Previously, on February 12, 1916, they had announced in *Das Volksrecht* that Hugo Ball was going to recite poems by Marinetti, Buzzi, and Palazzeschi. But a truly Futurist style of recitation came to be introduced by Spaini. We know that on May 12, 1917 he recited Meriano's *Gemma* and on April 14, 1917 he performed Marinetti's *Bombardment of Adrianopoli* that he had seen Marinetti recite on several occasions. It was through Spaini that Tzara made contact with a large number of artists, poets, and editors in Italy and acquired material from them, to be used in Dada soirées, publications, and exhibitions. Huelsenbeck remembered the visits of Futurist friends to Zurich, with whom they agreed in principle on their philosophy ("most public monuments should be smashed with a hammer") and artistic intentions ("our art had to integrate all the experimental tendencies of the Futurists and Cubists").[9] More personal connections were established when, in the summer of 1916, Tzara visited Italy. There, the artists he spoke to regarded Zurich Dada as Futurism with a German face ("Futurisme allemandisé"[10]). But once they had been enlightened about the new artistic movement, they considered launching an Italian branch of Dada.[11]

At the end of this chapter, we return to the question of Dada's originality and how it updated certain concepts and ideas that were first formulated by the Futurists. Prior to this, I should like to discuss some of the differences in the historical situation in which the two groups were operating, as it may prepare us for a better understanding of the Dada activities described in the next sections of this chapter.

Futurism was very much the product of the nineteenth century and of a country that had only belatedly and very moderately participated in the Industrial Revolution. Dada, on the other hand, came into existence in a developed capitalist world and as a reaction to World War I. Whereas Marinetti grew up in a positivist and materialist culture that firmly believed in the perfectibility of mankind through technological progress, the Dadaists had experienced a world that was falling apart, causing harrowing destruction and a mindless bloodbath:

> An epoch is collapsing. A culture that has lasted for a thousand years is collapsing. There are no longer pillars and buttresses and no foundations that have not been blasted to smithereens. . . . The principles of logic, centrality, unity and rationality have been recognized as postulations of a domineering theology. . . . Chaos unfolded. Turmoil unfolded. The world revealed itself as a blind flux of colliding and entangled forces.[12]

Modern science had shattered the epistemological and ontological foundations of the world (see above, pp. 26–33). Humans were adrift in a chaotic, irrational, incomprehensible universe. Huelsenbeck explained in his memoirs that rationalism, scientism, and technology have been the causes of the war and that Dada was an "insurrection of the intellect against the assault of a mechanical world, of life against paralysis."[13] To the artists who assembled in Zurich in 1916, the world that had run out of control could not be fitted any longer into the well-ordered parameters of conventional art. The old aesthetic system, together with the institutions and the society that supported it, had ceased to be a valid reference point: "Who on earth, in those days of collapse, was still ready to believe in 'eternal values,' in the 'canned goods' of the past, in the academies, the schools of art?"[14] Therefore, the Dadaists "tried to discover the essence of life behind the wall of rationality, an essence that cannot be captured in words, but only perceived through the symbolic language of art and religion."[15] Even Huelsenbeck, who was not a particularly religious man, wrote that Dada was "a protest of spiritual mankind, of the personality, of creative uniqueness against mass man and a world that has turned man into pulp and morals into their opposite."[16] He enlarged on this issue by writing:

> Dadaism was an expression of confusion, of lost values in a time of decay, but it was also more than that. Dadaism became a symbol of nihilism for all those

spirited humans who had recognized the chaotic situation . . . underneath the surface of convention. . . . It signified the aggressiveness, rage, grief and mental condition of a small circle of human beings, who did not want to identify with the general collapse of Europe. . . . They were excited by the magic of the word Dada as it encapsulated the destruction of the old and the hope for a new world. . . . The foundation of Dada was our feeling of anger against the war, our rejection of contemporary European civilization, our love of the primitive, our mockery and scorn of official European society.[17]

In the first part of this chapter, I show how this aim was pursued by the Dada groups in Zurich, Berlin, and Paris, especially in the area of performance. In the second part, I then analyze how a balance between art and anti-art emerged out of these experiences and how some key elements of Modernist performance art developed out of it. We shall then come back to the question of originality of Dada and the contribution it made to the development of modern theatre.

HUGO BALL, THE CABARET VOLTAIRE, AND ZURICH DADA

Hugo Ball, the founder of the Dada movement, was a man with considerable theatrical experience. From 1910 to 1911 he had been a student at Max Reinhardt's acting school in Berlin and had written for the famous director a tragicomedy, *Michelangelo's Nose*. His first employments were at the Stadttheater Plauen and the Lustspielhaus (Kammerspiele) in Munich. His official position was not only that of a dramaturg, but he also took small acting parts and worked as an assistant director. In November 1912, he saw Frank Wedekind for the first time on stage and was greatly taken by his visceral and physical acting style. At Hellerau, the German center of Jaques-Dalcroze's Eurhythmy movement, he experienced the concept of a festival theatre in action and was inspired to set up something similar in Munich.

As a student he had been a great admirer of Georg Fuchs's productions at the Münchener Künstlertheater (1908) and was influenced by the reform program Fuchs had outlined in his book, *Revolution des Theaters* (1909). In 1914, when the Arts Theatre came up for a new lease, Ball made a bid for the directorship and won the support of a committee, that tried to bring the theatre back under the control of local artists with an interest in continuing Fuchs's original theatrical concepts. Ball contacted Kandinsky, sought his permission to produce *The Yellow Sound* and to win him over as stage designer for *Kanadehon Chushingura (The Treasury of Loyal Retainers)*, a Bunraku play by Takeda Izumo. Unfortunately, the lease went to the Dumont-Lindemann company, but Ball wrote an interesting article for the theatre journal *Phoebus*, in which he discussed the topicality of Fuchs's concepts and the plans he had wanted to pursue at the theatre. Based on Nietzsche's writings,[18] Craig and Appia's concept of theatre, and his own studies of east-Asian theatre, Ball promoted a form of theatre that was not merely geared toward a reform of dramatic literature, of stage design or theatre architecture, but toward a "totally new form of the whole dramatic-scenic and theatrical art . . . , which is rooted in the primal generative soil of dramatic life and expresses itself simultaneously through dance, color, mime, music and speech."[19] His diary notes and letters from this period show that he was greatly taken by the concept of theatre as a Total Work of Art, organized as a festival outside the conventional institutional set-up, and aspiring toward "a rebirth of society through a union of artistic means and forces."[20] He detested both the commercial bourgeois theatre and the over-intellectual art theatre of his time, and instead sought to establish a stage art that worked with archetypes and the subconscious faculties. In his view, theatre had to touch human life in all its aspects and conjure up alternatives to the existing world, because "theatre alone is capable of forming a new society."[21] In order to further these aims, he planned the foundation of an International Society for New Art, which would act as a forum for the avant-garde in the performing and fine arts, and a publication, *Das Neue Theater* (The New Theatre), as a kind of counterpart to Kandinsky's *Blue Rider Almanach* of 1912.

In summer 1914, he spent much time with Kandinsky, who put him into contact with artists and theatre people in Russia and Paris. He planned six productions for the next season of the Kammerspiele that included Kandinsky's *Violet Curtain* and plays by Claudel and Kokoschka. He also intended to hold a Futurist matinée, probably in the format of the infamous *serate* (see pp. 101–111), with recitations of Futurist manifestos and poems that had been published in *Der Sturm* and *Die Aktion*. He may have received further texts and information from Herwarth Walden, whose *Sturm* Gallery had hosted the first Futurist exhibition in Germany, which Ball had seen in 1912 in Dresden and had reviewed in an ecstatic manner in the journal, *Revolution*.[22] In July 1914, he agreed with Walden to organize an exhibition of Cubist, Futurist, and Expressionist paintings in the Foyer of the Munich Kammerspiele. However, due to the outbreak of World War I, none of these plans came to fruition.

If Ball's artistic development took a new turn following his contacts with Futurism, his position became even more radical when he witnessed the mass killings on the western front. He wrote to his sister on August 7, 1914: "Art?

That's had its day and has become a laughing matter. It's cast to the winds and has no longer any meaning."[23] He noted in his diary: "The whole machinery and the devil himself have broken loose now. Ideals are only labels that have been stuck on. Everything has been shaken to its very foundation."[24] Like many intellectuals of his generation, Ball had grown up with the cultural norms of the prosperous middle classes and increasingly felt the chasm that had opened up between idealistic philosophy and social reality. He, therefore, came to reject the nineteenth-century view that the Industrial Revolution was bringing to completion the Enlightenment project of liberating humanity. Subjecting Nature and society to the forces of rational science and technology had not giving the individual autonomy and self-determination, but rather had brought about his deracination, atomization, alienation, and the like. The way *logos* had imposed itself on society had caused a downward spiral into entropic chaos. "The collapse is beginning to take on gigantic dimensions. We will no longer be able to refer to the authority of the old idealistic Germany . . . The whole civilization was ultimately only a sham."[25] Ball concluded from this: "One has to break with the system of reason, for the sake of a higher reason."[26]

In October 1914, Ball moved to Berlin, where intensive studies of Kropotkin, Bakunin, and other anarchist writers prepared him for "a new, anarcho-revolutionary life."[27] He frequented the political circles of Gustav Landauer, a prominent anarchist later to become a leader in the Munich Soviet. Else Hadwiger, the translator of Marinetti's *Futuristische Dichtungen* (1912), informed him about the theatre evenings that had caused such scandals in Milan, Florence, and Rome and inspired him to organize three similar soirées in Berlin. He was supported in this undertaking by Richard Huelsenbeck, an old friend from his Munich days, whom he introduced to the artistic tenets of Expressionism and Futurism.[28] Both sought to join the forces of the aesthetic and political avant-gardes and wrote to this end a manifesto, in which they expressed a pre-Dadaist position that was based on "Expressionism, colorfulness, adventurousness, Futurism, action."[29] The leaflet was distributed during a soirée held on February 12, 1915 at the Berlin Architektenhaus. A second soirée on March 26 at the Café Austria had a more sober, political orientation; but the next event at the Harmoniumsaal on May 12, 1915 included self-composed "Negro poems" by Huelsenbeck and contributions by Emmy Hennings, a cabaret singer who had become Ball's lover.[30] The atmosphere was such that the critic of the *Vossische Zeitung* could describe it as "a protest against Germany, in favor of Marinetti."[31]

A few days later, Ball and Hennings emigrated to Switzerland, a country that to them felt like "a bird-cage surrounded by roaring lions."[32] In Zurich, they made the acquaintance of Fritz Brupbacher, a Swiss anarcho-syndicalist and editor of the journal *Der Revoluzzer*. Together, they attended political meetings and participated in activities of revolutionary groups. The young couple's financial situation was desperate. Hennings earned some money as a singer in *Marcellis Damenensemble* and occasionally had to resort to prostitution to top up her meager income. In October 1915, both joined the Variety ensemble *Maxim* and toured up and down the country. Despite the peaceful surroundings, Ball had great difficulty finding a purpose for his artistic activities: "I am still concerning myself with theatre, and yet it all has no sense any more. Who wants to produce plays nowadays, or who wants to see them? . . . The theatre is like a man who has suddenly been decapitated. He might stand up again and walk a few steps. But then he will fall and lie there dead."[33]

The performances of the *Maxim* ensemble were a far cry from the artistic program Ball had promoted in Munich, or the radical soirées he had organized in Berlin. In Zurich he had to play ditties on the piano for eight hours a night, write low-brow texts and songs for an Apache and Harem sketch, hunt for silly costumes and revue props, and so on. Yet, he and Hennings enjoyed the vitality and spontaneity of Variety theatre and, therefore, explored the possibility of "having our own troupe, writing our own material, working towards having a real theatre: this is our ultimate ambition."[34] On December 17, 1915, they organized a literary soirée at the Zunfthaus zur Zimmerleuten, and in January 1916, they formed the *Arabella-Ensemble*, a small-scale touring cabaret. The next stage was to find a permanent venue. In December 1915, they had met Jan Ephraim, owner of the Meierei, a run-down bar in the disreputable Niederdorfviertel of Zurich, which in 1914 had hosted the Cabaret Pantagruel. The publican felt that Ball and Hennings had just the right background to set up a new enterprise to provide entertainment for his guests. Ball believed that it would provide him with a regular income and leave him with enough time to complete his doctorate in Zurich. On January 19, 1916, they submitted to the police an application to open an "artist's tavern" at the Meierei, as a "meeting place for artistic entertainment and intellectual exchange,"[35] and on January 28 they were given license to do so. A press notice of February 2 announced the opening of Cabaret Voltaire, a "centre for artistic entertainment . . . with daily meetings where visiting artists will perform their music and poetry. The younger artists of Zurich are invited to bring along their ideas and contributions."[36]

The cabaret was located in a small room next to the bar and had some 15–20 tables, giving it a capacity of not more than 50 per night. Although the walls had been decorated with what nowadays would be priceless paintings and collages, the stage was without décor and offered only a tattered screen

CHRONOLOGY 4.1: DADA IN ZURICH

February 5, 1916   Opening of the Cabaret Voltaire in Zurich

February 12, 1916   Recitation of Futurist poems by Ball, French poems by Tzara, French chansons sung by Mme. Leconte and German Lieder by Emmy Hennings

February 26, 1916   Huelsenbeck's début at the Cabaret Voltaire with a reading of his own poems accompanied by a big drum

February 29, 1916   First mention of the name Dada in a letter of Ball to Tzara

March 1, 1916   Ball and Hennings read from Andreyev's play, *The Life of Man*

March 4, 1916   Russian Soirée

March 5, 1916   Swiss Soirée

March 18, 1916   French Soirée

March 23, 1916   Carnival evening with performance of a Futurist play and Futurist noise music

March 30, 1916   Dance soirée. Huelsenbeck, Tzara, and Janco perform *L'amiral cherche une maison à louer* and *Chant Nègre I+ II*

May 31, 1916   Grand Soirée of Artist-Society Voltaire, with Ball's concert bruitiste, *Simultan Krippenspiel*, a masked dance, *Negermimus*, and simultaneous poems by Huelsenbeck, Tzara, and Janco

June 23, 1916   Ball as Magical Bishop reads his first sound poems, *Gadji beri bimba*, *Labadas Gesang an die Wolken* and *Karawane,* and lectures on "The Alchemy of Language"

End of June   Closure of Cabaret Voltaire

July 6, 1916   Charity Soirée with reading of Futurist, Dadaist, and Cubist manifestos, poetry readings, dances, and puppet theatre

July 14, 1916   First Dada Soirée at the Zunfthaus zur Waag with compositions by Heusser, a reading of the *First Dada Manifesto*, recitation of *Gadji beri bimba* by Ball, a Cubist dance by Ball, Hennings, Huelsenbeck, and Tzara, a simultaneous poem, static poem and gymnastic poem by Ball, Janco, Huelsenbeck, and Tzara, masked Dada dances by Hennings

July–December 1916   Ball and Hennings tour Switzerland with a program of "Modern Literary Cabaret Evenings" that repeats many of their contributions to the Cabaret Voltaire

January 12, 1917   First Dada Exhibition at the Galerie Corray

March 17, 1917   Ball and Tzara take over the Galerie Corray and change its name to Galerie Dada

March 29, 1917   Grand Opening of the Galerie Dada with poetry recitations, abstract dances (*Gesang der Flugfische und*

	Seepferdchen) by Taeuber, Expressionist dances by Claire Walther, and music by Heusser and Perrottet
April 14, 1917	*Sturm* soirée at the Galerie Dada with recitation of poems by Kandinsky, Apollinaire, Cendrars, Van Hoddis and Stramm, Ball reading Marinetti's *Manifesto of Futurist Literature*, masked "Negro" dances performed by five Laban pupils, and a scenic performance of Kokoschka's *Sphinx und Strohmann*
April 28, 1917	Third Dada Soirée of New Art at Galerie Dada with simultaneous poems, "Negro" dances, music by Suzanne Perrottet, Ball in costume reciting a prose text, *Grand Hotel Metaphysik*
May 12, 1917	Fourth Dada Evening of Old and New Art, with Ball reciting a Chinese fairy tale, "Negro" verses and own poems, lecture by Spaini on Gothic and Futurist poetry, reading of texts by Dürer, Böhme, and Nostradamus, Heusser playing Arabian dances
May 19, 1917	Repeat performance of Dada Evening of Old and New Art
May 25, 1917	Sixth Dada Soirée in honor of Hans Heusser, who plays his own compositions, including music for Kandinsky's *Yellow Sound*
May 27, 1917	Closure of Galerie Dada. Ball breaks with Dada and retreats to Vira-Magadino
July 16, 1917	Tzara launches the Mouvement Dada and publishes *Dada 1*
July 23, 1918	Seventh Dada Soirée at the Zunfthaus zur Meise, with Tzara reading his *Manifeste Dada 1918* and reciting his poetry
September 1918	Exhibition of New Art at Kunstsalon Wolfsberg
November 10, 1918 to December 1, 1918	First exhibition of Das Neue Leben group in Basle, with contributions by Dadaists
January 12, 1919 to February 5, 1919	Das Neue Leben exhibition at Zurich Kunsthaus, with contributions by Dada artists
Janvary 22, 1919 to February 8, 1919	Picabia's sojourn in Zurich
April 9, 1919	Eighth Dada Soirée at the Saal zur Kaufleuten with reading of manifestos by Richter, Serner and Tzara; compositions by Heusser; Katja Wulff reciting poems by Huelsenbeck, Kandinsky and Arp; simultaneous poem for 20 people, and dance for 5 persons
March 5, 1920	Grand Bal Dada at Salle Communale de Plainpalais in Geneva, organized by Serner and Schad, with bruitist Dada jazz band

for costume changes. Performances were given daily except Fridays, and instead of an entrance fee, a slightly raised cloakroom fee was charged. Later, when they had established themselves, they performed every night and even sold tickets via a travel agency in the main railway station. Judging by Huelsenbeck's memoirs, the audience consisted mainly of young people, often students, who had spent a raunchy night in the amusement venues of Niederdorf and dropped in to have a late night drink and look for easy girls. Other memoirs mention a petty-bourgeois clientele who had come to the Meierei because of its restaurant service and who stayed on for the cabaret just out of curiosity. These were the sections of the audience who voiced the strongest objections to the high-brow offerings on stage and had to be reprimanded: "The Cabaret Voltaire is not a common music-hall. We have not gathered here to offer you *frou-frous* and naked thighs and cheap ditties. The Cabaret Voltaire is a cultural institution!"[37] Then there was the motley crew of émigrés living in or near Zurich—artists, writers, dancers, and musicians—who were attracted to the cabaret because of its international ambience and wondered about the growing fame, or rather notoriety, of the enterprise.[38] Occasionally members of the high society also strayed in, whom Guggenheim described as "visitors in evening dress who seem to have descended to the lower depths after a classy dinner."[39]

The first evenings in February 1916 offered a mixture of light entertainment and poetry readings: Emmy Hennings sang her own chansons with guitar accompaniment; Hugo Ball recited texts by Voltaire and Wedekind and played the piano; a Balalaika orchestra manned by six Russian émigrés performed folk music; guests with a more solid musical training contributed works by Liszt, Rachmaninov, and Saint-Saëns. There were poetry readings of Expressionist texts, complemented by works of French authors such as Aristide Bruant, Blaise Cendrars, and Max Jacob. The group also presented writings by Italian Futurists, and some Russian guests recited works by Chekhov, Andreyev, and Kandinsky.

This relaxed and loose format of an artists' cabaret in the manner of the Munich Simplicissimus may have been to Mr Ephraim's satisfaction as it increased the turnover of his bar, but it did not live up to Ball's expectation. On February 8 he wrote to Käthe Brodnitz in Berlin: "Financially the venture is not yet running as it should do, at least not if one is to make a living from it. Most of the profit goes to the landlord."[40] Also artistically it was a far cry from Ball's aesthetic concept of a modern theatre, which in November 1915 he had described as an art "that follows the course of free, unfettered imagination . . . a living art that will be irrational, primitive, complex, and speak a secret language."[41] The venue had been set up as "a gathering place for all artistic trends, not just modern ones,"[42] and according to the *Volksrecht* of February 12, 1916, the local community of literati proposed more contributions than could possibly be accommodated. But Ball did not want to offer a platform for second-rate artists performing tedious acts. Rather, he intended the Cabaret Voltaire to be "a gladatorial gesture"[43] or "a kind of 'Candide' against our time,"[44] that is, a critical yet hopeful challenge to a civilization that had reached a cul-de-sac. This was clearly brought out in the "French Soirée" of March 18, when they performed excerpts of *Ubu Roi* and texts by Apollinaire, Jacob, Laforgue, Salmon, Suarés, Deubel, and Rimbaud. On March 23, they held a Futurist soirée with poems, plays, and noise music, and on March 30 they performed for the first time a program that truly deserved to be called "Dadaist." Huelsenbeck recited "Negro" poetry with trembling nostrils and raised eyebrows, a cane in his hand, to the accompaniment of a bass drum, and was received with shouting, whistling, and laughter from the audience.[45] He then performed, together with Tzara and Janco, the simultaneous poem *L'amiral cherche une maison à louer* in three different languages to the accompaniment of a whistle, rattle, and bass drum. Afterward, they dressed up in black cowls and sang/danced/recited *Chant nègre I* and *II*.

The Dada circus, which according to Ball was "both a buffoonery and a requiem mass,"[46] had begun. Although most of the audience enjoyed the unique and highly experimental presentations, others, who had come for some light entertainment, took objection to the high-brow poetry recitations and incomprehensible "negro songs." They shouted, booed, demanded their money back, but calmed down again when Emmy Hennings appeared on stage to deliver her chansons. As Hugo Ball said: "The people get terribly agitated, as they expect the Cabaret Voltaire to be a normal night club. One first has to teach these students what a political cabaret is."[47] However, not only the students took objection to the presentations, but the local press and the conservative bourgeoisie also began to regard Dada "as a dissolute monster, a revolutionary villain, a barbarous Asiatic."[48] This attitude was not astonishing, as Janco explained: "At the Cabaret Voltaire we began by shocking the bourgeois, demolishing his idea of art, attacking common sense, public opinion, education, institutions, museums, good taste, in short, the whole prevailing order."[49]

The new direction of the Cabaret Voltaire gave Ball a fresh lease of life. During the following months, the group extended their activities into the fine arts (founding of a Voltaire Art Society; exhibition of Dadaist and Cubist paintings and Futurist *parole in libertà* in the cabaret), masked dances (masks by Janco and "African" dances by students of the Laban school), noise music, preparation of an anthology (*Cabaret Voltaire*) and a magazine (*Dada*). Soon,

Hugo Ball was on the brink of exhaustion and nervous breakdown, and the motley group of exiled artists came increasingly under the influence of Tristan Tzara, who sought to transform Dada into a more tightly organized association with a resolutely antitraditionalist and antibourgeois attitude.

In July 1916, the Cabaret Voltaire closed its doors. Ball and Hennings, whose livelihood depended on their stage work, went on tour with a program of "Modern Literary Cabaret Evenings" that included many of the works they had performed at the Cabaret Voltaire. In January 1917, a Dada exhibition was held at the Galerie Corray, which for the next six months became their new headquarters. On March 17, 1917, they renamed the venue "Galerie Dada" and organized a mixed show of Expressionist, Cubist, Dadaist, Futurist, and "Negro" works. They also arranged lectures, afternoon teas, and guided tours for an audience that was very different from the one they had had at the Meierei. Huelsenbeck characterized it as "old ladies trying to revive their vanishing sexual powers with the help of 'something mad,' "[50] but reviews in the local press indicate that the educated middle classes as a whole became curious about the new association in their city and its artistic program.[51] As the six soirées that were held at the gallery were open to the public by invitation only, they found an enlightened audience who were supportive of art and literature even in their bizarre and Modernist constellations. This intimate circle of connoisseurs (50–100 per evening) was broken up when the gallery closed its doors at the end of May 1917.

In June 1917, Ball and Hennings moved into the Ticino. Following their departure, Tzara was the undisputed leader of the remaining Dadaists and performed the program of the seventh soirée at the Zunfthaus zur Meise on his own. A final Dada soirée was held in April 1919 at the Kaufleuten Hall, attracting no less than 1,000 people (probably because of a popular exhibition at the Kunsthaus Zürich, that had also given Dada artists a platform to show their works). According to Hardekopf, the soirée made a net profit of several hundred Swiss francs[52]—a clear sign that Dada had found an inroad into the mainstream. However, in the following months, the group lost several of its members and then disbanded. Tzara, who had established for himself the status of a guru, accepted invitations to Paris and founded a new center of Dada activities there.

DADA IN BERLIN

In December 1916, Huelsenbeck left Switzerland with the intention of taking his *Physikum* examinations at the University of Greifswald. His father's declining health prompted him to return to Berlin in January 1917. When he heard from Tzara of the success of the Galerie Dada, he considered going back to Zurich, but then he found new friends with similar artistic ideas in Wieland Herzfelde and Franz Jung. As he reported in autumn 1917 to his friends in Zurich, he was eager to organize a Cabaret Dada in order to propagate their ideas in Berlin. He also planned a Dada exhibition and a Dada issue of the journal *Neue Jugend*.[53] However, the first Berlin Dada event proper only took place on January 22, 1922, when Huelsenbeck gave a "First Dada Lecture in Germany," which consisted mainly of readings of Expressionist poetry and a report on the activities of the Dada group in Zurich. A few days later, in a press notice of January 27, 1918, the foundation of a Club Dada was announced, including as its members, among other, Grosz, Herzfelde, Jung, and Hausmann.

In April 1918, several publications presented the Club Dada as a formally organized institution, with proper management rules and terms of business. These, of course, were entirely fictitious (just as later were the Dada Advertising Agency, or the Dadaist Revolutionary Central Committee),[54] but the change of terminology from cabaret to club was significant, as in the German tradition—following the model set by the French Jacobins—a club was a revolutionary rather than an artistic group. Such clubs had played a significant rôle in the revolutions of 1830 and 1848, and several had sprung up in Berlin in the month preceding the November Revolution of 1918. This political engagement became a characteristic trait of Berlin Dada for most of its brief period of existence. "Dada fights on the side of the revolutionary proletariat," proclaimed a banner at the First Dada Fair;[55] several Dadaists joined the Spartakus movement and the newly founded German Communist Party; others were active in anarchist circles or the November Group. Huelsenbeck commented on the fundamental change that took place in the Dada movement after his move to Berlin: "The program of the Cabaret Voltaire was totally overhauled. There was no desire any longer to make 'the right art.' Art became a means of propaganda for a revolutionary idea."[56] Therefore, Dada magazines and manifestos were distributed in working-class districts and at factory doors,[57] which may explain that on more than one occasion Dada publications were confiscated and the responsible editors taken to court. In the extremely politicized climate of postwar Berlin, Dada took on a far more radical political character than it had possessed in Switzerland. This, however, was not detrimental to the festive, life-affirming quality of Dada, which had already been present in Zurich and was also celebrated with great zest at the Dada parties in Berlin.[58]

In the course of the years 1918–1920, the Club Dada organized six major theatrical programs in a variety of venues and a tour to six cities outside Berlin.

CHRONOLOGY 4.2:   DADA IN BERLIN

January 1917	Huelsenbeck arrives in Berlin
January 22, 1918	Expressionist soirée at the Galerie I. B. Neumann with Huelsenbeck giving a lecture on Cabaret Voltaire and reading from his *Phantastische Gebete*
January 27, 1918	*Vossische Zeitung* reports on the foundation of a Club Dada in Berlin
April 12, 1918	Poetry soirée at Neue Sezession with Huelsenbeck lecturing on Dada, Hadwiger reading Futurist verses, Grosz singing African American jazz songs. Hausmann's lecture on new painting drowns in general pandemonium
May 1918	Huelsenbeck drafted for service in a military hospital. A Dada soirée planned for May 1918 has to be canceled
June 6, 1918	Dada soirée at Café Austria, with Baader and Hausmann reciting their sound poetry (this event, mentioned by Hausmann, may be spurious)
June 16, 1918	Publications of Club Dada are confiscated and Hausmann is arrested
November 1918	Revolution in Berlin exacerbates the Dada split into a communist and anarchist wing
November 17, 1918	Baader action in Berlin Cathedral
February 6, 1919	Baader distributes *Dadaisten gegen Weimar* in the wine bar Rheingold, Bellevuestraße, and declares himself president of the Globe
February 15, 1919	The magazine *Jedermann sein eigener Fußball* distributed in a spectacular street action and immediately confiscated. Mehring is taken to court and Herzfelde imprisoned
March 12, 1919	Club der blauen Milchstraße at the Café Austria with Baader and Hausmann
April 30, 1919	Dada soirée at Graphisches Kabinett I. B. Neumann with Huelsenbeck, Hausmann, and Golyscheff performing simultaneous poems, bruitist poems, and an atonal anti-symphony, *Musikaische Kreisguillotine*
May 24, 1919	Grand Soirée Dada at Meistersaal, originally advertised for May 15. It repeated the program of April 30, plus satirical poems by Mehring, masked dances, Baader and Hausmann lecturing on politics, *Chaoplasma* and *Race between a Type Writer and a Sewing Machine*
July 16, 1919	Baader distributes Dada leaflets in Weimar National Assembly
July 19, 1919	Hausmann and Baader perform street action in honor of Gottfried Keller
November 30, 1919	Dada matinée at Tribüne theatre (repeated on December 7 and 13)

December 8, 1919	Cabaret Schall und Rauch performers Mehring's puppet play *Einfach klassisch!* with puppets made by Grosz and Heartfield. Some Dadaists protest against labeling this event "Dadaist"
January 19, 1920 to March 5, 1920	Dada tour to Dresden, Hamburg, Leipzig, Teplice Lázně, Prague, and Karlovy Vary
March 20, 1920	Dada cabaret and costume ball at the Gartensaal am Zoo
June 30, 1920 to August 25, 1920	First International Dada Fair at Galerie Otto Burchard
December 15, 1920	Literary soirée at Berliner Sezession, Kurfürstendamm, with Hausmann reading *Puffke propagiert Proletkult*
January 20, 1921	Dada-Faschingsball (Carnival event) at Marmorsaal am Zoo
February 8, 1921	Literary soirée at Berliner Sezession, with Mynona, Höch and Hausmann
April 20, 1921	Court case against Dada defamation of Reichswehr, that ends with Grosz and Herzfelde being condemned to pay high fines
September 6 and 7, 1921	Anti-Dada-Merz tour to Prague by Hausmann, Höch, and Schwitters. Hausmann presents his manifesto *Presentismus*, an "eccentric dance" and a Hindenburg satire, Schwitter reads from *Anna Blume*, and all three perform a sketch, *Der mechanische Mensch*

These events were complemented by street actions, publicity stunts, a Dada fair, and several artists' balls. Most of the theatrical soirées and matinées used a format that was similar to the ones developed in Zurich: a mixture of poetry recitations, reading of manifestos, dances, noise music, satirical sketches, and occasionally a dramatic text. Each of the events found a lively response in the local press, and the general curiosity was further fanned by sensationalist press notices, the launch of outrageous manifestos, and spectacular promotion campaigns. As a result, Dada was soon a phenomenon that caused a great deal of interest also outside artistic circles. The Dadaists had no problem filling large-scale venues, and as more than just the intellectual élite was curious to find out first-hand what all the fuss was about, they were able to make serious money from the soirées.[59]

As in the Futurist soirées, the atmosphere in the halls was usually explosive, especially when people turned up with plenty of ammunition and noise-producing instruments, ready to attack the performers at the first opportune moment. The Dadaists were prepared for these altercations and positively invited them. Therefore, the scenes that unfolded at some of the events resembled the worst excesses in prewar Italy. And like Marinetti and his companions, the Berlin Dadaists were extremely apt at handling audience reactions, stirring up emotions and giving riots the desired direction. It seems rather telling that reviews of the Dada events have often more to say on the scenes unfolding in the auditorium than on the individual numbers presented on stage. One write-up of the Neue Sezession soirée of April 12, 1918 neatly summed this up: "Dadaist art was not presented on stage. The illustration of the concept was handed over to the audience."[60] However, this was not always the case. For example, the soirée given on April 30, 1919 in the intimate surroundings of Israel Ber Neumann's Graphisches Kabinett had an élite audience typical of this Kurfürstendamm venue, who viewed the performance as burlesque antics of eccentric artists, "presented for their entertainment and hence greeted with stale, hollow, snobbish laughter."[61] Nothing could be more different than the soirée of May 24, 1919 at the Meistersaal near the Anhalter Bahnhof in the working-class district Kreuzberg. Hausmann, Huelsenbeck, and Golyscheff basically repeated the program they had previously presented at the West-End venue, but this time the reaction was very different. Additional material was provided by Walter Mehring, an experienced *Kabarettist* who provoked the audience with highly offensive poems, a Dada prologue, and a parody of a famous Goethe ballad. The latter was interrupted by the Dadaists who stormed the stage and shouted: " 'Hey, Walt, don't cast pearls before these swine!' And the whole Dada chorus added: 'Stop! Get out of here! Ladies and gentlemen, you are kindly requested to go to hell. If you are looking for amusement, why don't you go the Eros Halls?'—(Huelsenbeck:) 'Or to a Momas Thann lecture?' "[62] As they left the stage, they were attacked by some spectators. To cool everyone off, Mehring performed a few jazz tunes, and an unnamed person (possibly Valeska Gert or Raoul Hausmann) presented a masked dance. The audience began to get boisterous again when Baader presented a lecture on "Politics," in which the author declared himself president of the Earth and Universe. Then followed the simultaneous poem, "Chaoplasma," for ten actors, two big drums and ten rattles, which ended with a parody of the church hymn, "O Haupt von Blut und Wunden," here rendered as: Intestines Soaked in Blood and Sores. To irritate those spectators who did not respond to blasphemies, Hausmann read a political satire, "On the New and Free Germany," Golyscheff performed an anti-symphony, "Gasp Maneuver," and Grosz danced a "Negro Jig" to the sound of a scraping cello. When the exasperated audience believed that they had finally reached the end of the program, Hausmann and Huelsenbeck came back on stage and performed a "race between a type writer and a sewing machine," with Grosz acting as referee and Valeska Gert accompanying the sounds of the two machines with grotesque dances. While Huelsenbeck was feeding sheets of paper into his typewriter, Hausmann sewed an endless loop of mourning crape and was declared winner of the race. The whole performance was so chaotic that every participant remembered it in a different way. Apparently, the same kind of chaos reigned in the auditorium, so that nobody noticed when the actors left the hall and the soirée was over.

Although many of the texts that were used in Dada soirées were subsequently published (in the contemporary press, or in later critical editions), it is difficult to reconstruct how these texts were presented on stage, and well-nigh impossible to attempt a critical analysis of the performances. Therefore, rather than describing the soirées in terms of the material presented, I focus on what kind of audience reactions they elicited and how these were handled by the Dadaists. Such a "dramaturgy of audience manipulation" appears to have been the most significant factor for determining the "success" of the soirées, which in many ways came to resemble the early Futurist *serate*.

One of the key events in the Dada calendar of 1919 was the matinée held on November 30 at the Tribüne theatre. It caused such a commotion that it had to be repeated on December 7 and 13. The program offered again a judicious mixture of bruitist and simultaneous poems, sketches, dances, lectures, and cabaret songs. However, this time the actors increased the level of scorn and insult. This is an extract from a report published two days after the event:

> One artist after the other appears on stage, shouts a few words, is interrupted, scolded, commended, thrown out, fetched back, derided, praised. The Dadaists shout a few incoherent sentences about art, politics, ethics. The audience yells, whistles, screeches, stamps its feet, climbs on to the nice red velvet seats, demands its money back, and nearly storms the stage. . . . Insults of an increasingly abusive kind are flung from the stage. I cannot distinguish any longer from which side of the fence the insults are coming: "You are far too stupid!"—"Shut your trap, you idiot!"—"If you don't want to listen, why don't you go and commit suicide, you numskull?"[63]

The strategies that were employed to raise the heat in the auditorium were manifold. It could either be insolent affront of the kind George Grosz used to revel in: " 'Hey, you shitface down there,—yes you, the one with the umbrella, you stupid idiot! Don't laugh, blockhead!' If the people answered back, which they naturally did, the tirade continued, in Sergeant-Major fashion: 'Shut up, or you'll get a kick up your arse!' "[64] Or it might involve a contemptuous comment, as in one scene when a Dadaist came on stage, interrupted the show and shouted: "Stop! You don't want to entertain these idiots down there in the stalls, do you?" A more subtle way of provoking reactions was to present pantomimic acts such as the one Hannah Höch remembered: "The actors suddenly lined up on stage with the back to the audience. Each pulled a handkerchief from his pocket, placed it carefully on the ground, took his jacket off and laid it on the handkerchief. Then they lit a cigarette, smoked calmly for a while, until the situation became dangerous: people got out of their seats and wanted to storm the stage."[65] At the repeat performance at the Tribüne on December 7 they employed the old Futurist trick of raising ticket prices by a few hundred percent and then chiding spectators for being so stupid to pay such elevated prices.

One can imagine how these tactics fared when the Dadaists took their anti-art on tour to the provinces. Intensive advance propaganda attracted up to 2, 000 people for each event. In Dresden, one reporter wrote that the audience arrived with a curiosity normally reserved for visits to the zoological garden. The reputation of the "Dada circus" guaranteed that people came prepared for taking an active rôle in the proceedings. They entered the theatre equipped with alarm-whistles, sirens, toy horns, and buzzers, ready to produce a fitting echo to the big drum, cow horns, and cymbals on stage. It seems that in every respect the audience was determined to play a major part in the show: "Huelsenbeck began to read a manifesto in order to present the theory of Dadaism. He did not get very far. The audience wanted to participate as well. He was shouted down in true people's-assembly fashion."[66] According to the reviews, little of what was presented on stage could actually be understood: "For a good half hour, the meaningless and incomprehensible clamor surged up and down, until in the end a group of curly-locked youngsters stormed the stage."[67] The actors were given a sound thrashing that prompted Hausmann to exclaim: "This beating was a nice massage for us, but a disgrace for you. We shall now have a discussion, in which everyone in the audience shall have three minutes speaking time." This was not at all what the people had expected. Hausmann remembered: "Instantly, the first person started to shout: 'To the gallows with the Dadaists. We want to have old Kaiser Bill back!' Turmoil in the auditorium. The scene repeated itself five or six times. . . . Then Baron von Lücken, a poet, came up and said: 'I think Dada is wonderful, I had a great time this evening. I donate all money I have on me to the Dadaists. Here is five mark!' "[68]

Similarly, in Leipzig there was an audience of over 1,000 tightly packed spectators, who

created a tumultuous atmosphere right from the very start. A police lieutenant, who had turned up with a large posse of constables, warned the spectators in his introductory speech to refrain from any transgression and was only laughed at. . . . Hausmann danced his idiotic Dada-trot to gramophone music and a perfect accompaniment of shrill sounds produced by the audience on their house keys. The auditorium resembled a roaring ocean scourged by indignation, laughter and unveiled aggression. Some speakers stormed the stage and thundered out statements pro and con Dada, and this to the sound of a big drum and gong—it was an embarrassing picture of human degeneration.[69]

In Prague, things got even more out of hand. Two thousand five hundred spectators began the performance long before the curtain had risen. When the Dadaists stepped out, they stood in front of a seriously combative audience. Hausmann remembers: "The Czechs wanted to give us a thrashing because we were, unfortunately, German; the Germans believed we were Bolsheviks, and the Socialists threatened us with death and destruction, because they suspected us to be libertines."[70] In view of the threat to his life and limb, Baader deserted and was not seen again. Hausmann and Huelsenbeck managed to get through the program and even repeat it the next day at the Mozarteum. But as Hausmann reported back to Hanna Höch, it was "a lumberjack job . . . sweating in front of these fat lumps."[71] The next performance in Brno had to be canceled because the life of the performers was seriously at risk. A planned continuation of the tour through Moravia down to Vienna was called off, due to general exhaustion and a growing friction between the performers.

Although Berlin Dada continued to employ conventional performance spaces for their soirées, they also moved outside the traditional frame of theatre performances and engaged in what, in chapter 3, I have called "Action Theatre." The person who became most notorious for these events was Johannes Baader, an architect and one of the most eccentric animals in the Berlin Dada zoo. He had a manic-depressive personality and was repeatedly submitted to psychiatric treatment.[72] To what degree this messianic Dada prophet was actually *compus mentis* during his Berlin period is difficult to determine, as most of his phantasmagoric declarations were laced with irony and caustic humor as well as serious megalomania. But because of his madness and unpredictability, he was seen by many Dadaists as the living incarnation of the Dada spirit (hence his name "Oberdada"). He had been "discovered" by Hausmann and Jung in 1917, when they had planned a series of public actions to shake people out of their stupor and to subvert "the general subordination" and "silent paralysis of the big mass."[73] Baader considered the official certification of his insanity as a *Jagdschein*, an official permission to do whatever he liked without being held legally responsible for it. The first such public action took place on September 18, 1918, when Baader discovered by chance the Reichstag deputy Scheidemann in a tram and declared him, to the great amusement of the bystanders, an honorary member of Dada. On November 17, 1918, Baader interrupted morning mass at Berlin cathedral and gave a speech that ended with the declaration: "You don't care two hoots about Jesus Christ!" The congregation reacted with dismay, the priest was horrified and intoned the choral "Ein' feste Burg ist unser Gott." Baader was removed from the gallery and handed over to the police, where he was charged with blasphemy.[74] On February 6, 1919, on the day of the first meeting of the newly elected Reichstag, Baader distributed the flyer *Dadaists against Weimar* in the wine bar Rheingold and declared that the national assembly had been blown up, that the Club Dada had taken over the government, and that he had been appointed president of the Globe. On July 16, 1919, during the parliament's grand opening ceremony in the State Theatre, he secured a seat in the front row of the dress circle. He behaved impeccably until the national anthem had been sung. Then, during a lull in the official proceedings, he raised his stentorian voice like a preacher in the desert and began a speech that was soon cut short by the guests around him. Having foreseen this reaction, he threw a pile of flyers into the assembly that proclaimed: "On his white steed, the Apocalyptic Rider Johannes Baader enters the Weimar National Assembly and after opening the Seventh Seal declares it to be the revelation of Dadaism."[75] According to Hausmann, the flyer also announced: "REFERENDUM: Are the German people ready to hand over the reign to the Oberdada? Should they vote yes, then Baader shall create order, peace, freedom and bread . . . We shall blow up Weimar! Berlin is the seat of DA-DA!"[76] Less controversial was his last reported action. On the centenary of the birth of the Swiss novelist Gottfried Keller (July 19, 1919[77]), they stopped the traffic on the busy Rheinstraße in Friedenau for a quarter of an hour and read out excerpts from his novel, *Der grüne Heinrich*. But in true Dada style, they chopped the text into fragments of words and phrases and mashed these up into a stew of nonsense poetry that was "illuminated by our elevated delivery, animated by our elated spirit, tormented by new associations, meaningful beyond logic and rationality."[78]

Baader was not the only person to carry out Dada actions in the streets and public institutions. When the magazine *Everyone His Own Football* came off the press, the group decided to launch it in grand style. Harry Graf Kessler reports: "[Grosz] wants to ram home the first number with the public by adopting fair-ground methods and he plans to distribute it through street-vendors and soldiers, students in hansom-cabs, and copies handed from cars. . . . The principal aim will be, in Herzfelde's own words, 'to sling mud at everything that Germans have so far held dear,' meaning moribund 'ideals,' and thereby to let in a little fresh air and smooth the way for fresh ideas."[79] Mehring described in great detail what actually happened before the journal was confiscated by the police: The Club Dada hired a horse-drawn coach and a brass band, complete with frock coats and top hats, and the six editors marched through the West End, where only few copies found a buyer, and then through the working-class districts, where they were greeted with cheers and applause. According to Herzfelde, 7,600 copies were sold that day.[80] When the procession reached the government quarters, they were arrested. An examination of the issue resulted in a charge of defamation of the Reichswehr and distribution of obscene literature.[81]

DADA IN PARIS

News about the Dada activities in Zurich arrived in Paris throughout the year 1916 without causing much of a reaction. In 1917, Tzara sought the collaboration of several influential figures, such as Apollinaire, Albert-Birot, and Reverdy for his Dada publications and had several of his own works printed in *SIC* and *Nord-Sud*. This caught the attention of other writers, among them Cocteau, Soupault, and Breton. When *Dada 3* (December 1918) arrived at Adrienne Monnier's bookshop, Apollinaire passed it around his circle of friends, where it made an immense impression. Breton was particularly taken by the *Manifeste Dada 1918* and showed it to Braque, Soupault, Aragon, and others, who subsequently engaged in a lively and enthusiastic correspondence with Tzara.

In March 1919, Picabia returned from Zurich and planned a Paris edition of his journal *391*. He found a suitable collaborator in Georges Ribemont-Dessaignes, and together they issued a first French issue in November 1919. Also Janco spent a few weeks in Paris and reported in great detail to Picabia, Breton, and Soupault what exactly had happened at the Cabaret Voltaire. This gave rise, as Aragon put it, to an image of Dada emerging from "a whorehouse atmosphere with Tzara as leader of a mad orchestra casting into the world, to the sound of some car horns, his black gospel."[82] On January 4, 1920, Breton visited Picabia for the first time, and their meeting became "the true beginning of the Dada movement in Paris."[83] Now everybody was waiting for the arrival of the legendary Tristan Tzara, the new Messiah of modern literature. On January 17, 1920, Breton, Aragon, Soupault, and Fraenkel went to collect him from Gare de l'Est—and missed him. A few days later the official welcome took place in the house of Picabia's girlfriend, Germaine Everling. From now on, her Louis XV drawing room became an operational headquarters, from where a string of Dada events were organized.

CHRONOLOGY 4.3: DADA IN PARIS	
January 23, 1920	First Paris Dada event, *Le Premier Vendredi de Littérature*, at the Palais des Fêtes, with lectures, poetry readings, presentation of paintings, and musical performances
February 5, 1920	Manifestation Dada as part of the Salon des Indépendants at the Grand Palais, with six manifesto readings
February 7, 1920	Dada lecture at the Club du Faubourg in Puteaux
February 19, 1920	Dada soirée at the Université Populaire du Faubourg Saint-Antoine
March 27, 1920	Manifestation Dada at the Salle Berlioz of the Maison de l'Œuvre, with performances of Ribemont-Dessaigne's *Le Serin muet*, Breton and Soupault's *S'il vous plaît*, and Tzara's *La Première Aventure céleste de M. Antipyrine*
May 26, 1920	Dada Festival at the Salle Gaveau, with performances of Tzara's *La Deuxième Aventure céleste de M. Antipyrine*, and Breton and Soupault's *Vous m'oublierez*
December 9, 1920	Dada soirée at the opening of a Picabia exhibition at the Galerie de la Cible (Librairie Povolozky), repeated as a matinée on December 17
January 12, 1921	Disturbance of a presentation on Tactilism by the Futurist F. T. Marinetti at the Théâtre de l'Œuvre
April 14, 1921	First Dada excursion to Saint Julien le Pauvre
May 2, 1921	Dada soirée at the opening of a Max Ernst exhibition at Au Sans Pareil (Librairie Hilsum)
May 13, 1921	Trial of Maurice Barrès at the Salle des Sociétés Savantes
June 10, 1921	Dada soirée at the Galérie Montaigne, with a performance of Tzara's *Le Cœur à gaz*
June 17, 1921	Disturbance of a bruitist concert by the Futurist Luigi Russolo at the Théâtre des Champs-Elysées
June 18, 1921	*Grand Après-midi Dada* at the Galérie Montaigne sabotaged by Hébertot. Some 100 people, including the Dadaists, find the gallery closed
October 21, 1921	Zdanevitch and Charchoune organize at the Café Caméléon a cabaret evening of Dada works
July 6, 1923	*Soirée du Cœur à barbe* at the Théâtre Michel, with a new production of Tzara's *Le Cœur à gaz*. Due to the disturbances a second performance on July 7 had to be canceled
May 17, 1924	Théâtre de la Cigale shows Tzara's *Mouchoir de nuages*
December 4, 1924	The Ballets Suédois stage Picabia's *Relâche* at the Théâtre des Champs-Élysées

The *Littérature* group had recently set up a series of twice-monthly literary matinées, with the first to take place on January 23, 1920. Tzara's arrival in Paris caused a radical change in the program, and when the day of the performance arrived, Tzara gave his new friends a lesson on how to turn a genteel poetry recitation into a "anti-poetic event of the most violent order."[84] The *Premier Vendredi de Littérature* repeated the formula of the Zurich soirées, with poetry readings, musical performances, and presentation of paintings. But it seems that Breton and his colleagues did not muster the necessary confidence to confront their audience in a truly provocative manner. The élite audience gave their readings polite applause, and Breton's lecture on the paintings exhibited in the hall produced yawns and bored reactions. When Picabia's *The Double World* was presented, it took the audience a while to understand the pun behind the letters that had been drawn on the painting: L.H.O.O.Q.—"She has the hots in her arse." Consequently, a first commotion could be observed in the hall. But it was only when Tzara appeared on stage and, instead of the announced poem, read Léon Daudet's latest pro-royalist speech to the national assembly that pandemonium broke out and a mass exodus occurred.

The second Dada attack on the Paris art scene found a more heterogeneous audience, due to the fact that Tzara had announced in the papers of February 2 that Charlie Chaplin was going to join the Dada movement and would be present at the Dada event at the Grand Palais in order to support "his friends, the poets of the Dada movement." Needless to say, confusion reigned when the matinée began and there was no sign of the famous actor. The initial turmoil rekindled when the writers began their manifesto readings. The texts were chanted in various combinations of voices as if they were religious revelations. After a while, this became exceedingly boring and the audience started to throw all sorts of objects on to the stage. Eventually, this necessitated a suspension of proceedings. Clearly, the budding contingent of Parisian Dadaists lacked experience in audience control; but not so Tristan Tzara. Like Marinetti before him in the infamous *serate*, he challenged as well as entertained his spectators with statements such as: "I have written a manifesto as I have nothing to say!" "Literature exists, but only in the hearts of imbeciles!" "Museums are like Père Lachaise cemetery!" "Dada creations must not exist for any longer than six hours!"

After the tumultuous event at the Salon des Indépendants, Breton was approached by a person who introduced himself as the president of the Club du Faubourg, a Left-wing organization that met regularly in the Puteaux district. He asked whether the group would be willing to repeat the reading and make themselves available afterward for answering questions. On February 7, 1920,

Breton, Tzara, Ribemont-Dessaignes, and Aragon found themselves the high-light of a cultural program that was otherwise dedicated to conventional debates on art and politics. More than a thousand Left-wing intellectuals, trade-unionists, and politicians had gathered in the aisles of a disused church, curious to meet the group who so quickly had established a reputation for itself in Paris. When the four writers appeared on stage, they were greeted with shouts of "Dada, Agaga!," sarcastic comments, insults, and so on. Even before the first manifesto had been read, the audience had assumed the rôle of principal actor in the matinée. Aragon fueled the commotion by shouting invective at the audience and was supported in this by a group of anarchists, who believed Dada to be a libertarian organization.[85] However, when they heard Tzara's *Manifeste Dada* 1918, they revised their opinion and joined the socialists in the concert of catcalls and boos. Attempts by some liberal-minded visitors to salvage the situation bore little fruit, and in the end the whole affair closed in total confusion.

In the following days, as Tzara was marshalling his forces for a third Dada event, he received an invitation to explain the new art movement to the workers attending classes at an educational institute in the Faubourg Saint-Antoine. He agreed and wrote a tongue-in-cheek announcement that prom-ised a group discussion of the burning questions of "locomotion, life, Dada skating; pastry, architecture, Dada morals; chemistry, tattooing, finances and Dada typewriters." This time, the attempt to explain Dada to the working class was more successful than in Zurich, where a guided tour of the Dada Gallery specifically organized for the proletarian masses had only attracted one interested person. The Popular University was a well-organized institution; therefore, plenty of workers filled the hall and listened attentively to Tzara's attacks on Cubism and modern poetry. A reading of the *Manifesto of Mr Antipyrine* left them flabbergasted, and to challenge their passivity, Tzara began to harangue against Marx and Lenin. This did not exactly cause the expected riot, but the audience forced him to justify his political statements. Tzara was at pains to explain that, as an anti-bourgeois movement, Dada was in sympathy with the workers' anticapitalist sentiments. But his demands for the extermination not only of bourgeois culture, but also *all* culture, *all* order, *all* hierarchy did not win him many supporters. The lesson Tzara learned from the event was that the workers who favored a revolution in the political realm had little sympathy for a Dada revolution of the mind.

For the fourth Dada event, Tzara managed to book the Théâtre de l'Œuvre, where some 25 years earlier Alfred Jarry had evoked a proto-Dadaist atmosphere with his play, *Ubu Roi* (see above, pp. 47–50) Tzara may have hoped for a similar scandal when he devised a program for the evening, as the Parisians were known for their violent reactions to provocative stagings, as had been demonstrated with Marinetti's *Roi Bombance* (1909), Stravinsky's *The Rites of Spring* (1913), Picasso's *Parade* (1917), Apollinaire's *The Breasts of Tiresisas* (1917), and Cocteau's *The Cow on the Roof* (1920). To this illustrious pedigree of Modernist theatre, Tzara wanted to add his own contribution: *The First Celestial Adventure of Mr. Disprin.*[86] The play, which had been published in Zurich in 1916, was a "double quadralog" with characters spouting forth sentences that were as intelligible as their names: Mr. Bleubleu, Mr. Cricri, Mr. Antipyrine, Pipi, Npala Garroo, La Parapole, and the like. Part of the script was written in an invented African language, or in an automatic, associative manner that cannot be comprehended by the rational mind. There was no dramatic conflict, no apparent structure (although in the middle of the text a character called Tristan Tzara reads a manifesto), no psychology, no apparent relation to a real world.[87] This anarchical firework of sounds and gestures, devoid of any resemblance to dramatic convention, was given a static performance at the Maison de l'Œuvre by actors immersed in multicolored paper bags (costume and stage design: F. Picabia) and reciting the text in a lackluster fashion. Around their necks they wore placards on which the name of the character they were representing was written. Understanding the play was not exactly helped by the diabolic sound machine that Tzara had especially constructed for the occasion of the Paris première. Furthermore, visibility was low as the stage was bathed in green light. The décor consisted of a bicycle wheel, some clotheslines strung across the stage, and a few signs with hermetic inscriptions that announced: "Paralysis is the beginning of wisdom," "Stretch out your hands and your friends will cut them off," and so on. The audience, clearly, had no idea what they were witnessing. They reacted with hilarity and animated interjections to the actors' "boxing match with words"[88] and declarations that they had to be idiots to come and see a Dada play performed on stage. The same can be said about the two other plays on the program: Ribemont-Dessaignes' *The Mute Canary* and Breton/Soupault's *If you Please*. Cacophonic musical offerings, an exhibition of paintings, aggressive manifesto readings, a Dada fashion show, and parodistic sketches rounded off the program, which was a resounding success: a full house paid serious money for a decidedly unserious show that not only questioned dramatic and theatrical convention, but also dismantled the whole institution of "art."

Immediately afterward, preparations were underway for an even bigger event, a Dada festival, with more plays, more music, more poetry—and more bedlam. For this event, the group rented the large and rather plush Salle Gaveau—a sanctuary of classical music—and attracted a large crowd with a sensationalist program of 19 numbers, including "sodomist music, a symphony for twenty voices, a static dance, two plays," and the like. They also announced that finally the sex of Dada would be disclosed on stage and that all Dadaists would have their hair shorn *coram publico*. The sex of Dada turned out to be a phalliform paper cylinder held up by two balloons. To the great disappointment of the audience, there was no demonstration of what a Dada haircut would look like; but they were amply compensated by the curious costumes worn by the participants: Éluard in a tutu, Fraenkel with an apron, Breton with a revolver tied to each temple. A surviving photograph shows them in funnel-like cardboard suits (reminiscent of Ball's Magic Bishop costume; see figure 4.1) and some five-foot high, white top hats (figure 4.2). As a kind of sequel to the Œuvre evening, Tzara's *Second Celestial Adventure of Mr. Disprin* was performed, again with a play by Breton and Soupault as its counterpart (see figure 4.3), and various sketches by Ribemont-Dessaignes and Dermée. As can be imagined, a great deal of chaos reigned in the hall, and reviews do not always make it clear which stage action related to which item on the program. Improvisation was the order of the day, and the audience (which included many figures of the cultural élite) enjoyed the freedom of intervention they had been granted by the actors. To the horror and indignation of the Gaveau family, a large array of tomatoes, eggs, and oranges were hurled at the performers, with some missing their target and splashing Mme. Gaveau's evening dress. When Breton appeared on stage to read Picabia's *Festival-Manifeste-Presbyte*, he was dressed up as a sandwich-board man with a target painted on the front and a text that accused the audience of being "a bunch of idiots." Although audiences had arrived at the theatre with a good array of projectiles, they quickly ran out of ammunition and had to use the interval to run out and stock up their missiles. The musical offerings (*Le Pélican*, a popular fox-trot tune played on the grand organ of the hall; Ribemont-Dessaigne's aleatory pieces for piano, *Suspect Belly Button* and *Dance of the Curly Chicoré*; Tzara's *Vaseline Symphonique* intoned by ten voices) found strong competition from the audience, who had their pockets laden with toy instruments and other noise-producing utensils. The scenes that unfolded during the show lived up to the precedents, that had been set by the Futurists in their *serate*, and made the matinée a *succès de scandale*.

Preceding the festival, dissent had been rife in the group, and following it, the controversies widened into a schism. Tzara's idea of instituting regular Dada soirées as had been the custom in Zurich did not win much support. Some people even suggested that Dada had become too popular and needed to be laid to rest. Indeed, the Dadaists had developed scandal to a new art form, and Parisian high society began to see in it an amusing diversion. Dada

Figure 4.1 Hugo Ball as Magical Bishop, reciting his verses at the Cabaret Voltaire, June 23, 1916. Ball's recitation took him into a state of deep trance, where he could access a "primordial memory" usually repressed and buried by the rational mind. Like a "witch doctor" he served as a medium for spiritual forces and conducted a primitive worship that led his audience into "poetry's last and holiest precinct."

Figure 4.2 Tristan Tzara, *La Deuxième Aventure céleste de M. Antipyrine*, Festival Dada, Salle Gaveau, May 26, 1920. In this second adventure of the Anti-Headache Man, we see on stage Paul Éluard (Mr Absorption), André Breton (Ear), Marguerite Buffet (Mme Interruption), Georges Ribemont-Dessaignes (The Disinterested Brain), Théodore Fraenkel (Mr Saturn), and Louis Aragon (Mr Shit).

had become the talk of the town and serious newspapers and magazines dedicated many pages to discussing the group's latest exploits. The cultured classes were ready, as Ribemont-Dessaignes wrote, "to accept a thousand repeat performances of the selfsame spectacles. One therefore had to prevent at all cost this acceptance of scandal as an art form."[89] The Dadaists held several meetings in Picabia's salon and like a war council discussed strategies of how to hit the enemy where least expected. They certainly sought to avoid what was most expected of them: to repeat the success of the Œuvre and Salle Gaveau events. When no new and efficacious formulae for their next campaign could be found, the group disbanded for the summer holidays and avoided any further performances for nearly a year.[90]

In April, 1921, preparations were underway for a Max Ernst exhibition at Au Sans Pareil. On the verso of the invitation cards one could read the following announcement: "On 14 April 1921, opening of the Grand Dada Saison, with visits, a Salon Dada, a congress, commemorations, operas, plebiscites, requisitions, trial and judgments. Sign up at Au Sans Pareil." Maybe prompted by reports on the actions of the Berlin Dadaists in public spaces,

Figure 4.3 *Vous m'oublierez*, by André Breton and Philippe Soupault, performed at the Salle Gaveau, May 26, 1920. From Left to right: Paul Éluard (holding a picture, in the rôle of Sewing Machine), Philippe Soupault (on his knees, in the rôle of Dressing Gown), André Breton (in the armchair, in the rôle of Umbrella) and Théodore Fraenkel (as supernumerary).

the Paris group opened their 1921 season with a new avant-garde tactic: Dada excursions and tourist visits, the first to be held at Saint Julien le Pauvre on the afternoon of April 14, 1921. If the intention had been "to remedy the incompetence of suspect guides and cicerones,"[91] they failed miserably. Only some fifty visitors and two journalists turned up for the event, and due to weather inclemency, the dozen Dada escorts were soon bereft of an audience. The group was greatly disappointed and lay low for a while. To pull them out of their "collective nervous depression,"[92] Breton arranged a performance for which no audience was required: he rented a hall of the Learned Societies in rue Serpente and organized a trial of the well-known writer, Maurice Barrès, who was accused of treason for having become a champion of conformist values diametrically opposed to the revolutionary ideas of his youth and for being the mouthpiece of the reactionary newspaper, *L'Echo de Paris*. As it happened, a large audience showed up for this "inimitable spectacle of intellectual justice"[93] and watched Breton as presiding judge, Ribemont-Dessaignes as public prosecutor, Aragon and Soupault as defense councils cross-examining a phalanx of witnesses testifying to the public danger of the accused (who was represented by a tailor's dummy). Tzara, who had not been particularly supportive of the event, used his testimony to settle accounts with Breton on a number of issues and was chided for being "an utter imbecile."[94] Also Picabia, who was opposed to the whole event and had publicly renounced his membership to the Dada circle two days before the trial, unexpectedly showed up and expressed his animosity toward Breton, Aragon, and Soupault. Ribemont-Dessaignes, who had joined the affair on the understanding of performing a sarcastic rôle in a satirical comedy, was deeply disappointed by the tone of high seriousness with which Breton conducted the proceedings.

The relations between Breton and Tzara continued to be tense after the trial, and it fell to the rest of the group to organize the next Dada event, to coincide with an exhibition at the Galérie Montaigne. Breton refused to have anything to do with it, but Tzara used the opportunity to arrange a performance of his latest play, *The Gas Heart*. The accompanying program consisted of the usual mix of music, poems, sketches, and dances (executed on this occasion by the Russian avant-gardist Valentin Parnak) and resembled in many ways the performances at the Galerie Dada in Zurich. The repetitive note of the soirée (two more matinées were arranged for June 18 and 30, 1921, but were canceled by the owner of the gallery) caused widespread disagreement in the group, who felt tired of the labor involved in planning, and even more so in executing, the events. Conflicts were further exacerbated by the Congress of Paris, a grandiose gathering designed to unite progressive European artists of every Modernist persuasion. Most Dadaists objected to Breton's attempt to appoint himself as the Pope of Modernism, to the procedures and protocols, the meticulous organization of sections, papers, speeches, and so on. In the end, the vast undertaking folded, and with it the possibility of uniting the former members of Paris Dada on a common platform. Tzara and Breton indulged in personal vendettas and published spiteful invectives against each other in the press. Nominally, at least, the group organized a last joint event, the Man Ray exhibition at the Librairie Six (December 3–31, 1921). An attempt to achieve conciliation through a meeting at the Closerie des Lilas on February 17, 1922 only brought about the final break and signaled the end of the Dada group in Paris.

Figure 4.4 Tristan Tzara, *Le Cœur à gaz*, Théâtre Michel, Soirée du Cœur à Barbe, July 6, 1923, directed by Yssia Siderski, design by Alexander Granovski, costumes by Sonia Delaunay. This production by the Russian exile theatre company Tchérez, directed by Ilya Zdanevich, had an extremely basic and economical design. The Cubo-Futurist costumes made from cardboard restricted the actors' movements and gave the play a very static quality.

This, however, did not mean the end of Dada activities. And two of the most accomplished theatre events took place even later.[95] With the help of the Russian Futurist Ilya Zdanevich, who had been living in Paris since 1921 and was director of a theatre group, Tchérez, Tzara managed to rent the Théâtre Michel for a new production of his play, *The Gas Heart*, with costume designs by Sonia Delaunay (see figure 4.4). The poster announced films by Hans Richter, Man Ray, and Charles Sheeler, a dance by Lizica Codreano, piano music by Georges Antheil, a poetry recitation by Pierre Bertin, and several premières of compositions by Auric, Milhaud, Satie, and Stravinsky. With such a star-studded program, the event promised to be a "must" for everybody interested in avant-garde experimentation. Little did they know that they were about to witness the swan song of Paris Dada.

Soon after the first musical offerings and poetry readings, Breton took offense at a not particularly offensive line about Picasso, stormed the stage and sought to beat up the author, Pierre de Massot. In the ensuing brawl, Massot broke his arm and the audience, shocked by the outrageous behavior, seized Breton, who was now aided by Desnos and Péret. Tzara signaled to the police to intervene and to expel the troublemakers. During the next poetry recitation, Éluard and Aragon shouted invective at the poets on stage and had to be forcibly silenced. The screening of three short films and a projection of *zaum* poetry calmed the atmosphere, but not for long. The performance of *The Gas Heart*, which this time was given a full-scale scenic interpretation with an added dance interlude, was systematically sabotaged by Breton's claque. Therefore, if one wants to get an impression of the production and of the artistic ideas behind it, one has to turn to designs and photographs, rather than reviews or audience memoirs, as the spectators hardly had a chance to appreciate the artistic endeavor of the organizers.[96] The evening ended with violent altercations, police intervention, and general pandemonium. When the owner of the theatre inspected the damage to his fittings and fixtures, he canceled the second performance and thereby brought the Paris Dada seasons to a close.

DADA ART AND ANTI-ART

Much has been written about Dada's nihilism and destructive streak, about its negative stance toward art and art institutions and its anarchical attempt "to smash the moralistic, self-righteous bourgeois world with its own means."[97] Although these were undoubtedly key features of the Dada movement, they need to be seen in context with other, more positive aims.[98] In an interview with the BBC, recorded in 1959, Tristan Tzara explained at great length the position of the Dada artists concerning art and anti-art and deplored "the fact that there is confusion about our negativism, in the sense that we wanted to make a clean break with everything that existed before us, to see life and everything with new eyes, with new and fresh feeling."[99] Huelsenbeck repeatedly voiced the opinion that Dada's "demonstration of nothingness, of madness and destruction was a constructive task"[100] and that it was to be achieved "by poets who wanted to start afresh from the very beginning."[101] Also, Hans Richter emphasized Dada's "double nature in which the forces of dissolution were always matched with other forces seeking form and substance. Dada grew on the tension between the two, as long as they remained in equilibrium."[102] Dada creations were polemical and highly unorthodox, but as Richter rightly stressed, "in spite of all our anti-art polemics, we produced works of art."[103] Even Tzara, who issued some of the most provocative nihilistic statements, was convinced that art "makes man better," that it is "essential to the life of every organism," and that it is a valuable contribution to "the great cathedral of life which we are building."[104]

Dada art, it seems to me, should never be taken at its face value. The Dadaists did not embrace nihilism for its own sake, but mimed the nihilism of the bourgeoisie in order to expose the degradation of humanist values, the butchery of World War I, and the like. It is missing the point when one confounds rhetorical nihilism with professed nihilism. The strong *anti* stance found a dialectic counterbalance in an equally strong positive impulse. Although the Dadaists were vehemently opposed to art as a bourgeois institution, they nevertheless advocated art as a liberating, creative activity. Richter aptly captured this balance when he wrote: "We were all propelled by the same vital impulse. It drove us to the fragmentation or destruction of all artistic forms, and to . . . a raging anti, anti, anti, linked with an equally passionate pro, pro, pro!"[105] Tzara, in his first Dada manifesto, had described this positive aim as a search for the essence of life ("nous cherchons l'essence centrale");[106] Huelsenbeck wrote: 'We were looking for what cannot be defined: the essence, the meaning and structure of a new life."[107] Hugo Ball named it "the purity for which we are striving"[108] and Hans Arp summarized it in similar terms: "We were looking for a more elementary art to cure mankind of the madness of our times and to establish a new order."[109]

The process of demolishing the recognized structures was combined with "a desperate search for a reconstruction of the world that had gone to pieces."[110] Destruction was seen to be therapeutic, to be a cure for the constipation of the body and mind: "[Dada] fulfilled the useful function of a purgative . . . For our group Dada had already acquired a positive meaning, which was to make a fresh start, beginning with the babble of infants, and to construct a new plastic language of the forces of the subconscious."[111] Dada's negativistic stance was an act of defiance, a weapon wielded against the bourgeoisie and its cultural institutions. The Dadaists saw themselves as "representatives of an epoch that needed cynicism in order to transform itself,"[112] but "the *tabula rasa*, which [they] made the guiding principle of [their] activities, only had value in so far as it prepared the way for other things to follow."[113]

The Dadaists realized that art and society are always closely related to one another and that somebody could not reject the one and accept the other: "The artist never stands above his surroundings and the society of those who admire him. His small brain does not produce the content of his creations but merely processes the ideologies of his market (just as a sausage machine processes meat)."[114] So if they wanted to subvert bourgeois values, they had to subvert art itself. This did not mean the abolition of artistic creativity as such, but of the aura that surrounds it and of the artist's dependence on the bourgeois art market. The Dadaists felt that the beauty, harmony, and rationality of academic art had served far too long as a prop of bourgeois society.

What was considered "intelligent," was for the Dadaists nothing but "the triumph of good education and pragmatism."[115] To denounce the "official vocabulary of wisdom" and "the logical nonsense" of bourgeois philosophy, Dada "trumpeted the praises of unreason [and] gave the Venus of Milo an enema."[116] Consequently they put their emphasis on the nonrational, nonlogic, nonintelligent: "The unconscious is inexhaustible and uncontrollable. So let us do away with the conscious, with philosophy. What matters is: we *are*; we dispute, we agitate, we discuss . . . What we want now is spontaneity. Not because it is more beautiful or better than other things. But because everything that comes out of us freely without the intervention of the speculative mind is a representation of ourselves."[117]

Also Hans Arp had this idea of another life in mind when he spoke of "Dada as a crusade organized to win back the promised land of creativity."[118] But how was one to achieve this ideal? Arp's metaphor of a "crusade" was not chosen at random. Ball compared his position in Zurich to that of a fighter in the trenches,[119] and the bellicose language becomes even more obvious when one examines the Dada manifestos published in Berlin. The outbreak of the November Revolution in 1918 made the Dadaists realize that confronting the bourgeoisie in cabarets and galleries was not enough. They had to leave the closed world of art and literature behind and link up with the political events on the street: "We know that we have to be an expression of the revolutionary forces, an instrument of the masses and of the necessities of our times. We deny any similarity with the aesthetic profiteers and academics of tomorrow."[120] For a large number of artists, Dada was an important transitional period in their lives that caused a radical reorientation of their outlook on art and society. Many of the Berlin Dadaists later joined the Communist Party (Erwin Piscator, George Grosz, John Heartfield, Wieland Herzfelde, Franz Jung), as did Paul Éluard and Louis Aragon in Paris. Dada became a training ground for radical, politically active artists. Even the arch-bohemian, anarchist, and nihilist Tristan Tzara later turned socialist. Hugo Ball converted to Catholicism, but did not give up his belief "in a holy Christian revolution and a mystical union of a liberated world."[121]

DADA PERFORMANCE ART

Although the delicate balance between art and anti-art applied to all artistic media in which the Dadaists were active, the group had in Hugo Ball a leader with a particular affinity to the performing arts and an extensive historical, theoretical, and practical knowledge of theatre. Furthermore, the ephemerality of the performance medium prevents it from becoming a collectable art object. Dada theatre came into existence through the encounter of actor and spectator at a particular time and place. The Dadaists did not write many plays, and those that were performed at their soirées did not bear much relation to traditional drama. Although some of the presentational formats were derived from Futurist precedents, the specific quality of the interaction with the audiences in Zurich, Berlin, and Paris determined the emergence of a recognizable Dadaist performance art. This section will be concerned with establishing its key traits and main components.

Most of the texts presented at the Cabaret Voltaire and the Galerie Dada were poems, and the way in which they were performed became one of the trademarks of the movement. Dada poetry was not communicated through the medium of the printed word; rather, it realized its full artistic potential in a live performance. The theatrical representation made use of acoustic effects (produced by voice and instruments) and visual presentation (gesture, mime, and movement), so that the audience could actually *hear* and *see* the poem.

The most famous example of this type of poetry was Ball's *Gadji beri bimba*, presented on 23 June 1916 in the guise of a "magical bishop" (see figure 4.1). His body was hidden inside a cylindrical pillar of shiny blue cardboard, with only his head, arms, and feet sticking out. A huge red and golden collar and a blue-and-white-striped witch doctor's hat further restricted his movements and forced him into a quasi-religious intensity of his recitation. He made great efforts to find the right rhythm, inflexion, and accentuation for his verses, modulating his enunciation and projecting his voice in a manner that proved him to be a true pupil of the Max Reinhardt School. The poem culminated in a cadence inspired by liturgical chant, revealing the religious, magical, and irrational undertones in Ball's art. He did not just perform his poetry, but celebrated it with the dignity and solemnity of a high priest.[122]

Ball's poetry had its roots in the Expressionist response to the crisis of language. His rejection of the "language which has become spoiled by journalism and, therefore, made useless"[123] him prompted to search for an *Ursprache*, a primal language based on pure sound as a kind of equivalent to the drama of pure color in Kandinsky's abstract paintings.[124] Although Ball may have been familiar with Khlebnikov and Kruchenykh's *zaum* poems and Balla and Depero's *onomalingua*, he pursued a much more spiritualist concern than the Futurists. His initial attempts "to get rid of the dirt that sticks to this accursed language as if it came from stockbrokers' hands filthy from counting coins"[125] led him into a realm of magic and shamanic incantation. Poetry became for Ball a "retreat into the innermost alchemy of words"[126] and reciting these works was a means of reaching a state of deep trance. Like a "witch doctor" he served as a medium for spiritual forces and conducted a primitive worship that led his audience into "poetry's last and holiest precinct."[127] Here, they were able to gain access to a "primordial memory, a realm that has been repressed beyond recognition and buried, but which is liberated through the uninhibited enthusiasm of the artist . . . and offers the human being a lever for unhinging this exhausted world."[128] The African or, more often, pseudo-African poetry contained a naïve vitality that Ball and Huelsenbeck believed to be a characteristic of "primitive" people and that they sought to reinstate in their art.

A variant to the sound poems were the noise poems or "poèmes bruitistes," invented by the Futurists and introduced to the Zurich Dada circle by Richard Huelsenbeck, who considered this type of art to be a "direct objectivization of the dark, vital forces" and "a rather violent reminder of the colorfulness of life."[129] Here, the text was only a skeleton, a sort of libretto, that was overlaid with an orchestration of noises, produced on drums, rattles, whistles, pots, and pans. The performer would speak, shout, yodel, or sing at the top of his voice, and the result was seen as "an attempt to capture in a clear melody the totality of this unmentionable age, with all its cracks and fissures, with all its wicked and lunatic coziness, with all its noise and hollow din. The Gorgon's head of boundless terror smiles out of the fantastic ruins."[130]

The simultaneous poems, which could involve up to 20 people on the stage, had a similar function, as none of the text could possibly be understood. The only impression the audience was able to get was that of chaos and unbridled vitality. But this was, according to Huelsenbeck, exactly the intended effect: "Simultaneity is a direct reminder of life . . ., which defies formulation, because it is a direct symbol of action. And so ultimately a simultaneous poem means nothing but 'Long live life!' ('Es lebe das Leben')."[131] Of course, in a situation of war this emphatic praise of life was an action of protest, directed against "this mad simultaneous concert of butchery, cultural fraud, eroticism, and *schnitzel*."[132] The simultaneous poem was not only a symbol of life in an ossified, moribund society, but it also reflected the chaos in a war-stricken world and a civilization that was falling apart.

The stage has often been called a *theatrum mundi* that reflects the state and order of the world; the stage of the Cabaret Voltaire was a *circus mundi* reflecting the chaos of a world that had gone out of joint. The Dada encounter with the dark, irrational forces was enhanced by the use of primitive masks that forced the wearer into strange, dance-like movements that conveyed both a sense of possession and psychic release. There were several occasions when Emmy Hennings, Sophie Taeuber, and Claire Walther presented such masked dances. Mary Wigman, who was famous for this type of performance (see figure 2.7) and a frequent guest at the Cabaret Voltaire, agreed to participate, but due to some other engagement had to withdraw her offer, and some of Laban's younger pupils stepped in.[133] Also in Berlin, dances were an integral feature of the Dada soirées. Both Grosz and Hausmann developed considerable talent in this field, and on other occasions they engaged professional dancers, such as Valeska Gert and Sent M'ahesa (alias Else von Carlberg). In Paris, it was Valentin Parnak who helped to raise the profile of dance in the Dada spectrum of modern forms of artistic expression.

Another genre of Dada performance art resulted from the poetry recited to the accompaniment of certain movements ("gymnastic poems"). It depended on the performer's physical skill to combine his utterances with kinetic creations, which could be simple movements such as knee bending, or more complicated "dances." An explanation of these works was given by Tristan Tzara: "The gymnastic poem which we have invented is designed to accentuate and to articulate the meaning of words through primitive movements. What we want to represent is intensity. It is for this reason that we go back to primitive elements."[134]

A more refined version of these gymnastic poems was the dances carried out by members of the Laban school. Here, a professional dancer interpreted the rhythms and sounds of the poems kinetically and created a synaesthetic artwork that according to some descriptions must have looked very convincing indeed.

A further type of performed poetry was the static poem, "which" Tzara distinguished from the simultaneous poems thus: "Uniformly dressed people carry signs on which the words of the poem were written. They arrange and rearrange themselves in groups according to the (classic) law which I impose on them."[135] A variation on this form of performance was the static poem where the words were written on cardboards and rested on chairs arranged on the stage in a certain order. From time to time the curtain was lowered and the words were rearranged or exchanged. (This idea was taken up again in 1924 by Schlemmer in *Meta, or The Pantomime of Scenes*. See p. 214)

Audiences who tried to "understand" these works with the interpretative tools of the rational mind were at a loss and expressed their frustration through laughter and aggression. However, the Dadaists did not want to produce meaning in the traditional sense; rather, their art depended on the exclusion of distinct meanings and on the provocative effect this had on the unprepared onlooker. The "meaningless" of Dada art was only a camouflage for a new kind of meaning, hidden behind a surface of pure nonsense. The artists wanted to take art out of the hands of academic teachers and turn it into something personal again. Art had to be produced as a creative act, free of any restrictions normally imposed by taste, rules, logic, and so on.

The performer had to give in to his or her spontaneous impulses and create without premeditation, or let the scripted event transform itself under the imponderable influence of chance, the inspiration of the moment, and the unpredictable reactions of the audience: "All of our sketches were of an improvised nature, full of fantasy, freshness, and the unexpected."[136] What mattered was the creative process, and not the aesthetic quality of the final product. Tzara's well-known adage, "Thought is produced in the mouth,"[137] captures well the spontaneous nature of Dada performances that were usually presented by artists without any professional training or theatre experience.[138] When they went on stage, they did not exhibit a technically accomplished, rehearsed, and directorially fixed rôle, but rather a rendering of their own instantaneous feelings and ideas. Therefore, the performer did not *represent* a character, but rather *presented* him- or herself. The performance did not relate to any other place or time, but only to the here and now. "Here" normally meant a small, bare platform stage, without set and with only few props. Sometimes there was a backdrop, but this never related to the performance itself. Considerable effort, however, was put into the costumes and masks, which in Zurich were produced by Marcel Janco and in Paris by Francis Picabia and Sonja Delaunay. They greatly enhanced the effect of the productions and must be regarded as an important ingredient of Dada performances.

Although the actor's "self-exhibition" on stage was a largely improvised event, the overall structure of a soirée was nevertheless well organized. Richter, for example, recalled the "Non Plus Ultra Ninth [recte: Eighth] Dada Evening" in the Saal zur Kaufleuten (April 19, 1919): "Tzara had organized the whole thing with the magnificent precision of a ringmaster."[139] This in no way contradicted the improvised nature of the stage events themselves. Apart from allowing the performers room for creative self-expression, the soirées had the equally important function of provoking the largely bourgeois audience, and this could only succeed if the whole program was well planned.

Whatever happened on stage was directed toward an audience. The Dadaists did not experiment with the architectural structure of the theatre, but basically accepted the spatial differentiation between performers and spectators. However, in every major performance they challenged the forms of communication between stage and auditorium. After the first production of Kokoschka's *Strawman and Sphinx* at the *Sturm* soirée on April 14, 1917, Tzara wrote: "This performance decided the rôle of our theatre, which will entrust the stage direction to the subtle invention of the explosive wind, and the scenario to the audience."[140] The early soirées in the intimate setting of the Cabaret Voltaire and Galerie Dada displayed a great deal of serious intention and were generally appreciated by those members of the audiences who had an interest in modern art and literature and had not just dropped in for a beer and some light entertainment. However, the more public events in major halls and theatres aimed at shocking, provoking, and enraging audiences to such an extent that the direction of communication between stage and auditorium was reversed. The most important aspect of the soirée in the Salle Gaveau (May 26, 1920) was—according to Tzara—that "the spectacle took place in the auditorium. We were gathered on the stage watching the audience let loose."[141] Georges Charensol in *Comœdia* reported on the "Manifestation Dada" at the Maison de l'Œuvre: "The public booed, hissed and jeered at the Dadaists, who greeted the insults with grins on their faces. It felt like being in a madhouse, and the breeze of madness wafted across the stage as well as through the hall. The Dadaists have exasperated their spectators and this is exactly, I think, what they wanted."[142]

The situation was slightly different at the Kaufleuten soirée, where a certain section of the audience had become familiar with the Dadaists' provocations and had arrived with what the performers considered the "wrong" kind of expectation. Tzara decided that they needed "special treatment" and devised a program that delivered exactly the opposite of what these spectators had come for. Viking Eggeling introduced the evening with a serious lecture on abstract and constructivist art. After this prosaic beginning, which provoked simply by being so unprovocative, there followed a piano recital of music by Schoenberg, Satie and Cyril Scott, given by Suzanne Perrottet. Katja Wulff recited poems by Huelsenbeck, Arp and Kandinsky, which prepared the ground for Tzara's simultaneous poem for 20 performers, *The Fever of the Male*. This "hellish spectacle enraged the other half of the audience and unleashed the 'signal of blood.' Revolt of the past and of education."[143] The spectators were now in a state of agitation; but before they could bring the evening to a close, an intermission was called.

In the second half, the same defiance of expectations was repeated and brought the audience to new heights of indignation. There was a talk by Richter on Dadaism, which "cursed the audience with moderation," atonal music by Hans Heusser, a recitation by Arp from his *Cloud Pump*, and Wulff's *Black Cockatoo Dance*, performed by five dancers in black, oversized outfits. When Tzara read out his *Proclamation Dada 1919*, he was showered with coins, oranges, and similar objects. Among the booing and whistling, he hardly succeeded in making his manifesto heard. But things got even worse, when the climax of the evening arrived, the entrance of Walter Serner, a tall, elegant figure dressed in an immaculate black coat and striped trousers, with a gray cravat. When he read out the provocative statements of his Dada manifesto, *Final Dissolution*, he received such a tumultuous reception that he had to withdraw into the wings. When he finally returned to the stage, people expected him to proceed with the next item on the program, a recitation of his own poems. But instead, he carried a headless tailor's dummy, gave it a bunch of roses to smell, and placed the flowers at the mannequin's feet. He then brought a chair and sat astride it, but with his back to the audience. Hans Richter described the spectators' reaction to this act of defiance:

> The tension in the hall became unbearable. At first it was so quiet that you could have heard a pin drop. Then the catcalls began, scornful at first, then furious. "Rat, bastard, you've got a nerve!" until the noise almost entirely drowned Serner's voice, which could be heard, during a momentary lull, saying the words "Napoleon was a big strong oaf, after all." That really did it. What Napoleon had to do with it, I don't know. He wasn't Swiss. But the young men, most of whom were in the gallery, leaped on to the stage, brandishing pieces of the balustrade (which had survived intact for several hundred years), chased Serner into the wings and out of the building, smashed the tailor's dummy and the chair, and stamped on the bouquet. The whole place was in an uproar.[144]

So finally the provocation had worked. But this was only due to the fact that Tzara had masterminded the show with a clear vision of how the various sections of the program would affect the audience, who after three years of Dada activities were no longer naïve in their expectations, but arrived in order to be shocked and affronted. Once the spectators began to enjoy the spectacle on stage, and the conventional rôles of performers and onlookers were reinstated, Dada performance had failed in one of its major objectives: to provoke its bourgeois audience to the extent that they reversed the direction of theatrical communication and "performed the script in the hall."[145]

The later Dada performances were organized with the intention of attacking the audience, who was principally seen as an enemy[146] and considered philistine in its assumption that for a few francs or marks they could "buy" art. Ribemont-Dessaignes wrote a programmatic text, "Au public," that he shouted at the visitors to the Dada evening at the Grand Palais on February 5, 1920:

> Before descending amongst you in order to eradicate your decayed teeth, your scabby ears, your canker-ridden tongues—Before breaking your rotting bones, before opening your bilious stomach and removing, for use as fertilizer, your swollen liver, your ignoble spleen and your diabetic kidneys—Before ripping off your vile, incontinent and purulent sex . . .—Before all that, we shall take an enormous antiseptic bath—And we warn you—It is we who are the murderers.[147]

Huelsenbeck described such direct attacks on the spectators as "an educational measure . . . to enlighten them that their notion of art and culture was only an ideological superstructure under which they were hiding their daily profiteering. We wanted to direct them towards a new, primitive life, where the intellect dissolved and gave way to simple instinctual actions."[148] Seen in this context, the Dada provocation pursued a positive aim: releasing the spectators from the force of habit, jolting them out of their passivity, and allowing them to feel the psychic energies rising from the subconscious. However, Huelsenbeck's own performance experience showed him that appealing to the audience's basest instincts could be very dangerous indeed. For example, in Prague, the insults directed at a crowd of over 1,000 people caused a near-riot: "It was like the outbreak of a revolution. The mob was thirsty for violence. They were asking for clubs, legs of chairs, fire extinguishers. It was the hoarse scream of an overexcited mass. Now we had them where we wanted to. It was time to pour oil on the troubled waters."[149]

The clamorous and provocative soirées organized by the Dadaists in Zurich, Berlin, and Paris repeated a theatrical formula that had been developed by the Futurists in their *serate*. The sound poems recited on these occasions were very similar to works that had been written and performed by Balla and Depero on similar occasions in Rome. The gymnastic poems, which combined dance movements and poetic recitation, bore close resemblance to the ideas expressed in Marinetti's *Manifesto of Dynamic and Multichaneled Recitation Declamation* of March 1916 and the *Manifesto of Futurist Dance* of July 1917. Even the simultaneous poems, which the Dadaists developed into very original and highly creative performance pieces, had been preceded by similar experiments in Italy. Poets in either movement also wrote plays, but these were devoid of the staple ingredients of dramatic literature (plot, character, dialog, location) and were performed with a high degree of spontaneity and improvisation, indicating a clear preference for process over product.

Also, the reversal of the traditional stage–audience relationship followed a model established by the Futurists in 1910–1914. The Futurist manifestos suggested a variety of strategies of how the audience could be activated, for example, selling the same ticket to several people, spreading glue on some seats, sprinkling sneezing powder in the auditorium, reducing all of Shakespeare's plays to the length of a one-acter, having the actors recite a famous tragedy while being enclosed in a sack up to their necks. These and many other provocative ideas were carried out in the infamous *serate* and led to scenes as in the Teatro Verdi in Florence (December 12, 1913), where the performers stood on stage, smoking a cigarette and watching the main action unroll in the stalls.[150] This could equally have taken place during the performance of Tzara's *First Celestial Adventure of Mr. Disprin*, where "the actors began to insult the audiences and welcomed their catcalls with a smile,"[151] or the soirée at the Salle Gaveau (May 26, 1920), where the performance took place in the auditorium and the artists on stage watched the audience take over the proceedings. Hannah Höch remembered seeing such scenes several times in Berlin: "The audience and the actors on stage incited each other, and when the spectators began to join into the action or to vent their anger, the actors stood calmly at the proscenium arch and let the players in the hall run the show for a while."[152]

In an essay for the popular magazine, *Reclams Universum*, Huelsenbeck compared Dada to other art movements of the time and found that the Futurists came closest to Dada because of their dynamic concept of the world and the way this was expressed in their theatre works. Furthermore, "Dada belongs on the stage, yes I would even say, on the streets, where it is surrounded by the noise of wheels and car horns. Everything in it aspires towards life."[153] Therefore, Dadaists undertook street actions like the one in Zurich on October 6, 1919, where they erected a fantastic, over-life-size mannequin on the busy Bahnhofstraße and announced Marinetti's conversion to Dadaism.[154] Also, in other cities, they emulated the Futurist concept of Action Theatre (see chapter 3) in streets and in public buildings. Above (pp. 153–154), I mentioned the actions of Johannes Baader. On other occasions, they invaded theatres and protested against certain works performed there: in Paris, they disturbed Marinetti's lecture on tactilism at the Théâtre de l'Œuvre on January 14, 1921, Russolo's *intonarumori* concert at the Théâtre des Champs-Élysées on June 17, 1921, and Cocteau's *Wedding on the Eiffel Tower* at the same theatre on June 18, 1921. In Cologne, on March 4, 1919, Max Ernst and several friends disturbed a performance of Raoul Konen's *The Young King* and sent an Open Letter to local newspapers, in which they criticized the municipal theatre's repertoire policy. The subsequent court case turned the Cologne theatre scandal into an effective publicity stunt for the Dadaists.[155]

DADA'S ORIGINALITY AND CONTRIBUTION
TO THE THEATRE

Given the extensive knowledge the Dadaists possessed of Futurist aesthetics and artistic practices, it is not astonishing that we find traces of the infamous *serate* in the Dada soirées organized in Zurich, Berlin, and Paris. Other similarities can be detected in Dadaist music, where the shadows of Pratella and Russolo fall heavily on Heusser's and Golyscheff's compositions and Huelsenbeck's noise instruments. Each of these composers worked with sounds of all kinds produced on all sorts of instruments, in an attempt to widen the concept of what may be called "music." In the field of literature, we can observe an early adaptation of the *parole in libertà* technique, of sound poetry and automatic writing, of the principles of primitivism, irrationality and the subconscious. Marinetti's concept of "poetry as an uninterrupted sequence of new images"[156] and of "untrammeled imagination, i.e. the absolute freedom of images or analogies, expressed by means of Words-in-Freedom, unencumbered by syntactical conductors or by punctuation"[157] propagated the same aims as the Dada poems that were unbridled expressions of subconscious charges of energy. Both Dada and Futurist artworks were informed by the concepts of dynamism, simultaneity, and fragmentation. The exchange of literary works between members of both movements is evident from the Futurist contributions to Dada publications and their typographical design, and, vice versa, from the Dada works printed in Futurist publications and those of their allies.

The question that automatically arises from such a comparison of analogous features is whether Dada was any more than an updated version of Futurism. Tzara, of course, did everything he could to show his absolute originality and Marinetti's old-fashionedness. On September 21, 1919, he declared to Breton that he and his friends "have nothing in common with Futurism."[158] In the broadsheet, *Dada soulève tout*, he stated "Futurism has died. Of what? Of Dada. . . . Dada runs everything through a new sieve." He even claimed retrospectively that the term Dada was coined to distinguish it more clearly from the Futurist movement.[159] This may be how Tzara felt in later years. But from today's vantage point we can see more clearly to what extent Dadaism was indebted to Futurism. Until 1918, there were close similarities between both movements both in spirit and artistic practice. Notwithstanding the Dadaists' roots in Expressionism, it was Futurism that came closest to their avant-garde concerns. The Dada soirées and public events were "Art as Action" in the manner Marinetti had developed in Italy. They were an expression of the same attitude of protest and rebellion against the autonomous position occupied by art in bourgeois society. Both movements displayed the same aggressiveness in their stance toward tradition and the values of the past; they showed the same contempt for traditional morality and received ideals of beauty, harmony, and so on; they embraced the same attitude of *épater le bourgeois* when they came into contact with the representatives of the old order.

Although indebted to Futurism in many ways, Dadaism did not, however, passively accept the ideas and forms of expression suggested by their Italian colleagues. The Zurich group took over many of the central tenets of Futurism, but step by step filled them with new meaning, or—one might say—they drained them of their old meaning and thereby moved beyond the parameters of what had been established by the Futurists. In the *Dada*

Manifesto of 1918, Tzara gave a clear reason for rejecting Futurism: "The modern artist protests; he does not paint any longer." For Tzara, Futurism even in its negative stance against bourgeois culture was still a system of thought based on the "investment of intellectual capital" in art. And he was right. Futurism was still entrenched in the philosophical traditions of a positivist age. The Futurists never questioned their fundamental ontological assumptions about reality and matter. They saw the world in a dynamic swirl, but behind this dynamism of the universe they still sought to discern some kind of unity and order: "There is with us not merely variety, but chaos and clashing of rhythms, totally opposed to one another, which we nevertheless assemble into a new harmony."[160]

Tzara and his fellow Dadaists, on the other hand, no longer believed in the existence of a stable matter or in finding harmony behind chaos. For them, the world around them had no rule, no plan, no meaning. Their philosophy was: nature equals chaos; the universe is in permanent flux; the unrelated energies do not fit into any cohesive pattern; there are no linear developments, and all constellations are unstable. For this reason, simultaneity or bruitism as artistic means of expression taken over from the Futurists took on a different rôle in Dadaism. These techniques, when used by the Dadaists, expressed a noncausal relationship between elements of reality, not a synthesis of parts related to each other by a mysterious cosmic plan.

Many of these dissimilarities can be explained by the changed historical situation; others were due to different ideological agendas, particularly with regard to the national question and the issue of war. Dada not only merged many aspects of its predecessors, but also developed them further and enriched them with elements that were typically theirs.

When Tzara moved from Zurich to Paris, he found a group of artists that had been primed for his artistic message by Futurism. There can be no doubt that the *Littérature* group was well informed about Marinetti's activities. Soupault himself confirmed: "We read the Futurist manifestos early on. It was Apollinaire who gave them to us."[161] It is not astonishing, therefore, that the influence of Futurist Synthetic Theatre, first shown in Paris in 1918, can be detected in the two plays by Breton and Soupault, *You Will Forget Me* and *If you Please*, written in 1919. The two authors had learned their lesson from the *sintesi* performed by the group *Art et Liberté* and the *Manifesto of Futurist Synthetic Theatre*, which Marinetti had issued in a French translation in response to the interest roused by the Synthetic Theatre productions in Paris. Breton's interest in Futurist Synthetic Theatre is further documented in his publishing a number of *sintesi* in his periodical *Littérature* (May 1, 1922). But he also followed with a keen eye the developments in Futurist literature.

Breton had plenty of occasions to study Marinetti's literary manifestos and was certainly familiar with his brochure *Les Mots en liberté* of 1919. Common objectives led to similar results. When he and Soupault composed the automatic text *The Magnetic Fields* (in May 1919), they employed methods that had been practiced by the Dadaists and Futurists before. But when Breton severed his contacts with Tzara and founded the Surrealist movement, he placed the greatest emphasis on his opposition to Futurism and on the originality of his movement: "One must be the most naïve of men to grant any attention to the Futurist theory of 'Words-in-Freedom' . . . We have opposed this theory, like many others that are no less precarious, with our automatic writing."[162] He had good reason for being so defensive. Although Surrealism undoubtedly possessed highly original features, the movement had not been created by Breton in a void. Futurism offered an important inspiration both in a direct and an indirect manner. But like Tzara before him, Breton must have felt a need to go beyond the literary and theatrical parameters established by Marinetti and his fellow Futurists. For this reason, he responded with great enthusiasm when he received the first Dadaist publications from Zurich. For him, they represented a new phase in the development of an avant-garde aesthetic that, initially, he welcomed and then, after 1922, he discarded to the dustbin of history. It is evident that the Surrealists pursued some interests that had been discarded by the Dadaists or never fully explored by the Futurists. Each movement borrowed elements from the preceding one and developed them further, while at the same time rejecting others or making them a minor concern. Given the osmosis of artistic ideas between the various movements of the historical avant-garde, their methods and directions were more often complementary than contradictory and were born from the same rationale: restoring life to art.[163]

In view of Dada's radical opposition to the artistic institutions of its time, it is not astonishing that it left few recognizable traces in the contemporary theatre world. Cocteau, who was despised by most Dadaists, possibly received some inspiration from them for his plays, *The Cow on the Roof* (1920) and *The Wedding on the Eiffel Tower* (1921). Léger, who was a friend of Duchamp's, shared the Dadaists' love of primitivism and incorporated it in his ballet, *The Creation of the World* (1923); but in other respects he was closer to the Futurists, Cubists, and Purists. The only work with strong Dada roots to have been produced in a mainstream theatre was *Relâche*, written by Picabia with music by Satie and film projections by René Clair, staged by the Ballets Suédois at the Théâtre des Champs-Élysées in 1924.

Dada's lasting influence was certainly not to be found among actors and theatre directors, but rather in postwar Performance Art and some postmodern artists. The émigrés to the United States often mixed Dada aesthetics with Expressionist and Surrealist components and introduced this mélange into the curriculum of art schools, such as the Black Mountain College and the Chicago Bauhaus. The concepts of chance, collage, fragmentation, and simultaneity became an integral element of the work of artists who had received their training in these institutions or were in close contact with their teachers. The music of John Cage, the dances of Merce Cunningham and the Happenings of Allan Kaprow would have been unthinkable without the inspiration received from the Dada movement. Motherwell's anthology of Dada writings, *The Dada Painters and Poets*, first issued in 1951, made a large number of theoretical and historical texts for the first time available in translation and found an avid readership among the Happening and Fluxus community, who often referred to themselves as "Neo-Dada." But most of all, Dada left a lasting mark on all subsequent art movements and schools by its radical redefinition of what constitutes art and what it meant to be an artist.[164]

5. Constructivism ✣

TERMINOLOGY AND GENERAL INTRODUCTION

The term "Constructivism" gained currency in the early 1920s and was based on aesthetic principles established by a previous generation of artists, with roots going back as far as Cézanne. Kandinsky had developed a Utopian and often mystical concept of construction and composition; analytic and synthetic Cubism had made abstract and geometric principles of construction a basis of painting and sculpture; the Futurists Balla and Depero had promoted a project of "re-constructing the universe" and Prampolini had published some very profound reflections on the material aesthetics and elementary components of the arts. These predecessors of a fully developed Constructivist style applied constructive principles both to the creative process and to the internal order of the work of art, without necessarily exploring them in a systematic and comprehensive manner. In the course of the 1910s, some of these ideas and concepts were taken up by Russian artists, and it was here that a first formulation of a Constructivist aesthetics could be found before it was adopted by an international movement spanning from Russia to Holland with a particularly active phase in the years 1922 to 1928. In fact, Stephen Bann goes as far as saying that "these generalized tendencies toward constructive art and constructive attitudes would, in all probability, have given rise to no coherent movement if the Soviet example had not acted as a galvanizing force."[1]

The first congress of the International Union of Progressive Artists in Düsseldorf (March 1922) brought together leading Constructivists from eastern, and western, and central Europe and led to the foundation of a Constructivist Internationale (KI). In the second half of the 1920s, the center of the Constructivist movement shifted to Germany and incorporated many artists, who had moved from the Soviet Union to the West because of their political opposition to Lenin's style of Communism and the productivist orientation of Russian Constructivism. Consequently, the International Constructivist movement became less political and operated in more traditional artistic domains. When it merged with Purism, Concretism, and other nonfigurative movements, a rather heterogeneous form of Constructivism came into existence. The rise of Stalinism and of Fascist régimes discredited the Utopian concept of "social Constructivism," and with the deteriorating political climate in the early 1930s, the hub of the Constructivist movement moved from eastern and central Europe to Paris, where the groups Cercle et Carré and Abstraction-Création continued to promote Constructivism as a generalized aesthetic of geometric abstraction. After World War II, an aesthetically and politically diluted version of Constructivism formed part of an abstract, nonobjective branch of Late-Modernism.

Originally, Constructivism was not an artistic style, but a fundamental approach to the organization of the creative process, often combined with a redefinition of the rôle of the artist and the function of art in society. Instead of the intuitive approach and subjective grounding that had been typical of Expressionist art, the Constructivists promoted a scientific, rationalist method of construction and applied functional aspects of engineering to the arts. The artist was put on a par with the scientist and engineer and was incorporated into production processes that were typical of the industrial age. The resulting principles of Constructivist art (economy of materials, precision, geometric forms, pure colors, rational order, clarity of organization, realization of the natural propensities of the materials used, etc.) stood in marked contrast to the ornamental excesses of Art Nouveau, the *l'art pour l'art* attitude of the Symbolists, the emphasis on intuition and lyrical values in Expressionism, and the metaphysical and spiritual orientation of Kandinsky's Abstractionism.

CONSTRUCTIVISM IN RUSSIA

In her study on Russian Constructivism, Christine Lodder distinguished between (a) the evolution of a formal language of nonutilitarian constructions in the 1910s, based to a large degree on Cubism and Futurism and expressing the dynamic aspects of a society determined by industrialization, technology, and science, and (b) the development of a Constructivist theory and practice with strongly utilitarian purpose harnessed to the needs of a Communist society after the October Revolution of 1917.[2]

In the power vacuum after the February Revolution of 1917, the conservative élite and moderate Modernists occupied all influential positions in the Russian cultural administration, much to the chagrin of the avantgardists, who saw themselves forced into an oppositional position to the government. Futurists, Suprematists, and other Left-wing artists had good reason to fear that the new authorities would fail to embark on the cultural renewal of the country and impose administrative control over cultural institutions, thus restricting artistic freedom rather than fostering creativity in tune with the new times. After the October Revolution, avant-garde artists and members of the intelligentsia found themselves even more pushed to the margins, as the revolting masses had little respect for "superfluous" parasites and "unproductive" servants of the bourgeois class.

Lunacharsky, the People's Commissar of Enlightenment, was a man of conservative tastes and more interested in revitalizing the traditions of Realist art than in promoting avantgardism. When he tried to enter into a dialog with the Modernists, they were suspicious and declined his advances. This opened up negotiations between Bolsheviks and conservatives and led, ironically, to a very moderate profile of appointments in the new governing bodies of artistic institutions. Recognizing their errors, the Left-wing avant-gardists changed direction and sought to conquer positions of influence in the various departments of the People's Commissariat of Enlightenment (Narkompros). By mid-1918, Shterenberg, Punin, Altman, Tatlin, Malevich, Rodchenko, Udaltsova, Kandinsky, and other members of the avant-garde managed to occupy important posts in government and administrative offices, which they used for promoting their concepts of art and culture. But this, of course, did not necessarily mean that their ideas were accepted by their colleagues or by the public.

After the revolutions of 1917 and the Civil War of 1918–1920, Russian artists found themselves confronted with a new reality that seriously questioned their self-image and rôle in society. The demise of the bourgeoisie and aristocracy had deprived them of their old patrons, and the deeply rooted antipathy of the common people against the intelligentsia prevented them from finding access to a new market. Under these conditions, it became a matter of necessity to give up the idealistic notions of artistic autonomy, to prove the artist's usefulness to society, and to produce works that had practical benefits in an everyday setting. The shift from artist to "maker of useful objects" was therefore more than a voluntary adjustment caused by revolutionary enthusiasm.

In November 1918, Narkompros organized a conference at the old Winter Palace on the theme of "Temple or Factory?" Punin gave a speech in which he presented the artist of the "New Era" as a "constructor" executing socially relevant commissions, and not a maker of pretty objects for the bourgeoisie, nor a creative genius giving expression to his subjective feelings. This vision of an "artist-engineer" fulfilling "constructive tasks" was a major departure from the predominantly "destructive" attitude that had led the Futurists into the ranks of the Bolsheviks. Although there existed a certain continuity and even partial overlap between both movements, Constructivism was an artistic school more attuned to the changed conditions of post–Revolutionary Russia and earned it a great deal of sympathy from the new government.

The First Working Group of Constructivists was set up in March 1921[3] in INKhUK (Institut Khudozhestvennoi Kul'tury; Institute of Artistic Culture), a school that had been founded at the initiative of Wassily Kandinsky, Alexander Rodchenko, and Varvara Stepanova in 1920, when the government had dissolved the Professional Union of Artist and Painters. Kandinsky drew up the school's teaching program[4] and statutes (approved on May 26, 1920) and acted as chairman of the collective Presidium. However, Kandinsky's psycho-physiological approach was soon felt to be incompatible with the demands of the new, Communist era, and he was forced to resign his post on January 27, 1921.[5] Subsequently, he was invited by Walter Gropius to become a teacher at the Bauhaus and left Russia in December 1921.

Following Kandinsky's departure from INKhUK, the school's emphasis shifted toward a more materialist approach to the basic components of a work of art (the object) and a devaluation of the aesthetic and psychological aspects of production and reception (the process). A General Working Group of Objective Analysis, directed by Rodchenko, established clear distinctions between primary (material) and secondary (representational) elements and instigated a protracted debate about the differences between composition and construction.[6] Whereas the former was seen to be a contemplative activity, using aesthetic principles for defining the relationship between form and structure, the latter was regarded as an active process, employing the material properties of the elements to establish a system of structural relationships between the forces of line, plane, and space. This approach was a far cry from Kandinsky's focus on the subjective components in the composition and reception process, or on the expressive elements and psychological effects of the work of art (see above, pp. 52–54). As the term "construction" had many associations with technology and engineering, it fitted in with the overall intention of the Fine Arts Department of Narkompros to promote a stronger scientific-technological thinking in the art institutions.

In the first years of INKhUK, one could observe three different lines of thought:

Constructivism:	taking a scientific approach to the analysis of the material and formal qualities of a work of art and seeking to construct a new synthesis from these basic elements
Objectivism:	undertaking scientific analyses of utilitarian and aesthetic objects, of the manifestations of their materials and their

	underlying constructional principles, but excluding from the investigations the emotional and representational dimensions of art and any questions of taste and psychology
Productivism:	focusing exclusively on the production of utilitarian objects and seeking to turn the artist into a technician-engineer

Between September 1921 and October 1922, the Working Group of Constructivists at INKhUK organized a series of lectures that was widely discussed and inspired a whole spate of other publications on the emerging Constructivist aesthetics.[7] Stepanova's talk, "On Constructivism," gave a definition that appears to have been widely accepted in the group: "Constructivism is an inventive, creative activity, embracing all those fields which relate to the question of external form, and which implement the results of human ideas and their practical application through construction."[8] She summarized the key features that characterized the new artistic departure as: Constructivism does not seek to transform traditional aesthetics of taste but to replace it with an intellectual production based on analytical methods, objective knowledge, and technical necessity. It abandons introspection, contemplation, and figurative representation as well as the conventions of style and the old formulae of eternal and ideal beauty. Conscious analytical methods (intellect) replace subconscious inspiration (the soul). Once art has been stripped of its metaphysical, philosophical, and aesthetic excrescences, its material foundations can be discerned. From the proper analysis of its basic elements, a new construction that serves society can be synthesized. Art no longer functions as a drug or ornament, but has a utilitarian purpose. The construction of objects and apparatuses will, therefore, not be judged by their stylistic traits but rather by their usefulness. Constructivism is a social rather than aesthetic theory; its creations are not art for art's sake in the guise of craftsmanship, but conscious actions and interventions in the laboratory of life. And life in the new era was not to replicate the alienated state of existence in capitalist society, but become a liberated, creative everyday reality purged of the last remnants of bourgeois consciousness.

Stepanova, Rodchenko, and Gan were the principal architects of the Constructivist definition of the three principles involved in the act of creation: *tektonika* (ideological and formal conception of the work), *faktura* (the choice and handling of the material), and *konstruktsia* (the process of giving form, structure, unity, and organic coherence to it). Many discussion papers, essays, and book chapters revolved around these "three pillars" of Constructivism, to which another key issue must be added: the new rôle of the artist. Many Constructivists renounced the autonomous position of art embraced by the early historical avant-garde and sought to play an active rôle in the transformation of society. From now, they rejected easel painting or decorative sculpture in favor of constructions and designs of more utilitarian function (architecture, typography, photography, textile, ceramics, theatre, etc.). They sought to fuse politics and aesthetics and integrate the artist into the industrial process. The productivists even went a stage further. They believed that Constructivism should not be "a new and modern trend in art but . . . a dialectical transcendence of art." Consequently, they invented the slogan, "Constructivism—gravedigger of art,"[9] abandoned their studios, and became "workers specializing in intellectual production."

The great verve, enthusiasm, and optimism of the Russian Constructivists were soon thwarted by political, social, and economic realities, which forced many of them into resignation, emigration, or a radical change of direction. In the early years of the Soviet Union, little progress was made with industrialization and collectivization; central planning was largely absent and pre-revolutionary conditions prevailed in most sectors of the economy. In 1921, Lenin introduced a New Economic Policy (NEP) in order to overcome the acute crisis that resulted from the Civil War and the intervention of the Western powers. It brought a new class of managers into industry, who were more concerned with profitability than providing Constructivists with testing grounds for their artistic ideas. In the social domain, the primary consumers of artistic products, including those of the avant-garde, were now the new bourgeoisie (the "NEPmen") rather than the proletariat. Paul Wood, in his assessment of the Constructivists' utilitarian endeavors of the early 1920s, comes to the following sobering conclusions:

> It was the "authorities" who appeared to frustrate the artist-constructors in their attempts to turn art into production, not the sheer impracticality of the projects in the first place. And these were managers of NEP concerns whom it behooved to make a profit rather than build a new society. . . . Constructivism in these conditions, trying to push ahead with the sociopolitical transformation put on the agenda by the October Revolution but subsequently marginalized by the New Economic Policy, had more the quality of a rearguard than an avant-garde action.[10]

This Constructivist attempt to create a new artistic vocabulary and a synthesis of art and technology found its most productive application in the VKhUTEMAS (Vysshie Khudozhestvenno-Tekhnicheskie Masterskie, Higher Artistic and Technical Workshops). This school had been set up in 1920 to transform industrial culture and technical design and to promote an "art in production [. . . that is] closer to human life than pure art."[11] It absorbed the former School of Applied Art and the Moscow School of Painting, Sculpture and Architecture. During the period 1920–1930, they trained several thousand artist, who entered industry as designers and other art institutions as instructors. When the Constructivists joined the school, their ideas and concepts became absorbed in several areas of teaching and made a particularly strong impact in the Basic Course and the typography, woodwork, and metal workshops.

The VKhUTEMAS had a multidisciplinary orientation and did not uphold the old distinctions between fine art and applied art. Before students could specialize in a discipline most suited to their talents, they received a sound grounding in the fundamental aspects of all arts and crafts. During this foundation year, the school offered training in objective analysis of the artistic elements (color, plane, volume, space), their function in an artistic construction, the chemical and physical properties of materials, and social and political issues. These skills were taught in a manner that they could be applied to the more specialized disciplines of fine art, design, and architecture, and therefore provide a "basis for the new synthetic art."[12] This integration of basic and applied expertise and the merging of artistic media under a technological umbrella was a groundbreaking approach to artistic training, which had profound influences on other institutions such as the Bauhaus. An important intermediary between both institutions was, of course, Kandinsky. He had been an instructor at the VKhUTEMAS and the guiding light behind the innovative Basic Course. Soon after his return to Germany, he became a Master of Form at the Bauhaus (June 1922), where he suggested to his colleagues an official exchange scheme between the two institutions. But before examining the teaching program at the Weimar school, we need to examine, more closely, the dissemination of Constructivism in the wider European arena.

INTERNATIONAL CONSTRUCTIVISM

Until 1920, the West-European public largely identified Russian art with Sergej Diaghilev's Ballets Russes and the painters of *Mir isskustva*. The Modernist schools, from Cubo-Futurism via Suprematism to Constructivism, were largely unknown until a series of exhibitions offered the Western public an opportunity to inform themselves about the recent developments in Russian and Soviet art.

The Russian Constructivists first made their presence felt in Berlin,[13] where Puni arrived in 1920 and, in February 1921, held an exhibition at the *Sturm* Gallery. A Russian Club at the Café Leon set up a number of meetings between German and Russian artists, and in early 1922, a German

Constructivist group was founded in the studio of Gert Caden.[14] In February 1922, the Hungarian Constructivists Moholy-Nagy and Péri showed their work at the *Sturm* Gallery. In October 1922, a major and highly influential exhibition with many key Constructivist works opened at Galerie van Diemen, followed, in 1923, by three Constructivist shows at the *Sturm* Gallery. The popular success of these events, combined with the political repression and economic hardship artists had to endure in the Soviet Union, caused a phenomenal growth of the Russian community in Berlin. In 1923, no less than 300,000 Russians lived in Berlin and ran 87 publishing houses, 20 bookshops, 3 daily newspapers, a Russian writers' club, an arts center, a cabaret, and several cafés.[15]

East-European Constructivism offered great inspiration to Western artists dissatisfied with the late offshoots of Expressionism and Dadaism, with the subjective and intuitive approach to art to be found in Surrealism and Metaphysical Painting, and the mystical and spiritualist foundations of Abstractionism. Even before Constructivism became known in the West, the famous *rappel à l'ordre* (call for a return to order) could be heard, leading to the establishment of De Stijl (1917), the *Esprit Nouveau* group (1918), and Mondrian's Neoplasticism (1919). From this situation, two dominant trends emerged. On the one hand, there were the groups and cenâcles to whom the bold experiment of Communist reconstruction in Russia served as a model for redefining their own position in society and finding for themselves a new rôle in life. Participation in the "Great Construction," that is, the building of a Communist society, promised to give concrete reality to the old dream of the avant-garde to merge art with life and to turn the artist into a constructor, who gives *Gestalt* to a new edifice that is life itself. On the other hand, there were a significant number of artists who subscribed to the Constructivists' rational, analytical, and elementary method of creation without, however, sharing their overtly ideological concerns. Consequently, the aims and objectives of the Russian Constructivists mixed and mingled with a more general trend in Western art toward a purist, objective, and universal language, for which technology and science provided the model.

During the first congress of the International Union of Progressive Artists (Düsseldorf May 29–31, 1922), Lissitzky and Ehrenburg rejected the "subjective mystical world view" and instead promoted "the universal— unambiguous—real" that was "objective like science and constructive like Nature."[16] An "International Faction of Constructivists" signed a manifesto that protested "against the predominance of subjectivity in art and against the arbitrariness of lyrical values." In its stead, they wanted to establish "a new principle of creation based on the systematic organization of the means of expression and producing an art that is universally comprehensible."[17] The Düsseldorf congress was a key event for forging an international axis of Constructivism (*KI: Konstruktivistische Internationale*), whose founding manifesto promoted the concept of a rationally thinking and logically planning artist, who worked collectively, employed universal means of expression, and produced works that had a positive relationship to life in its entirety.[18]

Also the Dadaists developed an increasing sympathy with the aims of Constructivism.[19] Many of them realized that as a pure protest the movement had outlived its usefulness and had become an anachronism. The balance between anti-art and art, which had already been an important feature of their activities (see above, pp. 166–168), had more and more tilted toward the latter. In 1924, Van Doesburg declared categorically: "The epoch of destruction has come to an end. A new epoch has begun: the great epoch of construction."[20]

But where were the Constructivists going to find their new aesthetic principles? Clearly not in nineteenth-century values of representation. The Futurist artist Enrico Prampolini had proposed, in *Pure Painting* and *A New Art? Absolute Construction of Noise in Motion,*[21] "constructions" entirely derived from the *intrinsic* values of the material. The Dadaists had used in their collages *objets trouvés* (found objects) as material to define the aesthetic qualities of the work of art. Dada art of the later period was less determined by the desire to destroy the old forms than to explore the new elementary language that Ball had already spoken of in 1916. In 1921, Hausmann and Arp joined Puni and Moholy-Nagy in a "Call for an Elementary Art," in which they demanded that art has to be "created out of its own means."[22] This was the beginning of *Materialästhetik*, an aesthetics derived from the material qualities of its constituent components, which dominated artistic debates over the next ten years and was of major significance in the theatre as well.

THE BAUHAUS

The most important institution to spread the ideas of Constructivism among the young generation of western Europe was the Bauhaus. It had been founded in March 1919 by Walter Gropius and a group of like-minded artists and craftsmen, as a bold experiment that united the former Grand-Ducal School of Arts and Craft in Weimar (which had been closed during the war) with the Saxon Academy of Art. Their aim was to reform art education by bringing together different artistic disciplines and to overcome the divide that traditionally separated the arts from the crafts. The name "Bauhaus" created an associative link to the medieval "Bauhütte," a cooperative association between the various crafts required for the construction of major edifices such as cathedrals and castles. This symbol of the interaction between different arts and crafts inspired Gropius to write in his first Bauhaus manifesto:

> Today the arts exist in isolation, from which they can be rescued only through the conscious, cooperative effort of all craftsmen. Architects, painters, and sculptors must recognize anew and learn to grasp the composite character of a building. . . . The ultimate, if distant, aim of the Bauhaus is the unified work of art.[23]

The principal aims of the Bauhaus that transpire from this and other publications were:

- to overcome the divide between artist and craftsman, between fine arts and applied arts
- to reunify the artistic disciplines in a Total Work of Art
- to close the divide between teacher and pupil through collective working methods in workshops
- to reform society through a new concept of artistic creation

During its first phase in Weimar, the Bauhaus was led by a group of artists who had been politically active in the November Revolution and who pursued a program of renewal and social reform based on Expressionist principles. But with the famous *rappel à l'ordre* and the emerging trend toward a New Sobriety, the artistic and political orientation of the school's founding fathers became an anachronism and made them loose their appeal to young students. When, in September 1922, the KI met in Weimar, the attitude of the group (which had among its participants Van Doesburg, Lissitzky, Moholy-Nagy, Richter, Tzara, Arp, and Schwitters) toward the still Expressionist orientation of the Bauhaus was derogatory and condescending: "The Bauhaus is an hotel for invalid artists; many suffer from Mazdaznan illness of the tongue and hi-tech Expressionism."[24] However, the year 1922 was in many ways a transition period for the Bauhaus and the latest artistic developments did not pass it unnoticed. A group of some 15 loosely organized Constructivists (the KURI group under the direction of Farkas Molnár[25]) had been founded in December 1921 and was given reinforcement by Van Doesburg's De Stijl course held in Weimar from March 8, to July 8, 1922.[26] In October 1922, Itten handed in his resignation and was replaced, in March 1923, by Moholy-Nagy. In the stage workshop, Schlemmer succeeded Schreyer, and at the summer exhibition of 1923, the theme of "Art and Technology—A New Unity" served as an indicator that the transformation of the Bauhaus into a Constructivist institution was taking shape.

Between 1922 and 1925, the Bauhaus remodeled its curriculum and based it on principles that came close to those of the Constructivists at INKhUK. Increased contacts with industry brought in new commissions and a closer contact with the requirements of a democratic society recovering from the devastations of World War I. The fundamental guideline of the teaching program at the Bauhaus was to combine theoretical enquiry with practical experimentation. After deconstructing a work of art and stripping it down to its basic components, these constituent parts were then reassembled according to the principles of *elementare Gestaltung* and *Materialästhetik*. Initial instruction was carried out in a foundation course that bore much resemblance to the Basic Course at the VKhUTEMAS. Students were taught to recognize and analyze the elementary components of all art forms, to understand their material characteristics, and to investigate how the material affected the artistic forms derived from it. Successful completion of the six-month probation period (twelve months as of 1925) in the foundation course allowed them to enroll for training with a chosen master in one of the workshops disciplines. This involved:

- practical tuition: construction of objects supervised by master craftsmen specializing in mural painting, woodcarving, stonemasonry, metalwork, cabinet making, weaving, printing, and bookbinding;
- notation: drawing, painting, and sculpting as basic forms and communication, complementing verbal and written explanations; and
- theory: art history, composition, structural analysis, material science, anatomy, chemistry, and optics.

Each workshop was run in tandem by an artist (Master of Form) and a craftsman (Workshop Master), who taught the students the intellectual concepts and practical skills of their given discipline. In the course of their studies at the Bauhaus, students could progress from apprentice via journeyman to junior master. After the foundation course, they were admitted to the vocational courses on a trial period. If they proved suitable, they signed an apprenticeship agreement and enrolled for a minimum period of one year. The maximum stay at the Bauhaus was four years. Depending on available space and consent from the Workshop Master, students were allowed to change direction.[27] This, together with the foundation course, gave students an astounding versatility. In the 14 years of its existence, the Bauhaus taught some 1,250 students, many of whom made a major contribution to artistic developments in the twentieth century.

CHRONOLOGY 5.1:   RUSSIAN CONSTRUCTIVISM

March 13, 1920	First meeting of the collective Presidium at INKhUK chaired by Kandinsky
November 23, 1920	General Working Group of Objective Analysis founded at INKhUK
January 27, 1921	Kandinsky resigns from his post at INKhUK
February 4, 1921	Rodchenko appointed president of INKhUK
March 18, 1921	First Working Group of Constructivists founded at INKhUK
September 18–	5+5=25 Exhibition held in Moscow. The five works each
October 20, 1921	by five artists (Stepanova, Vesnin, Rodchenko, Popova, and Exter) were a culmination of the early phase of Constructivism in Russia
December 1921	Kandinsky leaves Russia for Germany, where on January 16, 1922 he is appointed Master of Form at the Bauhaus.
December 22, 1921	Stepanova's talk "On Constructivism" at INKhUK
February 4, 1922	G. and V. Stenberg and Medunetskii present a paper entitled "Constructivism" at INKhUK
February 8, 1922	Tairov's *Phèdre* designed by Alexandr Vesnin at the Kamerny Theatre
March 1922	First number of *Veshch—Gegenstand—Objet*
April 25, 1922	Meyerhold's *The Magnanimous Cuckold*, with designs by Popova, at the former Zon Theatre, reopened under the name The Actor's Theatre
October 15, 1922	First Russian Exhibition opens at Galerie van Diemen in Berlin
November 24, 1922	Meyerhold's *Tarelkin's Death* designed by Stepanova at the Zon Theatre (The Actor's Theatre)
March 4, 1923	Meyerhold's *Earth in Turmoil* (*Earth Rampant*) at The Meyerhold Theatre, adapted by Sergej Tretyakov from Marcel Martinet's *La Nuit*, designed by Popova
March 6–23, 1923	Kamerny Theatre at the Théâtre des Champs Élysées with a repertoire that includes *Phèdre*, subsequently taken on tour to Germany and Austria (April–August 1925) and Europe and South America (March–August 1930)
March 1923	First number of *LEF*
May 11, 13, 30, 1923	Khlebnikov's *Zangezi*, directed and designed by Tatlin, at the Experimental Amateur Theatre of the Museum of Artistic Culture in Petrograd
November 8, 1923	Meyerhold's *Lake Lyul* at the Theatre of Revolution, designed by Viktor Shestakov
December 6, 1923	Tairov's *The Man who Was Thursday* at the Kamerny Theatre, designed by Alexandr Vesnin

CONSTRUCTIVIST THEATRE IN RUSSIA

In the first decade after World War I, European theatre underwent a profound transformation and began to adopt many ideas and techniques first developed by the Expressionists, Futurists, and Cubists. Theatre began to liberate itself from the tyranny of the playwright and the scene painter. Actors and directors rediscovered the fundamental elements of the theatrical act— the physicality of the actor, the director as an arranger of dramatic material, the designer as a constructor of sets and scenic spaces. This trend was less obvious in the commercially run, private theatres of the period (although many attempts were made here to show a decidedly "modern" face and to adopt elements from the avant-garde that had acquired a fashionable status), but could be widely encountered in the State-subsidized theatres of Russia and Germany.

In Russia, Meyerhold prepared the birth of a new theatricality with his innovative productions of the 1910s and, possibly more significantly, the new training methods developed in his studio. When this new breed of actors joined forces with the young artists from INKhUK, a stimulating environment for exciting lines of experimentation came into existence. The new theatrical arts of Soviet Russia, which until 1921 had been strongly influenced by Cubo-Futurist aesthetics, came after 1922 under the control of the Constructivists, who applied the basic principle of "construction as the suitable organization of material elements"[28] to the stage event and shaped it according to the tenets of *faktura, tektonika,* and *konstruktsia.* The conscious use of the mechanical functions of the body and of the material characteristics of the other stage components resulted in works that were seen to be "not a representation of life, but an organization of the exemplary and significant aspects of life."[29] With this approach, they purged the theatre of its naturalistic clutter and aesthetic ornaments and brought to a conclusion the rejuvenating process that Cubo-Futurism had set in motion in the 1910s.

In the first decade after the October Revolution, Russia had no less than 3,000 professional theatre organizations, 20,000 amateur theatre clubs, and 40 theatre journals. The government's new subvention policies facilitated free or cheap access to performances, and the experimental theatres, due to the prorevolutionary sentiments of its Left-wing leaders, found themselves propelled into positions of artistic preeminence. With the appointment of Meyerhold to the directorship of the Theatre Department in the People's Commissariat of Education (1920), the theatrical avant-garde suddenly assumed control and power. The resulting *Teatralny oktyabr* as an artistic equivalent to the political October Revolution unleashed a "civil war" in theatrical institutions.

Whereas before, the avant-garde could only *declare* the old theatrical arts to be outdated, its shift from a position of opposition to one of authority gave it an opportunity to fight the "old masters" in their "nests of reaction" with concerted means of propaganda and fiscal might.

Many of the artists who were responsible for the theatrical revolution were young men and women in their mid- to late twenties. Their boldness, energy, and radicalism often clashed with the more balanced and moderate views of Commissar Lunacharsky, who propagated the need to "maintain the traditional theatres" and "preserve whatever is old and good."[30] Nonetheless, for a while the artistic revolutionaries were furnished with an apparatus that allowed them to put onstage experimental productions that were an artistic equivalent to the revolution undertaken by the Bolsheviks in the political domain. Whereas in Germany the theatrical avant-garde remained entrenched in the margins of the cultural scene, in Russia they took charge of major playhouses and employed all their resources (small to begin with, but increasing in line with the box-office takings) for the mounting of large-scale spectacles.

Meyerhold's First Constructivist Productions

Popular mythology has it that Constructivism entered Russian theatre when Meyerhold visited the 5+5=25 exhibition in October 1921. He was so impressed with the works on display that he asked Popova to design his next show, Crommelynck's *Le Cocu Magnifique*.[31] This unexpected marriage of Constructivism and the Soviet theatre caused quite a stir in Moscow art circles. The productionist branch of the Constructivists had rejected the theatre together with all other arts as useless or even detrimental to the development of a utilitarian, proletarian culture. "Abandon stages and theatrical performances," Boris Arvatov had exhorted actors and directors. "Go into life and re-educate yourselves and others. Be the engineers, the orchestrators of everyday life."[32] Even revolutionary theatre as an equivalent to the political revolution of 1917 was categorized as detrimental to proletarian class consciousness: "It is preposterous for Constructivism, as the formal expression of intellectual and material production, to participate in either the performance of bucolic pastorals or new productions of the theatrical October Revolution."[33] Nonetheless, one Constructivist after another entered the bourgeois factory of make-believe and transformed it into a laboratory of social and aesthetic construction. While Tatlin's tower, Vesnin's Palace of Labor or Rodchenko's Workers' Club never made it beyond the drawing board or model stage, Constructivist theatre productions—which clearly had the advantage of costing much less than an apartment block or cultural center—realized, in an experimental manner, a fusion of the artistic media in a total work of art that could lay claim to offering a model for real life.

The working relationship between Meyerhold and Popova began a good year before they presented the fruits of the collaboration in *The Magnanimous Cuckold*. While in post as head of the Theatre Department of NARCOMPROS, Meyerhold had sought to open an acting school attached to his theatre. With his demission in February 1921 this became impossible, but in autumn 1921 he was appointed director of a newly formed State Graduate Theatre Workshop (GVYTM). It was briefly incorporated into the GITIS (State Institute of Theatrical Arts) and, in 1923, broke away to form the Meyerhold State Experimental Theatre Workshop as an integral part of his theatre. The State Graduate Workshop of Theatre had some 100 students, and many of these were introduced by Meyerhold to the principles of Biomechanics and by Popova to scenic Constructivism.[34] The technique of Biomechanics[35] was a "scientific" organization of the actor's body based on Constructivist principles:

> In art the constant concern is the organisation of raw material. Constructivism has forced the artist to become both artist and engineer. Art should be based on scientific principles; the entire creative act should be a conscious process. The art of the actor consists in organising his material: that is, in his capacity to utilise correctly his body's means of expression.[36]

The streamlined body purged of everything superfluous could operate in a highly efficient manner. Movements and gestures were consciously shaped to achieve universal rather than individualistic expression. The journal *Zrelishcha* called the technique "visual Taylorism in motion" and explained: "Biomechanics strives to create a man who has studied the mechanism of his construction, and is capable of mastering it in the ideal and of improving it. Modern man living under conditions of mechanization cannot but mechanize the motive elements of his organism."[37] Meyerhold also made frequent references to Frederick Winslow Taylor and his Russian disciple Aleksei Gastev in order to show that his scientific approach to actors' training met the demands of a mechanical-industrial age and was therefore much superior to Stanislavsky or Tairov's systems. Some of these claims were clearly exaggerated. Meyerhold's method was as much based on his pre-revolutionary work on commedia *lazzi* and Constant Benoît Coquelin's nineteenth-century acting manuals as it was on Taylorism and Behaviorism.[38] But in the period of Constructivism's greatest success it seemed appropriate to demonstrate that pre-revolutionary aesthetics of theatre had been thoroughly overcome.

Figure 5.1   Émile Verhaeren, *The Dawns*, directed by Meyerhold, design by Vladimir Dmitriev (1920). A first attempt at creating a Constructivist set devoid of naturalistic paraphernalia. A "lean" functionalism tailored toward the actor's needs eliminated the dogma of providing a time and place setting for a play.

Since the closure of the First Theatre of the RSFSR on September 6, 1921, Meyerhold had been without a playhouse. In February 1922, he moved with his students into the former Zon Theatre and reopened it under the name "The Actor's Theatre." In a symbolic "clearing out" action they emptied "the whole stage in the huge theatre of 'junk,' as the master put it. . . . A pillar of dust arose when the accumulated sets and stage furniture from decades of performance were thrown out in the courtyard. We simply tossed out the bourgeois theatre with all its crockery."[39]

Already in previous productions, Meyerhold had been a chief proponent of the battle against illusionism and aestheticism in the theatre. His attempts to revive the simple fit-up format of fairground booths and street theatre, of Italian *commedia dell'arte* and Russian *balagan*, had found reflection in productions such as *The Fairground Booth* (1906, 1914), *Columbine's Veil* (1910), *Don Juan* (1910), *Harlequin, the Marriage Broker* (1911), and *Masquerade* (1917).[40] In *The Dawns* (premièred November 7, 1920) (figure 5.1), the opening performance of the "Theatre October," he had renounced the principle of reproducing the time and place setting of a drama (in this case: Verhaeren's *Les Aubes*) and stripped the stage of all illusionistic paraphernalia.[41] A set of cubes, cylinders and triangles was lit by simple searchlights and served the actors, who wore no make-up, as a structural device from which they could exhort, chorus-like, the audience in direct addresses. This setting, which was variously referred to as Cubist or Futurist, was described by Meyerhold as "a first attempt at building Constructivist sets on the stage."[42] In a speech of 1920, he explained that they stripped down the play to its plot line and eliminated all "flabby material" that was merely literature: "Thus, this scenario, this skeleton of *The Dawns*, in losing its surplus weight, has developed a lean body." The same approach was taken to the stage set: "For us the art of manufacture is more important than any tediously pretty patterns and colors. What do we want with pleasing pictorial effects? What the *modern* spectator wants is the placard, the juxtaposition of the surfaces and shapes of *tangible materials*!"[43] In *Mystery-Bouffe* (premièred May 1, 1921), he again placed on stage an assembly of multileveled platforms interconnected by steps, and abolished the proscenium by making a ramp lead down into the auditorium. As one critic commented: "This is no 'temple' with its great myth of the 'mystery' of art. This is the new proletarian art."[44] It also convinced other critics that the time of illusionistic sets had definitely passed: "The theatre does not need painters' canvasses. This means that the theatre needs real space—not illusionary space; it does not need pictorial representations of objects but the materiality of objects."[45]

The production of *Mystery-Bouffe* was one of the last theatrical manifestations of Futurism in the Russian theatre. Constructivism turned out to be more in step with the new political trends. It also fitted in with the practical necessities of Meyerhold's young troupe, who intended to present their first production, Crommelynck's *The Magnanimous Cuckold*, in a variety of locations, not only theatres with a fully equipped stage apparatus. Also financial considerations spoke for the elimination of illusionistic sets and solid stage furniture. One can therefore assume that both economic and aesthetic reasons gave rise to the production's simple, functional, and utilitarian stage design. Its principal features were developed in teamwork by Meyerhold, Popova, Ivan Aksyonov, and Vladimir Lyutse, but the final shape was determined by Popova.[46] In a presentation of her concept at INKhUK on April 27, 1922, she outlined the key intentions behind her design as (a) "shifting the problem from an aesthetic to a productivist level"; (b) "organizing the material elements of the production . . . according to utilitarian and not formal-aesthetic criteria"; (c) "introducing material elements into the working process that would not only function as stage décor but also as active, kinetic components of the stage action"; (d) "creating costumes that serve equally

Figure 5.2   Fernand Crommelynck, *The Magnanimous Cuckold*, directed by Meyerhold, design by Popova (1922). This was the first truly successful demonstration of scenic Constructivism. The functionalist structure provided a "trampoline for the actor . . . without any pretence of decorative significance" (A. Gvozdev).

well as ordinary clothes and workshop attire . . . and eliminating the distinction between male and female clothes."[47]

The Magnanimous Cuckold (figure 5.2) was premièred at The Actor's Theatre on April 25, 1922 and derived its theatrical power not least from the combination of a new acting technique with a new principle of set construction.[48] Popova eliminated all reminiscence of the locations in Crommelynck's play and reduced the watermill setting to a "machine" that provided all components required for the performance (doors, windows, stairs, platforms, etc.). Like a structure in a playground, it did not mean anything but offered plenty of scope for physical actions carried out by the biomechanically trained performers ("A trampoline for the actor . . . without any pretence of decorative significance," it was called by the critic Aleksei Gvozdev[49]). The decentralized scaffold placed a number of elements in a nonhierarchical order. Decorative painted canvas as a means of representing other worlds had been relinquished in favor of a three-dimensional structure for the actors to operate in. Due to its kinetic quality, the set could also take on an active rôle in the dramatic action itself and assume functions that were on a par with those of the human actors. Reducing the specific denotations of an illusionistic set to a poly-semantic abstract skeleton, the construction offered the potential for creating a variety of meanings depending on how it was used by the actors. For example, the turning wheels and sails invited associations with a windmill. But they also commented on the action by moving at increased speed in moments of heightened tensions; or when Stella confronted the cowherd and slapped him in the face, the wheels began to turn in opposite directions. The set thereby assumed a catalyzing function for the actors and became a springboard for the spectators' power of imagination.

Placed on a bare stage with only a red brick wall at the back and lit by means of bright military searchlights, this set eschewed all associations of false theatricality. It was used to its maximum potential by actors clad in simple work overalls (*prozodezhda*, also designed by Popova) and wearing no make-up. This brought out the performers' joyous physicality and confident display of craftsmanship. The functionalist apparatus of the set joined forces with the biomechanically trained apparatus of the body, and both operated in harmony with each other like a compact machine. The whole ensemble turned into a "factory" of Constructivism, uniting in its mechanism "the material elements of theatre (dynamics of light, color, line, volume in general, and, in particular, that of the human body)."[50] However, in the discussion paper for her INKhUK colleagues, Popova admitted that her utilitarian intention had not been fully realized, as "the visual, farcical character of the stage action made it impossible for her to treat the whole thing like a shop-floor operation, and this endowed it with an essentially aesthetic character."[51]

On November 24, 1922, Meyerhold's production of *Tarelkin's Death* by Alexander Sukhovo-Kobylin, designed by Vera Stepanova, opened at the Zon Theatre.[52] Meyerhold's treatment of the play was typical of "Circusization" and "Eccentrism," a fashion made popular by the director Sergei Radlov and the Petrograd FEKS studio. *Tarelkin's* clowning and knockabout humor was very popular with audiences, but artistically it fell a stage behind what Meyerhold had achieved with *The Magnanimous Cuckold*. Vera Stepanova's designs were again decidedly Constructivist. The stage had been emptied of everything one would expect to find in a theatre: curtains, footlights, prompt-box, decorations, and the like. Instead, there were several mobile "acting instruments" that could be assembled in different forms according to the requirements of the scene. Stepanova described her intention in an interview with Aleksei Gan: "I wanted to produce . . . a total environment in which the living human material was to act."[53] Part of the action took place in a police station, and in reference to the brutal practices of Tsarist Russia, Stepanova constructed a machine that was half cage, half meat-mincer. The furniture consisted of folding chairs and tables, which had capricious lives of their own. They were all made from the same, standardized wooden slats, painted white, and looked like objects defined purely by their function. The costumes (simple work clothes decorated with geometric patterns of stripes and patches[54]) were meant to visually underline the actors' movements. Depending on how the groups positioned themselves on stage, the patterns formed a living Constructivist structure. But the shapeless, baggy material also made the actors' acrobatic movements look less impressive than they should have been.

In 1923, Meyerhold became the director of two playhouses: the remodeled Zon Theatre (now called Meyerhold Theatre) used for experimental productions, and the Theatre of the Revolution, used for large-scale productions of popular appeal. In the former venue, he mounted a spectacle originally intended for the fifth anniversary of the October Revolution. *Earth in Turmoil (Earth Rampant)* was adapted by Sergej Tretyakov from a verse drama by Marcel Martinet *La Nuit*[55] and was designed by Ljubov Popova in a manner that made it possible to take the production to open-air locations. It was premièred with some delay on March 4, 1923 as a revue of "numbers," each summed up in a slogan that was projected onto screens (this novel technique was one of the reasons why Brecht later called Tretyakov his "teacher"[56]). The theatre looked like an empty factory hall. Popova had renounced on any idea of aestheticism in her stage set and had constructed a system of open platforms, placed in front of the theatre's back wall and illuminated by searchlights. This Constructivist "machine" was supplemented by other machinery taken from real life: cars, motorcycles, a threshing machine, a field telephone, and the like. Over the stage hung a large gantry crane, and in one scene, an army lorry drove through the central gangway of the auditorium.[57] In a note on the stage set, Popova wrote that she had relinquished any aesthetic considerations and created a set that had only one function: to serve a propagandistic purpose. All props were taken from real life in order to comment on real life: the Red Army, the electrification and industrialization of the Soviet State, the mechanization of agriculture, the development of a transportation system, and so on. Her rôle as designer was merely "to select and combine the material elements of the production with the aim of accomplishing the most effective propaganda."[58] The use of projections together with Tretjakov's "Epic" montage of the scenes gave the production a strongly cinematographic feel and caused the reviewer of *Zrelishcha* to comment: "With this production, theatre has for the first time defeated cinema."[59]

Alexander Tairov Adopts the Constructivist Style

Ironically, this attempt to merge life and theatre by excluding any hint of aestheticization and incorporating real objects from everyday life into the production created a new type of realism,[60] which indirectly strengthened a development toward an aesthetic and representational type of Constructivism. The person largely responsible for giving this trend a major force was Meyerhold's antipode, Alexander Tairov. Through his collaborations with the designer Alexandra Exter, Tairov had prepared the ground for the advent of Constructivism in the theatre. *Famira Kifared* (1916), *Salome* (1917), and *Romeo and Juliet* (1921) had designs that relinquished all painted scenery and replaced it with solid three-dimensional constructions.[61] They have variously been described as "a triumphal parade of Cubism" (Rudnitsky[62]), "a triumph of Cubofuturism" (Ciofi degli Atti[63]), or "the first authentically 'constructivist' approach to the staging of a play" (Worrall[64]). Exter as a partisan of Cubism and Futurism[65] worked with plastic stylizations of geometric shapes and rhythmic arrangements of space, which were principally abstract in form but still fulfilled representational functions (e.g., an assembly of cubes and cones could provoke associations of a landscape with rocks and cypresses). She was a true scenic architect in the sense of Tairov's adage: "The theatre does not need the artist-painter but the artist-builder."[66] She constructed evocative spaces *inside of which* the actor could move (rather than painted prospects *against which* the actor would move). She also applied the same principles to costume design and created clothes that turned the actor into a mobile sculpture.

In 1922, Tairov moved a stage further from these "proto-Constructivist" productions of the Kamerny Theatre with his production of *Phèdre*, designed by Alexandr Vesnin.[67] This remarkable production was a kind of endpoint of a development that had begun with Craig and Appia's "reform stage" and now incorporated the latest research undertaken by the Constructivists. Vesnin produced a number of sketches, ranging from a fairly realistic representation of a ship on which the whole play was to be performed, to a totally abstract, Cubist rendering of volumes and platforms set at oblique angles. In the end, he opted for a semi-abstract version of the ship theme, with geometric planes, cutting angles, and allusions to riggings, sails, and a triangular stern-frame. A few monumental columns gave a vague indication of a palace façade. The design made no direct reference to classical Greece or Neoclassical France, thus complying with Tairov's principle, "the place of action is a prejudice which must be eliminated. . . . The only place of action in theatre is the stage." Nonetheless, the austere simplicity and geometric purity of Vesnin's stage bore a great deal of similarity with the mathematical harmonies of (Neo)classical architecture. The tilting stage floor with the three terraces descending into the auditorium gave the production a menacing quality, and the splashes of color (golden and crimson draperies against a light-blue backcloth) foreboded the tragic passions that propel the action to its cataclysmic end. Alisa Koonen, who played Phèdre, remembered: "The stage floor was lightly tilted, giving the impression of a pitching boat deck; the outlines of the sails and ropes added to this impression. In the background the sober and striking vastness of the sea was rendered by a remarkable stage backcloth. . . . The stage floor was divided on three levels. It is on this broken diagonal that Phèdre advances slowly in her first entrance on stage."[68] She wore a highly stylized, dark-red cloak and, like the other characters, a remarkable headdress that translated the already flamboyant helmets customary in ancient Greece into large, geometric shapes.[69] Stylized gestures added to the plasticity of the movements, and the simplicity of the multileveled planes gave the remarkably sculptured volumes of the actor's body a highly flexible kinesphere, which fully realized Vesnin's goal "to lay bare the actor and his movements."[70] The production was a resounding success and, according to Abram Efros, "the Chamber Theatre's most remarkable production. . . . It was 'classic avant-garde' in the true sense of the term."[71] When it was taken on tour to France and Germany, the reception was equally enthusiastic and set the tone for a popular fashion of Constructivist stage designs in European theatre.[72]

On December 6, 1923, the Kamerny Theatre opened with Tairov's adaptation of G. K. Chesterton's detective novel, *The Man who Was Thursday*, designed by Alexander Vesnin (figure 5.3).[73] In 1922–1923, many Constructivists adopted modern technology as a subject matter of the theatre and constructed "machines" that all had a great deal of similarity with each other. Chesterton's urban theme suggested to Vesnin a schematized city architecture. The small stage of the Kamerny only measured 6 × 8 meters and forced Tairov to employ the height of the theatre as well. Vesnin used the logic of an architectural order to fill the whole space of the stage with a construction that in a frontal view looked like the façade of a three-story modern building. But in this production, Vesnin was not only the architect and designer, but also the engineer of an amazing "machine" comprising of two lifts, one elevator, a crane, turning cogwheels, a drawbridge, a moving sidewalk with luminous advertisements, and so on. Platforms could be raised and moved and allowed the action to shift smoothly from one stage to another. The dynamic dimension was amplified by the actors' hectic style of movements and rhythmic, monotone voices, the ceaseless activities in various parts of the architecture, and the mechanical billboard men who walked sporadically across the stage. The microcosm of this capitalist city sometimes gave the impression of an anthill, and actors had to be lit by spotlights to allow the audience to pick out the main action on stage.

Figure 5.3 Gilbert K. Chesterton, *The Man who Was Thursday*, directed by Tairov, design by Alexander Vesnin (1923). The theatre as a Constructivist machine reflected on the "mechanical" life in Capitalist countries.

Tatlin's Scenic Architecture and its Popular
Counterparts of 1923

Vladimir Tatlin, the most important father figure of Constructivism, had come to the theatre at the very beginning of his artistic career. His early stage designs were strongly influenced by Futurism,[74] but in 1913–1915 he began to explore the spatial implications of Cubism and arrived at proto-Constructivist build-ups of the whole stage. In Glinka's *A Life for the Czar* (*Ivan Susanin*, 1913), he worked with intersecting planes at different levels, geometric shapes, stairs, and platforms. In *The Flying Dutchman* (1915–1918), he rejected a painterly treatment of Wagner's themes and envisaged building an enormous ship with intersecting decks, tilting planes, and tall masts and sails that gave the whole stage, including its height, a dynamic rhythm.[75] None of these sets were ever built, but they may have been seen by Meyerhold, who considered Tatlin as designer for *Mystery-Bouffe* and *The Dawns*[76] Tatlin was working at that time with Khlebnikov on a production of *Zangezi*, which had to be postponed due to Khlebnikov's death in 1922.[77] The same year, Tatlin established the Petrograd Museum of Artistic Culture as an equivalent institution to INKhUK in Moscow, and it was here, as part of an anniversary celebration dedicated to Khlebnikov's memory, that *Zangezi* was given three performances on May 11, 13, and 30, 1923. Tatlin attempted to find a "material construction" that would correspond to Khlebnikov's "architecture made of words," a dream about the future of humankind written in *Zaum* style.[78] For this purpose, he returned to the idea of a ship with masts and sails, which in the model were reduced to a mast with a few ropes, placed center stage right, and some irregularly shaped cloths hung from an obtusely angled pole. The actual construction[79] resembled Tatlin's corner reliefs: a cylinder and several blocks served as steps and platforms that led up to the tower where Zangezi, played by Tatlin himself, delivered his speeches (see figure 5.4). Several narrators gave an expressive reading of the other texts, which were also written out on long scrolls so that the audience could participate in the recitation. A long wooden triangle leaned from a downstage left position across the stage against the top of the tower. Apparently, 14 different surface textures were chosen to correspond to the textures of the sounds. Two spotlights were used to focus attention on key scenes, to throw dynamic shadows, and to enhance the textures of the materials. A photograph of the performance shows that Tatlin also incorporated the architectural features of the assembly hall in which the poem was performed. Unfortunately, no information is available on the machines designed to move in parallel to the action and to fuse with it. Apparently, a breakdown of the cable system rendered them

Figure 5.4 Velimir Khlebnikov's *Zangezi* directed, designed, and performed by Vladimir Tatlin at the Petrograd Museum of Artistic Culture (1923). Tatlin built a "material construction" corresponding to Khlebnikov's "architecture made of words," written in *Zaum* style. This "astral language" was accompanied by music specially written by M. S. Druskin.

wholly ineffectual. The performers were taken from the Experimental Amateur Theatre Group of the Museum of Artistic Culture in Petrograd, as Tatlin believed that the poem was too advanced for professional actors trained in the conventional theatre. The "astral language" of the poem was accompanied by music specially written by Mikhail Seminovich Druskin.

In the course of 1923, the Moscow studio theatres increasingly offered cabaret and music-hall material for a NEPmen audience or reverted to dramatic offerings of an increasingly conventional type. The agit-prop and political-rally types of shows, which even inveterate party members had grown tired of, gave way to entertainment with a political tinge, and then to pure entertainment of a predominantly Western, "jazz-age" variety. Meyerhold had to steer a careful course between Scylla and Charybdis when he produced *Lake Lyul*, a romantic melodrama by the young Soviet dramatist Aleksei Faiko, designed by Viktor Shestakov and premièred on November 8, 1923 at the Theatre of Revolution.[80] He produced, on the one hand, a melodramatic adventure yarn with elements of a detective story, pseudo-Expressionist "Big-City" horrors, capitalist bacchanalia, and so forth, and at the same time offered a critique of exactly those elements the NEPmen in the audience may have found most attractive. The leading character's search for head-spinning earthly pleasures and the leading lady's seductive lures (played by a stunning Ida Ormond in decadent and luxurious attires in the latest Western style) were presented in a dynamic action-film manner that had "the brash coherence of a motion picture" and caused critics to marvel at "Meyerhold's techniques of cinema montage."[81] Yet at the same time, what superficially looked like the NEPmen's dream of American-style High Life was cloaked in a "flavor of doom, of disaster looming over the inhabitants of this imaginary center of capitalist culture," as the critic Boris Alpers wrote.[82]

Viktor Shestakov's set design bore such a remarkable similarity to Vesnin's *Man who Was Thursday* that it provoked a fierce argument between the two artists as to who had copied whom. As Vesnin completed his model in May 1923, that is, four months before *Lake Lyul* opened, the charge of plagiarism was certainly unfounded.[83] In fact, it may have been Vesnin who inspired Popova to the first such machines used in *The Magnanimous Cuckold*, as they collaborated in spring 1921 on a mass spectacle for the third Comintern congress, the unperformed *Struggle and Victory*, which was to employ openwork iron constructions, transmission wheels, tent-riggings, flying buttresses, skeletal bridges, and so on.[84] Shestakov's design for *Lake Lyul* consisted of a construction of platforms arranged on three levels and interconnected by a lift that allowed the action to transfer smoothly from one location to another.

It was described by the author in the following words:

> The entire monumental back wall of the theater was exposed, metal fittings stuck out and cables and wires hung challengingly. The center stage was occupied by a three-story construction with corridors leading into the back, with cages, ladders, platforms, and elevators running not only vertically but horizontally. Slides with signs and advertisements were projected, silver screens shone from within. In contrast, against this background flickered the colored spots of rather unusual costumes.[85]

What in the model looked like a plain and sober system of steps, ladders, and platforms, was turned by the actors into a multifaceted urban landscape, where scenes could be switched in montage-fashion from one location to the other, or even played simultaneously. Although the set was not representational in itself, it still conjured up a Western city, mainly due to the hectic movements, advertising hoardings, and street noises.

As various contemporary and modern critics have observed, by the end of 1923, Constructivism made the transition from an artistic *method*, which was symbolic of the new order emerging from the chaos and turmoil of the Revolution, to a new and fashionable *style*. After 1923, it was no longer the INKhUK purists who determined the Constructivist trend in the theatre, but a whole phalanx of designers operating with a functionalist aesthetics that reduced illusionist or decorative sets into simple architectural structures. Such utilitarian "workplaces" became popular not only in Russia, but also in West-European countries, with a particularly strong tradition emerging in Germany.

THEATRE AT THE BAUHAUS

The Bauhaus, established under entirely different social and political circumstances from the VKhUTEMAS, played a distinguished rôle in consolidating a Constructivist tradition in western Europe. Soon after the school's inception, a stage workshop was formed to complement the institution's interdisciplinary curriculum. Given that the architecture workshop, which had been promised in the foundation manifesto of April 1919, did not come into existence until 1927, theatre as an art that combined several disciplines could take over some of its functions. It not only symbolized the syncretistic orientation of the Bauhaus, but also offered practical fields of exploration for the collaboration of artists of different backgrounds and artistic inclinations.

CHRONOLOGY 5.2:   GERMAN CONSTRUCTIVISM AND THE BAUHAUS

December 7, 1916	First public performance of the early version of Schlemmer's *Das Triadische Ballett* in Stuttgart
March 1919	The government of Saxony approves the foundation of the Staatliches Bauhaus in Weimar
April 1, 1919	Gropius appointed director of the Bauhaus. Later in the month he publishes the Program of the Bauhaus
November 24, 1920	Schlemmer accepts appointment at the Bauhaus, where he is put in charge of the mural workshop as of January 1, 1921. On March 15, 1921, he becomes Master of Form at the stonemasonry workshop
October 1, 1921	Lothar Schreyer appointed director of the stage workshop at the Bauhaus
December 1921	Kandinsky leaves Russia for Germany, where on January 16, 1922 he is appointed Master of Form at the Bauhaus. In June 1922, he moves to Weimar and takes over the direction of the mural workshop
March 1922	First number of *Veshch—Gegenstand—Objet*
March 8 to July 8, 1922	Van Doesburg's De Stijl course in Weimar
May 29–31, 1922	First congress of the International Union of Progressive Artists in Düsseldorf
September 25–27, 1922	Congress of the Constructivist Internationale in Weimar
September 30, 1922	Première of Schlemmer's *Das Triadische Ballett* at Württembergisches Landestheater Stuttgart
October 4, 1922	Itten hands in his resignation and leaves the Bauhaus in March 1923
October 15, 1922	First Russian Exhibition opens at Galerie van Diemen in Berlin
February 17, 1923	Abortive performance of Schreyer's *Mondspiel*, leading to his resignation on March 5
March 1923	Schlemmer becomes provisional director of the stage workshop
March 31, 1923	Moholy-Nagy appointed at Bauhaus to replace Itten on the foundation course. He works initially at the metal workshop and in October 1923 takes over the remodelled foundation course, now extended to one year and partly taught by Kandinsky and Itten
July 1923	First number of *G: Zeitschrift für elementare Gestaltung*
August 15– September 30, 1923	Bauhaus Week with exhibition of works from all workshops

August 16, 1923	Schlemmer's *Das Triadische Ballett* at the National Theatre in Weimar; on August 25–26, at the Jahresschau in Dresden; subsequently on tour to Hanover, Celle, Hamburg, and Bremen
August 17, 1923	*The Mechanical Cabaret* at the Municipal Theatre Jena. Performances include Schlemmer's *Figurales Kabinett*, Schwerdtfeger's *Reflektorisches Lichtspiel*, and Schmidt/Telscher's *Mechanisches Ballett*
October 1923	With the new semester, Schlemmer, becomes director of the Bauhaus stage workshop
April 29, 1924	Bauhaus Festival at "Ilmschlößchen" with performances of Schmidt/Telscher's *Mechanisches Ballett*, Schmidt's *Mann am Schaltbrett*, Schawinsky's *Circus*, and Bogler's *Rokokokokotte*
September 1924	Performances of Schmidt/Telscher's *Mechanisches Ballett* in Berlin
September 24, 1924	Opening of International Exhibition of New Theatre Technology in Vienna, organized by Friedrich Kiesler, with several Bauhaus contributions
November 29, 1924	Fifth Anniversary Festival of Bauhaus with performances of Schmidt/Telscher's *Mechanisches Ballett*
December 26, 1924	Bauhaus staff tender their resignation with effect from April 1, 1925
March 24, 1925	The Bauhaus is integrated into the School of Arts, Crafts and Trade in Dessau
April–October 1925	Exposition Internationale des Arts Décoratifs et Industriels Modernes in Paris
June 1925	Schlemmer is offered a teaching post at the new Bauhaus in Dessau, to be furnished with a studio theatre, which he accepts in September 1925
October 14, 1925	Teaching starts at the new Bauhaus in Dessau, with Schlemmer as director of the theatre workshop
February 27–March 15, 1926	International Theatre Exposition in New York, organized by Friedrich Kiesler and Jane Heap
March 20, 1926	White Festival in Dessau, with performance of Schlemmer's *Salonstück*, a section of *Das Triadische Ballett*, and scenes from Schawinsky's *Feminine Repetition*
July 1926	Performances of *Das Triadische Ballett* at Donaueschingen Festival, then in Frankfurt/M and Berlin
December 6, 1926	Formal opening of the new Bauhaus building in Dessau, containing a small studio theatre designed by Schlemmer. The stage workshop performs six pieces during the opening celebrations: Schlemmer's *Raumtanz, Formtanz, Gestentanz, Lichtspiel*, and *Musikalischer Clown*, and a collective work, *Circus*
March 16, 1927	Bauhaus stage workshop perform a series of scenic studies to the Friends of the Bauhaus

May–September 1927	Bauhaus stage workshop presents several designs at the German Theatre Exhibition in Magdeburg. Schlemmer edits for this occasion a special issue of the Bauhaus magazine dedicated to theatre. Plans to perform some Bauhaus dances at the First German Dance Congress in Magdeburg (June 21–24) do not come to fruition
July 9, 1927	Bauhaus stage workshop, supplemented by three professional dancers and actors, performs a program of 12 dances and mimes in Dessau, including excerpts from *Das Triadische Ballett* and new versions of *Gestentanz*, *Musikalischer Clown*, and *Das Figurale Kabinett*
February 4, 1928	Gropius resigns from his post as director of the Bauhaus and leaves Dessau on March 24, 1928. On April 1, 1928, Hannes Meyer is appointed new director.
February 21, 1928	Bauhaus stage workshop and a professional dancer perform Schlemmer's *Illusionstanz* and Schawinsky's *Olga Olga* in Dessau
April 4 and 11, 1928	Kandinsky's *Pictures at an Exhibition* at Friedrich-Theater Dessau
June 25, 1928	Bauhaus stage workshop performs *Stäbetanz*, *Baukastenspiele*, *Gliedertanz*, and *Gestentanz* at the Dance Congress in Essen
July 7, 1928	Bauhaus stage workshop performs at their studio theatre *Stäbetanz*, *Maskenchor*, *Bühnenmechanik*, *Musikalischer Clown*, *Schwarz-Weiß-Trio*, and *Farbtanz*
February 9, 1929	Metallic Festival at the Bauhaus, with performances of *Musikalischer Clown*, *Sketsch*, *A-B-C-Bau*, *Frauentanz*, *Kulissentanz*, *Metalltanz* and *Glastanz*
March 3–April 30, 1929	Bauhaus stage workshop performs 12 dances at Volksbühne Berlin and goes on tour to Breslau, Frankfurt/M, Stuttgart, and Bâle
April 1929	The new leadership at the Bauhaus opposes Schlemmer's theatre work. In July 1929, he accepts a professorship at Breslau Academy of Arts
August 1, 1930	Hannes Meyer has his contract terminated by the Mayor of Dessau and is replaced, on August 5, by Mies van der Rohe
October 1, 1932	Discharge of the entire teaching staff of the Bauhaus on instigation of the NSDAP
October 18, 1932	Opening of the Berlin Bauhaus, which is closed by the Gestapo on April 11, 1933

"A yearning for synthesis dominates today's art and calls upon architecture to unite the disparate fields of endeavor. This yearning also reaches out for the theater, because the theater offers the promise of total art."[86]

Lothar Schreyer had been invited in summer 1921 to become director of the stage workshop, and he took up his post at the beginning of the winter semester of 1921. Gropius had been impressed by Schreyer's work in Berlin and Hamburg (see chapter 2) and in particular the score of *Crucifiction*. In *The Bauhaus Stage: First Communication*, of December 1922, Gropius formulated a program for the stage workshop and emphasized the need for a "purification and renewal of today's theatre" by combining (a) "a fundamental clarification of the manifold problems of the stage," and (b) "making manifest a metaphysical idea." He expanded on the former task by saying: "We research the discrete problems of space, body, movement, form, light, color and sound. We shape the movements of the organic and mechanical body, the vocal and musical sound, and build the stage space and the stage figures. Conscious application of the laws of mechanics, optics and acoustics is determining the form of our stage."[87] This statement attempted to brush over two very contradictory tendencies at the stage workshop: one represented by Schreyer's religiously motivated Expressionism, and the other by Schlemmer's Constructivist approach, which as yet played only a subservient rôle at the Bauhaus.[88] Given Schlemmer's teaching obligations in the stone-masonry and metal workshops and his preparatory work for the première of the *Triadic Ballet* in Stuttgart, Schreyer was in charge of the day-to-day running of the stage workshop and could give it his personal stamp. Admission was only possible after successful attendance of the foundation course, and as the workshop did not offer any vocational training for the theatre profession, it was frequented only by students officially registered in one of the other workshops.

Various reports of pupils and visiting friends indicate that only part of Schreyer's time was actually dedicated to teaching; otherwise he was occupied with editing religious literature, and writing poems inspired by the Baroque mystics Jakob Böhme and Angelus Silesius. There were only a few students attending his classes, with whom in the autumn of 1921 he staged his *Song of Mary*, a *Dance of Wind Spirits*, and a *Mercenary's Dance*.[89] Most of the practical studies were focused on Expressionist speech techniques, primitive dances accompanied by African rhythms, and experiments with colored lights. He worked with Hans Haffenrichter and Eva Weidemann on masked dances, which he planned to perform at the *Sturm* gallery in Berlin. Some of these ideas were incorporated into Schreyer's *Moon Play*, which his students worked on in the course of 1922. This lyrical and highly static drama dealt with Man's mystical redemption through the cosmic forces of a "heavenly virgin" and a "loving redeemer"[90] and was conceived as a "unified artwork of the stage as a living, material expression of the human participation in the divine revelation and the renewal of the cosmos."[91] The work was going to be premièred at the first Bauhaus Festival in August 1923, but several students, among them the Constructivist KURI group, made a petition to the Council of Masters on December 14, 1922 and demanded a trial performance at the Bauhaus. This took place on February 17, 1923 and found an extremely negative response. There was a clear feeling that Schreyer's artistic and spiritual orientation was at odds with the new direction of the Bauhaus. Soon afterwards he drew the necessary consequences and tendered his resignation.

The Weimar Stage Workshop under the Direction of Oskar Schlemmer

With the demise of the Expressionist heritage of the Bauhaus and the departure of Lothar Schreyer, Oskar Schlemmer became director of the theatre workshop, initially on a provisional basis (he continued to be Master of Form in the woodcarving and stonemasonry workshops until 1925; as of October 1923 he acted as official director of the stage workshop). Schreyer's "cultic theatre" was replaced with a Constructivist theatre, which focused on a rational analysis of basic elements of the stage and their synthesis according to materialist principles developed in the theoretical workshop classes. In spring 1923, Schlemmer submitted to the Council of Masters a program for the work of the stage workshop, which foresaw as the key fields of investigation the basic elements of stage production and design: space, form, color, sound, movement, and light. Preparation of designs and models was combined with practical classes in making costumes, stage constructions, masks, and festival décor. It also foresaw student placements on external productions of plays, operas, ballets, circus, variety shows, and films.[92]

In the following months, Schlemmer supervised the student productions that were going to be presented at the Bauhaus Festival in summer 1923. This debut of the stage workshop on August 17, 1923 at the Stadttheater Jena included five presentations, two of which were short cabaret numbers designed to fill the gap between the three main items on the program. The first was Kurt Schwerdtfeger and Ludwig Hirschfeld-Mack's *Reflective Light Play*.[93] Inspired by the experience of light–dark contrasts in film projections and grown out of experiments with a shadow play for the Bauhaus lantern festival of June 21, 1922, the two students developed a simple machine that allowed the projection of light through stencils and colored glass panes onto a transparent screen. The movement of the templates and the superimpositions of different colors followed a precise score and produced the effect of an abstract cinema, without the use of scrolls or colored celluloid (as the Futurists and Dadaists had employed) and always as live performances (and therefore not reproducible in a mechanical fashion). In a second stage, these kinetic compositions were complemented by music, which Hirschfeld-Mack composed and played on a piano, thus adding a further note to this entirely nonrepresentational color symphony, developed from the absolute qualities of the material used and from the complex correlations between optical and acoustical elements, form and color, pitch, and light intensity, musical and visual rhythm, and the like. Four of the light plays were performed in Weimar in 1923 and 1924 and taken on tour to Berlin (1924 and 1925), Vienna, Leipzig, Hanover (all 1925), Nuremberg (1926), Hamburg (1927), and various smaller cities in Germany. Reviews of these events indicate that the plays were either seen to be representative of the occult-spiritual tendency in abstract art, or of the integration of art and technology as propagated by the Bauhaus.

The second major piece of the festival was Kurt Schmidt and Georg Teltscher's *Mechanical Ballet*,[94] originally a "free" work created outside the stage workshop and in some ways conceived as an alternative to Schreyer's Expressionist predisposition. Schmidt had entered the mural workshop in 1921 and was active in the KURI group in 1921–1923. In the autumn of 1922, he started work on a construction that demonstrated the dynamic forces inherent in abstract forms and colors. In the course of the winter 1922–1923, Schmidt thought of ways of enhancing the dynamic aspects of his constructions by setting them in motion. He assembled some man-sized shapes made up of circles, triangles, squares, rectangles, and trapezoids, and painted them in the primary colors yellow, red, and blue. They could be fastened to a body with leather straps in a manner that made the person completely disappear behind them. Hans Heinz Stuckenschmidt provided a primitive musical accompaniment that corresponded to the geometric forms. What initially had been an improvised affair was later scored for violin and piano, and after two or three weeks of rehearsals, the 30-minute action of the *Mechanical Ballet* had been worked out.[95] Although the constructions bore some vague resemblance to human figures, the "dancers" themselves were invisible and only functioned as motors for the flat, cut-out shapes. The music proved to be essential for turning a nonrepresentational play of shapes and colors into a ballet depicting the relationship between man and machine in the industrial age. A heavy, machine-like rhythm formed the basis of the movements of three figures representing the forces of the mechanical world. The contrasting figure was danced by a young boy and had a much lighter touch, supported by jazz music. A fifth figure appeared in the final scene, where a red square danced a *pas de deux* with a blue square. The juxtapositions of human and mechanical elements, the ingenious narrative and psychology behind the "characters" gave the piece a suggestive charm and led to several repeat performances.

The last item on the program was a revised version of Schlemmer's *Figural Cabinet*, a mechanical theatre some 4 m high and 5 m wide. Some of the figures were mounted on a conveyer belt, others were hand-held and executed either in relief, quarter-relief, or as full-figure puppets. The plot was a mixture of sense and nonsense that combined man with machine, geometric shapes with archetypal fairground figures, and surrealist magic with cabaret satire.[96]

The stage workshop at the Weimar Bauhaus under the direction of Oskar Schlemmer developed only a handful of productions that were deemed advanced enough to be presented to the public. In spring 1924, they performed *Meta*, a short pantomime by Schlemmer, in which four actors mimed a series of actions, whose significant dramatic moments (e.g., "rise of tension," "passion," "conflict," "suspense," "climax") were announced on signboards. A longer program was presented at the Bauhaus Festival at the "Ilmschlößchen" on November 29, 1924, which included a repeat performance of Schmidt/ Telscher's *Mechanical Ballet* and three new pieces. Schmidt/Bogler's *Man at the Control Desk* was a mimed dance concerned again with the technological age and the danger of humans becoming trapped in a robotic existence. Two dancers in highly abstract, geometric costumes and devoid of any individual features carried out a number of actions, which were triggered and controlled by a de-humanized engineer. In the end, the characters staged a revolution against the "demon" at the control desk and let him vanish in a big explosion.[97] Bogler's *Rokokokokotte* reduced human figures to simple geometric shapes. Set in the eighteenth century, it translated extravagant court attire into exaggerated papier-mâché costumes, which were moved around on stage in a satire on the dictates of social manners. Schawinsky's *Circus* was equally humorous, with cut-out shapes of animal figures and geometric-plastic costumes given life by actors in a piece of "visual theatre, a realization of painting and constructions in motion."[98]

Schlemmer's diary notes from this period show that he was very unhappy about the limited financial resources allocated to his workshop. In autumn–winter 1924–1925, further cuts in the Bauhaus budget and a smear campaign from Right-wing circles in Thuringia pushed the Bauhaus into a serious economic and political crisis. A national support group, "Friends of the Bauhaus," was set up and brought in offers of a new home in Frankfurt am Main, Hagen, Mannheim, Darmstadt, and Dessau. At the end of 1924, the Bauhaus staff tendered their resignations and most of them moved to Dessau, where on March 24, 1925 they were integrated into the School of Arts, Crafts and Trade.

The Bauhaus in Dessau and the Maturation of
Constructivist Theatre

In his diary notes of spring 1925, Schlemmer reflected on Constructivism and welcomed its effort to replace illusionistic pictorial elements with real objects of clear and simple form. He saw the same trend toward simplification and abstraction in his own work, but he also noticed his desire to use these elements in order to portray and convey things and make them "the carrier of spiritual dynamics."[99] During the following months, he sought to apply the principles of Constructivism to the theatre. He drew up a detailed work schedule and curriculum for the new Bauhaus in Dessau. On July 13, he noted in his diary: "Theater! Music! My passion! . . . Free run for the imagination." And on July 14: "Painting or the stage! I really want very much to do 'metaphysical theater.' " However, negotiations for his "experimental theatre at the new Bauhaus" did not progress as expected. Schlemmer's successful stage designs of Carl Hauptmann's *The Disloyal Tsar*, Leonid Andreyev's *King Hunger*, and Friedrich Wolf's *Poor Conrad* brought him the offer of a post at the Volksbühne Berlin, which he declined.[100] The prospect of a teaching position at the Stuttgart Academy failed to materialize. So he stayed in Weimar until September 1925, when Gropius made him a final offer of a free apartment and a theatre under his exclusive control in the new Bauhaus building in Dessau.

The year 1925 brought a restructuring of the Bauhaus both in terms of personnel and curriculum. The dual leadership of workshops was given up in favor of a single professor, who was responsible for both practical and theoretical instruction. Many of them were "Young Masters," that is, former students from the Weimar years. Kandinsky and Klee gave lessons in painting and taught a compulsory theory course; Albers and Moholy-Nagy ran the Foundation Course, now extended to two semesters. Instruction in the fine arts was cut back in favor of "industrial form construction." The new purpose-built facilities, ready for the beginning of the academic year 1926–1927 and inaugurated in December 1926, indicated most clearly with its streamlined, functionalist style that the institution had come of age and had entered the Constructivist, industrial era. A newly founded "Bauhaus GmbH" as an incorporated society provided a vital feedback to industry, distributed novel design products on the general market, and helped to supplement the grant from the city council.

Following his official appointment as director of the stage workshop, Schlemmer developed plans for the new studio theatre, which finally became available in October 1926.[101] It was situated in a 13 m-wide wing between

the Studio and Workshop Buildings, wedged between the canteen and auditorium maximum. It was lifted 47 cm above ground and was 5 m high. The
main stage measured 8.48 m by 7.27 m, the two side-stages 3.30 m by
7.27 m. Movable walls, sliding doors, and curtains could be used to open up
or close off any of the adjacent rooms. Such flexibility opened up opportuni-
ties for overcoming the restrictions of a proscenium arch theatre (e.g., the
side-stages could be used as auditoria); but the lack of a proper trapdoor and
revolve, of a treadmill and an elevator imposed other limitations.[102]

Schlemmer also devised a new and more comprehensive curriculum[103]
that was taught in two classes: one for stage designers and technicians;
another for actors, dancers, and directors. Students were only admitted after
completion of the Foundation Course and had to commit themselves to a full
year's work in the workshop. There were three categories of students: (a) those
studying exclusively at the stage workshop,[104] (b) those studying at one of the
other workshops and taking theatre as a subsidiary subject; (c) occasional
students from outside the Bauhaus. The aim of the course was to explore the
fundamental laws of stage performances both on a theoretical and practical
level. The key areas of investigation were the problems of space, movement,
form, color, speech, and sound, and the applications of the laws of mechanics, geometry, and acoustics to the stage. This involved practical classes in
model-making, stage and costume design, making of props, masks, instruments and stage constructions, movement and voice training, improvisation,
and notation (choreography, scores, diagrams). Analysis of the elementary
forms of theatre was combined with the reintegration of these components in
a new synthesis by applying theatrical ideas and compositional principles.
Schlemmer called the basic elements "the theatrical ABC"[105] and sought to
create from them a new grammar of the stage, which would help to reform
the theatre of his age still rooted in illusionism and false naturalism.

This curriculum offered tuition in all technical and aesthetic aspects of
theatre, but it was not geared toward a specialized training of dancers, actors
or stage designers. Rather, it gave students a comprehensive introduction to
the fundamental aspects of theatrical creation and opportunity for experi-
menting with these components in order to arrive at new forms of theatrical
expression. The starting point of most classes was architectural space as a container for the movement of bodies and the oscillations of light and sound.
Then followed studies of the body of the actor as a volume in space, of the
mechanical laws of movement, and of the forces of gravity. They also explored
the psychological dimensions of space, for example, the impact of open or
closed space on the stage action. Students were given an introduction to theatre technology and the mechanical aspects of stage machinery. They carried

out experiments with marionettes and mechanical forms of theatre in order to gain insight into the organic components of the stage that could not be mechanized. Finally, the transformational aspects of theatre, the actor turning into a different being, theatre as a ludic game, the rôle of fantasy and imagination all formed part of the curriculum.

The first results of the new experiments of the stage workshop were demonstrated to the outside world at the White Festival in March 1926. Schlemmer danced sections of his *Triadic Ballet* and presented a satire on conventional salon comedies. More interesting were two scenes from Schawinsky's *Feminine Repetition*: an eccentric step dance with a Constructivist costume, and a machine-like dance of flat, geometric shapes in the style of the Tiller Girls.[106] As part of the opening celebrations of the new Bauhaus building in December 1926, the stage workshop performed six pieces: Schlemmer's *Space Dance, Form Dance, Light Play*, and *Gesture Dance*; Weininger's *Clown Game*, and a collective work, *Circus*. The first three of these were simple demonstrations of the spatial explorations of the stage by three dancers, of the use of props and geometric objects, and of the fundamental significance of light. *Gesture Dance* was a more complex dramatic piece and less abstract in form and meaning. It presented three "characters" clad in red, blue, and yellow costumes carrying out actions such as walking, sitting, lying, and using a vocal register and gestural language that tied in with their phlegmatic, sanguine, and choleric personality types. A scenario suggested a comic fusion of the formal elements in a synthesis, which illustrated Schlemmer's concept of "modern theatre as an organism that employs all technical and functional elements in order to create a platform for the free play of imagination and a corresponding poetic-dramatic style of representation."[107] Schlemmer's *Musical Clown* was presented by Andreas Weininger, who wore a costume similar to the Abstract One in *Triadic Ballet*, but furnished with all sorts of instruments and objects. Formal elements of Constructivist costume design were combined with comical and grotesque actions taken from circus and variety theatre, thus presenting a ludic form of theatre unencumbered by narrative and illusionistic representation.[108]

On March 16, 1927, the workshop performed a series of scenic studies to the Friends of the Bauhaus. The main theme was again the relationship between body space and scenic space, clarified here by floor grids and ropes stretched diagonally across the stage. Following this visualization of the "mathematics of dance" and the dimensions, proportions, and sensations of space,[109] the students demonstrated the transformation of the human body by means of masks and costumes. Other exercises dealt with the ordering of the space through flats and building blocks, the significance of light in the creation of scenic space, the quality of gesture and movement in relation to the handling of props and objects, and the creation of types and stereotypes by means of costumes.[110]

In all these projects developed under the aegis of Oskar Schlemmer, the actor did not treat the body as a medium of individual expression but rather as a mechanism interacting with space and props. The idea behind this approach was to demonstrate either formal characteristics of the body in motion, derived from the elementary components of form, color, space, and material, or basic behavioral patterns, which have social or metaphysical meaning. Schlemmer saw in the underlying formal unity of the dances a reflection of a higher order that dominates all Being. Others, who did not share his philosophical viewpoint, found aesthetic pleasure in the highly sophisticated play with pure forms, colors, and rhythms. As Schlemmer explained in an essay for *Schrifttanz*, the starting point of these dances could either be the body, with the dance developing gradually from the physical material, or a formal idea, with the dance being realized by means of the dancer's body. As the former point of departure was the norm in conventional dance, the Bauhaus workshop placed more emphasis on the latter, but still attempting to achieve a balance.[111] Schlemmer therefore rejected the epithet "mechanical theatre," which journalists and dance critics often attached to his theatre. Although workshop exercises and some of the demonstrations were primarily concerned with formal investigations, Schlemmer saw his dance performances to be intimately wound up with the social trends of the period:

> Our age is called the Technical Age. It could also be called the scientific or mathematical age. . . . Is it astonishing that these contemporary trends also find a reflection in the arts? We cannot close our eyes to the fact that we are surrounded by iron constructions, concrete buildings, cars, aeroplanes etc. and that this modern world of technology and inventions also affects our emotions and the arts, whether we like it or not.[112]

However, Schlemmer's metaphysical concerns, his love of the ludic aspects of theatre and his focus on "human and artificial figures"[113] was not shared by everybody at the Bauhaus. Although over the years a considerable number of students passed through the stage workshop, only few of them pursued their theatre studies for more than two semesters. On the other hand, there were students enrolled in other workshop disciplines with an interest in the theatre, who felt that the stage workshop under Oskar Schlemmer's direction did not offer them sufficient scope to develop their ideas and concepts. This, of course, meant that some regulations of the theatre curriculum became irrelevant, as there were not enough students to turn them into reality. One way out of this dilemma was to complement Bauhaus students with those of other institutions interested in the Constructivist orientation of the stage workshop. Already the statutes of 1925 had allowed the engagements of outside guests for performances; but in May 1927, Schlemmer suggested for the first time to separate the workshop group from a performance group, which would be able to travel to other theatres in Germany, represent the Bauhaus at festivals and congresses, and act as a go-between to the "industry."[114] However, as long as the theatre workshop eeked out a meager existence on the sidelines of the Bauhaus,[115] received a budget of only 25 Marks when the metal workshop, for example, was given 1,000 Marks,[116] and had a "shifting and unpredictable"[117] student population, Schlemmer could hardly produce more than small-scale dances with cheaply produced costumes and minimalist stage sets.

New Experiments with a Mechanical Form of Theatre

The budgetary restrictions of the stage workshop came to be felt particularly inhibiting to students, who took an interest in the domain of mechanical theatre (e.g., Joost Schmidt and Andreas Weininger) and who were only allowed to demonstrate their advanced ideas in the form of drawings and models rather than fully realized constructions. Quite a few of these frustrated students suggested that the lack of scope and opportunity in the stage workshop was not just caused by its limited financial and material resources, but also by the limited horizon of its director. This, of course, was not entirely justified, as Schlemmer had repeatedly demonstrated an interest in the mechanical aspects of the theatre.[118] But he always saw the mechanical and organic features of the human body and the stage in relation to each other and was opposed to reducing theatre to purely "mechanical effects . . . , which naturally suits the craftsmanship-oriented Bauhaus students better than acting."[119] Consequently, many of the Bauhaus projects in the field of mechanical theatre remained on the drawing board or were published in the books and journals issued by the school's directorate. Others were taken outside the Bauhaus and given realization in other institutions.

Moholy-Nagy belonged to the new generation of teachers appointed to the Bauhaus in order to strengthen the anti-Expressionist faction among staff and students. He took a particular interest in mechanical theatre and represented a thinking that was only partially explored in the stage workshop run by Schlemmer. Moholy-Nagy's Constructivism dates back to his Berlin years, when together with a small group of Hungarians (Kemény and Péri were his close collaborators then) he developed a project, which had its roots in Tatlin's spiral tower, Naum Gabo's kinetic constructions and Lissitzky's Prouns,[120] and led to a semi-theatrical "dynamic-constructive system of forces," where "the spectator, hitherto merely receptive in his contemplation of artworks, experiences a greater heightening of his powers than ever before and becomes an active factor of the unfolding forces."[121] This dynamic construction was not just a static assembly of material, but a conveyor of energy that embodied the dynamics of life and the vital principle of human and cosmic development. A first experimental demonstration of the interrelations among material, energy, and space combined film projections with a suspended sculpture moving freely in space. He published the design for another demonstration device, *Kinetic Constructive System* (dated 1922), in 1928. It was a huge spiral tower with an elevator, inner and outer path for moving up and down, creating an organism that interacted with the physical and intellectual forces of its users. This would foster their creative energies and aid in the "construction" of a dynamic (revolutionary) humanity.[122]

His *Mechanical Eccentricity*, dated 1922 and published in a pamphlet of 1924, was a "stage action in its purest form,"[123] in which the human being had been expelled from the stage in order occupy a place at the control board. The mechanical actions unrolled simultaneously on three stages to a musical accompaniment of a strictly mechanical nature: a lower one for large forms, a middle one for musical and noise instruments, and a top one with smaller forms. The back wall provided a fourth "stage" that was used for projections. The score foresaw actions such as rotating discs, colored grids shooting up and down, arrows hitting various mobile shapes that explode and give off phosphorescent light, wheels turning accompanied by thunder and lightning, and so on. Whereas the Russian Factory of the Eccentric Actor, which also dates from 1922, still employed human beings, Moholy-Nagy felt that human *Exzentrik* was inadequate. He therefore demanded "a precise and fully controlled organization of form and motion, intended to be a synthesis of dynamically contrasting phenomena (space, form, motion, sound, and light)."[124]

The *Light-Space-Modulator*, which Moholy-Nagy began in 1922 and completed in 1930, was a highly innovative intermedia construction situated somewhere between kinetic sculpture, abstract cinema, and mechanical theatre. In its final form, it consisted of a 120 cm by 120 cm big cube furnished with many colored light sources shining on a continually moving mechanism made from a three types of materials (transparent, semi-translucent, reflective metal) and shaped into disks, spirals, rods, and so on. Light projected onto the rotating shapes placed at oblique angles and on different planes passed through three metal screens and was reflected on surrounding walls. The movements of the construction and the lighting schemes are precisely programmed to produce an infinite variety of modulations (captured by Moholy-Nagy on the film, *Lightplay: Black-White-Gray*, 1930). It was, as Krisztina Passuth said, "the machine as spectacle"[125] and as such one of the most refined realizations of the Constructivist avant-garde. When it was exhibited in summer 1930 at the Werkbund Exhibition at the Grand Palais in Paris, it was named *Licht Requisit einer elektrische Bühne* (Light-Space Modulator for an Electric Stage), which indicates that at one point he had indeed intended it to be used in a theatrical context.[126]

Moholy-Nagy's concept of a Total Theatre[127] reintroduced the human being, but subjected the individual to the "great, dynamic-rhythmic form-giving process . . . which unites the accumulated means in compressed form." The human actor has an important rôle to play in the complex and manifold interrelationships of light, space, form, movement, sound, and color, but "solely as the bearer of functional elements organically appropriate to him." In such a "theatre of totality" the director has at his command a sophisticated technology, which emphasizes the contrast between human being and mechanical stage elements. To overcome the peep-show principle of the proscenium arch theatre and to close the gap between an active stage and a passive audience, he suggested to have suspended bridges and drawbridges run horizontally, vertically, and diagonally through the whole theatre; platforms would jut far into the auditorium and runways would connect the stage with the balcony, boxes, and dress circle; stage objects and scenery would be organized on various levels allowing both horizontal and vertical movement; film projections would add a further layer to the human and mechanical actions on stage; new lanterns and reflectors would create a dynamic space and give light a dramatic rôle of equal importance to the other media; an amplification system would allow sounds to issue from unexpected positions throughout the theatre; masks and costumes would be made from metal and synthetic substances and be capable of sudden transformations. This complex organism of manifold form-giving media would be unified in a harmonious whole that is given perfect equilibrium by a "new theatre maker" (*ein neuer Theatergestalter*).

Another attempt to unite stage and auditorium was the *U-Theater* by Farkas Molnár, one of Gropius's collaborators in the unofficial architecture studio. This U-shaped amphitheatre had three stages at the ground level, vaguely responding to the *platea*, *proscenium*, and *scaena* of classical times. A fourth stage was suspended over the proscenium. A cylindrical construction could lift people and equipment from the *platea* to a balcony, function as a lighting rig, and offer fixtures for aerial acrobatics. The audience was seated on five levels, with adjustable and rotating seats. The third-level balcony was connected via bridges to the hydraulic cylinder, allowing some mid-air actions to run across the whole theatre space.[128]

In 1926–1927, Andreas Weininger designed a Spherical Theatre[129] that modified several features of Moholy-Nagy and Molnár's concepts by giving the theatre a ball-like shape.[130] The audience was arranged on a dozen concentric rings along the inner wall of the sphere and had an all-encompassing view on "concentric, eccentric, multi-directional, mechanical spatial-stage events" in the center. Weininger's drawing indicated that the stage, which stretched from a circular floor to the apex of the sphere, had various platforms, spiral-like connections between different levels, and bridges running across to the balconies to allow the simultaneous actions to move in all directions. Thus it would "educate human beings through the creation of new rhythms of motion to new modes of spectatorship."

Best known of all the Utopian theatre designs developed at the Bauhaus is undoubtedly Walter Gropius's own Total Theatre of 1927.[131] Here the auditorium was arranged as a shell-like oval overlooking three fully flexible and transformable stages. The proscenium stage in the form of a disk was arranged on a platform that could be lowered and raised and turned by 180 degrees to fill up the center of the auditorium. Depending on the stage-configuration, the audience was seated in an amphitheatre or arena format. Scenes could shift in mid-action from one stage to another. Instead of constructed scenery, screens would be placed all around the auditorium and used for projections. Wherever spectators would be seated, they had a perfect view of all stage actions, which were to unfold in close physical proximity and mobilize their attention. This playhouse would have been "a great keyboard for light and space, so objective and adaptable in character that it would respond to any imaginable vision of a stage director: a flexible building, capable of transforming and refreshing the mind by its spatial impact alone."[132]

Like the great architectural plans for an advanced, electromechanical theatre, many of the small-scale projects of a mechanical stage show, which developed in parallel to them and were partly inspired by them, remained unrealized. Some of them were at least presented in Bauhaus publications or exhibitions, and it is from those that I have selected three for a brief discussion.

Weininger's *Mechanical Stage Revue* of 1926–1927[133] combined the author's early Bauhaus studies with his experiences as a cabaret performer in Hamburg (see figure 5.5). According to his testimony, Schlemmer never took much of an interest in this work, but Kandinsky, who was then working on *Pictures at an Exhibition*, scrutinized the plans in great detail and inquired

Figure 5.5   Andor Weininger, *Mechanical Stage Revue* (1926). Weininger produced a large number of design sketches for this "Abstract Revue of Moving Surfaces," first conceived in 1923 when he was working for a Hamburg cabaret. The ludic play of colored strips shooting out of the wings and revolving contraptions on stage was combined with various figures appearing from the flies or rising from the stage floor, all to the sound of mechanical noise music.

how he intended to put the forms in motion and relate them to the music.[134] The piece bore a certain resemblance to Schmidt/Telscher's *Mechanical Ballet*, but here the abstract colored shapes were shifted electromechanically by 23 small motors, and figurative rôles were taken by marionettes. Similarly, in Heinz Loew's *Model for a Mechanical Stage* (1927) the action unrolled mechanically on a three-track system and was mounted on invisible stage wagons and transmission belts.[135] Both theatres were presented at the German Theatre Exhibition in Magdeburg (1927), where they received considerable interest despite the fact that Thomas Mann referred to them in his opening address as a "guillotine of poets." My third example comes from Roman Clemens, who entered the Bauhaus in 1927 and established contacts with the Friedrich Theater Dessau in 1928, where Kandinsky was directing *Pictures at an Exhibition*. This inspired him to design a similar abstract piece of theatre, called *Play of Form, Color, Light and Sound* (1929) (see figure 5.6).[136] To the accompaniment of five pieces of music (Foxtrot, Russian folk song, Tango, German children's lullaby, Slow-Fox) a dynamic, Constructivist stage set of abstract shapes and colors created a very attractive kaleidoscope of highly graphic kinetic images. The designs were shown at a Bauhaus

Figure 5.6   Roman Clemens, *Play of Form. Color, Light and Sound.* Stage design for an unperformed Bauhaus piece, 1929. This totally abstract, mechanical performance was Clemens's diploma piece supervised by Wassily Kandinsky and inspired by his *Pictures at an Exhibition*. Clemens devised a choreography for five kinetic stage actions set to music by a large jazz orchestra. Unfortunately, it never made it beyond the drawing board stage.

exhibition in travel 1929, which secured him a post as assistant stage designer at the Friedrich Theater, followed by a successful career at the Zurich opera house.

In view of the many unrealized projects mentioned above, it is understandable that Kandinsky never attempted to produce any of his plays at the Bauhaus. Although in 1927 he published excerpts from his play *Violet* in the Bauhaus journal, there is no indication that he considered having it staged at the school. But soon after examining Weininger's project of an abstract-mechanical revue he showed the artistic director of the Dessau municipal theatre a series of sketches inspired by Mussorgsky's composition, *Pictures at an Exhibition*.[137] The production he had in mind reflected some of his early suggestions on a Total Work of Art (see pp. 52–54) as well as his more advanced theories developed during his Bauhaus years.

Pictures at an Exhibition was based on Mussorgsky's music of the same name, which reflected impressions and feelings stimulated by a series of paintings by Viktor Hartmann. Kandinsky did not know Hartmann's works and "translated" the music back into a visual medium in the form of (a) paintings and (b) an abstract, mechanical stage show.[138] Kandinsky's endeavor to reduce painting to its innate basic principles had led him, in 1909, to the creation of his first abstract painting, which he regarded as an equivalent to musical compositions. Sounds, like pure colors, were seen to be expression of an absolute spirit. However, the time dimension of music could only be insufficiently captured in the static, two-dimensional frame of a painting. Hence his move into "stage-compositions," the first of which, *The Yellow Sound*, was published in 1912. In 1923, Kandinsky issued an essay, "On the Abstract Stage Synthesis," which developed further his ideas set forth in "On Stage Composition" (1912) and gave them a twist that reflected his experiences at INKhUK and the Bauhaus. It presented architecture and theatre as the only two arts that bring together different disciplines. He suggested that following the "ruthless dissection" of the individual arts and the analysis of their elementary means, a rebuilding process, leading to "the great synthesis," had to take place. Although each art has a language of its own, the theatre has the magnetic power to reassemble all these languages and to form "a monumental abstract art" that is the sum of the abstract "sounds" in each individual art. The individual arts will serve the theatre purely as components of an overarching scheme, renounce their own goals, and subject themselves to the law of stage composition. The resulting "synthetic theatre" will be a "construction" made up of "basic and auxiliary elements" and held together by "the inner goal of the work—composition."[139]

Pictures at an Exhibition allowed Kandinsky to set forms and colors into motion and to interpret musical structures as a painting evolving in time. The production at the Friedrich Theater in Dessau was aided by Paul Klee's son Felix, who arranged the music and served as production assistant and stage manager. Kandinsky designed the stage construction, the lighting score, and the costumes for the two dancers who appeared in scenes 10 and 12. Although Mussorsky's music falls into the category of "program music," it could not suggest to Kandinsky any narrative development. Nor did he feel tempted to structure the movements of the shapes on stage in line with the musical rhythms. He adhered to his principle of convergence and divergence, which avoided the Wagnerian fault of expressing ideas several times over in parallel media. This created a complex web of temporal interaction between music and the theatrical means of space, light, form, color, and movement and resulted in a performance full of surprise and unexpected constellations.

The composer Ludwig Grote reviewed the production and was particularly impressed by the lighting design, which gave the drama of form and color an unreal and magic quality. He concluded:

> The hovering, sliding and resting of forms, the change of quality and intensity in the colors became a dramatic action of heightened tension. The images were in constant motion and each moment was experienced pictorially. Once a movement came to a standstill, the structure of the composition was completed and a dramatic climax was reached. The kinship with the artistic form of drama revealed itself in the most unexpected manner.[140]

Arthur Seidl saw in the production a "significant first phase of a total revolution and inner transformation of the formal language and design of the stage." However, this "advance into virgin territory" was already at this stage "technically immaculate and executed with impeccable perfection."[141] Most of the stage construction consisted of flat cutouts of forms and figures, which were carried by invisible stagehands or flown in. The effect was, as Kandinsky had intended: a "development of *pictures in time*, i.e. the gradual assembling and dissolving of colored forms, as the music unfolds"[142] (see figure 5.7).

The Demise of the Bauhaus and the Last Performances of the Stage Workshop

With the arrival of the Swiss architect Hannes Meyer at the Bauhaus, the already strong trend toward a rationalist and productivist brand of Constructivism gained further impetus. On February 4, 1928, Gropius resigned from his post and on April 1, 1928, Hannes Meyer officially became the new director of the Bauhaus. He immediately undertook a reorganization of the institution and its teaching program. Architecture now became the center of activities and other workshops were forced to adapt to the practical requirements of industry and society. Fine arts and free creation were wound back and interior design, town planning, sociology, engineering, economic management, photography, and so on were given a more prominent place on the curriculum.

The conflict that Schlemmer had experienced in 1927 with some of his workshop members, who deemed his theatrical research to be too formalistic, a-political, and irrelevant for the problems of everyday life, was exacerbated by the lack of technical and financial support for his teaching projects. Schlemmer had long felt that theatre was being treated like the "fifth wheel on the Bauhaus cart";[143] but now he feared the death sentence for his department. However, contrary to all expectations, the stage workshop scored some

Figure 5.7 Wassily Kandinsky, *Pictures at an Exhibition*. Painting of 1930, based on scene 16: *The Great Gate of Kiev*, performed at the Friedrich Theater in Dessau in 1928. The interaction between Mussorgsky's music and the theatrical means of space, light, form, color, and movement produced a performance full of surprise and unexpected constellations.

major successes in 1928–1929. The new Bauhaus timetable, which was divided into two art and theory days and three workshop days, allowed Schlemmer to introduce a new course called "Man," dedicated to an integrated investigation of human existence from an analytic and synthetic viewpoint.[144] This innovative concept allowed him to place dance and the formal aspects of the stage into a wider social and philosophical framework and to relate it organically to workshop explorations and rehearsals. The new emphasis on productive relations to industry helped Schlemmer to consolidate the Bauhaus performance group he had founded in May 1927 and to focus their minds on professional performances that could compete with the schools of, for example, Laban, Palucca, or Wigman. At one point he even suggested to turn the stage workshop into a professional theatre school without, understandably, finding much support for that idea.

In the summer and autumn of 1928, he focused his mind on a series of semi-professional dance performances, the first of them to be performed at the Essen Dance Congress on June 25, 1928. This turned out to be a major success and encouraged Schlemmer to put together an even more ambitious program for a performance at either Piscator's Theater am Nollendorfplatz or the Volksbühne in Berlin. In a position paper presented to the Bauhaus Council on September 26, 1928, he justified the focusing of all resources on the planned Berlin performance and the engagement of additional dancers in order to give the production the necessary professional polish.[145] When, in October 1928, the Volksbühne sent an official confirmation for a Bauhaus matinée, with a payment of 1,200 Marks attached, Schlemmer was given the necessary support by Meyer and other professors in order to turn this event into a major showcase for the school.

Some of the dances selected for the planned performance were given a trial run on July 7, 1928 at the Bauhaus studio theatre, and a few more at the Metallic Festival on February 9, 1929. The workshop now possessed a repertoire of over 15 so-called Bauhaus Dances, from which they selected 12 for the performance in Berlin. The matinée at the Berlin Volksbühne on March 3, 1929 reached an audience of over 2,000 and was probably the stage workshop's greatest success. It led to invitations to repeat the performance in several other towns and a subsequent tour to Breslau, Frankfurt/M, Stuttgart, and Bâle. The program presented in Berlin and the other cities consisted of: *Metal Dance, Space Dance, Form Dance, Wing Dance, Glass Dance, Gesture Dance, Slat Dance, Block Dance, Hoop Dance, Women's Dance, Masked Chorus,* and *Sketch.*[146] Four of these works—*Metal Dance, Glass Dance, Slat Dance, Hoop Dance*—belonged to the group of "material dances," in which the scenic form and the dancer's actions were entirely dictated by the material. In the *Metal Dance,* the actor operated in narrow space determined by three metallic elements: a flat sheet on the floor, two corrugated sheets at the side, and four pillars at the back. A female figure clad in white body stockings, her head and hands encased in silver globes, performed crisp movements to a "metallic" sounding music and produced a myriad of light reflexes and shadow effects. In *Glass Dance,* the material was incorporated into the costume: a bell jar covered the head; a bracket with small glass balls attached rested on the shoulders; a hoop around the hips had long glass rods suspended from it; and in her hands, the dancer held a glass club and a glass sphere. Movements were restricted to slowly walking, rocking, bowing, turning according to clearly defined choreographic patterns. Unpredictable light reflexes enhanced the "glassy" atmosphere conjured up by the music played on a celesta and triangle. In the *Slat Dance,* the dancer's limbs had been extended by 12 long phosphorized slats, which cut through space with each movement and visualized the work of each joint in a highly graphic fashion. The amazing combinations of geometric shapes underlined the close relationship between the organic body and the surrounding space. The effect of the *Hoop Dance* rested in the dexterous manipulation of wooden hoops in front of a "curtain" of hoops suspended from the flies. In one of the four-part dances a male and a female puppet made from hoops and two further "curtains" were lowered from the flies in center stage and downstage positions. The juggling with the hoops was combined with the effect of an inventive lighting design and created as many black shadows as there were white hoops on stage.

In the *Space Dance*, three dancers in padded body suits explored the spatial dimension of the stage, aided by a floor grid and rhythmic music. Different qualities of movement tied in with the dancers' "characters" indicated by the colors red, blue, and yellow. The dance illustrated Schlemmer's theory of the most elementary dramatic conflict: the tension resulting from a body entering space. The architecture of the stage was shown to be physically compelling and to make the actors become "bewitched" by the space that surrounded them. In the *Form Dance*, the same actors were given some simple props: a short baton and a big white ball for the red dancer, a long wooden slat for the blue dancer, a short stick and a small silver ball for the yellow dancer. These props became the deciding factor for suggesting gliding, swinging, and angular movements. In a new version of the *Gesture Dance*, Schlemmer added three pieces of stage furniture (a bench, a stool, and a chair), three character masks, and "narrative" music. Abstract forms were combined with dramatic characterization in a humorous, semi-narrative fashion.

In the *Dance of the Stage Wings*, the three actors wore neutral black leotards but showed their faces. Four colored flats partitioned the space and created corridors, in which the actors could demonstrate the effects of walking in front, behind, through, and along a spatial organism. Percussive instruments added rhythm to the vocal enunciations (either inarticulate sounds or combinations of numerals). Apart from the movements in relation to the flats there were irregular appearances of hands, feet, heads, and cards. Words shooting out from behind the panels gave the dance a comic and mysterious quality. In the *Dance with Building Blocks*, the actors threw to each other a number of blocks in bricklayer fashion and arranged them on stage in varying formations. In one section, called *Step Joke*, the blocks formed three symmetrical steps and one of the dancers explored the "sculpture" with the curiosity of a child or animal.

Three of the items on the Berlin program were short theatre pieces that had already been performed before. *Masked Chorus* was also known as *Dinner Society* and had 12 actors perform a social ritual that consisted of three solemn drinking ceremonies and the formal procedures of arrival and leave-taking.

The costumes were neutral work clothes, but each of the masks was given an individual character. The *Women's Dance* was presented by three "actoresses," who satirized behavior generally considered to be "typically female." Opulent, "baroque" costumes with hats, parasols, fans, lorgnons, and so on created a festive, if not pompous atmosphere, which was further accentuated by the manner of walking and the musical accompaniment. The three scenes of the piece showed the "dames" parading in an affected manner, greeting each other and acquaintances in the audience, doing up their hair at a dressing table, and having their photograph taken. The parodistic touch of the piece with its exaggerated movements, costumes, and masks had nothing to do with formal investigation, but rather belonged to the section in the curriculum dedicated to the transformational aspects of the theatre. *Sketch* was the longest piece on the Berlin program and the only one in which spoken language played a major rôle. It was inspired by some of Schwitter's *Merz* dramas and Tairov's principle of using different acting levels.[147] Performance spaces of varying height (ladders, steps, platforms, a trap door, and a column) were allocated in different scenes to the four characters (a young girl, a gigolo, a crook, and a policeman), who engaged in a hackneyed love drama accompanied by piano music full of references to opera arias and popular songs.

Reviews of the Berlin performance indicate that the audience thoroughly enjoyed the judicious mixture of dance and theatre pieces representing different aspects of the Bauhaus stage workshop. Most critics responded positively and praised the high quality of conception and execution of the pieces. Although some of them noticed that the technical demands on the performers was relatively low (reflecting that most actors came from a technical rather than performance background), they nevertheless commended the tight construction and precise execution of the works. The performance showed that a purified theatre centered on elementary means and abstract forms could indeed create a new synthesis, provided that a sufficient measure of imagination was involved.

CONSTRUCTIVISM CONQUERS THE MAINSTREAM

The pioneering rôle of the Bauhaus in the development of architecture and design and the school's impact on contemporary and subsequent generations is well known. Also in the theatre one can find wide-reaching influences, both in the areas of design and performance. Several of the Bauhaus masters and students (Schlemmer, Moholy-Nagy, Kandinsky, Schmidt, Weininger, Schawinsky, Clemens, etc.) undertook work in the professional theatre; and vice versa, theatre directors, actors, dancers, and choreographers came to see

Figure 5.8 Max Brand, *Machinist Hopkins*, Stadttheater Duisburg (1929), directed by Saladin Schmitt, designed by Johannes Schröder. This was one of the most popular *Zeitopern* of the Weimar Republik, with a stage design that revealed the influence of Constructivism and New Sobriety.

the performances in Weimar and Dessau or those given in other German cities. After 1922, the Expressionist fashion in German theatre began to wane and came to be replaced, from 1924 onwards, by New Sobriety. Bertolt Brecht and Erwin Piscator were probably the best-known representatives of this trend, and both availed themselves of designers well versed in the principles of Constructivism. In the opera houses, a whole wave of *Zeitopern* (operas on contemporary topics) was given a visual appearance that was rooted in the aesthetics of the machine age (see figure 5.8). Of course, not all of these stage designs can be classified as "Constructivist." Already in the previous decade one could observe a trend toward rationalization of means and elementary forms of visual expression. Therefore, not every production working with the principles of simplification and abstraction deserves to be called Constructivist. But some influential designs that were clearly based on Constructivist models first presented in Russia and at the Bauhaus stand out as masterpieces of their time: Lyonel Feininger's *Spiegelmensch* (Werfel) in Düsseldorf 1922; Heinrich Campendonk's *Magic* (K. G. Chesterton) in Krefeld 1925; Reinhold Schön's

Franziska (Wedekind) in Berlin, Theater am Nollendorfplatz 1926; Lothar Schenck von Trapp's *Hin und Zurück* (Hindemith) in Darmstadt 1927; Ewald Dülberg's *Fidelio* (Beethoven) at the Kroll Oper in Berlin 1927.[148]

When the Bauhaus closed its doors in Dessau (September 30, 1932), and when its short-lived successor in Berlin was also shut down by the Nazis (April 11, 1933), many Bauhaus members emigrated and introduced, as architects, designers, performers, and filmmakers, some of the most advanced forms of experimentation that had emerged during the interwar years to the United States and other countries. Russian Constructivism did not survive long during the Stalin years and was replaced by Socialist Realism. Some of the émigrés, such as Moholy-Nagy and Naum Gabo, continued to propagate Constructivist concepts abroad, where they merged with other purist and nonobjective trends, like those of De Stijl and the École de Paris. Little of this made inroads into theatre in the late 1930s or 1940s, but in the 1950s it came to resurface again in the wake of the Modernist revival. The generalized aesthetics of simple, functionalist stage design, which played a major rôle in Western theatre of the past fifty years, had its roots ultimately in the historical avant-garde discussed in this and the previous chapters.

6. Epilog: The Postwar Revival of Modernism and of the Avant-garde ⟡

The period of the historical avant-garde was a time of great cultural achievements as well as political crises and mindless destruction. The conservative nature of bourgeois society forced artists with an interest in creative experimentation and innovation into an oppositional position vis à vis "the establishment." A large number of novels and plays written between 1890 and 1914 still serve as a reminder for how traditionalist European middle-class society was at that time. The "official" culture of the Belle Époque reflected the Age of Imperialism and triumphant capitalism. The lofty realms of the arts served as a retreat from the abject realities of life in the lower depth of society; it eulogized the material achievements of the bourgeoisie, and it described, in a nostalgic vein, the glories of previous epochs. For this reason, any artist seriously engaged in developing the content and style of his or her medium of expression could not help but clash with the representatives of mainstream culture.

As a great deal of these creative activities was linked to the salient features of modernity, we are wont to describe this complex terrain outside official culture as "Modernism." After World War I, the most reactionary forces of the Old Europe and their militaristic underpinning went into decline and Modernism made its first inroads into the mainstream. For a period of some ten years, the *esprit nouveau* in European society allowed a flourishing of a Modernist culture that was no longer driven by an oppositional spirit, but a desire to make use of the advances in the social, political, economic, and technological domains. As I discussed in my introductory chapter, the avant-garde was firmly imbedded in this Modernist aspiration for renewal, although it often preceded it by years and always distinguished itself by a more radical, intransigent, and uncompromising stance. In the 1920s, the avant-garde remained an interest of a minority,—a minority of artists / dealers / buyers / viewers. By definition, it was the concern of an élitist circle of connoisseurs. As such, it was most heavily hit by the economic crisis toward the end of the 1920s and was practically eliminated by the subsequent conservative turn. With the increased influence of Nationalist and Fascist movements and, in the 1930s, the establishment and consolidation of Fascist régimes, the avant-garde was silenced and many artists were forced to emigrate to the more liberal climes of North America.

Modernism as a cultural force survived during the 1930s and 1940s, albeit in a rather constrained manner and in quite narrowly defined domains.[1] A large number of artists and writers preferred to escape the overwhelmingly conservative atmosphere in Fascist Europe and, consequently, the hub of artistic creativity shifted to the United States, where New York took on the rôle of international center of artistic research. Until then, the United States had been relatively unaffected by Modernism, as it was generally considered élitist and incompatible with the American sensibility. Instead, artists sought to immerse themselves into the "native land" and detached themselves from all foreign influences, thus maneuvering U.S.-American art into a provincial and isolationist position. The 1913 International Exhibition of Modern Art in New York (better known as the Armory Show[2]) and the 1915 Panama-Pacific International Exposition in San Francisco came more of a shock than a revelation to the American public, but among the younger generation it fostered a serious interest in international Modernism and led to a brief flowering of Synchromism, Precisionism, and New York Dada. During World War II, the majority of artists and the mainstream public lost interest in Modernist experimentation or simply regarded it as a foreign aberration. In 1944, Royal Cortissoz could unambiguously state in the last sentence of his updated edition of Samuel Isham's *History of American Painting*: "The bulk of American painting is untouched by modernism." This, however, was not to remain so for long.

The single most important factor for this change was the exodus of thousands of artists from totalitarian régimes and war-torn Europe. Many key figures of the prewar avant-garde settled in the United States or remained there for as long as it was unsafe to return to their homelands. Suddenly, the second- and third-hand knowledge of Modernism, which had produced so many misunderstandings in the 1910s and 1920s, gave way to informed, authentic voices, who through their exhibitions, writings and teaching activities introduced the American public to the great artistic achievements of the early twentieth century. The Museum of Modern Art began to exhibit major artists from the Modernist schools of Europe. The Solomon R. Guggenheim

Museum, inaugurated in 1939, followed suit, and several private galleries (some of them founded by émigrés) held exhibitions of significant figures of the European avant-garde. The catalogs published on these occasions contained, often for the first time, translations of key texts and manifestos, which were complemented by essays and reproductions in the "Little Magazines" of the period. Several art historians and critics among the émigrés found teaching positions at American universities, and leading artists of the avant-garde conveyed their rich knowledge and experience to the younger generation at art colleges or through private teaching. The New Bauhaus in Chicago provided a whole phalanx of artists with a formative training in modern art, and the émigrés at the Black Mountain College gave artists from a variety of disciplines a fundamental introduction to avant-garde concepts of experimentation, which prepared them for the major rôles they were later going to play in dance, theatre, and music.

These displaced Europeans transported across the Atlantic not only skill and knowledge, but also a different rôle model for what it meant to be an artist. For a while, it seemed as if the bohemian community of Montmartre had found a new home in Greenwich Village. A closely knit artist community came into existence—often referred to as the New York School—where, after an initial stage of absorbing the rich inheritance of European Modernism, an originally American brand of vanguard art came into existence. Artists and critics returning to the United States after several years of military service found that Social Realism and American Scene painting had been replaced by Surrealist and abstract art as the dominant trend in New York galleries. For example, Milton W. Brown noted in 1946: "I have returned to find with some surprise that in the interim the dark horse of abstraction has swept into the lead. . . . All along the streets are evidences that the vogue today is for abstraction. Three years ago this tendency was evident; today it is swarming all over the stage."[3] Abstract Expressionism, Action Painting, and Color-Field Painting were the first U.S.-American contributions to Late-Modernism. The works created in the 1940s and 1950s were very distinct from those created by their predecessors in the 1910s and 1920s, yet at the same time unthinkable without their European pedigree (in fact many members of the new schools had studied in Europe, or with European émigrés, or were of European extraction).

Also in Europe, the avant-garde went through a series of permutations and transformations. After years of pseudo-Realism and "heroic" idealism imposed by Fascist bureaucrats, the return of Modernism seemed like an act of liberation. Europeans were looking across the Atlantic and found inspiration from the artists of the New York School. Their popularity was, no doubt, strengthened by a general admiration for the American Way of Life, which due to the low standard of living in the ruins of postwar Europe appeared like a progressive culture worth striving for. The banning of Modernist and U.S.-American culture during the Fascist era had awakened a natural curiosity in the works of, say, Aaron Copland, George Gershwin, Gian Carlo Menotti, Thornton Wilder, Eugene O'Neill, Tennessee Williams, John Steinbeck, William Faulkner, Ernest Hemingway, and so on. The United States responded to this interest in their cultural foreign policy and organized a number of high-profile festivals and touring programs, thus giving representatives of recent American art prominent showcases in Berlin, Paris, Milan, Madrid, and so on.[4]

By the 1950s, the New York School was considered to be on an equal footing with prewar Modernism centered on Paris, Berlin, and Rome. The international success of modern U.S.-American culture suggested that the most innovative developments in the arts were now to be found in the United States rather than Europe. But whereas the founding fathers of American Modernism had been motivated by deeply personal and often existential reasons, the second generation was much more propelled by commercial motivations. This laid the ground for what Harold Rosenberg in 1959 could refer to as "the tradition of the new."[5] The changed conditions of a highly commercialized art market imposed on the avant-garde, which for many intellectuals had functioned as an *ersatz* religion, a process of secularization. Modernists, who had achieved bourgeois respectability and were now fêted by bankers, industrialists, and conservative politicians, relinquished their commitment to political causes and social change. "The modern artist is apolitical. . . . Political expertise belongs to the politician. As with art, only the full-time career can yield results," was the advice Allan Kaprow gave to his fellow artists.[6] The old commandment "Thou shouldst not contaminate art with gain" was overturned; bohemian artists turned into businessmen, and creativity came to be judged by the criteria of commercial success. During the first ten years of the Cold War, hardly any artist driven by a genuine quest for the betterment of society could maintain a position on the West-European art market. The often messianic visions of Expressionists and Constructivists, who in their majority had belonged to the Left-wing, and often Communist, community of artists, gave way to a rather inane Utopian optimism and to works of austere minimalism, which bore no relation to any kind of experienceable reality. Late-Modernism as a watered-down version of "classic" Modernist art was predominantly supported and bought by pretentious connoisseurs of middle-class origin. There was certainly nothing disturbing or scandalous about the "corporate Modernism" of the 1950s, which graced the walls of banks, boardrooms, and bourgeois villas. The former avant-garde, which had defined itself through its opposition to society and its artistic institutions, had moved from the margins of society into the mainstream. It became an object of "smart investment,"[7] was absorbed by academic institutions, and ended up as an integral element of the culture industry. The last permutations of Modernism produced a never-ending supply of "-isms," a scrambling for novelty and an unrelenting quest for the New, which could be exploited by the art market and commended to the bourgeoisie as the latest fashion fad and lifestyle accessory. A form of Modernism where form dominated over content had become a "modern tradition" functioning as the "official" art in advanced capitalist countries.

In the mid-1950s, the pendulum swung back again in the other direction, and a return to Realist means of representation could be observed in both Europe and the United States. Slowly but steadily, the trickle of figurative paintings inspired by the new urban culture of the postwar period swelled in size. What initially had been a faint counter-trend to high-Modernist abstraction became a rising tide, for which Lawrence Alloway in 1958 coined the term "Pop-Art."[8] In France, the new trend was called "Nouveau Réalisme." Artists as far afield as London, Paris, Düssseldorf, and Milan turned toward this new form of Realism without ever developing much of a group mentality or common program. Pierre Restany, who functioned for a while as an unofficial mouthpiece of this trend and who penned several of its most influential manifestos, organized two immensely important exhibitions of American Pop artists in Paris (July 1961 at the Galérie Rive Droite) and of French New Realists in New York (October 1962 at the Sydney Janis Gallery). In the following years, this led to the beginnings of a new performance art in Europe, which is usually referred to with the term "Happening and Fluxus," but was equally well-known as Neo-Dada.

Needless to say, the influx of European Modernism into the United States did not trigger a replication of its forms and functions. The Chicago Bauhaus was not an imitation of the Dessau Bauhaus; Lee Strasberg's Expressionism bears only superficial resemblance to Lothar Schreyer's training methods in Berlin, Hamburg, or Weimar; George Maciunas and Nam June Paik's use of the term Neo-Dada in their event art of 1962 was little more than a nod in the direction of a historical source of inspiration; and when the avant-garde performer Michael Kirby compiled a book of scripts, manifestos, and critical essays by and on Italian Futurism,[9] he did so with the aim of fostering an awareness of historical precedence rather than suggesting a copying of Marinetti's concepts and ideas. Similarly, the reception of Modernism in Asia and Africa was a complex process of cross-cultural appropriation that preserved indigenous traditions as well as adapting imported concepts and techniques. The Japanese avant-garde, for example, strove to create works that were modern in a Japanese way, incorporating and opposing at the same time local and Western influences. Not unlike Baudelaire a hundred years earlier (see p. 18–19), Japanese artists and writers believed in a timeless essence of tradition that interacted with the ever-changing constellations of the modern. So even when accepting certain aspects of Western Modernism, the artists avoided wholesale acceptance, second-hand adaptation, or uncritical emulation of Western models. By incorporating autochthonous elements, they added an Eastern perspective on the global practices of Modernist and avant-garde experimentation.

Western art of the 1950s and 1960s recuperated many essential character-istics of prewar Modernism, drew on the achievements of the Historical Avant-garde, and continued to incorporate these into mainstream culture. Under the changed conditions of a post-Fascist, liberal democracy, this revival had a significant political function and possessed a number of novel and innovative features. Both in Europe and in the United States, Late-Modernism constituted an important phase in twentieth-century art, literature, music, and theatre. To a considerable degree, it revealed that Expressionism, Futurism, Dada, Surrealism, and Constructivism were not just artistic schools restricted to their original time and society, but in a more metaphorical sense represented general aspects of modern art and were transferable to other times and cultures.

Notes ⁓

PREFACE

1. The term is used by David Graver in his study *The Aesthetics of Disturbance: Anti-Art in Avant-garde Drama*, which analyzes several such plays.
2. Although directors—myself included—have created theatrical performances based on such dramas, these cannot be considered realizations of the texts, as there is no authoritative voice of the playwright who could act as a guide to the director.
3. I have given a detailed consideration to this complex web of interconnections in an essay, "Futurism, Dada, and Surrealism: Some Cross-Fertilizations among the Historical Avant-garde," in Berghaus, *Futurism in Arts and Literature*, pp. 271–304.

1 INTRODUCTION

1. See the chapter "The Ancients and the Moderns," in Ernst Robert Curtius, *European Literature and the Latin Middle Ages*, London: Routledge and Kegan Paul, 1963, pp. 251–254; Hans Robert Jauß, "Literarische Tradition und gegenwärtiges Bewußtsein der Modernität: Wortgeschichtliche Betrachtungen," in Hans Steffen, ed., *Aspekte der Modernität*, Göttingen: Vandenhoeck & Rupprecht, 1965, pp. 150–197; Martini, "Modern. Die Moderne"; Pochat, "Moderne gestern: Eine begriffsgeschichtliche Untersuchung"; Gumbrecht, "Modern, Modernität, Moderne"; Japp, *Literatur und Modernität*.
2. *Œuvres du Sieur Théophile, Seconde Partie*, Paris: Billaine, 1632, p. 18; reprinted in Théophile de Viau, *Œuvres*, ed. Guidi Saba, vol. 2, Rome: Ateneo & Bizzarri, 1978, p. 14.
3. See Robert Muchembled, *L'Invention de l'homme moderne: Sensibilités, mœurs et comportements collectifs sous l'Ancien Régime*, Paris: Fayard, 1988.
4. For a general introduction to the history of urbanization in Europe see Lewis Mumford, *The City in History: Its Origins, Its Transformations, and Its Prospects*, New York: Harcourt Brace Jovanovich, 1961; Jan de Vries, *European Urbanization 1500–1800*, London: Methuen, 1984; Paul M. Hohenberg and Lynn Hollen Lees, *The Making of Urban Europe, 1000–1950*, Cambridge, MA: Harvard University Press, 1985; Gary Bridge and Sophie Watson, eds., *A Companion to the City*, Oxford: Blackwell, 2000.

5. See Donald J. Olsen, *The City as a Work of Art: London, Paris, Vienna*, New Haven, CT: Yale University Press, 1986.

6. Frances Trollope, *Paris and the Parisians in 1835*, vol. 1, London: Bentley, 1835, p. 356. On the housing conditions of the Parisian poor see, in particular, Ann-Louise Shapiro, *Housing the Poor of Paris, 1850–1902*, Madison, WI: University of Wisconsin Press, 1984.

7. Catherine Gore, *Paris in 1841*, London: Longman, Brown, Green, and Longmans, 1842, p. 12.

8. See the evocative description in Auguste Luchet, *Paris: Esquisses dédiées au peuple parisien*, Paris: Barbezat, 1830, p. 159.

9. See Johannes Willms, *Paris Capital of Europe: From the Revolution to the Belle Époque*, New York: Holmes & Meier, 1997, p. 213.

10. Adeline Daumard, *La Bourgeoisie parisienne de 1815 à 1948*, Paris: S.E.V.P.E.N., 1963, p. 8.

11. See Willms, *Paris Capital of Europe*, pp. 162–165.

12. See the *Journal de la Société de Statistique* (October 1836), quoted in Daumard, *La Bourgeoisie parisienne*, p. 11.

13. Luchet, *Paris: Esquisses dédiées au peuple parisien*, pp. 11–13. As Léon Colin made it very clear in his study, *Paris, sa topographie, son hygiène, ses maladies*, Paris: Masson, 1885, pp. 117 and 134–152, the situation improved markedly in the inner city as a result of Haussmannization, but continued to be equally appalling in the working-class districts outside the old city walls.

14. Jeanne Gaillard, *Paris, la Ville, 1852–1870: L'Urbanisme parisien à l'heure d'Haussmann*, Lille: Atelier Reproduction des Thèses, 1976, p. 9.

15. Edward King, e.g., used this term in *My Paris: French Character Sketches*, Boston, MA: Loring, 1868, p. 159. On Haussmann's modernization project see the studies of David H. Pinkney, *Napoleon III and the Rebuilding of Paris*, Princeton, NJ: Princeton University Press, 1958; David P. Jordan, *Transforming Paris: The Life and Labors of Baron Haussmann*, New York: Free Press, 1995.

16. See Anthony Sutcliffe, *The Autumn of Central Paris: The Defeat of Town Planning, 1850–1970*, London: Arnold, 1970, pp. 80–84, 155. For a contemporary account, see Ernest Fouinet, "Un voyage en Omnibus," in *Paris, ou Le Livre des cent-et-un*, vol. 3, Paris: Ladvocat, 1831, pp. 59–82.

17. Alfred Martin, *Étude historique et statistique sur les moyens de transport dans Paris*, Paris: Imprimerie Nationale, 1894, pp. 84 and 103. See also Claude Lucas, *Les Transports en commun à Paris: Étude économique et sociale*, Paris: Jouve, 1911; Louis Lagarrigue, *Cent Ans de transports en commun dans la région parisienne*, 2 vols, Paris: Régie Autonome des Transports Parisiens, 1956; *Analyse historique de l'évolution des transports en commun dans la région parisienne de 1855 à 1939*, Paris: Conservatoire National des Arts et Métiers, 1977.

18. See Maxime du Camp, *Paris, ses organes, ses fonctions et sa vie dans la seconde moitié du XIXe siècle*, vol. 1, Paris: Hachette, 1869, p. 259.

19. Gore, *Paris in 1841*, p. 267.

20. For a general discussion of the revolution in the transportation system see Wolfgang Zorn, "Verdichtung und Beschleunigung des Verkehrs als Beitrag zur Entwicklung der 'modernen Welt'", in Reinhard Koselleck, ed., *Studien zum Beginn der modernen Welt*, Stuttgart: Klett-Cotta, 1977, pp. 115–134.

21. Théophile Gautier, Preface to Édouard Fournier, *Paris démoli*, 2nd ed., Paris: Aubry, 1855, p. XI. The essay appeared originally in the *Moniteur universel* of January 21, 1854 and has also been published under the title "Mosaique de ruines," in *Paris et les Parisiens*, Paris: Morizot, 1856, pp. 38–43.

22. See Pinkney, *Napoleon III and the Rebuilding of Paris*, pp. 105–173, and Willms, *Paris Capital of Europe*, pp. 221–225 and 277–280.

23. Gaslights were first introduced in 1829; by 1850 there were 9,000 of them, in 1860 17,538, and in 1880 41,921. See Eugène Defrance, *Histoire de l'éclairage des rues de Paris*, Paris: Imprimerie Nationale, 1904, p. 88 and Henry Besnard, *L'Industrie du gaz à Paris depuis ses origines*, Paris: Domat-Montchrestien, 1942.

24. By the 1870s, nearly all modern houses had been supplied with gas mains. In 1872, Du Camp counted 94,774 subscribers to the municipal gas company. See Du Camp, *Paris, ses organes, ses fonctions, etc.*, vol. 5, Paris: Hachette, 1873, pp. 354–410.

25. Jules Vallès, "Le Tableau de Paris IV: Du Boulevard des Capucines à la Madeleine," *Gil Blas*, March 2, 1882, in J. Vallès, *Œuvres complètes*, vol. 3, Paris: Livre Club Diderot, 1969, p. 747.

26. Julien Lemer, *Paris au gaz*, Paris: Dentu, 1861, pp. 15 and 28.

27. Jules Janin, *Un hiver à Paris*, Paris: Curmer & Aubert, 1843, p. 192. I quote from the English edition, *The American in Paris*, London: Longman, Brown, Green, and Longmans, 1843, pp. 162–163. See also the chapter on "L'art de la flânerie," in Victor Fournel, *Ce qu'on voit dans les rues de Paris*, Paris: Delahays, 1858, pp. 261–263; Louis Huart, *Physiologie du Flâneur*, Paris: Aubert & Lavigne, 1841; M. A. Bazin, "Le Flâneur," in Anaïs Bazin de Raucou, ed., *L'Époque sans nom: Esquisses de Paris 1830–1833*, 2 vols, Paris: Mesnier, 1833, at vol. 2, pp. 295–323.

28. King, *My Paris*, p. 45. Very similar statements on the spectacle of the street can be found in Jules Vallès, "Le Tableau de Paris," *Œuvres complètes*, vol. 3, p. 739 ("il ne reste qu'à repaître ses yeux du spectacle que donnent les passants"); Gustave Fraipont, *Paris à vol d'oiseau*, Paris: Librairie Illustrée, 1889, p. 5 ("Ce qui donne à ces plaisirs [i.e. cafés, bals, théâtres, etc.] un ton particulier, c'est la liberté d'allure qui règne à Paris, et qui ne règne qu'ici, il faut bien le dire, et qui fait de la grande Ville un spectacle toujours vivant, animé, joyeux"); Georges Montorgueil, *La Vie des boulevards*, Paris: Librairies Imprimeries Réunies, 1896. ("Le spectacle vraiment parisien est où nous l'avons trouvé: dans la rue, aux terraces, au restaurant . . . c'ést la comédie humaine en action, qui se jou là, dans un décor superbe," pp. III and 141.)

29. See Alf Kjellén, *Flanören och hans storstadsvärld: Synpunkter på ett litterärt motiv / The Flâneur and His Urban World: Aspects of a Literary Theme*, Stockholm: Almqvist & Wiksell, 1985; Eckhardt Köhn, *Straßenrausch: Flanerie und kleine*

Form. Versuch zur Literaturgeschichte des Flaneurs von 1830–1933, Berlin: Das Arsenal, 1989; Keith Tester, ed., The Flâneur, London: Routledge, 1994.

30. A colorful impression of life on the boulevards is given in the exhibition catalogs, *Les Grands Boulevards*, Paris: Musée Carnavalet, 1985, and *Les Grands Boulevards: Un parcours d'innovation et de modernité*, ed. Bernard Landau, Claire Monod, and Évelyne Lohr, Paris: Action Artistique de la Ville de Paris, 2000, and the monograph by Patrice de Moncan, *Les Grands Boulevards de Paris: De la Bastille à la Madeleine*, Paris: Les Editions du Mécène, 1997.

31. "Le Flâneur, par un Flâneur," in *Paris, ou Le Livre des cent-et-un*, vol. 6, Paris: Ladvocat, 1832, pp. 95–110, at 96–97.

32. Henry T. Tuckerman, *Papers about Paris*, New York: Putnam, 1867, pp. 25–26.

33. The figure is given by E. King, *My Paris*, p. 112. The clubs were a fashion introduced from England and were considered by some to be "une innovation dangereuse, une concurrence fatale pour les salons." *Paris et les Parisiens*, Paris: Morizot, 1856, p. 440. This publication is more positive about the *dansomanie*, which it judged to be "le sport des femmes et le culte du Paris mondain" (ibid., p. 303).

34. For upper-class lifestyles see the figures in Gore, *Paris in 1841*, pp. 245 and 257–258 and the comments in Trollope, *Paris and the Parisians in 1835*, vol. 1, p. 351–353. A useful comparison of the cost of living in low, middle, and upper-class households around 1850 can be found in Jarves, *Parisian Sights*, pp. 201–203. Equally informative are Pierre Bleton, *La Vie sociale sous le Second Empire: Un étonnant témoignage de la Comtesse de Ségur*, Paris: Les Éditions Ouvrières, 1963, and Maurice Allem, *La Vie quotidienne sous le Second Empire*, Paris: Hachette, 1948, pp. 99–106.

35. Maxime du Camp, *Paris, ses organes, ses fonctions et sa vie*, vol. 6, Paris: Hachette, 1876, p. 233. King, *My Paris*, pp. 333–335 also speaks of 40 regular theatres, but adds that they offered mainly "glittering spectacles and trashy melodramas" (p. 333).

36. These figures are given by James Jackson Jarves, *Parisian Sights and French Principles, Seen through American Spectacles*, New York: Harper & Brothers, 1852, pp. 192–194.

37. James Dabney McCabe, *Paris by Sunlight and Gaslight*, Philadelphia: National Publishing Company, 1869, pp. 64–65. This author also compiled a number of other useful statistics on Parisian social life.

38. See Michael Robert Marrus, ed., *The Emergence of Leisure*, New York: Harper and Row, 1974; Hugh Cunningham, *Leisure in the Industrial Revolution c. 1780—c. 1880*, New York: St. Martin's Press, 1980; Rosalind H. Williams, *Dream Worlds: Mass Consumption in Late Nineteenth-Century France*, Berkeley, CA: University of California Press, 1982; Alain Corbin, ed., *L'Avènement des loisirs, 1850–1960*, Paris: Aubier, 1995.

39. For an excellent study of bourgeois lifestyles of the period see Daumard, *La Bourgeoisie parisienne de 1815 à 1848*.

40. See Walter Benjamin's unique collection of material, displayed in arcade-style fashion, *Das Passagen-Werk*, published as vol. 5 of his *Gesammelte Schriften*, Frankfurt/M: Suhrkamp, 1982, and the more recent studies of Johann Friedrich Geist, *Arcades: The History of a Building Type*, Cambridge, MA: MIT, 1983; Bertrand Lemoine, *Les Passages couverts en France*, Paris: Délégation à l'Action Artistique, 1989; Patrice de Moncan, *Le Guide des passages de Paris: Guide pratique, historique et littéraire*, Paris: SEESAM-RCI, 1991; Jean-Claude Delorme, *Passages couverts parisiens*, Paris: Parigramme, 1996.

41. Gore, *Paris in 1841*, p. 220. A good description of the arcades, "où l'on flâne, où l'on se promène, tout comme sur les boulevards" is given in an illustrated volume published on the occasion of the Exposition Universelle of 1889, *Paris à vol d'oiseau*, ch. 10: "Passages" (pp. 115–121).

42. Auguste Luchet, "Les Passages," in *Nouveau tableau de Paris aux XIXe siècle*, vol. 6, Paris: Charles-Béchet, 1835, pp. 97–113, at p. 107. See also his essay, "Les Magasins de Paris," in *Paris, ou Le Livre des cent-et-un*, vol. 15, Paris: Ladvocat, 1834, pp. 237–268.

43. Luchet, "Les Passages," p. 112.

44. See his department store novel, *Au Bonheur des Dames* (1883), in *Œuvres complètes*, vol. 4, Paris: Cercle du Livre Précieux, 1967, p. 888. On p. 711 he speaks of the department store as a "chapelle élevée au culte des grâces de la femme."

45. See George d'Avenel, "Le Mécanisme de la vie moderne I: Les grands magasins," *Revue des deux mondes*, 64e année, 4e période, vol. 124 (July 15, 1894), pp. 329–369; H. Pasdermadjian, *The Department Store: Its Origins, Evolution and Economics*, London: New Books, 1954; Jeanne Gaillard, *Paris, la Ville, 1852–1870*; 2nd ed. Paris: L'Harmattan, 1997, pp. 524–558; Alison Adburgham, *Shops and Shopping 1800–1914*, London: Allen and Unwin, 1964; Michael B. Miller, *The Bon Marché: Bourgeois Culture and the Department Store, 1869–1920*, Princeton: Princeton University Press, 1981; Philip G. Nord, *Paris Shopkeepers and the Politics of Resentment*, Princeton, NJ: Princeton University Press, 1986.

46. In the course of his research for the novel *Au Bonheur des Dames*, Zola discovered that in the early 1880s the Bon Marché had 2,500 employees, who served 10,000 customers on an ordinary day and 70,000 on a special sales day, with a receipt of 300,000 and 1,000,000 Francs respectively. The figures for the Magasin du Louvre were even higher. See Colette Becker and Jeanne Gaillard, *Au Bonheur des Dames: Analyse critique*, Paris: Hatier, 1982, p. 18.

47. Zola described the "splendeur féerique d'apothéose, sous cet éclairage nouveau" in *Au Bonheur des Dames, Œuvres complètes*, vol. 4, p. 1038.

48. Gaslights were first introduced in London theatres in 1817, became widely adopted in Europe in the 1820s, and developed their full technical potential in the 1840s.

49. Maude Annesley, *My Parisian Year*, London: Mills and Boon, 1912, p. 80. A contemporary observer contributing to a multivolume, panoramic picture of Parisian modernity remarked: "The mass of people only came to press their nose

against the door but did not enter." Amédée Kermel, "Les Passages de Paris," in *Paris, ou Le Livre des cent-et-un*, vol. 10, Paris: Ladvocat, 1833, pp. 49–72, at 58.

50. The parallels between these two types of exhibition have been elaborated in Saisselin, *The Bourgeois and the Bibelot*, pp. 41–49.

51. Benjamin, *Das Passagen-Werk* A4,1, in *Gesammelte Schriften*, vol. 5, p. 93. The comparison can also be found in contemporary literature; e g., Gore, *My Paris*, p. 259, observed that public recreations were offered to the lower classes as part of a *panem et circenses* policy of the State. The socialist Vallès remarked caustically: "La peuple n'a pas encore le pain; mais on lui a rendu les spectacles." Jules Vallès, "Le Tableau de Paris: Les Foires, I." *Gil Blas*, April 6, 1882, in *Œuvres complètes*, vol. 3, Paris: Livre Club Diderot, 1969, p. 774. J. J. Jarves, drawing on official statistics, wrote in 1852 that the State paid theatres a yearly subsidy of 648,420 Francs, 65,790 Francs for concerts, and 8,593 Francs for exhibitions. *Parisian Sights*, p. 143.

52. Henri Lefebvre, *Everyday Life in the Modern World*, New Brunswick, NJ: Transaction, 1984, p. 90. See also Judith Wechler, "The Spectator as Genre in Nineteenth-Century Paris," in Marc Bertrand, ed., *Popular Traditions and Learned Culture in France*, Saratoga, CA: Anma Libri, 1985, pp. 227–236; Martin Roberts, "Mutations of the Spectacle: Vitrines, Arcades, Mannequins," *French Cultural Studies*, 2 (1991), pp. 211–249; Christopher Prendergast, *Paris and the 19th C*, Oxford: Blackwell, 1992, pp. 31–45; Vanessa R. Schwarz, *Spectacular Realities: Early Mass Culture in Fin-de-siècle Paris*, Berkeley, CA: University of California Press, 1998.

53. King, *My Paris*, p. 271. Other marketing devises were described by Auguste Luchet, "Les Magasins de Paris," in *Paris, ou Le Livre des cent-et-un*, vol. 15, Paris: Ladvocat, 1834, pp. 237–268.

54. *Le Petit Journal* became the emblem of the popular press and in 1886, reached a circulation of one million copies. It was soon overtaken by the *Petit Parisien*, which at the height of its success sold 1.8 million copies every day. The success was emulated by others, and in 1899 Paris had some 60 newspapers costing one sou. See Claude Bellanger et al., *Histoire générale de la presse française, vol. 2: De 1814 à 1871*, Paris: PUF, 1969; *vol. 3: De 1871* à 1940, Paris: PUF, 1972.

55. Act II, sc. 7, in *Théâtre complet*, vol. 2, Paris: Clamann-Lévy, 1923, p. 289.

56. See Ann Martin-Fugier, *La Bourgeoise: Femme au temps du Paul Bourget*, Paris: Grasset, 1983, pp. 157–179. The opposite can be observed in rural areas, where the bourgeois woman became more restricted to reproductive and domestic functions than before. See Bonnie G. Smith, *Ladies of the Leisure Class: The Bourgeoises of Northern France in the Nineteenth Century*, Princeton, NJ: Princeton University Press, 1981.

57. Camille Debans, *Les Plaisirs et les curiosités de Paris: Guide humoristique et pratique*, Paris: Kolb, 1889, p. 14.

58. *Cassell's Illustrated Guide to Paris*, London: Cassell, 1884, p. 65.

59. Although shopping can be seen as a purposeful activity and hence incompatible with *flânerie*, the popular pastime of window-shopping and aimlessly strolling

through passages and department stores does, however, fulfill some of the criteria of *flânerie*. On the female *flâneuse* see Saisselin, *The Bourgeois and the Bibelot*, ch. 2 and 3; Rachel Bowlby, *Just Looking: Consumer Culture in Dreiser, Gissing and Zola*, New York and London: Methuen, 1985, ch. 2; Janet Wolff, "The Invisible *flâneuse*: Women and the Literature of Modernity," *Theory, Culture and Society*, 2:3 (1985), pp. 37–48; Anne Friedberg, *Window Shopping: Cinema and the Postmodern*, Berkeley, CA: University of California Press, 1993, ch. 1 and 2; Anke Gleber, "Female Flanerie and the *Symphony of the City*," in Katharina von Ankum, ed., *Women and the Metropolis: Gender and Modernity in Weimar Culture*, Berkeley, CA: University of California Press, 1997, pp. 67–88; Deborah L. Parson, *Streetwalking the Metropolis: Women, the City, and Modernity*, Oxford: Oxford University Press, 2000.

60. Balzac in a letter of September 1, 1837, in *Lettres à Mme Hanska*, vol. 1, Paris: Éditions du Delta, 1967, p. 534.

61. He used the terms "ungestalte Kolossalität," "moderne Monstruositäten," "chaotisch ist der Charakter der Modernen." See also the following entries in Friedrich Schlegel, *Fragmente zur Poesie und Literatur. Teil 1* (= vol. 16 of *Kritische Friedrich-Schlegel-Ausgabe*, ed. Ernst Behler), Paderborn: Schöningh, 1981 (references refer to page and entry numbers): 44/114, 92/79, 104/236, 110/307, 127/512, 159/866, 332/925, 375/106. The later notebooks in vol. 17 of the *Kritische Friedrich-Schlegel-Ausgabe*, Paderborn: Schöningh, 1991 are less interesting, except nos. 242–244 on p. 82.

62. See the excellent index in Schlegel, *Fragmente zur Poesie und Literatur. Teil 1* (=vol. 16 of *Kritische Friedrich-Schlegel-Ausgabe*).

63. "Erste Vorlesung," in A.W. Schlegel, *Vorlesungen über dramatische Kunst und Literatur*, ed. Edgar Lohner, vol. 1, Stuttgart: Kohlhammer, 1966, p. 21.

64. See his *Racine et Shakespeare (Œuvres complètes*, vol. 37), Geneva: Le Cercle du Bibliophile, 1970, pp. 45.

65. *Histoire de la peinture en Italie*, vol. 2 (*Œuvres complètes*, vol. 26), Geneva: Le Cercle du Bibliophile, 1969, p. 111. See also *Stendhal: Du Romantisme dans les art*, ed. Juliusz Starzynski, Paris: Hermann, 1966, and Emile J. Talbot, *Stendhal and Romantic Aesthetics*, Lexington, KE: French Forum Publishers, 1985.

66. *Racine et Shakespeare*, pp. 39, 46 and 146.

67. Emile Deschamps, *Études françaises et étrangères*, Paris: Canel, 1828, p. XVI. The preface of this anthology was a veritable manifesto of Romanticism and has been reissued as *Un Manifeste du romanticism: La préface des études françaises et étrangères*, ed. H. Girard, Paris: Les Presses Françaises, 1923. The quote can be found at p. 17.

68. "Du Romantisme, considéré historiquement" has been reprinted in Pierre Trahard, *Le Romantisme défini par "Le Globe,"* Paris: Les Presses Françaises, 1924, pp. 72–82.

69. Charles Baudelaire, "Qu'est-ce que le Romantisme?," ch. 2 of "Salon de 1846," in *Œuvres complètes*, Paris: Éditions de Seuil, 1968, pp. 878–879.

70. See the judgments in contemporary criticism discussed in Isabel Valverde, *Moderne/Modernité: Deux notions dans la critique d'art française de Stendhal à Baudelaire, 1824–1863*, Frankfurt/M: Lang, 1990, pp. 310–315.

71. Maxime du Camp, *Les Beaux Arts à l'Exposition Universelle de 1855*, Paris: Librairie Nouvelle, 1855, p. 407.

72. Ibid., p. 226.

73. See, e.g., Brian Rowley, "Anticipations of Modernism in the Age of Romanticism," in Garton, ed., *Facets of European Modernism*, pp. 17–30; Gerhard Schulz, "Eine Epoche die sobald nicht wiederkehrt: Zu den Anfängen der Moderne in der deutschen Literatur um 1800," in Elm and Hemmerich, ed., *Zur Geschichtlichkeit der Moderne*, pp. 135–151; Dieter Bänsch, ed., *Zur Modernität der Romantik*, Stuttgart: Metzler, 1977; Japp, *Literatur und Modernität*, ch. 7: "Modernität als Progression: Romantische Konjekturen," pp. 185–225; Andrea Gogröf-Voorhees, *Defining Modernism: Baudelaire and Nietzsche on Romanticism, Modernity, Decadence, and Wagner*, New York: Lang, 1999, ch. 1 and 4; Deniz Tekiner, *Modern Art and the Romantic Vision*, Lanham, MD: University Press of America, 2000; Vietta, *Ästhetik der Moderne*.

74. See Calinescu, *Five Faces of Modernity*, pp. 41–58.

75. See Gérard Froidevaux, *Baudelaire: Représentation et modernité*, Mayenne: Corti, 1989; Félix de Azúa, *Baudelaire y el artista de la vida moderna*, Pamplona: Pamiel, 1991; Gogröf-Voorhees, *Defining Modernism*. On his relationship to the modern city see Marc Eli Blanchard, *In Search of the City: Engels, Baudelaire, Rimbaud*, Saratoga, CA: Anma Libri, 1985; Reinhard H. Thum, *The City: Baudelaire, Rimbaud, Verhaeren*, New York: Lang, 1994; David Carrier, *High Art: Charles Baudelaire and the Origins of Modernist Painting*, University Park, PA: Pennsylvania State University Press, 1996.

76. Charles Baudelaire, "De l'héroisme de la vie moderne," ch. 18 of "Salon de 1846," in *Œuvres complètes,* Paris: Gallimard, 1961, p. 951.

77. "La Modernité," ch. 4 of "Le Peintre de la vie moderne," in *Œuvres complètes*, pp. 1152–1192, at p. 1163.

78. The preface to the first edition (Paris: Michel Lévy, 1855) was also reprinted in the *Revue de Paris* of February 14, 1855.

79. Maxime du Camp, *Les Chants modernes. Nouvelle édition revue et corrigée*, Paris: Bourdilliat, 1860, pp. 9–10.

80. Du Camp, *Les Beaux Arts à l'Exposition Universelle de 1855*, pp. 27–28.

81. Maxime du Camp, "De l'union des arts et de l'industrie," *Revue de Paris*, June 1, 1857, pp. 384–405, at p. 389–405.

82. See "De l'art moderne," *L'Artiste*, ser. V, vol. 10 (1853), pp. 135–136, at p. 136.

83. Théophile Gautier, "Le Chemin de fer," in *Fusains et eaux-fortes*, Paris: Charpentier, 1880, pp. 197–195. The essay was originally published in *La Charte de 1830* of October 15, 1837.

84. "L'Art en 1848," *L'Artiste*, ser. V, vol. 1 (May 15, 1848), pp. 9–11.

85. "La Poésie dans l'art. I. Ary Scheffer," *L'Artiste*, ser. V, vol. 16 (1855–1856), pp. 309–311, at p. 309.

86. Sainte-Beuve in a letter of April 22, 1862 to Charles Duveyrier, quoted in Claude Pichois, *Littérature et progrès: Vitesse et vision du monde*, Neuchâtel: Baconnière, 1973, pp. 41–42, and reported by Champfleury in "Courbet en

1860," *Grandes figures d'hier et d'aujourdhui: Balzac, Gérard de Nerval, Wagner, Courbet*, Paris: Poulet-Malassis et de Broise, 1861; repr. in *Le Réalisme*, ed. Geneviève and Jean Lacambre, Paris: Hermann, 1973, p. 185.

87. Auguste Comte, *Cours de philosophie positive*, 6 vols, Paris: Bachelier, 1830–1842, at vol. 1, pp. 4–5.

88. Hippolyte Taine, Introduction to *Histoire de la littérature anglaise*, vol. 1, Paris: Hachette, 1863, pp. XXII–XXXIII.

89. "L'école naturaliste affirme que . . . son unique but est de reproduire la nature en l'amenant à son maximum de puissance et d'intensité; c'est la vérité s'equilibrant avec le science." Jules-Auguste Castagnary in his review, "Salon de 1863: Les Trois Écoles contemporaines," *in Salons: 1857–1870*, Paris: Charpentier, 1892, pp. 100–106; at pp. 105–105.

90. See Émile Zola's preface to the second edition of *Thérèse Raquin*: "Mon but a été un but scientifique avant tout . . . J'ai simplement fait sur deux corps vivants le travail analytique que les chirurgiens font sur des cadavres." *Œuvres complètes*, ed. Henry Mitterand, 15 vols, Paris: Cercle du Livre Précieux, 1965–1971, at vol. 1, p. 520. In *Le Roman expérimental* he speaks of "L'idée d'une littérature déterminée par la science" and maintains that "le roman expérimental est une conséquence de l'évolution scientifique." *Œuvres complètes*, vol. 10, pp. 1175 and 1186.

91. Timothy James Clark, *The Painting of Modern Life: Paris in the Art of Manet and His Followers*, London: Thames and Hudson, 1985, pp. 10 and 12.

92. See Bonner Mitchell, ed., *Les Manifestes littéraires de la Belle Epoque 1886–1914: Anthologie critique*, Paris: Seghers, 1966, and Joachim Schultz, *Literarische Manifeste der Belle Epoque, Frankreich 1886–1909*, Frankfurt/M: Lang, 1981.

93. "Un Referendum artistique et social," *L'Ermitage* 4:7 (July 1893), pp. 1–24. The summary on p. 23 established 53% in favour of anarchism, 24% undecided, 23% against it.

94. Maffeo-Charles Poinsot, *Littérature sociale*. Paris: Bibliothèque Générale d'Édition, 1907, p. 56. See also Richard D. Sonn, *Anarchism and Cultural Politics in Fin de Siècle France*, Lincoln, NE: University of Nebraska Press, 1989; David Weir, *Anarchy and Culture: The Aesthetic Politics of Modernism*, Amherst, MA: University of Massachusetts Press, 1997; Dieter Scholz, *Pinsel und Dolch: Anarchistische Ideen in Kunst und Kunsttheorie 1840—1920*, Berlin: Reimer, 1999.

95. See Arno Holz, *Die Kunst: Ihr Wesen und ihre Gesetze*, Berlin: Issleib, 1891, p. 117, reprinted in Arno Holz, *Das Werk*, vol. 10, Berlin: Dietz, 1925, p. 89. In the shorthand formula "art = nature − X" the factor X includes the skill, knowledge, and state of mind of the artist as well as the objective conditions of the material he chooses to work with (stone, canvas, words, etc.).

96. Arthur Rimbaud, "Adieu" (*Une Saison en enfer*), in *Œuvres complètes*, Paris: Gallimard, 1972, p. 116.

97. See Wunberg, *Die literarische Moderne and Die Wiener Moderne*; Sprengel, *Berliner und Wiener Moderne*; Schütte and Sprengel, *Die Berliner Moderne 1885–1914*; Schmitz, *Die Münchener Moderne*; Merlio and Pelletier, *Munich 1900 site de la modernité*.

98. Leo Wulff, ed., *Die Insel der Blödsinnigen: Die Tollheiten der Moderne in Wort und Bild*, Berlin: Verlag der "Lustigen Blätter," 1901. There was also a sequel: *Der Drehwurm im Ueberbrettl: Der Insel der Blödsinnigen anderer Theil*, Berlin: Verlag der "Lustigen Blätter," 1902.

99. Michael Georg Conrad, *Von Emile Zola bis Gerhard Hauptmann: Erinnerungen zur Geschichte der Moderne*, Leipzig: H. Seemann Nachfolge, 1902.

100. Samuel Lubinsky, *Die Bilanz der Modern*, Berlin: Cronbach, 1904.

101. Lubinsky, *Der Ausgang der Moderne: Ein Buch der Opposition*, Dresden: Reissner, 1909.

102. D. H. Lawrence, Letter of June 5, 1914 to Edward Garnett, in *The Letters of D. H. Lawrence*, vol. 2, ed. G. J. Zyttaruck and J. T. Boulton, Cambridge: Cambridge University Press, 1981, p. 183.

103. Max Planck, *Where is Science Going?*, London: Allen and Unwin, 1933, p. 65. See also p. 51 for Kandinsky's response to the disintegration of the materialist-positivist worldview.

104. "The Second Coming" (1916), in *The Variorum Edition of the Poems of W.B. Yeats*, ed. P. Alt and R. K. Alspach, New York: Macmillan, 1957, p. 402.

105. John Donne, "The First Anniversary: An Anatomie of the World," in *The Variorum Edition of the Poetry of John Donne*, vol. 6. Bloomington, IN: Indiana University Press, 1995, p. 12, lines 212–213.

106. Kurt Pinthus, ed., *Menschheitsdämmerung: Ein Dokument des Expressionismus*, Berlin: Rowohlt, 1920, p. X (in the reprint of 1959, pp. 25).

107. In the period 1875–1910, the number of independent intellectuals (writers, journalists, etc.) in European countries experienced a rise of 219% in France, ca. 180% in Germany, ca. 170% in Britain, and ca. 160% in Italy. See Christophe Charle, *Les Intellectuels en Europe au XIXe siècle: Essai d'histoire comparée*, 2nd rev. ed., Paris: Seuil, 2001, pp. 174–175. The expansion was even higher among those employed at universities. Between 1864 and 1909 they experienced a growth rate of 714% in Britain, 259% in Germany, and 244% in France. See ibid., p. 179.

108. Theodor W. Adorno, *Aesthetic Theory*, London: Routledge & Kegan Paul, 1984, p. 31.

109. See Berghaus, *The Genesis of Futurism*, p. 58, and *Italian Futurist Theatre*, pp. 43–45, 68–79.

110. See, e.g., Germain Bazin, *Histoire de l'avant-garde en peinture du XIIIe au XXe siècle*, Paris: Hachette, 1969.

111. Étienne Pasquier, *Des Recherches de la France*, Paris: Longis and Le Manier, 1560, quoted in Calinescu, *Five Faces of Modernity*, p. 98.

112. "L'Organisateur" (1819) in *Œuvres de Saint-Simon*, vol. 4, Paris: Dentu, 1869 [this forms vol. 20 of the *Œuvres de Saint-Simon et d'Enfantin*, 47 vols, Paris: Dentu, 1865–1878], pp. 24, 42, and 184.

113. *Lettres de Henri Saint-Simon à Messieurs les Jurés*, Paris: Corréard & Pélicier, 1820. These letters have not been included in the Dentu edition, but have been

reprinted in *Œuvres de Claude-Henri de Saint Simon*, vol. 6, Paris: Éditions Anthropos, 1966, pp. 399–433, at p. 422.

114. "De l'organisation sociale" (1825), in *Œuvres de Saint Simon*, vol. 10, Paris: Dentu, 1875 [= vol. 39 of the standard edition, *Œuvres de Saint Simon et d'Enfantin*], p. 137.

115. [Olinde Rodrigues], "L'Artiste, le savant et l'industriel," in Henri, Comte de Saint Simon, *Opinions littéraires, philosophiques et industrielles*, Paris: Galérie de Bossange Père, 1825, pp. 331–392, at p. 341. In *Œuvres de Saint-Simon*, vol. 10, Paris: Dentu, 1875 [= vol. 39 of the *Œuvres de Saint-Simon et d'Enfantin*], pp. 210–211.

116. Excerpts from the essay have been reprinted in Hardt, *Literarische Avantgarden*, pp. 17–25.

117. During the revolution of 1848, a newspaper called *L'Avant-garde* was published in Paris; in the *Communist Manifesto*, Marx and Engels defined the Communists as "the most advanced and resolute section of the working class parties"; in 1878, Kropotkin edited a magazine called *L'Avant-garde*, and Lenin spoke in *What Is to Be Done* of the Communist Party as the avant-garde of the working class. A good survey of such usage of "avant-garde" in nineteenth-century revolutionary circles is given by Holthusen, "Kunst und Revolution," in Holthusen, ed., *Avantgarde: Geschichte und Krise einer Idee*, pp. 7–44; Egbert, "The Idea of 'Avant-garde' in Art and Politics"; Calinescu " 'Avant-garde': Some Terminological Considerations"; and Weisgerber, *Les Avantgardes littéraires*, vol. 1, pp. 7–24.

118. See "Mon Cœur mis à nu," § XXIII, fol. 39–41, in *Œuvres complètes*, Paris: Gallimard, 1961, p. 1285.

119. Mann, *The Theory Death of the Avant-Garde*, p. 47.

120. Marinetti propagated this concept in "Il proletariato dei geniali," in *Democrazia futurista*, Milan: Facchi, 1919, pp. 133–142, reprinted in *Teoria e invenzione futurista*, pp. 350–354. His proposals were repeated in a slightly altered wording in *Al di là del comunismo*, Milan: Edizioni de La Testa di Ferro, 1920, reprinted in *Teoria e invenzione futurista*, pp. 409–424.

121. Huelsenbeck, *Reise bis ans Ende der Freiheit*, p. 120.

122. F. T. Marinetti, "Uccidiamo il chiaro di luna," in *Teoria e invenzione futurista*, p. 22; *Selected Writings*, p. 52.

123. F. T. Marinetti, "Fondazione e manifesto del futurismo," in *Teoria e invenzione futurista*, p. 10; *Selected Writings*, p. 42.

124. F. T. Marinetti, Preface to *Mafarka il futurista*, in *Teoria e invenzione futurista*, p. 217.

125. F. T. Marinetti, "Fondazione e manifesto del futurismo," in *Teoria e invenzione futurista*, p. 13; *Selected Writings*, p. 43.

126. E. Settimelli, *Inchiesta sulla vita italiana*, Rocca San Casciano: Cappelli, 1919, p. 97.

127. Arp, "Emmy Hennings und Hugo Ball," in Ball/Hennings, *Damals in Zürich*, pp. 179–182, at p. 181.

128. "I want to suffer, I don't want to skive off. I'm no shirker. Don't you believe this! I too am standing in the trenches, but a different kind of trenches. I am not a deserter, I am fighting." Letter to his sister of December 19, 1916 in Ball/ Hennings, *Damals in Zürich*, p. 118.

129. "Pamphlet gegen die weimarische Lebensauffassung," in Hausmann, *Am Anfang war Dada*, pp. 74–77, at p. 77.

130. Otto Dix et al., "Offener Brief an die Novembergruppe," *Der Gegner* 2 (1920–1921), pp. 297–301, at p. 300.

131. See Marinetti's collection of essays, *Guerra sola igienie del mondo* (1915), reprinted in *Teoria e invenzione futurista*, pp. 201–293.

132. See Berghaus, *Italian Futurist Theatre*, p. 53, note 4.

133. Raoul Hausmann, "Dada ist mehr als Dada," in Hausmann, *Am Anfang war Dada*, pp. 83–89, at p. 89.

134. Marcel Janco, "Creative Art," in Verkauf, ed., *Dada: Monograph of a Movement*, pp. 42 and 44.

135. G. Maciunas, Letter of March 7, 1962 to La Monte Young, reproduced in Achille Bonito Oliva, ed., *Ubi Fluxus ibi modus 1990–1962*, Milan: Mazzotta, 1990, p. 119.

136. Huelsenbeck, *Mit Witz, Licht und Grütze*, pp. 81 and 85; *Memoirs of a Dada Drummer*, pp. 54 and 57.

137. Emmett Williams in an interview with Kirsten Martins, in Kirsten Martins and Peter J. Sohn, eds., *Performance: Another Dimension*, Exh. cat. Berlin: Künstlerhaus Bethanien, Berlin: Frölich and Kaufmann, 1983, p. 213.

138. Umberto Eco, *A Theory of Semiotics*, Bloomington, IN: Indiana University Press, 1976, p. 272.

139. George Steiner, *After Babel: Aspects of Language and Translation*, London: Oxford University Press, 1975, p. 465.

140. Pratella, *Autobiografia*, p. 121.

141. See Berghaus, *Futurism and Politics*, pp. 47–110, and Emilio Gentile, "Political Futurism and the Myth of the Italian Revolution," in Berghaus, ed., *International Futurism in Arts and Literature*, pp. 1–14.

142. The Futurist came closest to this ideal of merging radical art with intransigent politics in the Fiume Revolution of 1919–1921. See Berghaus, *Futurism and Politics*, pp. 134–143.

143. F. T. Marinetti, "Al di là del comunismo," in *Teoria e invenzione futurista*, pp. 422–424; *Selected Writings*, pp. 155–157.

144. F. T. Marinetti, "Il proletariato dei geniali," in *Democrazia futurista*, pp. 133–142; reprinted in *Teoria e invenzione futurista*, at p. 354.

145. See Jost Hermand, "Expressionismus als Revolution," in Jost Hermand, *Von Mainz nach Weimar*, Stuttgart: Luchterhand, 1969, 298–355; Wolfgang Frühwald, "Kunst als Tat und Leben: Über den Anteil deutscher Schriftsteller an der Revolution in München 1918/1919," in W. Frühwald and G. Niggl, eds., *Sprache und Bekenntnis: Hermann Kunisch zum 70. Geburtstag*, Berlin: Duncker & Humblot, 1971, pp. 361–389.

146. See Robert S. Short, "The Politics of Surrealism 1920–36," *Journal of Contemporary History* 1:2 (1966), pp. 3–25; Jack J. Roth, "The 'Revolution of the Mind': The Politics of Surrealism Reconsidered," *South Atlantic Quarterly* 76:2 (Spring 1977), pp. 147–158; Marguerite Bonnet, ed., *Archives du Surréalisme, vol 2: Vers l'action politique*, Paris: Gallimard, 1988; Helena Lewis, *Dada Turns Red: The Politics of Surrealism*, Edinburgh: Edinburgh University Press, 1990.

147. Alfred Jarry, "Questions de théâtre," *Œuvres complètes*, vol. 1, p. 418.

148. F. T. Marinetti, "Fondazione e manifesto del futurismo," in *Teoria e invenzione futurista*, p. 12; *Selected Writings*, p. 43.

149. "En avant Dada," in Motherwell, *Dada Painters and Poets*, p. 44.

150. See Sanouillet, *Dada à Paris*, p. 155.

151. Ferdinand Hardekopf in a letter of May 13, 1917 to Olly Jacques, in Richard Sheppard, "Ferdinand Hardekopf und Dada," *Jahrbuch der Schillergesellschaft* 20 (1976), p. 135.

152. "En avant Dada," in Motherwell, *Dada Painters and Poets*, p. 45.

153. Albert Gleizes and Jean Metzinger, "Cubism, 1912," in H. B. Chipp, *Theories of Modern Art*, Berkeley, CA: University of California Press, 1970, p. 214.

154. Rimbaud in his letters to Georges Izambart of May 13, 1871 and Paul Demeny of May 15, 1871, in *Œuvres complètes*, ed. Antoine Adam, Paris: Gallimard, 1972, pp. 249 and 250.

155. This applies in the first instance to the Futurist *serate* and Dada *soirées*. However, the historical avant-garde did not abolish the concept of "production" altogether. There are many examples of performances that were rehearsed and designed, but not for the sake of arriving at a fixed "product" organized for passive consumption, but rather to create events that might provoke, challenge or rouse an audience.

156. See the testimonies in Arnauld, *Alfred Jarry*, pp. 216–221.

157. See Jarry's critical writings on the theatre, collected in *Œuvres complètes*, vol. 1, pp. 399–423, and partly translated in *Selected Works of Alfred Jarry*, ed. Shattuck and Taylor, pp. 65–90.

158. His demands were very similar to those of the Futurists some 15 years later. See the *Futurist Playwrights' Manifesto* and the *Manifesto of Dynamic and Synoptic Declamation*, discussed in Berghaus, *Italian Futurist Theatre*, pp. 157–161 and 172–175. Like Jarry, Marinetti gave a first foretaste of this style of acting in the soirées of the Mercure de France.

159. See the letters to Lugné-Poë of July 29, and August 1, 1896, in *Œuvres complètes*, vol. 1, pp. 1049–1050.

160. "Questions de théâtre," *Œuvres complètes*, vol. 1, p. 416.

161. For primary sources see the Folio edition of 1978, the summaries provided by Arnauld, *Alfred Jarry*, pp. 312–322, P. Lié, "Comment Jarry et Lugné-Poe glorifièrent Ubu à l'Œuvre," and Lié, "Notes sur la seconde représentation d'Ubu Roi."

162. See the testimonial of Georges Rémond, "Souvenirs sur Jarry et autres," *Mercure de France*, 323:1099 (March 1, 1955), pp. 426–446; 323:1100 (April 1, 1955), pp. 656–677, at pp. 664–665.

163. See Rémond, "Souvenirs sur Alfred Jarry," pp. 664–665. This appears to have developed into a constituent feature of many avant-garde performances, as can be seen in chapters 3 and 4 on Futurism and Dada.

164. Henry Fouquier in his review of December 13, 1896, quoted in Beaumont, *Alfred Jarry*, p. 102. A detailed analysis of the press response has been given by Robillion, "La Presse d'Ubu Roi."

165. See Berghaus, *The Genesis of Futurism*, pp. 28–29, and *Italian Futurist Theatre*, pp. 30–31.

166. See Sixten Ringbom, "Kandinsky und das Okkulte," in Armin Zweite, ed., *Kandinsky und München: Begegnungen und Wandlungen, 1896–1914*, Munich: Prestel, 1982, pp. 85–101, and Ringbom, "Die Steiner-Annotationen Kandinskys," in ibid., pp. 102–105.

167. W. Kandinsky, "Rückblicke," in *Die Gesammelten Schriften*, vol. 1, p. 33; *Complete Writings on Art*, p. 364 (all translations here are my own).

168. The discovery of the spontaneous breaking up of certain atoms into smaller particles (natural radioactivity) by Becquerel (1896) and the Curies (1898) led to Rutherford's first atomic model of 1911. See pp. 29 and 31.

169. See Ringbom, *The Sounding Cosmos,* and the catalogs *The Spiritual in Art: Abstract Painting 1890–1985*, ed. Maurice Tuchman, Los Angeles: Los Angeles County Museum of Art, 1986; New York: Abbeville Press, 1986; *Okkultismus und Avant-garde*, ed. Veit Loers, Frankfurt: Schirn Kunsthalle, 1995; Ostfildern: Cantz, 1995.

170. The first of these took place around 1909, according to Briesch, *Wassily Kandinsky (1866–1944): Untersuchungen zur Entstehung der gegenstandslosen Malerei*, p. 187. See also *Towards a New Art*, Tate Gallery, 1980; Cheetham, *The Rhetoric of Purity*, and Brucher, *Wassily Kandinsky: Wege zur Abstraktion*.

171. See *Über das Geistige in der Kunst*, 1952 ed., pp. 44–47; *Complete Writings on Art*, pp. 146–148.

172. See Weiss, "Kandinsky: Symbolist Poetics and Theater in Munich."

173. A second, also aborted, production was set up in 1914 by the Kreis für Kunst in Cologne, to coincide with their Kandinsky exhibition. Equally unsuccessful were the attempts to produce the drama in 1922 at the Berlin Volksbühne and at an unknown venue with Oskar Schlemmer as director. See Kandinsky's letter of January 24, 1937 to Hans Hildebrandt in "Drei Briefe von Kandinsky," *Werk* 42:10 (October 1955), pp. 327–331, at p. 330, and Boissel, "Solche Dinge haben eigene Geschicke," pp. 249–250.

174. On Steiner's plays, *Die Pforte der Einweihung, Die Prüfung der Seele, Der Hüter der Schwelle* and *Der Seelen Erwachen* see Rudolf Steiner, *Das literarische und künstlerische Werk*, Dornach: Rudolf Steiner Nachlaßverwaltung, 1961, pp. 40–41

and 144; Robb Creese, "Anthroposophical Performance," *The Drama Review* 22:2 (T78) (June 1978), pp. 45–74; Johannes Hemleben, *Rudolf Steiner: An Illustrated Biography*, London: Sophia Books, 2000, pp. 121–128; Edmund B. Lingan, "Reincarnation and Individuality: Rudolf Steiner's 'Mystery Dramas' in the New Millennium," *Western European Stages* 13:2 (Spring 2001), pp. 73–78. As Washton Long pointed out (*Kandinsky: The Development of an Abstract Style*, p. 56), Emy Dresler from Kandinsky's Künstlervereinigung designed the sets and costumes for Steiner's productions in Munich.

175. Kandinsky, "Über die abstrakte Bühnensynthese," *Staatliches Bauhaus in Weimar 1919–1923*, pp. 142–144, partly reprinted in *bauhaus* 3 (1927), p. 6; *Complete Writings on Art*, pp. 504–507.

176. Ibid.

177. See Kandinsky, "Rückblicke," *Die Gesammelten Schriften*, vol. 1, p. 33; *Complete Writings on Art*, pp. 363–364.

178. Kandinsky, "Über die Formfrage," *Complete Writings on Art*, pp. 235–257, at p. 235.

179. Kandinsky, 'Über Bühnenkomposition', *Complete Writings on Art*, pp. 257–265, at p. 257.

180. See Kandinsky, "Rückblicke," *Die Gesammelten Schriften*, vol. 1, p. 45; *Complete Writings on Art*, p. 376.

181. Kandinsky, "Rückblicke," *Die Gesammelten Schriften*, vol. 1, p. 47, note. 1; *Complete Writings on Art*, p. 379, note.

2 EXPRESSIONISM

1. Herwarth Walden, "Erster Deutscher Herbstsalon," *Der Sturm* 4:180/181 (October 1913), p. 106.

2. Diebold in a review of Kornfeld's *Die Verführung*, *Frankfurter Zeitung*, December 10, 1917.

3. See his essay "Die Seele ist es, die da spielt," *Schauspielernotizen, Zweite Folge*, Berlin: Reiss, 1915, reprinted in Friedrich Kayssler, *Gesammelte Schriften*, vol. 3, Berlin: Horen-Verlag, 1929, pp. 190–195, at p. 192.

4. See the excellent essay by Denis Calandra, "Georg Kaiser's 'From Mourn to Midnight': The Nature of Expressionist Performance."

5. Herbert Jhering, *Die Zwanziger Jahre*, Berlin: Aufbau, 1948, p. 38.

6. See "Von der Natur der Gesichte," *Schriften*, pp. 337–341; *Das Schriftliche Werk*, vol. 3, pp. 9–12.

7. Kokoschka, *My Life*, p. 29.

8. Ibid., p. 30.

9. Kokoschka saw Wiesenthal on the stage of the Cabaret Fledermaus in 1908 and was deeply impressed. See his letter to Erwin Lang in Kokoschka, *Briefe*, vol. 1, p. 8.

10. Kokoschka, *My Life*, p. 26.

11. Ibid.

12. Kokoschka, "Vom Erleben," *Schriften 1907–1955*, pp. 50–51.
13. Quoted in Schweiger, *Der junge Kokoschka*, p. 106.
14. Kokoschka, *My Life*, p. 28.
15. Schweiger, *Der junge Kokoschka*, p. 106.
16. Kokoschka, *My Life*, p. 29.
17. The newspaper notices can be found in Schweiger, *Der junge Kokoschka*, pp. 111–113.
18. Kokoschka, *My Life*, pp. 28–29.
19. Diary note of September 26, 1904, quoted in Keith-Smith, *Lothar Schreyer: Ein vergessener Expressionist*, pp. 9–10.
20. L. Schreyer, "Vom Verfall der Bühnenkunst," *Xenien* 5 (1912), pp. 102–107, 166–170, at p. 105.
21. L. Schreyer, "Die jüngste Dichtkunst und die Bühne," *Die Scene: Blätter für Bühnenkunst* 5 (1915), pp. 171–172, 6 (1916), pp. 37–38, 101–102, at p. 102
22. Ibid., p. 102.
23. L. Schreyer, "Expressionistische Dichtung," *Sturm-Bühne* 4–5 (1918), pp. 19–20, 6 (1919), pp. 21–23, at p. 23.
24. L. Schreyer, "Hilfsdienst des Theaters," *Blätter des Deutschen Schauspielhauses in Hamburg* 2 (1917–1918), pp. 145–147, at p. 147.
25. Several reviews of the event are printed in Pirsich, *Der "Sturm" und seine Beziehungen zu Hamburg*, pp.103–109.
26. See "Aufruf," *Der Sturm* 8 (1917–1918), p. 94.
27. It was based on a series of lectures given under the auspices of *Der Sturm* and was published in several installments in *Der Sturm* 7 (1916/17), pp. 50–51, 8 (1917/18), pp. 18–22, 36–40. It was also incorporated into a 196-page book manuscript of 1917, entitled *Die Befreiung der Bühnenkunst*. I am glad to report that shortly after completing the manuscript of this volume, the Edwin Mellen Press issued the complete theatre essays of Lothar Schreyer, including unpublished manuscripts like the one above. I am indebted to Brian Keith-Smith for providing me with an advance copy of his edition.
28. See Schreyer's letter to Walden of September 19, 1919, quoted in Keith-Smith, *Lothar Schreyer: Ein vergessener Expressionist*, p. 110.
29. See Herbert Jhering, "Theater der Expressionisten," *Berliner Börsen-Courier*, October 16, 1918; Stefan Großmann, "Theaterstürmchen," *Vossische Zeitung*, October 16, 1918; frd, "Sturmbühne," *Vorwärts*, October 17, 1918; Hans Benzmann, "Die Dichter des Sturm," *Die Flöte* 1 (1918/19), p. 194 and *Westermanns Monatshefte* 64:127 (1919/20), p. 199.
30. "Versuch um das Mysterienspiel," in Schreyer, *Theateraufsätze*, pp. 579–586, at pp. 584–585.
31. William Wauer competed with Schreyer for the leadership of the Sturmbühne and apparently tried to oust him from the *Sturm* circle. See Pirsich, *Der Sturm*, pp. 467–468.
32. In *Expressionistisches Theater*, p. 198 Schreyer speaks of "200 friends of Expressionism, to which in the course of the following year some 100 were

added," whereas in a Kampfbühne announcement of August 1921 he mentions "over six hundred members." In an undated manuscript written later in his life, "Spielgang der Bühnenspiele," he even states: "In 1918–1921 we worked in a select circle of around 2,000 friends of the new art under exclusion from the public." See Schreyer, *Theaterschriften*, pp. 591, 617.

33. See Schreyer's letters of November 13, 1919 and March 26, 1920, quoted in Keith-Smith, *Lothar Schreyer: Ein vergessener Expressionist*, pp. 111–112.

34. *Mann* was actually premièred on May 16, 1920 at the Kammerspiele in Berlin. In Hamburg, only a Nativity Play was presented to a wider audience, on Boxing Day 1919 at St Catherine's Church. For the dates of performances, see Pirsich, *Der "Sturm" und seine Beziehungen zu Hamburg*, pp. 27–28 and Pirsich, *Der Sturm*, pp. 504–505.

35. These are the measurements given in the Spielgang for *Kreuzigung*. Schreyer in a letter to Wasserka said they were more likely to have been $4.5 \times 2 \times 1$ m. Wasserka, *Die Sturm- und Kampfbühne*, p. 203, note 69.

36. The one exception (on *Haidebraut* and *Kräfte*) can be found in the Expressionist journal, *Die rote Erde*, and has been reprinted in Pirsich, *Der 'Sturm' und seine Beziehungen zu Hamburg*, pp. 110–111.

37. The papers are now preserved in the Deutsches Literaturarchiv Marbach. Some of the manuscripts relevant to the theatre have been published by Brian Keith-Smith in Schreyer, *Theateraufsätze*. For a detailed examination of the performance scores, see Wasserka, *Die Sturm- und Kampfbühne*.

38. L. Schreyer, "Mensch und Maske," Ludwig Pallat and Hans Lebede, eds., *Jugend und Bühne*, Breslau: Hirth, 1924, pp. 189–194, at p. 192.

39. Schreyer, *Expressionistisches Theater*, pp. 200–201.

40. See Brian Keith-Smith, "Lothar Schreyer's Theatre Works and the Use of Masks." Schreyer published some of his general thoughts on the topic in the essay, "Mensch und Maske."

41. "Das Wesen des Körperlichen," *Sturm-Bühne* 4–5 (September 1918), p. 1.

42. For Laban's biography, see Preston-Dunlop, *Rudolf Laban: An Extraordinary Life*. Unfortunately, this informative study lacks any critical apparatus. For Laban's early period, her fully annotated series of essays in *Dance Theatre Journal* is therefore still an important source of information.

43. See Preston-Dunlop, "Rudolf Laban: The Making of Modern Dance," p. 12.

44. One of the best introductions to the system and a well-considered reflection of its genesis is Vera Maletic, *Body–Space–Expression: The Development of Rudolf Laban's Movement and Dance Concepts*.

45. For her biography, see Müller, *Mary Wigman*, and Manning, *Ecstasy and the Demon*.

46. See Hélène Emma Brunet-Lecomte, *Jaques-Dalcroze: Sa vie, son œuvre*, Geneva: Jeheber, 1950; Gernot Giertz, *Kultus ohne Götter: Emile Jaques-Dalcroze und Adolphe Appia. Der Versuch einer Theaterreform auf der Grundlage der rhythmischen Gymnastik*, Munich: Kitzinger, 1975; Irwin Spector, *Rhythm and Life: The Work of Emile Jaques-Dalcroze*, Stuyvesant, NY: Pendragon Press, 1990.

47. See Müller, *Mary Wigman*, p. 43.

48. See Curl, "Philosophical Foundations."
49. See Laban, *A Life for Dance*, p. 177. I wish to express my gratitude to Valerie Preston-Dunlop, who not only provided me with many unpublished documents from the Laban Archive in London, but also allowed me to see many of her recreations of Laban's dances from the early 1920s.
50. Quoted in Steffens, *Expressionistische Dramatik*, p. 140. Many reviews of the early Expressionist productions have been reprinted by Günther Rühle, *Theater für die Republik*, Frankfurt am Main: Fischer, 1967 and Hugo Fetting, *Von der Freien Bühne zum Politischen Theater*, Leipzig: Reclam, 1987.
51. "Reinhard Johannes Sorge: Der Bettler," *Der Tag*, 28 December 1917.
52. *Der Sohn* I,1; Hasenclever, *Sämtliche Werke Bd. II.1: Stücke bis 1924*, Mainz: Hase und Köhler, 1992, p. 237.
53. Richard Weichert, "Hasenclevers 'Sohn' als expressionistisches Regieproblem," *Die Scene: Blätter für Bühnenkunst* 8 (1918), pp. 65–67, at pp. 65–66.
54. Hasenclever, *Briefe Bd. 1: 1907–1932*, Mainz: Hase und Köhler, 1994, p. 250. See also *Stücke bis 1924*, p. 564.
55. *Menschheitsdämmerung* (Twilight of Humanity) was the title of the most important anthology of Expressionist poetry, edited by Kurt Pinthus in 1920.
56. Their artistic program was presented by Karl von Felner, "Die Tribüne," *Das deutsche Drama: Zeitschrift für Freunde dramatischer Kunst* 2 (1919), pp. 250–255 and quoted verbatim in *Das literarische Echo* 21:19 (July 1, 1919), col. 1213. The following quotes are taken from these statements.
57. Alfred Kerr, "Ernst Toller: 'Die Wandlung,' " *Berliner Tageblatt*, October 1, 1919.
58. Emil Faktor, "Ernst Toller: Die Wandlung," *Berliner Börsen-Courier*, October 1, 1919.
59. Emil Faktor, "Der zweite Tribüne-Abend: Nachlese," *Berliner Börsen-Courier*, October 1, 1919.
60. Herbert Jhering, " 'Die Wandlung': Uraufführung in der Tribüne," *Der Tag*, October 2, 1919.
61. The playhouse has been described and documented in Walter R. Fuerst and Samuel J. Hume, *Twentieth Century Stage Decoration*, London: Knopf, 1928; Richard and Helen Leacroft, *Theatre and Playhouse*, London: Methuen, 1984; George C. Izenour, *Theatre Design*, New York: McGraw Hill, 1977.
62. See Padmore, "German Expressionist Opera"; Mauser, *Das expressionistische Musiktheater der Wiener Schule*; Mauser, "Expressionismus als Musiktheater."
63. See Von Troschke, *Der Begriff "Expressionismus" in der Musikliteratur*; Crawford, *Expressionism in Twentieth-Century Music*; Poirier, *L'Expressionisme et la musique*.
64. Fritz Kortner, *Aller Tage Abend*, Munich: Kindler, 1959, p. 480.

3   FUTURISM

1. More information on these activities can be found in Berghaus, *The Genesis of Futurism* and *Futurism and Politics*.

2. Marinetti wrote in the chapter, "Prime battaglie futuriste," in *Guerra sola igiene del mondo*, that on October 11, 1908 he recognized for the first time the need to "lay siege to the theatres and introduce the fist into the struggle for art. . . . This new formula of art-as-action was a guiding rule for mental health." Marinetti, *Teoria e invenzione futurista*, p. 201.

3. For a detailed discussion of the political manifestos, the Futurist participation in regional and general elections, and the political links with the extreme Left see my studies *Futurism and Politics*, and "The Futurist Political Party," in Sascha Bru and Gunther Martens, eds., *The Invention of Politics in the European Avant-Garde, 1905–1940*, Amsterdam & New York: Rodopi (forthcoming).

4. See Carpi, *L'estrema avanguardia del Novecento*, and Ciampi,*Futuristi e anarchisti*.

5. Maria Rygier, "Futurismo politico," *L'agitatore* (Bologna), August 7, 1910.

6. Leda Rafanelli, "Futuristi," *Il novatore* (Milan), 3rd series, vol. 3, no. 1, July 29, 1911.

7. See "I futuristi," published in the *Corriere Universitario*, reprinted in *Cronache Torinesi, 1913–1917*, ed. S. Caprioglio, Turin: Einaudi, 1980, pp. 6–9, translated in Gramsci, *Selections from Cultural Writings*, Cambridge, MA: Harvard University Press, 1985, pp. 46–49. On the relationship between Gramsci and Futurism see also Renzo Martinelli, "Gramsci e il 'Corriere universitario' di Torino," *Studi storici* 14 (1973), pp. 906–920; Edo Bellingeri, *Dall' intellettuale al politico: Le 'Cronache teatrali' di Gramsci*, Bari: Dedalo Libri, 1975; Jean Thibaudeau, "Le futurisme dans les écrits de Gramsci," in G. Lista, ed., *Marinetti et le futurisme*, Lausanne: L'Age d'Homme, 1977, pp. 115–121; Daniela Quarta, *Gramsci e il futurismo*, Copenhagen: Romansk Instituts, 1987; Umberto Carpi, "Gramsci e le avanguardie intellettuali," *Studi storici* 21 (1980), pp. 19–29; Robert S. Dombroski, *Antonio Gramsci*, Boston: Twayne, 1989, pp. 94–99.

8. "Against Love and Parliamentarianism," *Teoria e invenzione futurista*, p. 252, *Selected Writings*, p. 74.

9. "The book, static companion of the sedentary, the nostalgic, and the Neutralists, can neither amuse nor stimulate the new Futurist generations, who are drunk on revolutionary, warlike dynamism." F. T. Marinetti et al., "The Futurist Cinema," *Teoria e invenzione futurista*, p. 118, *Selected Writings*, p. 130.

10. See the "Synthetic Theatre Manifesto," *Teoria e invenzione futurista*, p. 98, *Selected Writings*, p. 123.

11. "Azione politica e azione teatrale nel futurismo di Marinetti," in C. Vicentini, *La teoria del teatro politico*, Florence: Sansoni, 1981, pp. 45–82, at p. 71.

12. It was published in several Left-wing journals and reprinted in Marinetti, *Democrazia futurista*, ch. 23.

13. See Altomare, *Incontri con Marinetti*, p. 19.

14. Palazzeschi, preface to Marinetti, *Teoria e invenzione futurista*, p. XIII. A copy of the leaflet, in French, has been reproduced in Salaris, *Storia del futurismo*, 2nd ed., p. 33. Marinetti says that of this manifesto 300,000 copies were distributed. See *Teoria e invenzione futurista*, p. 510.

15. Marinetti, "Prima spedizione punitiva artistica," *Teoria e invenzione futurista*, p. 514.

16. Letter of October 15, 1913, printed in Giuseppe Miligi, *Prefuturismo e primo futurismo in Sicilia, 1900–1918*, Messina: Sicania, 1989, p. 292.

17. The text is reproduced in *Teoria e invenzione futurista*, pp. 280–281. For an English translation see *Selected Writings*, pp. 62–63. Although the text is dated "20 September," it was already distributed four days earlier. According to Marinetti's letter to Folgore of November 5, 1914, they had printed 20,000 copies of it. See Francesco Muzzioli, ed., *Luciano Folgore & F. T. Marinetti: Carteggio futurista*, Rome: Officina, 1987, p. 70.

18. Boccioni in a letter to his family of September 22, 1914, in Drudi Gambillo and Fiori, ed., *Archivi del futurismo*, vol. 1, p. 347.

19. "Le Mouvement poétique en Italie," *La Vogue*, April 1899, p. 61.

20. F. T. Marinetti, "Vittorio Pica," *Anthologie-Revue*, 2:7 (May 1899), p. 131.

21. F. T. Marinetti, "*Una Tempesta*, tragédie moderne en cinq actes, par E. A. Butti," *L'Art dramatique et musical*, December 1901, p. 701.

22. See Marinetti, *La grande Milano*, p. 84. The reason for the negative reaction was, as he put it in his review of the production in *La Revue blanche* of June 1, 1901, "the unquestionable beauty of his elevated poetry, which the normal audience is unable to appreciate."

23. "*Una Tempesta*," pp. 698–701. See also F. T. Marinetti, "Mouvement théâtral: Drames nouveaux. *Lucifero*, drame en quatre actes, par E. A. Butti," *L'Art dramatique et musical*, February 1901, pp. 118–121.

24. See his letter in Jarry, *Œuvres complètes*, vol. 3, pp. 635–636.

25. See *Teoria e invenzione futurista*, p. 507.

26. Achille Tedeschi called the work "Un bel titolo, molto promettente" in his review for *L'illustrazione italiana*, January 24, 1909.

27. See the extracts in Berghaus, *Italian Futurist Theatre*, pp. 33–35.

28. See Antonucci, *Cronache del teatro futurista*, p. 24, and Gigi Livio, *Il teatro in rivolta*, Milan: Mursia, 1976, p. 13.

29. Vaccari, *Vita e tumulti di F. T. Marinetti*, p. 195.

30. All quotation from reviews of the production are taken from the documentation Marinetti compiled in *Poesia* 5: 3–6 (April–July 1909), pp. 38–51.

31. This seemed to have applied only to the first night, because *Gil Blas* reports: "The two performances which the Œeuvre gave afterwards at the Théâtre Marigny were much calmer."

32. F. T. Marinetti, "Les Funérailles du *Roi Bombance*," *L'Intransigeant*, April 12, 1909; reprinted in Marinetti, *Teatro*, vol. 2, pp. 476–477.

33. See "Prime battaglie futuriste," in *Teoria e invenzione futurista*, p. 201. A similar idea was expressed in an interview with Jannelli for *L'avvenire* of Messina, February 23, 1915: "When I created this effective propaganda in the form of the Futurist *serate*, Futurism became a sign of war bursting into the field of art."

34. "In tema del futurismo," *La diana* 1:1 (January 1915), pp. 27–29, at p. 28.

35. Ibid. The same phrases were repeated a month later in "Il valore futurista di guerra," *L'avvenire*, February 23, 1915.

36. "The destructive gesture of freedom-bringer" (*il gesto distruttore dei libertarî*) he called it in *Foundation and Manifesto of Futurism*. See *Teoria e invenzione futurista*, p. 10, *Selected Writings*, p. 42.

37. "The Pleasure of Being Booed," in *Teoria e invenzione futurista*, p. 267, *Selected Writings*, p. 114.

38. "Un movimento artistico crea un Partito Politico," in *Teoria e invenzione futurista*, p. 298.

39. F. T. Marinetti, "Gli sfruttatori del futurismo," *Lacerba* 2:7 (April 1, 1914), pp. 108–107, reprinted in *Teoria e invenzione futurista*, pp. 92–94.

40. F. T. Marinetti, Preface to *Mafarka il futurista*, reprinted in *Teoria e invenzione futurista*, p. 217.

41. Claudio Vicentini, "Arte, politica e guerra nel futurismo di Marinetti," *Rivista di estetica* 2 (June 1979), pp. 62–87, at pp. 78–79.

42. Cangiullo, *Le serate futuriste*, pp. 113–114.

43. A list of source materials on which my descriptions are based can be found in Berghaus, *Italian Futurist Theatre*, p. 151, note. 98 and p. 152, note. 126.

44. Altomare, *Incontri con Marinetti*, p. 52.

45. Vaccari, *Vita e tumulti di F. T. Marinetti*, p. 288.

46. Alberto Viviani, *Giubbe rosse*, Firenze: Vallecchi, 1983, p. 66.

47. Ardegno Soffici, *Fine di un mondo*, Florence: Vallechi, 1955, p. 328.

48. Cangiullo, *Le serate futuriste*, pp. 160–161.

49. F. T. Marinetti, "Discorso del Teatro Verdi," *Teoria e invenzione futurista*, p. 499.

50. Ottone Rosai, *Pagine di memorie*, unpublished manuscript in the Gabinetto Vieusseux, Archivio Contemporaneo, Fondo Rosai, Cassetta 17, Inserto 8, pp. 112–115.

51. Soffici, *Fine di un mondo*, p. 330.

52. Carrà, *Tutti gli scritti*, p. 663.

53. F. T. Marinetti, "Synthetic Theatre Manifesto," *Teoria e invenzione futurista*, p. 98, *Selected Writings*, p. 123.

54. Papini, "Contro il futurismo," *Lacerba* 1: 5 (March 15, 1913), p. 45.

55. "Chronique zurichoïse," in Tzara, *Œuvres complètes*, vol. 1, p. 564.

56. "Le Surréalisme et l'après-guerre," in Tzara, *Œuvres complètes*, vol. 5, p. 67.

57. Richter, *Dada: Art and Anti-Art*, p. 77.

58. "The Futurist Playwrights Manifesto" of 11 January 1911, later reissued as "The Pleasure of Being Booed," in *Teoria e invenzione futurista*, p. 268, *Selected Writings*, p. 114.

59. "Synthetic Theatre Manifesto," in *Teoria e invenzione futurista*, p. 101, *Selected Writings*, p. 126.

60. Ibid.

61. Ibid.

62. "Variety Theatre Manifesto," in *Teoria e invenzione futurista*, pp. 72–73, *Selected Writings*, p. 118.

63. Ibid., in *Teoria e invenzione futurista*, p. 75, *Selected Writings*, p. 119.

64. "Futurist Playwrights' Manifesto," in *Teoria e invenzione futurista*, p. 269, *Selected Writings*, p. 115.
65. "Synthetic Theatre Manifesto," in *Teoria e invenzione futurista*, p. 100, *Selected Writings*, p. 125.
66. For a more detailed discussion of these and other works see Berghaus, *Italian Futurist Theatre*.
67. Reprinted in Drudi Gambillo and Fiori eds., *Archivi del futurismo*, vol. 1, pp. 48–51. An English translation can be found in Apollonio, *Futurist Manifestos*, pp. 197–200.
68. Balla's "noise forms," which he reflected on in his notebooks and his paintings "Line of Speed + Forms + Noise" and "Rhythm + Noise + Car Speed" of 1913 (see the Balla catalog, Oxford 1987, p. 88) were inspired by Russolo's manifesto *The Art of Noise* of March 1913 and the subsequent presentation of the noise-intoners in the Modena *serata* of June 2, 1913.
69. See Cangiullo, *Le serate futuriste*, pp. 173–174.
70. Balla and Depero, "Futurist Reconstruction of the Universe," in Apollonio, ed., *Futurist Manifestos*, p. 198.
71. This is Balla's characterization quoted in Léonide Massine, *My Life in Ballet*, London: Macmillan, 1968, p. 107.
72. "Transcendentalismo fisico. Roma 1915. Discussione con Umberto Boccioni sul quadro mobile," in Fortunato *Depero nelle opere e nella vita*, p. 234.
73. Depero, "Transcendentalismo fisico."
74. Foreword to the 1916 exhibition catalog, reprinted in *Depero Futurista*, Milano: Dinamo, 1927, p. 116.
75. It was first published in Giani, *Fortunato Depero Futurista*, ill. 26. A transcript can be found in the catalog *Fortunato Depero 1892–1960*, Bassano del Grappa: Museo Civico, 1970, pp. 138–140.
76. "Complesso plastico-mobile," in *Fortunato Depero 1892–1960*, Bassano del Grappa catalog, p. 158.
77. For a detailed description of these projects and performances see Berghaus, *Italian Futurist Theater*, pp. 297–315.
78. See "Mondo e il teatro plastico," *In penombra*, April–May 1919, pp. 20–22 and "Il teatro plastico Depero: Principî e applicazioni," *Il mondo* 5:17 (April 27, 1919), pp. 9–12. Both essays were reprinted in Passamani, *Depero e la scena*, pp. 95–97 and pp. 98–100.
79. "Scenografia e coreografia futurista" was reprinted in ten other journals and newspapers of the period, and was reissued in *Enrico Prampolini*, ed. Palma Bucarelli, pp. 41–44 and most other collections of Prampolini's theoretical writings. A shortened translation can be found in Apollonio, *Futurist Manifestos*, pp. 200–202.
80. See, e.g., Marinetti's letter to Cangiullo of April 26, 1914, where he arranged the publicity for the *pomeriggio futurista* of May 14, including a *lancio di manifesti*. Francesco Cangiullo and F. T. Marinetti, *Lettere, 1910–1943*, ed. by Ernestina Pellegrini, Florence: Vallecchi, 1989, p. 73.

81. Testimonial of Giuseppe Sprovieri, owner of the first permanent Futurist gallery in Rome, published in Fagiolo dell'Arco, *Esposizione di pittura futurista*, pp. 93–96.

82. The text was published as a brochure by the Edizioni di "Poesia" in 1916. Cangiullo had also planned to turn the piece into a ballet. Diaghilev, who had attended the performance in Naples, expressed an interest in the project and discussed with Stravinsky the possibility of setting the piece to music. See Cangiullo, *Le serate futuriste*, p. 231, and Vicente García-Márquez, *Massine*, New York: Knopf, 1995, p. 48. On Casavola's score *for Piedigrotta* see Pierfranco Moliterni, "Una Piedigrotta ritrovata," in *Marinetti e il futurismo a Napoli*, Roma: De Luca, 1996, pp. 99–106.

83. Huelsenbeck, *En avant Dada*, p. 30.

84. Ball, *Flucht aus der Zeit*, p. 79 (entry for March 12, 1916).

85. Huelsenbeck, *En avant Dada*, p. 30.

86. See Berghaus, *Italian Futurist Theatre*, pp. 384–395, and Berghaus, "The Futurist Banquet," pp. 3–17.

87. "Grande Cotillon patriottico," *Il piccolo*, September 21, 1922.

88. "Inaugurazione alla casa d'arte Bragaglia," *Il tempo*, April 18, 1922.

89. Antonio Aniante, "Una notte da Bragaglia," *La nuova Italia*, January 2, 1926.

90. See Berghaus, *International Futurism in the Arts and Literature*.

91. Francesco Flora, *Dal romanticismo al futurismo*, Piacenza: Porta, 1921, pp. 150–153.

92. These were the words of the henceforth well-known philosopher, Giacomo Donati Spartaco, quoted by Carpi, *L'estrema avanguardia del Novecento*, pp. 27–28.

93. Antonio Cervi in *Il resto del Carlino*, February 6, 1915; quoted in Antonucci, *Cronache del teatro futurista*, p. 84.

94. The relationship between Diaghilev and the Futurists has been discussed in Berghaus, *Italian Futurist Theatre*, pp. 253–259, 277–278, 300–309.

95. See Günter Berghaus, "Futurism, Dada, and Surrealism: Some Cross-Fertilizations among the Historical Avant-garde," in Berghaus, *International Futurism in Arts and Literature*, pp. 271–304.

4 DADAISM

1. See John White, "Futurism and German Expressionism," in Berghaus, *International Futurism in Arts and Literature*, pp. 39–74.

2. See Bergius, *Das Lachen Dadas*, p. 54.

3. See his diary entry in *Flucht aus der Zeit* (1946 edition), p. 35. There is a further entry on the *parole in libertà* on June 18, 1916. Marinetti's accompanying letter of July 5, 1915 was published by Schrott, *Dada 15/25*, p. 22. See also Ball's letter to Tzara of September 27, 1916, published in Schrott, *Dada 15/25*, pp. 66–67.

4. *En avant Dada* (1984 edition), p. 11; in Motherwell, *The Dadaist Poets and Painters*, pp. 24–25. See also his reflections on Futurism in the essay, "Die dadaistische

Bewegung," in *Die neue Rundschau* 31:8 (August 1920), p. 975, and in his memoirs, *Reise bis ans Ende der Freiheit*, pp. 67, 123, 130–131, 139–140, 168–169.

5. Glauser, *Dada, Ascona und andere Erinnerungen*, p. 46.

6. Zürcher, *Scharfrichter der bürgerlichen Seele*, p. 234.

7. Tzara called them "cartes-poèmes géographiques futuristes: Marinetti, Cangiullo,
   Buzzi" in his "Chronique zurichoïse," *Œuvres complètes*, vol. 1, p. 561. See also
   Ball's description of the hall in his letter of February 8, 1916 to Käthe Brodnitz,
   printed in Sheppard, "Hugo Ball and Käthe Brodnitz," p. 52.

8. No details of the evening are available, but it is likely to have been a performance
   of some *sintesi* from the collection *Teatro futurista sintetico*, published in
   November 1915.

9. Huelsenbeck, "Dada Lives," in Motherwell, *The Dada Painters and Poets*,
   pp. 279–280.

10. Evola summing up an essay by Margherita Sarfatti. Quoted without giving the
    exact source of reference in Lista, "Tzara et le dadaisme italien," *Europe* 53:
    555–556 (July–August 1975), pp. 173–192, at p. 178.

11. Tzara in a letter of Meriano of June 12, 1917 asked his Italian friend if he would
    be prepared to launch officially the Dada movement in Italy. See Giovanni
    Lista, "Encore sur Tzara et le futurisme," *Les Lettres nouvelles*, December 1974,
    pp. 114–149, at p. 140.

12. H. Ball, "Kandinsky," in Ball, *Künstler und Zeitkrankheit*, p. 41.

13. Huelsenbeck, *Mit Witz, Licht und Grütze*, pp. 113, 132; *Memoirs of a
    Dada Drummer*, pp. 76, 88. See also Huelsenbeck, *Reise bis ans Ende der Freiheit*,
    p. 321.

14. Marcel Janco, "Creative Art," in Verkauf, *Dada: Monograph of a Movement*,
    pp. 26–46, at p. 38.

15. Huelsenbeck, *Reise bis ans Ende der Freiheit*, p. 96.

16. Huelsenbeck, *Mit Witz, Licht und Grütze*, pp. 113, 132; *Memoirs of a Dada
    Drummer*, pp. 76, 88. See also Huelsenbeck, *Reise bis ans Ende der Freiheit*, p.
    321.

17. Huelsenbeck, *Reise bis ans Ende der Freiheit*, pp. 63, 129.

18. In 1909 he had begun a doctoral thesis on Nietzsche. For the draft of the study,
    see Ball, *Der Künstler und die Zeitkrankheit*, pp. 61–101.

19. Ball, "Das Münchener Künstlertheater," *Phoebus* 1:1 (April 1914), pp. 68–74,
    at p. 73.

20. Ball, *Flucht aus der Zeit*, p. 10.

21. Ibid., p. 11.

22. Ball, "Die Reise nach Dresden," *Revolution* 1:3 (November 15, 1913), reprinted
    in Ball, *Der Künstler und die Zeitkrankheit*, pp. 11–14.

23. Ball, *Briefe 1911–1927*, pp. 34–35.

24. Ball, *Flucht aus der Zeit*, p. 14 (November 1914).

25. Ibid., pp. 38–39 (November 18, 1915).

26. Ibid., p. 15 (November 25, 1914).

27. "Hier geht ein neues Leben los: anarcho-revolutionär." Letter of December 18, 1914 to August Hofmann in Ball, *Briefe 1911–1927*, p. 36.

28. See Huelsenbeck, *Reise bis ans Ende der Freiheit*, pp. 64–67.

29. The manifesto was first published by Gerhard Schaub, "*Dada avant la lettre:* Ein unbekanntes 'literarisches Manifest' von Hugo Ball und Richard Huelsenbeck," *Hugo Ball Almanach* 9–10 (1985/86), pp. 63–180, at p. 86. A facsimile has been reproduced in Bergius, *Das Lachen Dadas*, p. 57.

30. Hennings had led a gypsy-like existence for many years, performing in road shows, operettas, and nightclubs in Moscow, Budapest, and Cologne. She met Ball in autumn 1913 while performing at the Café Simplicissimus in Munich and joined him in Berlin in November 1914. See Rugh, "Emmy Hennings and the Emergence of Zurich Dada," in Sawelson-Gorse, *Women in Dada*, pp. 519–524, and Schwab, "Emmy Ball-Hennings."

31. F[ritz] St[ahl]: "Expressionisten-Abend," *Vossische Zeitung* [Abendausgabe], May 14, 1915. The review, together with several others of the event, was reprinted in Füllner, *Dada Berlin in Zeitungen*. See also Bergius, *Das Lachen Dadas*, pp. 58–59, and Reinhard Nenzel, "Hugo Ball und Richard Huelsenbeck: DADA-Kunst gegen Kunst. Aspekte ihrer Beziehung," *Hugo Ball Almanach* 14 (1990), pp. 115–226, at p. 148.

32. Ball, *Flucht aus der Zeit*, p. 47 (October 15, 1915). Similarly, Huelsenbeck wrote: "Those who had reached Zurich had rescued themselves, albeit only for a short while, from an ocean of blood. Here reigned an atmosphere of a holiday from death." "Dada in Zürich," *Die Weltbühne* 23:31 (August 2, 1927), p. 172.

33. Ball, *Flucht aus der Zeit*, pp. 21–22 (April 11, 1915).

34. Ball, Letter to Maria Hildebrand-Ball, November 12, 1915, in Ball/Hennings, *Damals in Zürich*, p. 28.

35. The text of the application has been printed in Meyer, *Dada in Zürich*, pp. 155–156.

36. Ball, *Flucht aus der Zeit*, p. 71.

37. Huelsenbeck, *Reise bis and Ende der Freiheit*, p. 114.

38. See the chapter, "Publikum und Presseberichte" in Bolliger, Magnaguagno and Meyer, *Dada in Zürich*, pp. 54–63, and Sheppard's collection, *Dada Zürich in Zeitungen*.

39. Kurt Guggenheim, *Alles in allem*, vol. 2, Zurich: Artemis, 1953, p. 184.

40. Sheppard, "Hugo Ball and Käthe Brodnitz," p. 52.

41. Ball, *Flucht aus der Zeit*, p. 70 (November 25, 1915).

42. Huelsenbeck, *Mit Witz, Licht und Grütze*, p. 33. *Memoirs of a Dada Drummer*, p. 19.

43. Ball, *Flucht aus der Zeit*, p. 91 (June 12, 1916).

44. Ibid., p. 94 (June 16, 1916).

45. See his description in *Reise bis ans Ende der Freiheit*, p. 121 and Ball, *Flucht aus der Zeit*, pp. 77–78 (March 11, 1916).

46. Ball, *Flucht aus der Zeit*, p. 78 (March 12, 1916).

47. Huelsenbeck, *Reise bis ans Ende der Freiheit*, p. 115.

48. Arp, *On My Way*, p. 48.

49. Janco, "Dada at Two Speeds," in Lippard, *Dadas on Art*, p. 36.

50. Huelsenbeck, *En avant Dada*, p. 18, translated in Motherwell, *The Dada Painters and Poets*, p. 33.

51. Suzanne Perrottet characterized the audience of the soirée on April 28, 1917: "The audience consisted mainly of young people, students, artists, the *crème de la crème* of Zurich, intellectuals, psychologists, teachers and many curious citizens." *Ein bewegtes Leben*, p. 138.

52. See his letter of April 19, 1919 to Olly Jacques, in Richard Sheppard, "Ferdinand Hardekopf und Dada," p. 145.

53. See his letters of February 16 and August 2, 1917 to Tzara in Sheppard, *Zürich—"Dadaco"— "Dadaglobe,"* pp. 10–12. The opening of a Cabaret Dada was considered again in winter 1918. See ibid., p. 14.

54. See Herzfelde, *Der Malik-Verlag 1916–1947*, p. 24.

55. See the illustration in Altshuler, *The Avant-garde in Exhibition*, p. 102.

56. Huelsenbeck, "Die dadaistische Bewegung," *Neue deutsche Rundschau* 31:8 (August 1920), p. 978.

57. This may have been a necessity, rather than an option, as Harry Graf Kessler reports in his diary on April 12, 1919: "In the afternoon Wieland Herzfelde brought me the third issue of *Pleite*. Street-vendors, he reported, are afraid to handle it; they might be killed. But he is having four to five thousand copies distributed in factories." *The Diaries of a Cosmopolitan, Count Harry Kessler, 1918–1937*, ed. Charles Kessler, London: Weidenfeld and Nicolson, 1971, p. 94. On May 3, he reports that 10,000–12,000 copies of *Die Pleite* had been distributed. Ibid., p. 100.

58. These have been brilliantly conjured up in a letter of George Grosz to Otto Schmalhausen, in Grosz, *Briefe 1913–1956*, Reinbek: Rowohlt, 1979, pp. 65–66, and emended in Bergius, *Das Lachen Dadas*, p. 30.

59. The evening at the Neue Sezession made a net sum of 500 marks. Hausmann was, therefore, keen to open a Galerie Dada in Berlin as a serious competition to Walden's *Sturm* Gallery. See his letter to Hannah Höch of May 3, 1918, quoted in Thater-Schulz, *Hannah Höch: Eine Lebenscollage*, vol. I.1, p. 330.

60. "Da-Da. Literatur-Narrheiten in der Sezession," *Berliner Börsen-Courier*, April 13, 1918, quoted in Füllner, *Richard Huelsenbeck*, p. 165.

61. Udo Ruckser, "Dada," *Freie Zeitung* (Berlin), May 8, 1919, quoted in Bergius, *Das Lachen Dadas*, p. 339. In 1923, Neumann emigrated to New York, where under the name Joseph B. Neumann he ran a successful gallery that played an important rôle in introducing Expressionist art to American audiences. See Platt, *Modernism in the 1920s*, pp. 28–30.

62. Mehring, *Berlin-Dada*, p. 52. Thomas Mann had at that time already achieved the status of a Prince of Letters. The offensive poems can be found in Mehring's *Chronik der Lustbarkeiten*, pp. 45–46, 47–48, 55–57.

63. E. Neuhahn, "Dada Matinee," *Hannoverscher Kurier*, December 2, 1919, reprinted in Bergius, *Das Lachen Dadas*, p. 347.

64. Grosz, *Ein kleines Ja,* p. 130.

65. H. Höch, "Erinnerungen an DADA: Ein Vortrag 1966," in *Hannah Höch 1889–1978: Ihr Werk, Ihr Leben, Ihre Freunde,* pp. 206–207.

66. *Dresdner Nachrichten,* January 21, 1920, quoted in Füllner, *Richard Huelsenbeck,* p. 196.

67. *Dresdner Nachrichten,* January 21, 1920, quoted in Bergius, *Das Lachen Dadas,* pp. 353–354.

68. Hausmann, "Wer gegen Dada ist, ist Dadaist," *Am Anfang war Dada,* p. 116. According to the socialist *Unabhängige Volkszeitung* of January 22, 1920, the attack had been premeditated by right-wing elements and was brought under control by young socialists. See Füllner, *Richard Huelsenbeck,* p. 198.

69. "Vortragsabend der Dadaisten," *Leipziger Neueste Nachrichten,* February 25, 1920, quoted in Bergius, *Das Lachen Dadas,* pp. 354–355. The figure of 1,000 spectators is given in the *Leiziger Tageblatt* of January 21, 1920.

70. Hausmann, "Wer gegen Dada ist, ist Dadaist," *Am Anfang war Dada,* p. 118.

71. Letter of March 3, 1920, printed in Thater-Schulz, *Hannah Höch: Eine Lebenscollage,* vol. I.2, pp. 647–648.

72. He stopped working as an architect in 1914 and after his return from the front line in Belgium, he never returned to full-time employment.

73. Hausmann, *Am Anfang war Dada,* p. 55. See also Heartfield's account in *Der Malik-Verlag 1916–1947,* pp. 24–26.

74. Several Dada memoirs related the event in different forms. The most reliable is the report that appeared in the *Deutsche Zeitung* of November 18, 1919, reprinted in Baader, *Das Oberdada,* p. 118.

75. This is the version of events given by Mehring, *Berlin-Dada,* pp. 56–60.

76. Hausmann, *An Anfang war Dada,* p. 56. Part of this text also appears on the flyer *Dadaisten gegen Weimar,* written by Baader and signed on behalf of the "Dada Central Committee of World Revolution," and the special issue of *Grüne Leiche.* This may indicate that all three leaflets were thrown into the assembly.

77. Hausmann gives the year 1918, but since Keller was born on July 19, 1819, this would have been his ninety-ninth birthday, an unlikely date for the commemoration. The centenary was the topic of many articles in the German press and the cause of several official ceremonies.

78. Hausmann, *An Anfang war Dada,* p. 57.

79. Kessler, *The Diaries of a Cosmopolitan,* p. 62. However, it needs to be pointed out that *Jederman sein eigener Fussball,* like *Die Pleite* and *Der blutige Ernst,* was not a Dada magazine strictly speaking but a satirical review written by artists also active in Dada.

80. Herzfelde, "George Grosz, John Heartfield, Erwin Piscator, Dada und die Folgen," p. 1240. The figure mentioned here seems rather high and is probably exaggerated.

81. Mehring, *Berlin-Dada,* pp. 67–69.

82. "Tristan Tzara arrive à Paris," in Aragon, *Projet d'histoire littéraire contemporaine,* p. 58.

83. Sanouillet, *Dada à Paris*, p. 132.

84. "Premier Vendredi de *Littérature*," in Aragon, *Projet d'histoire littéraire contemporaine*, p. 66.

85. Aragon gave a detailed report on the event in "Manifestation de la rue de Puteaux," *Les Écrits nouveaux* 7:1 (January 1921), pp. 61–64.

86. Georges Charensol in his review, "A la Maison de L'Œuvre: Manifestation Dada," *Comœdia* 14:2660 (March 29, 1920), p. 2, recalled the "séances désormais historiques" of *Ubu Roi* and *Roi Bombance* and suggested that the audience in the overcrowded theatre expected something of a similar kind to happen at the Dada event.

87. A modern edition can be found in Tzara, *Œuvres complètes*, vol. 1. Attemps to interpret the text have been undertaken by Béhar, *Le Théâtre dada*, Berghaus, "Dada Theatre," Kümmerle, *Tristan Tzara: Dramatische Experimente*, Matthews, *Theatre in Dada*, and Peterson, *Tzara*.

88. This is Tzara's description in his "Memoirs of Dadaism," p. 307.

89. Ribemont-Dessaignes, *Déjà jadis*, pp. 85–86.

90. I purposely disregard here a soirée and matinée held as part of the Picabia exhibition at Povolozky's bookshop in December 1920, as they attracted only a limited number of invited guests, and the offerings were humorous rather than provocative (Cocteau directing a jazz band with the help of a big drum, cymbals, and castagnettes; Tzara demonstrating his method of creating a Dada poem with the help of a newspaper and a pair of scissors). A similarly exclusive audience was present at the soirée given at the opening of a Max Ernst exhibition in May 1921.

91. This was the purpose of the visits as stated on the invitation flyer.

92. Ribemont-Dessaignes, 'Histoire de Dada', *Nouvelle Revue française* 19:214 (July 1931), p. 46.

93. Ibid., p. 47.

94. See the excerpts of the speeches in Nadeau, *The History of Surrealism*, p. 66.

95. The second event was Picabia's *Relâche*, which does not truly qualify to be called "Dadaist," as Picabia had by then left the group and the Ballets Suédois were a modern dance troupe rather than a Dada company.

96. See the excellent exhibition catalog, *La Rencontre Sonia Delaunay—Tristan Tzara*, Paris 1977.

97. Hausmann, "Was will der Dadaismus in Europa?," *Prager Tageblatt*, February 22, 1920, reprinted in a shortened form as "Dada in Europa," *Der Dada* 3 (April 1920), p. 3. Hausmann, *Texte bis 1933*, vol. 1, pp. 94–100, at p. 95.

98. For a more detailed discussion of this issue, see Berghaus, "Dada Theatre, or The Genesis of Anti-bourgeois Performance Art."

99. "Art–Anti-Art. Interview par Olivier Todd," in Tzara, *Œuvres complètes*, vol. 5, pp. 431–440, at pp. 431–432.

100. Huelsenbeck, *Mit Witz, Licht und Grütze*, p. 81. *Memoirs of a Dada Drummer*, p. 54.

101. Huelsenbeck, "Der Dadaismus," *Reclams Universum* 4:40 (July 4, 1918), pp. 679–689, at p. 679.

102. Richter, *Art and Anti-Art*, p. 185.

103. Idid., p. 59.

104. Tzara, "Note 2 sur l'art" and "Notes: Pierre Reverdy," in *Dada 2* (December 1917), pp. 2, 18.

105. Richter, *Art and Anti-Art*, p. 35.

106. "Manifeste de Monsieur Antipyrine," in Tzara, *Œuvres complètes*, vol. 1, pp. 357–358, at p. 357.

107. Huelsenbeck, *Reise bis ans Ende der Freiheit*, p. 109.

108. Ball, *Flucht aus der Zeit*, p. 229 (December 28, 1919).

109. "Dadaland," in Arp, *Unsern täglichen Traum*, pp. 51–61, at p. 51.

110. "Kandinsky," in Ball, *Der Künstler und die Zeitkrankheit*, p. 42.

111. Janco, "Creative Art," in Verkauf, *Dada: Monograph of a Movement*, pp. 42, 44.

112. Huelsenbeck, *Mit Witz, Licht und Grütze*, p. 120 and *Memoirs of a Dada Drummer*, p. 80.

113. "Le Surréalism et l'après-guerre," in Tzara, *Œuvres complètes*, vol. 5, pp. 59–108, at p. 68.

114. Georg Grosz and John Heartfield, "Der Kunstlump," *Der Gegner* 1 (1919/1920), pp. 48–56, at p. 54.

115. Tzara, "Conferénce sur Dada," p. 420.

116. Arp, *On My Way*, p. 48. This statement was originally published in El Lissitzky and Hans Arp, eds., *Die Kunstismen*, Erlenbach-Zürich: Rentsch, 1925, p. X.

117. Tzara, "Conferénce sur Dada," p. 421.

118. Arp, "Emmy Hennings and Hugo Ball," in Ball/Hennings, *Damals in Zürich*, pp. 179–182, at p. 181.

119. "I want to suffer, I don't want to skive off. I'm no shirker. Don't you believe this! I too am standing in the trenches, but a different kind of trenches. I am not a deserter, I am fighting." Letter to his sister of December 19, 1916 in Ball/Hennings, *Damals in Zürich*, p. 118.

120. Otto Dix et al., "Offener Brief an die Novembergruppe," *Der Gegner* 2 (1920/21), pp. 297–301, at p. 300.

121. Ball, *Flucht aus der Zeit*, p. 233 (June 5, 1919).

122. See Ibid., pp. 98–100. He performed the poem again on July 14 at the Dada Soirée at the Zunfthaus zur Waag, this time with a longer introduction that explained the purpose of the recitation (see *Der Künstler und die Zeitkrankheit*, pp. 39–40). A photograph of Ball wearing a long, dark gown that reached to the floor, a white, cylindrical cardboard tube around his head with the figure 13 written on it, a top hat and white gloves that hold a flag with three stripes (see Ribemont-Dessaignes, *Déjà jadis*, opposite p. 80; Schrott, *Dada 15/25*, p. 54), has often been related to this performance. However, I doubt this, as it would have been very difficult to recite the poem with the head stuck in a tube. Perrottet describes him as having worn again a simple cardboard costume: "He

stood there like a priest, dressed in a cardboard costume, in front of him a lectern. On it lay a thick book, like a Bible, from which he read out what Dada wanted." *Ein bewegtes Leben*, p. 135.

123. Ball, *Flucht aus der Zeit*, p. 100 (June 24, 1916).
124. Ball refers to this parallel between Kandinsky's painting and his decision "to eliminate language from poetry" in his diary entry of March 5, 1916, *Flucht aus der Zeit*, pp. 76–77.
125. "Das erste dadaistische Manifest," in Ball, *Der Künstler und die Zeitkrankheit*, pp. 39–40, at p. 40.
126. Ball, *Flucht aus der Zeit*, p.100 (June 24, 1916).
127. Ibid.
128. Ibid., p. 104 August 8, 1916.
129. Huelsenbeck, *En avant Dada*, pp. 30, 14. He even defined bruitism as "life itself" (p. 15: "Bruitismus ist das Leben selbst").
130. Ball, *Flucht aus der Zeit*, p. 145 (March 29, 1917).
131. Huelsenbeck, *En avant Dada*, p. 30.
132. Huelsenbeck, *Dada siegt*, p. 21 (in the 1985 edition p. 28).
133. See Wigman's letter to Tzara, June 26, 1916: "I shall probably be unable to participate in your next performance, as much as I should like to be part of it...But I hope that there will be another occasion to bring the planned dance to fruition." Schrott, *Dada 15/25*, p. 45. On the dance performances at the Cabaret Voltaire, see also Naima Prevots, "Zurich Dada and Dance: Formative Ferment," *Dance Research Journal* 17:1 (Spring/Summer 1985), pp. 3–8; Valerie Preston Dunlop, "Rudolf Laban: The Nightmare Years in Zurich 1914–1919," *Dance Theatre Journal* 10:3 (Spring/Summer 1993), pp. 14–19.
134. "Le poème bruitiste," in Tzara, *Œuvres complètes*, vol. 1, Paris 1975, pp. 551–552, at p. 552.
135. Tzara, *Œuvres complètes*, vol. 1, p. 551.
136. Marcel Janco in a personal letter to Elmer Peterson, quoted in Peterson, *Tristan Tzara: Dada and Surrational Theorist*, p. 9.
137. "Dada manifeste sur l'amour faible et l'amour amer," in Tzara, *Œuvres complètes*, vol. 1, pp. 337–387, at p. 379.
138. The musicians were certainly masters on their instruments, but for the production of their cacophonic "musique bruitiste" no more skills were required than the average person in the street could muster. An exception to the rule of unprofessionalism was the Laban dancers, who performed in several of the Dada shows. But they never considered themselves to be Dadaists.
139. Richter, *Art and Anti-Art*, p. 77.
140. "Chronique zurichoïse," in Tzara, *Œuvres complètes*, vol. 1, pp. 561–568, at p. 564.
141. "Le Surréalism et l'après-guerre," in Tzara, *Œuvres complètes*, vol. 5, pp. 59–108, at p. 67.
142. G. C., "A la Maison de L'Œuvre: Manifestation Dada," *Comœdia* 14:2660 (March 29, 1920), p. 2. It needs to be stated that newspaper reviews are, on the

whole, more reliable sources for the Dada soirées than the memoirs of their protagonists. Especially Huelsenbeck and Hausmann indulged in mystification, half-truths, and, in some instances, replacing intention with realization.

143. "Chronique zurichoïse," in Tzara, *Œuvres complètes*, I, p. 567.

144. Richter, *Art and Anti-Art*, pp. 78–79.

145. "Chronique zurichoïse," in Tzara, *Œuvres complètes*, I, p. 564.

146. See Huelsenbeck, *Bis am Ende der Freiheit*, pp. 109, 156.

147. "Au public," *Littérature* 2:13 (May 1920), p. 18; "An das Publikum," *Dada Almanach*, Berlin: Reiss, 1920, pp. 98–99, reprinted in Ribemont-Dessaignes, *Dada: Manifestes, poèmes, articles, projets, 1915–1930*, pp. 11–12, and Motherwell, *The Dada Painters and Poets*, p. 109.

148. Huelsenbeck, "Die dadaistische Bewegung," *Neue deutsche Rundschau* 31:8 (August 1920), p. 979.

149. Huelsenbeck, *Mit Witz, Licht und Grütze*, p. 103; *Memoirs of a Dada Drummer*, p. 68. See also his description in *Reise bis ans Ende der Freiheit*, pp. 154–156.

150. See Berghaus, *Italian Futurist Theatre*, pp. 122–128.

151. Hugnet, "Dada à Paris," *Cahiers d'art* 9:1–4 (1934), pp. 109–114, at p. 113.

152. H. Höch, "Erinnerungen an DADA: Ein Vortrag 1966," in *Hannah Höch 1889–1978: Ihr Werk, Ihr Leben, Ihre Freunde*, p. 204.

153. "Der Dadaismus," *Reclams Universum* 34:40 (July 4, 1918), pp. 679–689.

154. See "Dadaismus in Zürich," *Berliner Zeitung am Mittag*, October 7, 1919 and "Eine Ehrung Marinettis durch die Dadaisten," *Berliner Börsen-Courier*, October 7, 1919, reprinted in Serner, *Das Gesamte Werk*, vol. 2, pp. 52–53.

155. See the essay by Angela Merte, "Dilettanten erhebt euch—Dada siegt: Dada Kölns aktionistische Momente," in Riha and Schäfer, *Fatagaga-Dada*, pp. 59–68, and Vitt, *Bagage de Baargeld*, pp. 19–22.

156. "Manifesto tecnico della letteratura futurista," in Marinetti, *Teoria e invenzione futurista*, p. 42; *Selected Writings*, p. 85. See also his comments on "l'ispirazione incosciente" in his response to the critics of his manifesto, in "Riposte alle obiezioni," Marinetti, *Teoria e invenzione futurista*, p. 49.

157. "Distruzione della sintassi—Immaginazione senza fili—Parole in libertà," in Marinetti, *Teoria e invenzione futurista*, p. 63; Apollonio, *Futurist Manifestos*, p. 99.

158. Quoted in Richard Sheppard, "Dada und Futurismus," in Paulsen and Hermann, *Sinn aus Unsinn: Dada international*, pp. 29–70, at p. 47. A detailed examination of Tzara's anti-Futurist tendencies has been offered by Sandro Briosi, "Un nodo dell'avanguardia storica: Tzara e Marinetti," *Il lettore di provincia* (Ravenna) 13:49–50 (June–September 1982), pp. 35–58.

159. See his letter to Breton of September 21, 1919 in Sanouillet, *Dada à Paris*, pp. 448–450.

160. "The Exhibitors to the Public" (Preface to the catalog of the exhibition of Futurist painting in Paris, February 1912), in Apollonio, *Futurist Manifestos*, pp. 45–50, at p. 49.

161. Soupault in a personal communication to Giovanni Lista, quoted in Lista, "Marinetti et le surréalisme," *Surrealismo*, Rome: Bulzoni, 1974, pp. 121–149, at p. 128.

162. André Breton, *Légitime Défense*, Paris: Éditions Surréalistes, 1926; English translation in *What is Surrealism*, p. 37.

163. For a more detailed discussion of this complex field of interconnections and mutual influences, see Berghaus, "Futurism, Dada, and Surrealism: Some Cross-Fertilisations among the Historical Avant-gardes," in Berghaus, *International Futurism in Arts and Literature*, pp. 271–304.

164. Some of these connections between the interwar and postwar avant-gardes have been discussed in my study, *Avant-garde Performance: Live Events and Electronic Technologies* 60–78.

5   CONSTRUCTIVISM

1. Bann, *The Tradition of Constructivism*, p. XXIX.

2. See Lodder, *Russian Constructivism*, p. 3.

3. See the "Program of the Constructivist Working Group of INKhUK," in *Art into Life: Russian Constructivism 1914–1932*, p. 67.

4. See "Program for the Institute of Artistic Culture," Kandinsky, *Complete Writings on Art*, pp. 455–472.

5. For a detailed analysis of the conflict see Khan-Magomedov, *Rodchenko*, pp. 55–71. A more general assessment of Kandinsky's activities in Soviet Russia can be found in John E. Bowlt and Rose-Carol Washton Long, eds., *The Life of Vasilii Kandinsky in Russian Art*, Newtonville, MA: Oriental Research Partners, 1980, pp. 29–34, Hahn, *Kandinsky: The Russian and Bauhaus Years*, and Poling, *Kandinsky: Russian and Bauhaus Years*.

6. See the Work Plan of the group, printed in Khan-Magomedov, *Rodchenko*, p. 287. Some 24 other documents from these discussions have been published in *Art into Life: Russian Constructivism 1914–1932*.

7. See the list in Lodder, *Russian Constructivism*, p. 93. The papers were not published at the time, but have become partly available in monographs published on individual artists active in the group.

8. Varvara Stepanova, "On Constructivism," in Lavrentiev, ed., *Varvara Stepanova*, pp. 173–175, at p. 173.

9. Aleksei Gan in two essays on Constructivism, printed in *Zrelishcha* 78 and 80 (1924), quoted in Khan-Magomedov, *Rodchenko*, p. 99.

10. Paul Wood, "The Politics of the Avant-garde," *The Great Utopia*, pp. 1–24, at p. 11.

11. Lunacharsky in an address to the First All-Russian Conference on Art and Production in August 1919, quoted in Lodder, *Russian Constructivism*, p. 113. On the VKhUTEMAS see Khan-Magomedov, *VHUTEMAS*.

12. Policy statement on the aims of the Basic Division, quoted in Lodder, *Russian Constructivism*, p. 124.
13. See Fritz Mirau, *Russen in Berlin 1918–1933*, 2nd rev. ed. Weinheim: Quadriga, 1988; Irina A. Antonova and Jörn Merkert, eds., *Berlin—Moskau 1900–1950*, Exh. cat. Berlin: Martin-Gropius-Bau, 1995–1996; Munich: Prestel, 1995; Karl Schlögel, *Berlin Ostbahnhof Europas: Russen und Deutsche in ihrem Jahrhundert*, Berlin: Siedler, 1998; Marion von Hofacker, "Verbreitung konstruktivistischer Ideen in Berlin und Jena," in Finkeldey, ed., *Konstruktivistische Internationale*, pp. 203–206; Stephen Bann, "Russian Constructivism and Its European Resonance," *Art into Life: Russian Constructivism 1914–1932*, pp. 213–221. On the influential Great Russian Exhibition at the Van Diemen Gallery in October 1922, see also *The First Russian Show: A Commemoration of the Van Diemen Exhibition*; Steneberg, *Russische Kunst Berlin 1919–1932*; Lodder, *Russian Constructivism*, pp. 225–238; Eckhard Neumann, "Russia's Leftist Art in Berlin 1922," *Art Journal* 27:1 (1967), pp. 20–23; Naum Gabo, "The 1922 Soviet Exhibition," *Studio International* 182:938 (November 1971), p. 171.
14. See Kai-Uwe Hemken, " 'Muß die neue Kunst den Massen dienen?': Zur Utopie und Wirklichkeit der 'Konstruktivistischen Internationalen,' " in Finkeldey, ed., *Konstruktivistische Internationale*, pp. 57–67.
15. These figures are taken from Mirau, *Russen in Berlin 1918–1933*, 2nd rev. ed., pp. 259–261.
16. Die Redaktion des, *"Gegenstand,"* "Deklaration an den ersten Kongress fortschrittlicher Künstler, Düsseldorf," *De Stijl* 5:4 (April 1922), pp. 56–57.
17. Theo van Doesburg, El Lissitzky, Hans Richter, "Erklärung der internationalen Fraktion der Konstruktivisten," *De Stijl* 5:4 (April 1922), pp. 61–64.
18. Théo van Doesburg, El Lissitzky, Hans Richter, Karel Maes, Max Burchartz, "K.I.: Konstruktivistische Internationale schöpferische Arbeitsgemeinschaft," *De Stijl* 5:8 (August 1922), pp. 113–115. The magazine *De Stijl*, besides *Veshch—Gegenstand—Objet* (no. 1–2, March–April 1922, no. 3 May 1922), *LEF* (no. 1, March 1923—no.7, 1925) and *G: Zeitschrift für elementare Gestaltung* (no. 1, July 1923—5/6, 1926), became the official organ of the movement, with Lissitzky, Van Doesburg and Richter acting as key promoters. Through Prampolini and Vasari they tapped into the Futurist movement; Kassák with his magazine *Ma* and Teige with *Disk* built bridges to the South-Eastern countries.
19. See *Dada and Constructivism: The Janus Face of the Twenties*, Exh. cat. London: Juda Fine Art, 1984; Bergius, *Das Lachen Dadas*, pp. 302–309, 380–385; Maria Müller, "Dada—Merz—Konstruktivismus: Versuch einer Annäherung," in *Raumkonzepte*, pp. 373–379.
20. "Vers une construction collective," *De Stijl* 6:6–7 (1924), pp. 89–92, at p. 92.
21. "Pittura pura: Riposta a Kandinsky" was first published in *L'artista moderno* of January 1915, "Un'arte nuova? Costruzione assoluta di motorumore" in the same journal in March 1915. Both essays have been reprinted in Bucarelli, *Enrico Prampolini*, pp. 36–39.

22. "Aufruf zur elementaren Kunst," *De Stijl* 4:10 (October 1921), p. 156.

23. Walter Gropius, *Programm des Staatlichen Bauhauses in Weimar*, Weimar: Bauhaus, 1919, reprinted in Wingler, *The Bauhaus*, pp. 31–33.

24. Theo van Doesburg, "Internationaal Congres van Konstruktivisten en Dada 1922 in Weimar," *Mécano* 3 (1922), s.p., reproduced in Finkeldey, ed., *Konstruktivistische Internationale*, p. 65. The original wording was: "Hôtel des artistes invalides 'Bauhaus' (Baucoup des malades de pépie de Mazdaznan et de l'expressionisme sans fil)." Itten promoted the mystical Mazdaznan religion at the Bauhaus and increasingly maneuvered himself into an outsider position. *Télégraphie sans fil* was a popular catch phrase in the 1910s and 1920s with associations of hi-tech Modernism. Marinetti used it metaphorically in his manifesto on *L'Imagination sans fil* (1913), whereas van Doesburg intended it as a gibe at the impossible union of Expressionist primitivism and Bauhaus modernity.

25. The name KURI was an anagram of "Konstruktive, utilitäre, rationale Internationale." See Farkas Molnár, "KURI-Manifest," in Gassner, *Wechsel Wirkungen: Ungarische Avantgarde in der Weimarer Republik*, pp. 266–268; Kurt Schmidt, "Der Vorkurs von Johannes Itten und die Kuris am Bauhaus," *bauhaus* 2, Exh. cat. Leipzig: Galerie am Sachsenplatz, 1977, pp. 10–11, reprinted as "Die Kuris am Bauhaus," ICSAC-Cahier 6–7 (1987), 71–73; Kurt Schmidt, "Die Kuris am Bauhaus," *Kurt Schmidt* cat. Gera 1990, pp. 106–107; Monika Wucher, "Weltkuri! Der Beitrag einer Künstlergruppe zum gewandelten Konzept des Weimarer Bauhaus," in Finkeldey, ed., *Konstruktivistische Internationale*, pp. 178–181; Eva Bajkay-Rosch, "Die KURI-Gruppe," in Gassner, *Wechsel Wirkungen: Ungarische Avantgarde in der Weimarer Republik*, pp. 260–266.

26. See Peter Röhl, "Der Beginn und die Entwicklung des Stijl's in Weimar," *De Stijl* 79–84 (1927), col. 103–105; Kai-Uwe Hemken and Rainer Stommer, "Der 'De Stijl'-Kurs von Theo van Doesburg in Weimar (1922)," in Finkeldey, ed., *Konstruktivistische Internationale*, pp. 169–177; Weininger, "Bauhaus und Stijl."

27. For a detailed study of the Bauhaus pedagogy see the writings of Rainer Wick; various curricular regulations can also be found in Wingler, *The Bauhaus*.

28. This is the basic definition given by the First Working Group of Constructivists in 1921. See Khan-Magomedov, *Rodchenko*, p. 289 and the Programme of the Constructivist Working Group, published in *Art into Life: Russian Constructivism 1914–1932*, p. 67.

29. Popova in an unpublished manuscript quoted in Adaskina and Sarabianov, *Lioubov Popova*, p. 252.

30. *Puti razvitiia teatra*, p. 30 and *Teatr i revolutsiia*, p. 43, quoted in Gorchakov, *The Theatre in Soviet Russia*, pp. 112–113.

31. Meyerhold and Popova had already collaborated in spring 1921 on a mass spectacle for the third congress of the Comintern, *Struggle and Victory*. Originally, Meyerhold had asked Medunetzky and the Stenberg brothers to design the Crommelynck play. See Braun, *Meyerhold: A Revolution in Theatre*, p. 178.

32. *Literaturnye manifesty*, Moscow 1924, pp. 257–258, quoted in Rudnitsky, *Russian and Soviet Theatre*, p. 90.

33. Aleksei Gan, "Konstruktivizm. Otvet Lefu," *Zrelishcha* 55 (1923), p. 13, quoted in Elena Rakitin, "How Meyerkhol'd never Worked with Tatlin, and What Happened as a Result," in *The Great Utopia*, pp. 649–664, at p. 650.

34. Popova's teaching at the GVYTM, which ran parallel to her work at the VKhUTEMAS, has been analyzed in Adaskina and Sarabianov, *Lioubov Popova*, pp. 213–216.

35. See Braun, *The Theatre of Meyerhold*, pp. 164–168; Alma H. Law and Mel Gordon, *Meyerhold, Eisenstein, and Biomechanics*; Jörg Bochow, *Das Theater Meyerholds und die Biomechanik*.

36. Meyerhold in an opening speech of his first public demonstration of Biomechanics on June 12, 1922, translated in *Meyerhold on Theatre*, pp. 197–200.

37. Stinf, "Biomekhanika," *Zrelishcha* 10 (1922), p. 14, quoted in Rudnitsky, *Meyerhold the Director*, p. 294.

38. Foregger's training system *Tefiztrenazh* was inspired by similar motives and created group movements that were like those of a great stage machine. Describing them as "a plastic exercise in Constructivism," he claimed that he was creating a form of choreography that would assist the masses in mastering "the rhythm that is so essential in all labour processes." See Elizaveta Uvarova, *Russkaya sovetskaya estrada 1917–1929*, Moscow: Iskusstvo, 1976, p. 267, quoted by Edward Braun, "Futurism in the Russian Theatre, 1913–1923," in Berghaus, *International Futurism*, pp. 75–99, at 88–90.

39. Erast Garin, *S Meierkhol'dom*, Moscow 1974, pp. 44–45, quoted in Hoover, *Meyerhold and His Set Designers*, p. 126.

40. See Meyerhold's essay "The Fairground Booth" in his collection of writings, *O teatre* (St. Petersburg, 1913), translated in *Meyerhold on Theatre*, pp. 119–142. In his first theatre studio in St Petersburg, Meyerhold introduced commedia and mime techniques to the curriculum. See Braun, *The Theatre of Meyerhold*, pp. 125–126.

41. See the illustrations in *Meyerhold on Theatre*, opp. 145, Braun, *The Theatre of Meyerhold*, pp. 156 and 158; Rudnitsky, *Meyerhold the Director*, pp. 264–265; Rudnitsky, *Russian and Soviet Theatre*, pp. 86–87; Hoover, *Meyerhold*, p. 124.

42. The essay written to commemorate the fifth anniversary of The Meyerhold Theatre has been translated as "Über die Bühnenausstattung zu *Morgenröte*" in Meyerhold, *Schriften*, vol. 2, pp. 17–18. He also stated that the designer, Vladimir Dmitriev, stopped half-way on the path toward "eliminating the canons of decorative, Italianate theatre."

43. *Vestnik teatra* 72–73 (1920), pp. 8–10, translated as "On the Staging of Verhaeren's *The Dawn*," in *Meyerhold on Theatre*, pp. 170–173.

44. Emmanuel Beskin in *Internatsionalnyi teatr* 4 (1933), p. 45, quoted in Rudnitsky, *Russian and Soviet Theatre*, p. 63.

45. Abram Efros in an article on "The Painter and the Stage of 1921," quoted in Khan-Magomedov, *Alexandr Vesnin*, pp. 49–52.

46. See Elena Rakitina, "Über plastische Raumgestaltung, Konstruktion, Schönheit, Funktionalität und über zwei schöne russische Frauen," in *Die Maler und das Theater*, pp. 69–87, at p. 79. At a first stage of the production process, the

brothers Stenberg and Medunetsky worked on the set design. They came up with a realistic representation of the mill, which Popova successively reduced to a purely structural and functionalist model, in line with her idea of "shaping the material elements of a spectacle." See Adaskina and Sarabianov, *Lioubov Popova*, pp. 250–251 and the illustrations on pp. 258–260.

47. "Préambule à la discussion de l'INKhOUK sur le 'Cocu Magnifique,' " in Adaskina and Sarabianov, *Lioubov Popova*, pp. 378–379. A German translation can be found in the catalog *Ljubow Popova*, Cologne: Museum Ludwig, 1991, pp. 159–160.

48. For a more detailed discussion of the production see Alma H. Law, " 'Le Cocu magnifique' de Crommelynck"; Alma H. Law, "Meyerhold's *The Magnanimous Cuckold*"; Worrall, "Meyerhold's '*The Magnificent Cuckold*' "; Rudnitsky, *Meyerhold the Director*, pp. 289–310; Hamon-Siréjols, *Le Constructivisme au théâtre*, pp. 159–175; Adaskina and Sarabianov, *Lioubov Popova*, pp. 250–254; Braun, *Meyerhold: A Revolution in Theatre*, pp. 178–184; Leach, *Revolutionary Theatre*, pp. 110–113; Hoover, *Meyerhold*, pp. 125–128; Hoover, *Meyerhold and His Set Designers*, pp. 125–128, Rudnitsky, *Russian and Soviet Theatre*, pp. 92–93.

49. A. Gvozdev, *Teatr imeni Meierkhold'da*, Leningrad 1927, p. 28, quoted in Rudnitsky, *Meyerhold the Director*, p. 290.

50. Boris Arvatov, *Iskusstvo i klassy*, Moscow 1923, p. 85, quoted in Rudnitsky, *Meyerhold the Director*, p. 292.

51. Adaskina and Sarabianov, *Lioubov Popova*, p. 378; Dabrowski, *Liubov Popova*, rev. edn, Cologne, 1991, p. 160.

52. See Law, "The Death of Tarelkin"; Rudnitsky, *Meyerhold the Director*, pp. 310–313; Braun, *The Theatre of Meyerhold*, pp. 175–179; Picon-Vallin, *Meyerhold*, pp. 141–145; Lavrentiev, *Stepanova*, pp. 61–73; Hamon-Siréjols, *Le Constructivisme au théâtre*, pp. 175–176; Rudnitsky, *Russian and Soviet Theatre*, p. 95.

53. The interview in the journal *Zrelishcha* 16 (1922) is quoted in Lavrentiev, *Stepanova*, pp. 64–66.

54. See the designs and photos in Lavrentiev, *Stepanova*, pp. 61–73.

55. See Hamon, "La Terre Cabrée"; Rudnitski, *Meyerhold the Director*, pp. 313–316; Adaskina and Sarabianov, *Lioubov Popova*, pp. 255–257; Braun, *The Theatre of Meyerhold*, pp. 179–184; Picon-Vallin, *Meyerhold*, pp. 145–149; Hamon-Siréjols, *Le Constructivisme au théâtre*, pp. 182–192; Rudnitski, *Russian and Soviet Theatre*, pp. 102–103.

56. See B. Brecht, "Ist das Volk unfehlbar?," *Werke: Große kommentierte Berliner und Frankfurter Ausgabe vol. 14: Gedichte vol. 4*, Berlin: Aufbau and Frankfurt/M: Suhrkamp, 1993, pp. 435–436.

57. See the photographs of the set in Hamon, "La Terre Cabrée"; Rudnitski, *Russian and Soviet Theatre*, pp. 138–139; Rudnitsky, *Meyerhold the Director*, pp. 301–302; Picon-Vallin, *Meyerhold*, pp. 146–147.

58. Popova, "Exposition des éléments fondamentaux de la mise en forme matérielle du spectale 'La Nuit'," in Adaskina and Sarabianov, ed., *Lioubov Popova*, p. 382.

59. *Zrelishcha* 27 (1923); p. 7, quoted in Adaskina and Sarabianov, *Lioubov Popova*,
    p. 257. Picon-Vallin suggested that Popova had originally intended to use film
    projections in *Earth in Turmoil*, a concept Eisenstein took up in his "Montage of
    Attractions," *The Wise Man* (1923), which contained brief sequences ("Glumov's
    Diary") specially shot for the production. According to Picon-Vallin,
    Meyerhold's later use of film projections included *The Gun Shot* (1929), *The
    Second Army Commander* (1929), *The Final Conflict* (1931), and *D.E.* (1935
    version). See Béatrice Picon-Vallin, "Le Cinéma: Rival, partenaire ou instrument
    du théâtre meyerholdien?" in Amiard-Chevrel, ed., *Théâtre et cinéma années
    vingt*, vol. 1, pp. 229–262.

60. "Instead of having an aesthetic effect, the décor should force the spectator to
    make no longer a distinction with phenomena of real life . . . Costumes and
    props (big and small) are like those in life." "Sachliche Ausstattung," in
    Meyerhold, *Schriften*, vol. 2, p. 47.

61. See Cohen, "Alexandra Exter's Designs for the Theatre"; Worrall, *Modernism to
    Realism on the Soviet Stage*, pp. 27–37; Rakitina, "Über plastische
    Raumgestaltung," pp. 69–87; Rudnitski, *Russian and Soviet Theatre*, pp. 15–19,
    and the exhibition catalogs listed in the Bibliography under Exter. Popova's
    designs for the production, which were not adopted, have been discussed in
    Adaskina and Sarabianov, *Lioubov Popova*, pp. 217–219 and reproduced on
    pp. 226–234. Vesnin's designs, which elaborated Popova's concept and were
    equally discarded by Tairov, can be found in Khan-Magomedov, *Alexandr Vesnin*,
    pp. 64–66.

62. Rudnitsky, *Russian and Soviet Theatre*, p. 18.

63. *Alexandra Exter e il Teatro da Camera*, p. 28.

64. Worrall, *Modernism to Realism on the Soviet Stage*, p. 27.

65. See Bowlt and Drutt, *Amazons of the Avant-garde*, and the exhibition catalogs
    listed in the Bibliography under Exter.

66. Tairov, *Notes of a Director*, p. 123.

67. For a detailed description of the production see Khan-Magomedov, *Alexandr
    Vesnin*, pp. 74–81; Rudnitsky, *Russian and Soviet Theatre*, pp.104–106; Worrall,
    Modernism to Realism on the Soviet Stage, pp. 37–39.

68. A. Koonen, "Stranici iz žizni," *Teatr* 6 (1968), pp. 94–95, quoted in Khan-
    Magomedov, *Alexandr Vesnin*, p. 74. The full text of "Pages from a Life" has been
    published in Moscow: Iskusstvo, 1975.

69. See the photograph and sketch in Rudnitsky, *Russian and Soviet Theatre*, p. 150.

70. Vesnin at a discussion of his designs at INKhUK on May 4, 1922, quoted in
    Khan-Magomedov, *Alexandr Vesnin*, p. 78.

71. A. Efros, *Kamerny teatr i ego hudožniki*, Moscow 1934, p. 23, quoted in Khan-
    Magomedov, *Alexandr Vesnin*, p. 74.

72. See the reviews quoted in Khan-Magomedov, *Alexandr Vesnin*, pp. 79–81, *Paris—
    Moscou, 1900–1930*, Exh. cat. Paris: Centre Pompidou, 1979, pp. 390–391, and
    Antonova and Merkert, *Berlin—Moskau 1900–1950*, pp. 173–177.

73. See Khan-Magomedov, *Alexandr Vesnin*, pp. 91–108, and Hamon-Siréjols, *Le Constructivisme au théâtre*, pp. 241–249.
74. See the illustrations in Harten, *Vladimir Tatlin: Retrospektive*, pp. 205–241.
75. Both stage designs can be found in Harten, *Vladimir Tatlin: Retrospektive*, color plates 65 and 73, and Zhadova, *Tatlin*, ill. 137 and 157.
76. See Elena Rakitin, "How Meyerkhol'd never Worked with Tatlin, and What Happened as a Result," in *The Great Utopia*, p. 663, note 8.
77. See Zhadova, *Tatlin*, pp. 160–164, 248–249, 395–403; Kovtun, *Sangesi*, pp. 97–103; Gail Harrison Roman, "Vladimir Tatlin and *Zangezi*," in Bowlt, ed., *Twentieth Century Russian and Ukrainian Stage Design*, pp. 108–139; Hamon-Siréjols, *Le Constructivisme au théâtre*, pp. 292–293; Kovtun, *The Russian Avant-garde in the 1920s and 30s*, pp. 76–79. The often reproduced model from the Theatermuseum Wien (e.g., Hamon-Siréjols, *Le Constructivisme au théâtre* p. 288) is a later reconstruction and different from Tatlin's own model, reproduced in Harten, *Vladimir Tatlin: Retrospektive*, p. 267 and Zhadova, *Tatlin*, ill. 216.
78. See Tatlin, "O Zangezi," *Zhizn' iskusstva* 18 (1923), p. 15, translated, in Zhadova, *Tatlin*, pp. 248–249 and Kovtun, *The Russian Avant-garde in the 1920s and 30s*, pp. 77–78.
79. See the photograph in Zhadova, *Tatlin*, ill. 214, and Nikolai Lapshin's illustration in *ibid.*, no. 213.
80. See Rudnitski, *Meyerhold the Director*, pp. 354–358; 365; Picon-Vallin, *Meyerhold*, pp. 151–164; Braun, *The Theatre of Meyerhold*, pp. 184–186, Hamon-Siréjols, *Le Constructivisme au théâtre*, pp. 202–208, 227–228; Rudnitski, *Russian and Soviet Theatre*, pp. 101, 136–137.
81. Rudnitsky, *Meyerhold the Director*, p. 356. Meyerhold reiterated Marinetti's demand for a cinematization of theatre, made in the Variety Theatre Manifesto of 1913, in his essay of 1930, "The Reconstruction of the Theatre," where he wrote: "The theatre cannot afford to ignore the cinematograph; the action of the actor on stage can be juxtaposed with his filmed image on screen. . . . Let us carry through the 'cinefication' of the theatre to its logical conclusion, let us equip the theatre with all the technical refinement of the cinema." *Meyerhold on Theatre*, pp. 254–255.
82. Quoted in Rudnitsky, *Meyerhold the Director*, p. 357.
83. A color-reproduction of the model, now in the Theatermuseum Köln-Wahn, can be found in Hamon-Siréjols, *Le Constructivisme au théâtre*, p. 286.
84. See the models and drawings reproduced in Khan-Magomedov, *Alexandr Vesnin*, pp. 72–73 and Adaskina and Sarabianov, *Lioubov Popova*, pp. 245–246.
85. Aleksei Faiko, "Tri vstrechi," *Teatr* 10 (1962), p. 117, quoted in Rudnitsky, *Meyerhold the Director*, p. 356. See the photos in *ibid.*, p. 365; Rudnitsky, *Russian and Soviet Theatre*, pp. 136–137; Picon-Vallin, *Meyerhold*, pp. 152–153.
86. Schlemmer, *Letters and Diaries*, p. 127. Gropius described the theatre as being intimately related to architecture, as it forms "an orchestrated unity" where "a variety of artistic media are conjoined, according to a superior law, into a new

and larger ensemble." See "Idee und Aufbau des Staatlichen Bauhauses," in *Staatliches Bauhaus in Weimar 1919–1923*, pp. 7–18, at p. 17. Klee's 1922 diagram of the Bauhaus concept placed architecture and theatre ("Bau und Bühne") at the center of the institution. See Bothe, *Das frühe Bauhaus und Johannes Itten*, p. 322, ill. 250.

87. Walter Gropius, "Die Arbeit der Bauhausbühne," *Die Bauhausbühne. Leitung: Lothar Schreyer. Erste Mitteilung Dezember 1922.* It may be worth noting that my photocopy of this communication stems from the personal archive of Enrico Prampolini, who made several visits to the Bauhaus and took great interest in the theatre work going on there.

88. Schreyer said in his memoirs, *Expressionistisches Theater*, p. 207, that he ran the stage workshop jointly with Schlemmer. In a letter to Otto Meyer of March 13, 1922, Schlemmer wrote that he was in charge of "dance and the comic element," whereas Schreyer occupied himself with "the realm of the holy." *Letters and Diaries*, p. 116. The *First Communication* contained a brief essay by Schreyer, but none by Schlemmer (although he may have provided some of the wording in Gropius's statement).

89. See Hans Haffenrichter, "Lothar Schreyer und die Bauhausbühne," in Neumann, ed., *Bauhaus und Bauhäusler*, pp. 49–52.

90. Lothar Schreyer, "Mondspiel," *Der Sturm*, vol. 14 (1923), pp. 56–61. He described the Weimar production in a manuscript, now in the Deutsches Literaturarchiv Marbach and partly published in Bothe, *Das frühe Bauhaus und Johannes Itten*, pp. 345–346. A photograph of the production was published in Scheper, *Oskar Schlemmer*, p. 71. See also Schreyer, *Theateraufsätze*, pp. 602–603.

91. Schreyer, *Expressionistisches Theater*, p. 207.

92. Oskar Schlemmer, "Die Bühnenwerkstatt des Staatl. Bauhauses Weimar," draft manuscript published in Wingler, *The Bauhaus*, p. 59.

93. See Hirschfeld-Mack, *Farbenlicht-Spiele*; Gilbert, "The Reflected Light Compositions of Ludwig Hirschfeld-Mack"; Peter Stasny, *Die Farbenlichtspiele*, in *Ludwig Hirschfeld-Mack: Bauhäusler und Visionär*, pp. 94–112; Wingler, *The Bauhaus*, pp. 370–371, *Für Augen und Ohren*, Exh. cat. Berlin: Akademie der Künste, 1980, pp. 127–129; Moholy-Nagy, *Painting, Photography, Film*, pp. 79–85; Scheper, *Oskar Schlemmer*, pp. 107–111; Draffin, *Two Masters of the Weimar Bauhaus*, pp. 39–44; Wick, "Kurt Schwerdtfeger." The Light Plays were reconstructed in Darmstadt (1964) and Bozen (1999). The Bauhaus-Archive in Berlin preserves a film and video recording of the two reconstructions.

94. See Kurt Schmidt, "Das mechanische Ballett: Eine Bauhaus Arbeit," in Neumann, ed., *Bauhaus und Bauhäusler*, pp. 54–58; Kurt Schmidt, "Das mechanische Ballett: Entwurf und Choreographie," *ICSAC-Cahier* 6–7 (1987), pp. 67–70; Ulrike Rüdiger, "Die mechanische Aktion—Arbeit für die Bühne," *Kurt Schmidt*, Exh. cat. Gera: Kunstgalerie, 1990, pp. 30–41; Bothe, *Das frühe Bauhaus und Johannes Itten*, pp. 352–358; Scheper, *Oskar Schlemmer*, pp. 78–81; Finkeldey, *Konstruktivistische Internationale*, pp. 180, 186, 201–202. In 1961,

the ballet was presented again in Zurich as part of the exhibition, *Oskar Schlemmer und die abstrakte Bühne*. In 1987, the Theater der Klänge in Düsseldorf recreated the ballet with the support of Kurt Schmidt. See the programme, *Die mechanische Bauhausbühne*, Düsseldorf: Theater der Klänge, 1987. Performances were repeated at the Centre Georges Pompidou in 1994.

95. See Stuckenschmidt, *Musik am Bauhaus*, pp. 6–7.

96. See the description in Scheper, *Oskar Schlemmer*, pp. 73–76 and *Oskar Schlemmer: Tanz, Theater, Bühne*, p. 204.

97. See the descriptions in Scheper, *Oskar Schlemmer*, pp. 98–99 and the Gera catalog, *Kurt Schmidt*, pp. 38 and 73.

98. Schawinsky, "From the Bauhaus to Black Mountain," p. 33. See also *Xanti Schawinsky: Malerei, Bühne, Grafikdesign, Fotografie*, p. 48.

99. Schlemmer, *Letters and Diaries*, p. 166 (May 22, 1925).

100. There is an interesting note in his diary, where he writes that going to the Volksbühne, one of the most esteemed theatres in Germany, would mean "selling ninety-nine percent of my soul" and becoming "shoe-shine boy to the egocentric actors and directors." He obviously felt that his work on reforming the stage could only happen outside the world of professional theatre. Schlemmer, *Letters and Diaries*, p. 161 (February 17, 1925).

101. Until the studio theatre was completed, Schlemmer taught, supported by Xanti Schawinsky and Joost Schmidt, in the Dessau Kunsthalle.

102. See Schlemmer, "die bühne im bauhaus," *bauhaus* 1 (1926), p. 3 and "bühne," *bauhaus* 3 (1927), pp. 1–4.

103. "studienplan der versuchsbühne am bauhaus in dessau. leitung: oskar schlemmer," *bauhaus* 3 (1927), p. 6. It was based on an exposé dated June 18, 1925 and an appendix of June 28, 1925. See Scheper, *Oskar Schlemmer*, pp. 119–120.

104. During the Weimar period, when the stage workshop did not offer any vocational training, it was only frequented by students officially registered in one of the other workshops. Schlemmer commented on this in a diary note of April 6, 1923: "The great difficulties of getting ahead with the stage work at the Bauhaus are rooted in the fact that if students want to be successful in their theatre work, they have to be suspended from their official assignments in the other workshops." Scheper, *Oskar Schlemmer*, p. 76.

105. Schlemmer, *Letters and Diaries*, p. 185.

106. See *Xanti Schawinsky*, pp. 50 and 81. On the Tiller Girls as representatives of a "mechanistic age" see Günter Berghaus, " 'Girlkultur': Feminism, Americanism and Popular Entertainment in Weimar Germany," *Journal of Design History* vol. 1 (1988), pp. 193–220.

107. Oskar Schlemmer, "Moderne Bühnenmittel," *Scene* 19 (1929), pp. 258–261, at p. 260. The *Gesture Dance* became a popular piece of the Bauhaus stage and was reconstructed by Gerhard Bohner in 1974 and 1985, Debrah McCall in 1982 and Günter Berghaus in 1991. The version by McCall was filmed in

1986 and can be viewed at the New York Public Library; those by Bohner and Berghaus are available from Inter Nationes in Bonn.

108. A photograph of the costume is contained in *Andor Weininger: Vom Bauhaus zur konzeptuellen Kunst*, p. 46.

109. See Schlemmer's essay, "Tänzerische Mathematik," translated in Wingler, *The Bauhaus*, pp. 118–119.

110. See Scheper, *Oskar Schlemmer*, pp. 141–146. The evening was repeated on July 9, 1927 in a slightly expanded form, this time including professional dancers from outside the Bauhaus, who performed six scenes from the *Triadic Ballet*.

111. See O. Schlemmer, "Mißverständnisse," *Schrifttanz* 4:2 (October 1931), pp. 27–29. He had previously tried to explain his concept in the essay "Mensch und Kunstfigur," translated in *Theater of the Bauhaus*, pp. 19–20.

112. Schlemmer, "Neue Formen der Bühne: Eine Unterhaltung von Oskar Schlemmer," *Schünemanns Monatshefte* 10 (October 1928), pp. 1062–1072, at pp. 1067–1068.

113. See his essay "Mensch und Kunstfigur," translated in *The Theater of the Bauhaus*.

114. See Schlemmer, *Letters and Diaries*, pp. 207 and 213; Scheper, *Oskar Schlemmer*, pp. 151–152.

115. He felt that it was increasingly considered "peripheral" to the main activities of the Bauhaus. See Schlemmer, *Letters and Diaries*, p. 203 (April 17, 1927).

116. Schlemmer, *Letters and Diaries*, p. 213 (October 17, 1927).

117. Schlemmer, *Letters and Diaries*, p. 198 (December 21, 1926).

118. See, e.g., his diary entry of April 1926 on the issue of mechanization and metaphysics. Schlemmer, *Letters and Diaries*, p. 193.

119. Schlemmer, *Letters and Diaries*, p. 140 (Early June 1923).

120. Tatlin's *Monument to the Third International* dates from 1919 and was intended to rotate on its axis. Gabo's *Kinetic Construction* of 1919–1920 was exhibited in Berlin in 1922. The first model of his *Column* dates from 1920–1921, and the first actual constructions from 1921–1922. It is uncertain whether one of these was exhibited in the 1922 Berlin show. Lissitzky presented his Proun concept on September 21, 1921 at INKhUK and published his Proun manifesto in *De Stijl* 5:6 (June 1922), pp. 81–85, in which he described "a construction one needs to circle around, look at from all sides . . . and while moving around it we spiral up into space. . . . Material form moves along specific axes in space: across the diagonals and spirals of stairs, in the verticals of lifts, along the horizontals of tracks." An earlier project, called "Electric-Mechanical Spectacle" was developed in Moscow in 1920–1921 and published in the "music and theatre issue" of *Ma* in Vienna in 1924 (for an English translation see the Cambridge journal *Form* 3 (December 1966), pp. 12–14.

121. László Moholy-Nagy and Alfréd Kemény, "Dynamisch-konstruktives Kraftsystem," *Der Sturm*, 13:12 (December 1922), p. 186, translated in *Moholy-Nagy*, ed., R. Kostelanetz, p. 29.

122. "Kinetisch konstruktives System: Bau mit Bewegungsbahn für Spiel und Beförderung," in Moholy-Nagy, *Vom Material zur Architektur*, p. 205. See also Pontus Hultén, ed., *The Machine as Seen at the End of the Mechanical Age*, New York: Museum of Modern Art, 1968, p. 137 and *Raumkonzepte*, pp. 195-196.

123. The pamphlet has been reprinted in *Oskar Schlemmer und die abstrakte Bühne*, pp. 32–33. A revised and expanded version appeared in *Die Bühne am Bauhaus* (1925), translated in *The Theater of the Bauhaus* on pp. 52–54. In 1987, a recreation of the work was presented at the Junges Theater in Düsseldorf.

124. *The Theater of the Bauhaus*, p. 54.

125. Passuth, *Moholy-Nagy*, p. 52.

126. See László Moholy-Nagy, "Licht Requisit für eine elektrische Bühne," *Die Form* 5: 11–12 (1930), pp. 297–299; English translation in Passuth, *Moholy-Nagy*, pp. 310–311. The Paris version of the modulator had been constructed by the theatre department of the Berlin electricity company, A.E.G., who saw a range of theatrical applications of the product. See Weitemeier, *Licht-Visionen*, pp. 47–48, 62–63.

127. It was first presented in *Die Bühne am Bauhaus* (1925) and in altered form in *bauhaus* 3 (1927), p. 6 and *Blätter der Staatsoper und Städtischen Oper* 19 (1928/1929), pp. 14–16. See also the essay "Total Theatre Is the Theatre of the Future" (1927) in Passuth, *Moholy-Nagy*, pp. 299–301.

128. See the description and diagrams in *Die Bühne am Bauhaus* (1925). For a possible influence of the project on the design of Meyerhold's new theatre and Lissitzky's projected stage set of Tretyakov's *I Want a Child* see Braun, *Meyerhold: A Revolution in Theatre*, pp. 268–269.

129. Published in *bauhaus* 3 (1927), p. 2. See also *Andor Weininger: Vom Bauhaus zur konzeptuellen Kunst*, pp. 47–50, 55–57, 111–115 and *Raumkonzepte*, pp. 189–190 with some preparatory drawings.

130. In the earlier studies of 1926–1927, one can still see the spiraling inner axis that bore close resemblance to Moholy-Nagy's *Kinetic Constructive System* and Lissitzky's *Proun* concept referred to on pp. 220 and 279n120.

131. It was published in "Vom modernen Theaterbau, unter Berücksichtigung des Piscatortheaterneubaues in Berlin," *Berliner Tageblatt*, November 2, 1927, p. 5; *Die Scene*, 18:1 (1928), pp. 4–6; Erwin Piscator, *Das Politische Theater*, Berlin: Schultz, 1929, pp. 124–127. A later explanation given at the Volta Congress in Rome (*Convegno di lettere, 8–14 ottobre 1934: Il teatro drammatico*, Rome: Reale Accademia d'Italia, Fondazione Alessandro Volta, 1935) was reprinted in *The Theater of the Bauhaus*, pp. 11–14. See Stefan Woll, *Das Totaltheater: Ein Projekt von Walter Gropius und Erwin Piscator*, Berlin: Gesellschaft für Theatergeschichte, 1984. The design may also have been the basis of Marinetti's *Teatro Totale*, published in a manifesto of 1933. See Berghaus, *Italian Futurist Theatre*, p. 539, and the translation of the original manuscript in my edition of Marinetti's critical writings, New York: Farrar, Straus and Giroux (forthcoming).

132. *The Theater of the Bauhaus*, p. 12.

133. See *Andor Weininger: Vom Bauhaus zur konzeptuellen Kunst*, pp. 94–99, *Raumkonzepte*, pp. 183–185, *Andor Weininger zum 100. Geburtstag*, pp. 28–32 and *Andor Weininger: Works in the Busch-Reisinger Museum*, pp. 21, 49–50, 64. The revue was not performed at the time and received its first public perform-ance belatedly in 1993 in Graz, directed by the Viennese group of architects, Coop Himmelblau.

134. Weininger felt that some of his ideas became later incorporated into *Pictures at an Exhibition*. His testimony was printed in Kathrin Michaelsen, "Andor Weininger's Bühnenprojekte am Bauhaus," in Gassner, ed., *Wechsel Wirkungen: Ungarische Avant-garde in der Weimarer Republik*, pp. 427–434.

135. It was published in *bauhaus* 3 (1927), p. 2 and The *Theater of the Bauhaus*, p. 84. Further drawings and photographs can be found in Heinz Loew, "Die bewegliche Plastik und die mechanische Bühne," in Joost Schmidt, ed., *Lehre und Arbeit*, pp. 77–83.

136. The text has been published in Scheper, *Oskar Schlemmer*, p. 214. See also *Bühne und Raum: Roman Clemens* and Herold, *Roman Clemens*. A partial realization of the play was given in 1986 by the Zurich ballet director, Uwe Scholz.

137. Georg Hartmann, "Eine Inszenierung Kandinskys," *Der Querschnitt* 8:9 (September 1928), pp. 666–667.

138. Felix Klee's promptbook and production notes, now in the Centre Pompidou, enabled Martin Rupprecht in 1982 to reconstruct a performance for the Akademie der Künste Berlin. A film of the event was produced for Sender Freies Berlin in 1984 and is available from Inter Nationes in Bonn. Another, yet remarkably similar, reconstruction was produced by Der Rote Kreis in Dessau and recorded for ZDF and 3SAT in 1995.

139. W. Kandinsky, "über die abstrakte bühnensynthese," *Staatliches Bauhaus in Weimar 1919–1923*, pp. 142–144, partly reprinted in *bauhaus* 3 (1927), p. 6. An English translation can be found in Kandinsky, *Complete Writings on Art*, pp. 504–507 and Rischbieter and Storch, *Art and the Stage in the 20th Century*, p. 150.

140. Ludwig Grote, "Bühnenkomposition von Kandinsky," *i 10: Internationale Revue* (Amsterdam) 2:13 (1928), pp. 4–5; reprinted in *Raumkonzepte*, p. 170.

141. Arthur Seidl, "Bauhaus und Friedrich Theater," *Deutsche Tonkünstler Zeitung* 26:478 (July 5 1928), pp. 206–207.

142. Manuscript notes quoted by Jelena Hahl-Koch in *Kandinsky*, London: Thames and Hudson, 1993, p. 306.

143. Schlemmer, *Letters and Diaries*, p. 198 (December 21, 1926).

144. See O. Schlemmer, *Man: Teaching Notes from the Bauhaus*, eds. Heimo Kuchling and Janet Seligman.

145. See Scheper, *Oskar Schlemmer*, pp. 176–180.

146. For a detailed description of the dances see Scheper, *Oskar Schlemmer*, pp. 185–204. My summary here also draws on Bohner's reconstruction of 1977

and Susanne Lahusen's MA thesis presented at the Laban Centre for Movement and Dance in London.

147. See the chapter "Scenic Atmosphere," in *Notes of a Director*.

148. These have been documented in Walter René Fuerst and Samuel J. Hume, *Twentieth Century Stage Decoration*, London: Knopf, 1928 (reprinted New York: Blom, 1967); Bablet, *Les Révolutions scéniques du XXe siècle*, and the catalogs, *Die Maler und das Theater im 20. Jahrhundert*, and *Raumkonzepte*.

6   EPILOG

1. The rôle of Modernism in Fascist aesthetics has been the subject of extensive scholarly debate and investigation. See, e.g, Andrew Hewitt, *Fascist Modernism: Aesthetics, Politics, and the Avant-garde*, Stanford, CA, 1993, and Roger Griffin, *Fascism and Modernism* (forthcoming from Palgrave Macmillan).

2. See Milton W. Brown, *American Painting from the Armory Show to the Depression*, Princeton, NJ: Princeton University Press, 1955; Judith K. Zilczer, "The Armory Show and the American Avant-garde: A Re-evaluation," *Arts Magazine* 54 (September 1978), pp. 126–130; *The Shock of Modernism in America: The Eight and the Artists of the Armory Show*, Exh. cat. Roslyn,NY: Nassau County Museum of Fine Arts 1984; Milton W. Brown, *The Story of the Armory Show*, New York: Abbeville Press, 1988.

3. Milton W. Brown, "After Three Years," *Magazine of Art* (Washington) 39:4 (April 1946), pp. 138 and 166.

4. For the subsequent impact of U.S.-American culture on Europe see C. W. E. Bigsby, ed., *Superculture American Popular Culture and Europe*, London: Elek, 1975, and Rob Kroes et al., eds., *Cultural Transmissions and Receptions: American Mass Culture in Europe*, Amsterdam: VU University Press, 1993.

5. See Harold Rosenberg, *The Tradition of the New*, New York: Horizon Press, 1959.

6. Allan Kaprow, "Should the Artist Become a Man of the World?" *Art News* 63:6 (October 1964), pp. 34–37, 58–59, at p. 35.

7. See Eric Hodgins and Parker Lesley, "The Great International Art Market," *Fortune* 52:6 (December 1955), pp. 118–120, 150, 152, 157–158, 162, 169; 53:1 (January 1956), pp. 122–125, 130, 132, 134, 136. This essay was first pointed out to me by Stuart Hobbs, who dedicated a large chapter in *The End of the American Avant-garde* to the domestication of the avant-garde in the 1950s.

8. Lawrence Alloway, "The Arts and the Mass Media," *Architectural Design* 28:2 (February 1958), pp. 84–85.

9. Michael Kirby, *Futurist Performance*, New York: Dutton, 1971. As editor of *The Drama Review*, he was also responsible for the Historical Avant-garde section in this influential performance journal.

Bibliography ❧

This selective bibliography is arranged in sections that correspond to the main chapters of this volume. It contains both works quoted in the notes as well as titles that may be useful for further readings. Exhibition catalogs related to individual artists have been entered under the artist's name. Catalogs on general topics are entered under the name of editor or chief curator.

CONCEPTS OF MODERNITY, MODERNISM, AND OF THE AVANT-GARDE

Adorno, Theodor W., *Aesthetic Theory*, London: Routledge and Kegan Paul, 1984.

Albright, Daniel, *Untwisting the Serpent: Modernism in Music, Literature, and Other Arts*, Chicago: University of Chicago Press, 2000.

Altshuler, Bruce, *The Avant-garde in Exhibition: New Art in the 20th Century*, New York: Abrams, 1994; reprinted Berkeley, CA: University of California Press, 1998.

Asholt, Wolfgang and Walter Fähnders, eds., *Manifeste und Proklamationen der europäischen Avantgarde (1909–1938)*, Stuttgart: Metzler, 1995.

———, *Avantgarde: "Die ganze Welt ist eine Manifestation": Die europäischen Avantgarde und ihre Manifeste*, Darmstadt: Wissenschaftliche Buchgesellschaft, 1997.

———, *Avant Garde: Geschichte und Krise einer Idee. Vortragsreihe an der Bayrischen Akademie der Schönen Künste, November 1965 (Elfte Folge des Jahrbuchs Gestalt und Gedanke)*, Munich: Oldenbourg, 1966.

Avant-garde: Revue interdisciplinaire et internationale, Amsterdam: Rodopi, vols 0–15, (1987–2000).

Avant-garde & modernité, Paris: Champion-Slatkine, 1988.

Barck, Karlheinz, Dieter Schlenstedt, and Wolfgang Thierse, eds., *Künstlerische Avantgarde: Annäherungen an ein unabgeschlossenes Kapitel*, Berlin: Akademie-Verlag, 1979.

Baudrillard, Jean, "Modernité," *Encyclopedia Universalis*, vol. 11, Paris: Encyclopedia Universalis, 1975, 139–141.

Beebe, Maurice, "Introduction: What Modernism Was," *Journal of Modern Literature* 3:5 (July 1974), 1065–1084.

Béhar, Henri, *Littéruptures*, Lausanne: L'Age d'Homme, 1988.

Benjamin, Andrew, *Art, Mimesis and the Avant-garde: Aspects of a Philosophy of Difference*, London: Routledge, 1991.

Benjamin, Andrew, ed., *The Problems of Modernity: Adorno and Benjamin*, London: Routledge 1989.

Bergonzi, Bernard, ed., *Innovations: Essays on Art and Ideas*, London: Macmillan, 1968.

Berman, Marshall, *All That Is Solid Melts into Air: The Experience of Modernity*, New York: Schuster and Schuster, 1982.

Bernstein, Richard J., ed., *Habermas and Modernity*, Oxford: Polity Press, 1985.

Böhringer, Hannes, "Avantgarde: Geschichte einer Metapher," *Archiv für Begriffsgeschichte* 22 (1978), 90–114.

Bollenbeck, Georg, *Tradition, Avant-garde, Reaktion: Deutsche Kontroversen um die kulturelle Moderne 1880–1945*, Frankfurt am Main: Fischer, 1999.

Bradbury, Malcolm and James McFarlane, eds., *Modernism 1890–1930*, Harmondsworth: Penguin, 1976; 2nd rev. edn, 1983.

Brion-Guerry, Liliane, ed., *L'année 1913: Les Formes esthétiques de l'œuvre d'art à la veille de la Première Guerre Mondiale*, 3 vols, Paris: Klincksieck, 1971–1973.

Buchloh, Benjamin, "Theorizing the Avant-garde," *Art in America* 72:10 (November 1984), 19–21.

Buchloh, Benjamin H. D., Serge Guilbaud, and David Solkin, eds., *Modernism and Modernity: The Vancouver Conference Papers*, Halifax, NS: Press of the Nova Scotia College of Art and Design, 1983.

Bürger, Peter, *Theory of the Avant-garde*, Minneapolis, MN: University of Minnesota Press, 1984.

———, *The Decline of Modernism*, University Park, PA: Pennsylvania State University Press, 1992.

———, "Moderne," in Ulfert Ricklefs, ed., *Fischer Lexikon Literatur*, vol. 2, Frankfurt am Main: Fischer, 1996, 1287–1319.

Butler, Christopher, *After the Wake: An Essay on the Contemporary Avant-garde*, Oxford: Clarendon Press, 1980.

———, *Early Modernism: Literature, Music and Painting in Europe 1900–1916*, Oxford: Oxford University Press, 1994.

Calinescu, Matei, " 'Avant-garde': Some Terminological Considerations," *Yearbook of Comparative and General Literature* 23 (1974), 67–78.

———, "Avant-garde, Neo-Avant-garde, Post Modernism: The Culture of Crisis," *CLIO: An Interdisciplinary Journal* 4:3 (June 1975), 317–340.

———, *Faces of Modernity*, Bloomington, IN: Indiana University Press 1977; 2nd rev. edn under the title: *Five Faces of Modernity: Modernism, Avant-garde, Decadence, Kitsch, Postmodernism*, Durham, NC: Duke University Press, 1987.

Chefdor, Monique, Ricardo Quinones, and Albert Wachtel, eds., *Modernism: Challenge and Perspectives*, Urbana, IL: University of Illinois Press, 1986.

Clignet, Remi, *The Structure of Artistic Revolutions*, Philadelphia, PA: University of Pennsylvania Press, 1985.

Crouch, Christopher, *Modernism in Art, Design and Architecture*, New York: St. Martin's Press, 1999.

Crow, Thomas, "Modernism and Mass Culture in the Visual Arts," in T. Crow, *Modern Art and Common Culture*, New Haven, CT: Yale University Press, 1996, 3–37.

Crowther, Paul, *The Language of Twentieth-century Art: A Conceptual History*, New Haven, CT: Yale University Press, 1997.

Davies, Alistair, *An Annotated Critical Bibliography of Modernism*, Totowa, NJ: Barnes and Nobles, 1982.

Dawtrey, Liz, et al., eds., *Investigating Modern Art*, New Haven, CT: Yale University Press, 1996.

Debeljak, Aleš, *Reluctant Modernity: The Institution of Art and Its Historical Forms*, Lanham, MD: Rowman & Littlefield, 1998.

Deecke, Thomas, ed., *Avantgarden Retrospektiv*, Exh. cat. Münster: Westfälischer Kunstverein, 1980.

Drucker, Johanna, *Theorizing Modernism: Visual Art and the Critical Tradition*, New York: Columbia University Press, 1994.

Egbert, Donald D., "The Idea of 'Avant-garde' in Art and Politics," *The American Historical Review* 73 (1967), 339–366.

Elm, Theo and Gerd Hemmerich, eds., *Zur Geschichtlichkeit der Moderne: Der Begriff der literarischen Moderne in Theorie und Deutung. Ulrich Fülleborn zum 60. Geburtstag*, Munich: Fink, 1982.

Enzensberger, Hans Magnus, "Die Aporien der Avantgarde," H. M. Enzensberger, *Einzelheiten*, Frankfurt am Main: Suhrkamp, 1962, 290–315; "The Aporias of the Avant-garde," in Gregory T. Polletta, ed., *Issues in Contemporary Literary Criticism*, Boston, MA: Little, Brown & Co, 1973, 734–753.

Estivals, Robert, Jean-Charles Gaudy, and GabrielleVergez, *"L'Avant-garde": Étude historique et sociologique des publications périodiques ayant pour titre "L'Avant-garde,"* Paris: Bibliothèque Nationale, 1968.

Everdell, William R., *The First Moderns: Profiles in the Origins of Twentieth-Century Thought*, Chicago: University of Chicago Press, 1997.

Eysteinsson, Astradur, *The Concept of Modernism*, Ithaca and London: Cornell University Press 1990.

Fähnders, Walter, *Avantgarde und Moderne 1890–1933*, Stuttgart: Metzler, 1998.

Fokkema, Douwe and Elrud Ibsch, *Modernist Conjectures: A Mainstream in European Literature, 1910–1940*, London: Hurst, 1987.

Frisby, David, *Fragments of Modernity: Theories of Modernity in the Work of Simmel, Kracauer and Benjamin*, Cambridge, MA: MIT Press, 1986.

From Modernism to Postmodernism. Special issue of *Journal of Modern Literature* 3:5 (July 1973).

Gamache, Lawrence B., "Towards a Definition of 'Modernism,' " in Lawrence B. Gamache and Ian S. MacNiven, eds., *The Modernists: Studies in a Literary Phenomenon. Essays in Honor of Harry T. Moore*, Rutherford, NJ: Fairleigh Dickinson University Press, 1987, 32–45.

Gassner, Hubertus, Karlheinz Kopanski, and Karin Stengel, eds., *Die Konstruktion der Utopie: Ästhetische Avantgarde und politische Utopie in den 20er Jahren*, Marburg: Jonas, 1992.

Golding, John, *Visions of the Modern*, London: Thames and Hudson, 1994.

Goldmann, Lucien, "Avant-garde Literature and the Evolution of Capitalist Society," in David Daiches and Anthony Thoreby, eds., *The Modern World*, vol. 3, London: Aldus, 1975, 433–458.

Graevenitz, Gerhart von, ed., *Zur Ästhetik der Moderne: Für Richard Brinkmann zum 70. Geburtstag*, Tübingen: Niemeyer, 1992.

———, *Konzepte der Moderne: Germanistisches Symposion der DFG*, Stuttgart: Metzler, 1999.

Grimm, Reinhold and Jost Hermand, eds., *Faschismus und Avantgarde*, Königstein: Athenäum, 1980.

Grimminger, Rolf, *Literarische Moderne: Europäische Literatur im 19. und 20. Jahrhundert*, Reinbek: Rowohlt, 1995.

Gullón, Ricardo, *Direcciones del Modernismo*, Madrid: Alianza, 1990.

Gumbrecht, Hans Ulrich, "Modern, Modernität, Moderne," in Otto Brunner, Werner Conze, and Reinhart Koselleck, eds., *Geschichtliche Grundbegriffe: Historisches Lexikon zur politischen Sprache in Deutschland*, vol. 4, Stuttgart: Klett, 1978, 95–131.

Habermas, Jürgen, *Der philosophische Diskurs der Moderne: Zwölf Vorlesungen*, Frankfurt am Main: Suhrkamp 1985; English edn *The Philosophical Discourse of Modernity: Twelve Lectures*, Cambridge: Polity and Blackwell, 1987.

———, *Die Moderne—ein unvollendetes Projekt: Philosophisch-politische Aufsätze*, 3rd edn, Leipzig: Reclam, 1994.

Hadjinicolau, Nicos, "Sur l'idéologie de l'avant-gardisme," *Histoire et critique d'art* 2 (1976), 49–76; "On the Ideology of Avant-Gardism," *Praxis* (Los Angeles) 6 (1982), 38–70.

Haller, Rudolf, ed., *Nach Kakanien: Annäherungen an die Moderne*, Wien: Böhlau, 1996.

Hardt, Manfred, ed., *Literarische Avantgarden*, Darmstadt: Wissenschaftliche Buchgesellschaft, 1989.

Haug, Walter and Wilfried Barner, eds., *Ethische contra ästhetische Legitimation von Literatur. Traditionalismus und Modernismus: Kontroversen um den Avantgardismus. Akten des VII. Internationalen Germanisten-Kongresses, Göttingen 1985* [General editor: Albrecht Schöne], vol. 8, Tübingen: Niemeyer, 1986.

Heistein, Jósef, ed., *Décadentisme, symbolisme, avant-garde dans les littératures européennes: Recueil d'études*, Wrocław: Wydawnictwo Uniwersytetu Wrocławskiego, and Paris: Nizet, 1987.

Henríquez Ureña, Max, *Breve historia del modernismo*, México: Fondo de Cultura Económica, 1954; 2nd edn 1962.

Hess, Thomas B. and John Ashberry, eds., *The Avant-garde*, New York: Macmillan, 1968 [= *Art News Annual* 34 (1968)].

Hirdina, Karin, "Der Kunstbegriff der Avantgarde," *Weimarer Beiträge* 32 (1986), 1460–1485.

Holthusen, Hans Egon, *Avantgardismus und die Zukunft der modernen Kunst*, Munich: Piper, 1964.

Horowitz, Gregg, "The Aesthetics of the Avant-garde," in Jerrold Levinson, ed., *The Oxford Handbook of Aesthetics*, New York: Oxford University Press, 2003, 748–760.

Howe, Irving, ed., *The Idea of the Modern in Literature and the Arts*, New York: Horizon Press, 1967.

———, *Literary Modernism*, Greenwich, CO: Fawcett, 1967.

Huyssen, Andreas, "The Hidden Dialectic: The Avant Garde—Technology—Mass Culture," in Kathleen Woodward, ed., *The Myths of Transformation: Technology and Postindustrial Culture*, Madison, WI: Coda, 1980, 151–164.

Japp, Uwe, *Literatur und Modernität*, Frankfurt am Main: Klostermann, 1986.

Jauß, Hans Robert, "Literarische Tradition und gegenwärtiges Bewußtsein der Modernität: Wortgeschichtliche Betrachtungen," in Hans Steffen, ed., *Aspekte der Modernität*, Göttingen: Vandenhoeck & Rupprecht, 1965, 150–197.

Jäger, Georg, "Avantgarde," in Klaus Weimar, ed., *Reallexikon der deutschen Literaturwissenschaft: Neubearbeitung*, vol. 1, Berlin: De Gruyter, 1997, 183–187.

Jauss, Hans Robert, "Literarische Tradition und gegenwärtiges Bewußtsein der Modernität," in Hans Steffen, ed., *Apekte der Modernität*, Göttingen: Vandenhoeck & Rupprecht, 1965, 150–197.

Josipovici, Gabriel, *The Lessons of Modernism and Other Essays*, London: Macmillan, 1977.

Karl, Frederick R., *Modern and Modernism: The Sovereignty of the Artist 1885–1925*, New York: Atheneum, 1985.

Kermode, Frank, ed., "The Modern," in F. Kermode, *Modern Essays*, London: Collins, 1971, 39–70.

———, "Modernisms," in Bernard Bergonzi, ed., *Innovations: Essays on Art and Ideas*, London: Macmillan, 1968, 66–92.

Kirshner, Judith Russi, "The Possibility of an Avant-garde," *Formations* (Madison, WI) 2:2 (Fall 1985), 81–103.

Klotz, Heinrich, *Kunst im 20. Jahrhundert: Moderne, Postmoderne, Zweite Moderne*, Munich: Beck, 1994.

Kolocotroni, Vassiliki, Olga Taxidou, and Jane Goldman, eds., *Modernism: An Anthology of Sources and Documents*, Edinburgh: Edinburgh University Press, 1998.

Kostelanetz, Richard, "Avant-garde," *Avant Garde* 3 (1989), 109–112.

Kostelanetz, Richard, ed., *The Avant-garde Tradition in Literature*, Buffalo, NY: Prometheus Books, 1982.

Kostelanetz, Richard and Richard Carlin, eds., *Dictionary of the Avant-gardes*, Pennington, NJ: A Cappella, 1993.

Koster, Udo, "Die Moderne, die Modernisierung und die Marginalisierung der Literatur," in Jörg Schönert and Harro Segeberg, eds., *Polyperspektivik in der literarischen Moderne: Studien zur Theorie, Geschichte und Wirkung der Literatur. Karl Robert Mandelkow gewidmet*, Frankfurt am Main: Lang, 1988, 353–380.

Krysinski, Wladimir, "Manifestos, Avant-gardes, and Transgressive Modernity," *Aims and Prospects of Semiotics: Essays in Honor of Algirdas Julien Greimas*, vol. 1, ed. Herman Parret and Hans-George Ruprecht, eds., Amsterdam and Philadelphia, PA: John Benjamins, 1985, 41–51.

Kuspit, Donald, *The Cult of the Avant-garde Artist*, Cambridge: Cambridge University Press, 1993.

———, *Psychostrategies of Avant-garde Art*, Cambridge: Cambridge University Press, 2000.

Lefebvre, Henri, *Introduction à la modernité*, Paris: Éditions de Minuit, 1962; English edn *Introduction to Modernity: Twelve Preludes, September 1959–May 1961*, New York: Verso, 1995.

———, "Theses on Modernism," in Benjamin H. D. Buchloh, Serge Guilbaud, and David Solkin, eds., *Modernism and Modernity: The Vancouver Conference Papers*, Halifax, NS: Press of the Nova Scotia College of Art and Design, 1983, 3–12.

LeRoy, Gaylord and Ursula Beitz, "The Marxist Approach to Modernism," *Journal of Modern Literature* 3:5 (July 1973), 1158–1174.

Levenson, Michael, *The Cambridge Companion to Modernism*, Cambridge: Cambridge University Press, 1999.

Loevgren, Sven, *The Genesis of Modernism: Seurat, Gauguin, Van Gogh and French Symbolism in the 1880's*; 2nd rev. edn, Bloomington, IN: Indiana University Press, 1971.

Lüdke, W. Martin, ed., *"Theorie der Avantgarde": Antworten auf Peter Bürgers Bestimmung von Kunst und bürgerlicher Gesellschaft*, Frankfurt am Main: Suhrkamp, 1976.

Lukácz, Georg, "Die weltanschaulichen Grundlagen des Avantgardeismus," *Werke*, vol. 4: *Probleme des Realismus I*, Neuwied: Luchterhand, 1971, 467–499.

Lunn, Eugene, *Marxism and Modernism: An Historical Study of Lukácz, Brecht, Benjamin, and Adorno*, Berkeley, CA: University of California Press, 1982.

Mann, Paul, *The Theory Death of the Avant-garde*, Bloomington, IN: Indiana University Press, 1991.

Marchán Fiz, Simón, *Las vanguardias históricas y sus sombras, 1917–1930*, Madrid: Espasa Calpe, 1995.

Marchart, Oliver, *Neoismus: Avantgarde und Selbsthistorisierung*, Klagenfurt: Edition Selene, 1997.

Mariátegui, José Carlos, *Avanguardia artistica e avanguardia politica*, Milan: Mazzotta, 1975.

Marino, Adrian, "Modernisme et modernité: Quelques précisions sémantiques," *Neohelicon* 2: 3–4 (1974), 307–318.

———, "Essai d'une définition de l'avant-garde," *Explorations des avant-garde. Publié par le Centre d'Études des Avant-gardes Littéraires*. Special issue of *Revue de l'Université de Bruxelles* 1 (1975), 64–120.

————, "Comment définir l'Avant-garde?" in Béla Köpeczi and György M. Vajda, eds., *Actes du VIIIe Congrès de l'Association Internationale de Littérature Comparée, Budapest, 12–17 Août 1976*, vol. 1, Stuttgart: Kunst und Wissen E. Bieber, 1980, 889–895.

Martini, Fritz, "Modern. Die Moderne," *Reallexikon der deutschen Literaturgeschichte*, vol. 2, Berlin: De Gruyter, 1965, 391–415.

Meschonnic, Henri, *Modernité Modernité*, Lagrasse: Verdier, 1988.

Miller, Tyrus, *Late Modernism: Politics, Fiction, and the Arts between the World Wars*, Berkeley, CA: University of California Press, 1999.

Modernity and Modernism, Postmodernity and Postmodernism. Special issue of *Cultural Critique* 5 (1987).

Mouvements littéraires d'avant-garde, Lausanne: Grammont, and Barcelona: Salvat, 1976.

Mukařovský, Jan, "Dialectic Contradictions in Modern Art," in J. Mukařovský, *Structure, Signs and Function: Selected Essays*, New Haven, CT: Yale University Press, 1978, 129–149.

Münch, Richard, *Die Kultur der Moderne*, 2 vols, Frankfurt am Main: Suhrkamp, 1993.

Murphy, Richard, *Theorizing the Avant-garde: Modernism, Expressionism, and the Problem of Postmodernity*, Cambridge: Cambridge University Press, 1999.

Nicholls, Peter, *Early Modernism: A Literary Guide*, Houndmills: Macmillans, 1995.

Nochlin, Linda, "The Invention of the Avant-garde: France 1830–1880," *Arts News Annual* 34 (1968), 11–18; reprinted in L. Nochlin, *The Politics of Vision: Essays on Nineteenth-Century Art and Society*, London: Thames and Hudson, 1991, 1–18.

Noszlopy, George T., "The Embourgeoisement of Avant-garde Art," *Diogenes* 67 (Fall 1969), 83–109.

Osborne, Peter, "Modernity as a Qualitative, not a Chronological, Category: Notes on the Dialectics of Differential Historical Time," in Francis Barker, Peter Hulme, and Margaret Iversen, eds., *Postmodernity and the Re-Reading of Modernity*, Manchester: Manchester University Press, 1992, 23–45.

————, *The Politics of Time: Modernity and Avant-garde*, London: Verso, 1995.

Paszkiewicz, Piotr, ed., *Totenmesse: Modernism in the Culture of Northern and Central Europe*, Warsaw: Institute of Art, Polish Academy of Sciences, 1996.

Piechotta, Hans Joachim, Ralph-Rainer Wurthenow, and Sabine Rotheman, eds., *Die literarische Moderne in Europa*, vol. 2: *Formationen der literarischen Avantgarde*, Opladen: Westdeutscher Verlag, 1994.

Pellegrini, David and Dennis Kennedy, "Avant-garde," in Dennis Kennedy, ed., *The Oxford Encyclopedia of Theatre and Performance*, Oxford: Oxford University Press, 2003, 93–96.

Pippin, Robert B., *Modernism as a Philosophical Problem: On the Dissatisfactions of European High Culture*, Cambridge, MA: Blackwell, 1991.

Platt, Susan Noyes, *Modernism in the 1920s: Interpretations of Modern Art in New York from Expressionism to Constructivism*, Ann Arbor, MI: UMI Research Press, 1985.

Pleynet, Marcelin, "Les Problèmes de l'Avant-garde," *TelQuel* 25 (Spring 1966), 77–86.

Pochat, Götz, "Moderne gestern: Eine begriffsgeschichtliche Untersuchung," in Hans Holländer and Christian W. Thomsen, eds., *Besichtigung der Moderne: Bildende Kunst, Architektur, Musik, Literatur, Religion. Aspekte und Perspektiven*, Cologne: DuMont, 1987, 21–39.

———, "Charakteristika der Moderne," in Rudolf Haller, ed., *Nach Kakanien: Annäherung an die Moderne*, Vienna: Böhlau, 1996, 267–323.

Poggioli, Renato, *The Theory of the Avant-garde*, Cambridge, MA: Harvard University Press, 1968.

Rosa, Alberto Asor, "Avanguardia," *Enciclopedia Einaudi*, vol. 2, Turin: Einaudi, 1977, 195–231.

Rosenberg, Bernard and Norris Fliegel, *The Vanguard Artist: Portrait and Self-portrait*, Chicago: Quadrangle Books, 1965; 2nd edn, New York: New Amsterdam, 1990.

Russell, Charles, *Poets, Prophets, and Revolutionaries: The Literary Avant-garde from Rimbaud through Postmodernism*, New York and Oxford: Oxford University Press, 1985.

Sanguineti, Edoardo, "Pour une avant-garde révolutionnaire," *TelQuel* 29 (1967), 76–95.

Scheunemann, Dietrich, ed., *European Avant-garde: New Perspectives. Avantgarde–Avantgardekritik–Avantgardeforschung*, Amsterdam: Rodopi, 2000.

Schönert, Jörg, "Gesellschaftliche Modernisierung und Literatur der Moderne," in Christian Wagenknecht, ed., *Zur Terminologie der Literaturwissenschaft: Akten des IX. Germanistischen Symposions der Deutschen Forschungsgemeinschaft, Würzburg 1986*, Stuttgart: Metzler, 1989, 394–413.

Schulte-Sasse, Jochen, "Avant-garde," in Erik Barnow, ed., *International Encyclopedia of Communication*, vol. 1, New York: Oxford University Press, 1989, 162–166.

———, "Modernity and Modernism, Postmodernity and Postmodernism: Framing the Issue," *Cultural Critique* 5 (1987), 5–22.

Sheppard, Richard, *Modernism–Dada–Postmodernism*, Evanston, IL: Northwestern University Press, 2000.

Somol, Robert E., ed., *Autonomy and Ideology: Positioning an Avant-garde in America*, New York: The Monacelli Press, 1997.

Steffen, Hans, ed., *Aspekte der Modernität*, Göttingen: Vandenhoeck und Ruprecht, 1965.

Stephan, Rudolf, "Moderne," *Musik in Geschichte und Gegenwart: Sachteil*, 2nd edn, L. Fischer, ed., vol. 6, Kassel: Bärenreiter, 1997, 392–397.

Szabolcsi, Miklós, "L'Avant-garde littéraraire et artistique comme phénomène international," in Nikola Banaševi, ed., *Actes du Ve Congrès de l'Association Internationale de Littérature Comparée Belgrad 1967*, Belgrade: Université de Belgrade and Amsterdam: Swets and Zeitlinger, 1969, 317–334.

———, "Avant-garde, Neo-avant-garde, Modernism: Questions and Suggestions," *New Literary History* 3 (1971), 49–70.

Torre, Guillermo de, *Literaturas europeas de vanguardia*, Madrid: Caro Raggio, 1925.

———, *Historias de las literaturas de vanguardia*, Madrid: Guadarrama, 1965; 2nd edn in 3 vols, 1971; 3rd edn, 1974.

Vargish, Thomas and Delo E. Mook, *Inside Modernism: Relativity Theory, Cubism, Narrative*, New Haven, CT: Yale University Press, 1999.

Vietta, Silvio, *Die literarische Moderne: Eine problemgeschichtliche Darstellung der deutschsprachigen Literatur von Hölderlin bis Thomas Bernhard*, Stuttgart: Metzler, 1992.

———, *Ästhetik der Moderne: Literatur und Bild*, Munich: Fink, 2001.

Vietta, Silvio and Dirk Kemper, eds., *Ästhetische Moderne in Europa: Grundzüge und Problemzusammenhänge seit der Romantik*, Munich: Fink, 1998.

Weir, David, *Anarchy and Culture: The Aesthetic Politics of Modernism*, Amherst, MA: University of Massachusetts Press, 1997.

Weisgerber, Jean, ed., *Les Avant-gardes littéraires au XXe siècle*, 2 vols, Budapest: Akadémiai Kiadó, 1984.

Weston, Richard, *Modernism*, London: Phaidon, 1996.

Wild, David, *Fragments of Utopia: Collage Reflections of Heroic Modernism*, London: Hyphen Press, 1997.

Williams, Raymond, *The Politics of Modernism: Against the New Conformists*, London: Verso, 1989.

Wood, Paul, ed., *The Challenge of the Avant-garde*, New Haven, CT: Yale University Press, 1999.

Wunberg, Gotthardt, ed., *Die literarische Moderne: Dokumente zum Selbstverständnis der Literatur um die Jahrhundertwende*, Frankfurt am Main: Athenäum, 1971.

Yack, Bernard, *The Fetishisms of Modernity*, Notre Dame, IN: University of Notre Dame Press, 1997.

Zima, Peter V. and Johann Strutz, *Europäische Avant-garde*, Frankfurt am Main: Lang, 1987.

GENERAL ASPECTS OF AVANT-GARDE AND MODERNIST ART, THEATRE, AND PERFORMANCE

Bablet, Denis, *Les Révolutions scéniques du XXe siècle*, Paris: Société Internationale d'Art, 1975; English edn *The Revolution of the Stage: Design in the XXth Century*, Paris: Amiel, 1977.

Baltz-Balzberg, Regina, *Primitivität der Moderne 1895–1925: Am Beispiel des Theaters*, Königstein/Ts.: Hain, 1983.

Barthes, Roland, "A l'avant-garde de quel théâtre?" in R. Barthes, *Essaies critiques*, Paris: Seuil, 1964, 80–83; "Whose Theater? Whose Avant-garde?" in R. Barthes, *Critical Essays*, Evanston, IL: Northwestern University Press, 1972, 67–70.

Bell, John Thomas, *Mechanical Ballets: The Rediscovery of Performing Objects on European Stages from the 1890s to the 1930s*, Ph.D. Dissertation, New York: Columbia University, 1993.

Benson, Timothy O., ed., *Central European Avant-gardes: Exchange and Transformation, 1910–1930*, Exh. cat. Los Angeles: Los Angeles County Museum of Art, 2002; Cambridge, MA: MIT Press, 2002.

Berghaus, Günter, *Avant-garde Performance: Live Events and Electronic Technologies*, London: Palgrave Macmillan, 2005.

Brandt, Sylvia, *Bravo! & Bum Bum! Neue Produktions- und Rezeptionsformen im Theater der historischen Avantgarde: Futurismus, Dada und Surrealismus*, Frankfurt am Main: Lang, 1995.

Braun, Edward, *The Director and the Stage: From Naturalism to Grotowski*, London: Methuen, 1982.

Carlson, Marvin, *Performance: A Critical Introduction*, London: Routledge, 1996.

Chadwick, Whitney, "Modernism, Abstraction and the New Woman, 1910–25," in W. Chadwick, *Women Art and Society*, London: Thames and Hudson, 1990, 236–264.

Daval, Jean Luc, *Modern Art: The Decisive Years 1884–1914*, Geneva: Skira and London: Macmillan, 1979.

————, *Journal des avant-gardes: Les années vingt, les années trente*, Geneva: Skira 1980; English edn *Avant-garde Art 1914–1939*, Geneva: Skira, and New York: Rizzoli, 1980.

Davidson, Abraham, *Early American Modernist Painting 1910–1935*, New York: Harper, 1981.

Deepwell, Katy, ed., *Women Artists and Modernism*, Manchester: Manchester University Press, 1998.

DeKoven, Marianne, *Rich and Strange: Gender, History, Modernism*, Princeton, NJ: Princeton University Press, 1991.

Dubreuil-Blondin, Nicole, "Feminism and Modernism: Paradoxes," in Benjamin H. D. Buchloh, Serge Guilbaud, and David Solkin, eds., *Modernism and Modernity: The Vancouver Conference Papers*, Halifax, NS: Press of the Nova Scotia College of Art and Design, 1983, 195–214.

Fauchereau, Serge, *Expressionnisme, dada, surréalisme et autres ismes*, 2 vols, Paris: Denoël, 1976.

Felski, Rita, *The Gender of Modernity*, Cambridge, MA: Harvard University Press, 1995.

Fischer-Lichte, Erika, ed., *Theater Avantgarde: Wahrnehmung, Körper, Sprache*, Tübingen: Francke, 1995.

Folejewski, Zbigniew, ed., *Les Années folles: Les mouvements avant-gardistes européens/The Roaring Twenties: The Avant-garde Movements in Europe*, Ottawa, ON: Éditions de l'Université d'Ottawa, 1981.

Foster, Stephen C., ed., *"Event" Arts and Art Events*, Ann Arbor, MI: UMI, 1988.

Goldberg, RoseLee, *Performance: Live Art 1909 to the Present*, London: Thames and Hudson, 1979; 2nd rev. edn, 1988.

Graver, David, *The Aesthetics of Disturbance: Anti-Art in Avant-garde Drama*, Ann Arbor, MI: University of Michigan Press, 1995.

Griffin, Gabriele, ed., *Difference in View: Women and Modernism*, London: Taylor & Francis, 1994.

Harding, James M., ed., *Contours of the Avant-garde: Performance and Textuality*, Ann Arbor, MI: University of Michigan Press, 2000.

Harrison, Elizabeth Jane and Shirley Peterson, eds., *Unmanning Modernism: Gendered Re-readings*, Knoxville, TN: University of Tennessee Press, 1997.

Heistein Józef, *Le Drame d'avant-garde et le théâtre: Actes du colloque franco-polonais organisé par l'Université de Wrocław et l'Université de la Sorbonne Nouvelle, Paris IIIe*, Warszawa: Państwowe wydawnictwo naukowe, 1979.

Homer, William Innes, ed., *Avant-garde: Painting and Sculpture in America 1910–25*, Exh. cat. Wilmington, DE: Delaware Art Museum, 1975.

Jardine, Alice, *Gynesis: Configuration of Woman and Modernity*, Ithaca, NY: Cornell University Press, 1985.

Kahn, Douglas and Gregory Whitehead, eds., *Wireless Imagination: Sound, Radio, and the Avant-garde*, Cambridge, MA: MIT Press, 1992.

Kirby, Michael, *The Art of Time: Essays on the Avant-garde*, New York: Dutton, 1969.

———, "Avant-garde Theater: The Antagonistic and the Hermetic," *Formations* (Madison, WI) 2:2 (Fall 1985), 72–80.

Koneffke, Silke, *Theater-Raum: Visionen und Projekte von Theaterleuten und Architekten zum anderen Aufführungsort, 1900–1980*, Berlin: Reimer, 1999.

Labelle-Rojoux, Arnaud, *L'Acte pour l'art*, Paris: Evidant, 1988.

Lerman, Philip, *Theatricalism in European Avant-garde Drama 1918–1939*, Ann Arbor, MI: UMI, 1985.

McCarren, Felicia M., *Dancing Machines: Choreographies of the Age of Mechanical Reproduction*, Stanford, CA: Stanford University Press, 2003.

Mennemeier, Franz Norbert, Erika Fischer-Lichte, and Doris Kolesch, *Drama und Theater der europäischen Avant-garde*, Tübingen: Francke, 1994.

Merlio, Gilbert and Nicole Pelletier, eds., *Munich 1900 site de la modernité/München 1900 als Ort der Moderne*, Berne and New York: Lang, 1998.

Mersch, Dieter, "Ereignis und Aura: Radikale Transformation der Kunst vom Werkhaften zum Performativen," *Kunstforum International* 152 (October–December 2000), 94–103.

Meskimmon, Marsha, *We Weren't Modern Enough: Women Artists and the Limits of German Modernism*, London: I. B. Tauris, 1999.

Nam, Sang Sik, *Der Faktor "Publikum" in den Theatertheorien der europäischen Avantgarde zwischen 1890 und 1930*, Frankfurt am Main: Lang, 1997.

Passuth, Krisztina and Dominique Moyen, *Les Avant-gardes de l'Europe centrale, 1907–1927*, Paris: Flammarion, 1988.

Pauly, Danièle, *La Rénovation scénique en France: Théâtre années 20*, Paris: Institut Français d'Architecture, 1995.

Paz, Marga, ed., *El teatro de los pintores en la Europa de las vanguardias*, Exh. cat. Madrid: Museo Nacional Centro de Arte Reina Sofía, 2000; Madrid: Aldeasa,

2000; English edn *Painters in the Theater of the European Avant-garde*, Madrid: Aldeasa, 2001.

Perry, Gill, *Women Artists and the Parisian Avant-garde: Modernism and "Feminine" Art, 1900 to the Late 1920s*, Manchester: Manchester University Press, 1995.

Picon-Vallin, Béatrice, ed., *Les Écrans sur la scène: Tentations et résistances de la scène face aux images*, Lausanne: l'Âge d'Homme, 1998.

———, *La scène et les images*, Paris: Centre National de la Recherche Scientifique, 2001.

Poole, Ralph, *Performing Bodies: Überschreitungen der Geschlechtergrenzen im Theater der Avantgarde*, Frankfurt am Main: Lang, 1996.

Pollock, Griselda, "Modernity and the Spaces of Femininity," in G. Pollock, *Vision and Difference: Femininity, Feminism and the Histories of Art*, London: Routledge, 1988, 50–90; reprinted in Francis Frascina and Jonathan Harris, eds., *Art in Modern Culture: An Anthology of Critical Texts*, London: Phaidon, 1992, 121–135.

———, *Avant-garde Gambits 1888–1893: Gender and the Colour of Art History*, London: Thames and Hudson, 1992.

Rischbieter, Henning and Wolfgang Storch, eds., *Bühne und bildende Kunst im 20. Jahrhundert: Maler und Bildhauer arbeiten für das Theater*, Velber: Friedrich, 1968; English edn *Art and the Stage in the 20th Century: Painters and Sculptors Work for the Stage*, Greenwich, CT: New York Graphic Society, 1969.

Roters, Eberhard, ed., *Avantgarde Osteuropa 1910–1930*, Exh. cat. Berlin: Deutsche Gesellschaft für Bildende Kunst (Kunstverein Berlin) und Akademie der Künste, 1967; Berlin: Hartmann, 1967.

Schmitz, Walter, ed., *Die Münchener Moderne*, Stuttgart: Reclam, 1990.

Schober, Thomas, *Das Theater der Maler: Studien zur Theatermoderne anhand dramatischer Werke von Kokoschka, Kandinsky, Barlach, Beckmann, Schwitters und Schlemmer*, Stuttgart: M&P Verlag für Wissenschaft und Forschung, 1994.

Schütte, Jürgen and Peter Sprengel, eds., *Die Berliner Moderne 1885–1914*, Stuttgart: Reclam, 1987.

Scott, Bonnie Kime, ed., *The Gender of Modernism: A Critical Anthology*, Bloomington, IN: Indiana University Press, 1990.

Shapiro, Theda, *Painters and Politics: The European Avant-garde and Society 1900–1925*, New York: Elsevier, 1976.

Shattuck, Roger, *The Banquet Years: The Origins of the Avant-garde in France, 1885 to World War I*, New York: Harcourt, Brace, 1958; 2nd rev. edn, New York: Vintage Books, 1968.

Silver, Kenneth E., *Esprit de corps: The Art of the Parisian Avant-garde and the First World War, 1914–1925*, Princeton, NJ: Princeton University Press, 1989.

Smith, Terry, *Invisible Touch: Modernism and Masculinity*, Chicago: University of Chicago Press, 1997.

Sprengel, Peter, *Literatur im Kaiserreich: Studien zur Moderne*, Berlin: Schmidt, 1993.

———, *Berliner und Wiener Moderne: Vermittlungen und Abgrenzungen in Literatur, Theater, Publizistik*, Vienna: Böhlau, 1998.

Stahl, Enno, *Anti-Kunst und Abstraktion in der literarischen Moderne (1909–1933): Vom italienischen Futurismus bis zum französischen Surrealismus*, Frankfurt am Main: Lang, 1997.

Stanislawski, Ryszard and Christoph Brockhaus, eds., *Europa, Europa: Das Jahrhundert der Avantgarde in Mittel- und Osteuropa*, Exh. cat. Bonn: Kunst- und Ausstellungshalle der Bundesrepublik Deutschland, 1994; 4 vols, Bonn: Stiftung Kunst und Kultur des Landes Nordrhein-Westfalen, 1994.

Stationen der Moderne: Die bedeutenden Kunstausstellungen des 20. Jahrhunderts in Deutschland, Exh. cat. Berlin: Berlinische Galerie, Museum für Moderne Kunst, Photographie und Architektur, 1988.

Stein, Donna, ed., *Women Artists of the Avant-garde 1910–1935*, Exh. cat. New York: Rachel Adler Gallery, 1984.

Stephan, Inge and Sigrid Weigel, eds., *Weiblichkeit und Avantgarde*, Hamburg: Argument, 1987.

Suleiman, Susan Rubin, *Subversive Intent: Gender, Politics and the Avant-garde*, Cambridge, MA: Harvard University Press, 1990.

Tomkins, Calvin, *The Bride and the Bachelors: The Heretical Courtship in Modern Art*, New York: Viking Press, 1965; 2nd edn, *The Bride and the Bachelors: Five Masters of the Avant-garde*, Harmondsworth: Penguin, 1976.

Vaccarino, Elisa, Gabriella Belli, and Brunella Eruli, eds.,*Automi, marionette e ballerine nel teatro d'avanguardia: Depero Taeuber-Arp Exter Schlemmer Morach Schmidt Nikolais Cunningham*, Exh. cat. Trento: Palazzo delle Albere, 2000–2001; Milan: Skira, 2000.

Van Crugten, Alain, "Le Théâtre d'avant-garde," *Acta Universitatis Wratislaviensis* 462 (*Romanica Wratislaviensia* 15) (1979), 193–204.

Voss, Ursula, *Szenische Collagen: Theaterexperimente der europäischen Avant-garde zwischen 1913 und 1936*, Bielefeld: Aisthesis, 1998.

Vergine, Lea, *L'altra metà dell'avanguardia, 1910–1940: Pittrici e scultrici nei movimenti delle avanguardie storiche*, Milan: Mazzotta, 1980; French edn *L'Autre Moitié de l'avant-garde, 1910–1940*, Paris: Des Femmes, 1982.

Watson, Steven, *Strange Bedfellows: The First American Avant-garde*, New York: Abbeville Press, 1991.

Wolff, Janet, "Feminism and Modernism," in J. Wolff, *Feminine Sentences: Essays on Women and Culture*, Berkeley, CA: University of California Press, 1990, 51–66.

Wunberg, Gotthardt, ed., *Die Wiener Moderne: Literatur, Kunst und Musik zwischen 1890 und 1910*, Stuttgart: Reclam, 1981.

ALFRED JARRY

Arnaud, Noël, *Alfred Jarry: D'Ubu Roi au Docteur Faustroll*, Paris: La Table Ronde [1974].

Beaumont, Keith, *Alfred Jarry: A Critical and Biographical Study*, Leicester: Leicester Press, 1984.

Beaumont, Keith, *Jarry: Ubu Roi*, London: Grant and Cutler, 1987.

Béhar, Henri, *Jarry: Le monstre et la marionnette*, Paris: Larousse, 1973.

————, *Jarry dramaturge*, Paris: Nizet, 1980.

Béhar, Henri and Brunella Eruli, eds., *Jarry et Cie: Communications du colloque international, TNP, 12–13 mai 1985*, Tournées: L'Etoile-Absinthe, 1985.

Bordillon, Henri, *Gestes et opinions d'Alfred Jarry, écrivain*, Laval: Siloé, 1986.

Chauveau, Paul, *Alfred Jarry, ou La naissance la vie et la mort du père Ubu*, Paris: Mercure de France, 1932.

Cooper, Judith, *Ubu Roi: An Analytical Study*, New Orleans, LA: Tulane University, 1974.

Jarry, Alfred, *Œuvres complètes*, 8 vols, Monte-Carlo: Éditions du Livre, and Lausanne: Kaeser, 1948.

————, *Œuvres poétiques complètes*, ed. Henri Parisot, Paris: Gallimard, 1945.

————, *Selected Works of Alfred Jarry*, ed. Roger Shattuck and Simon Watson Taylor, London: Methuen, 1965; 2nd edn, 1980.

————, *Œuvres complètes*, ed. Michel Arrivé, 3 vols, Paris: Gallimard, 1988.

————, *Ubu Roi: Drama in 5 Acts*, trans. Barbara Wright, London: Gaberbocchus Press, 1951.

————, *King Turd*, trans. Beverley Keith and G. Legman, New York: Boar's Head Books, 1953.

————, *Tout Ubu*, ed. Maurice Saillet, Paris: Le Livre de Poche, 1962.

————, *The Ubu Plays*, ed. Simon Watson Taylor, London: Methuen, 1968.

————, *Peintures, gravures et dessins d'Alfred Jarry*, ed. Michel Arrivé, Paris: Collège de Pataphysique et Cercle Français du Livre, 1968.

————, *Ubu Rex: A Play*, trans. David Copelin, Vancouver: Pulp Press, 1973.

————, *Ubu: Ubu Roi, Ubu Cocu, Ubu Enchaîné, Ubu sur le Butte*, ed. Noël Arbaud and Henri Bordillon, Paris: Gallimard, 1978.

————, *Adventures in "Pataphysics,"* ed. Paul Edwards and Antony Melville, London: Atlas, 2001.

LaBelle, Maurice Marc, *Alfred Jarry: Nihilism and the Theater of the Absurd*, New York: New York University Press, 1980.

Lebois, Andrè, *Alfred Jarry, l'irremplaçable*, Paris: Cercle du Livre, 1950.

Lié, P., "Comment Jarry et Lugné Poe glorifièrent Ubu à l'Œuvre," *Cahiers du Collège de 'Pataphysique* 3–4 (October 27, 1950), 37–51.

————, "Notes sur la seconde représentation d'Ubu Roi," *Cahiers du Collège de 'Pataphysique* 20 (June 29, 1955), 47–52.

Perche, Louis, *Alfred Jarry*, Paris: Éditions Universitaires, 1965.

Rachilde [Marguerite Eymery], *Alfred Jarry; ou, Le Surmâle de lettres*, Paris: Grasset, 1928.

Robillion, Henri, "La Presse d'Ubu Roi," *Cahiers du Collège de Pataphysique* 3–4 (October 27, 1950), 73–88.

Schumacher, Claude, *Alfred Jarry and Guillaume Apollinaire*, Houndmills: Macmillans, 1984.

Stillman, Linda Klieger, *Alfred Jarry*, Boston, MA: Twayne Publishers, 1983.

Szeemann, Harald, ed., *Alfred Jarry*, Exh. cat. Zurich: Kunsthaus Zürich, 1984–1985.

WASSILY KANDINSKY AND EARLY ABSTRACTIONISM

Becks-Malorny, Ulrike, *Wassily Kandinsky, 1866–1944: The Journey to Abstraction*, Cologne: Taschen, 1994.

Berghaus, Günter, "A Theatre of Image, Sound and Motion,"*Maske und Kothurn 32* (1986), 7–28.

Bill, Max, *Wassily Kandinsky*, Paris: Maeght, 1951.

Boissel, Jessica, " 'Diese Dinge haben eigene Geschicke': Wassily Kandinsky und das Experiment 'Theater,' " *Der Blaue Reiter*, Exh. cat. ed. Hans Christoph von Tavel, Berne: Kunstmuseum, 1986–1987, 240–251; " 'Questo tipo di cose ha il suo destino': Kandinskij e il teatro sperimentale," *Vassilij Kandinskij*, Exh. cat. Verona: Galleria d'Arte Moderna e Contemporanea di Palazzo Forti, 1993; Milan: Mazzotta, 1993, 193–205.

Briesch, Klaus, *Wassily Kandinsky (1866–1944): Untersuchungen zur Entstehung der gegenstandslosen Malerei an seinem Werk von 1900–1921*, Ph.D. Dissertation, Bonn, 1955.

Brucher, Günter, *Wassily Kandinsky: Wege zur Abstraktion*, Munich: Prestel, 1999.

Cheetham, Mark A., *The Rhetoric of Purity: Essentialist Theory and the Advent of Abstract Painting*, Cambridge: Cambridge University Press, 1991.

Denkler, Horst, "Kandinsky et le théâtre," *Oblique* 6–7 (1976), 95–99.

Eller-Rüter, Ulrika-Maria, *Kandinsky: Bühnenkomposition und Dichtung als Realisation seines Synthese-Konzepts*, Hildesheim: Olms, 1990.

Grohmann, Will, *Wassily Kandinsky: Leben und Werk*, Cologne: DuMont, 1958.

Hahl-Koch, Jelena, "Kandinsky et le théâtre: Quelques aperçus," *Kandinsky à Munich*, Exh. cat. Bordeaux: Galerie des Beaux-Arts, 1976, 53–59.

———, *Kandinsky*, New York: Rizzoli, 1993.

Kandinsky, Wassily, *Über das Geistige in der Kunst*, Munich: Piper, 1912 [i.e. 1911]; 4th edn, Berne: Benteli, 1952; English edn *The Art of Spiritual Harmony*, London: Constable, 1914; *On the Spiritual in Art*, New York: Guggenheim-Foundation, 1946; *Concerning the Spiritual in Art, and Painting in Particular*, New York: Wittenborn, Schultz, 1947; New York: Dover, 1977.

———, *Essays über Kunst und Künstler*, ed. Max Bill, Stuttgart: Hatje, 1955; 2nd rev. edn, Berne: Benteli, 1963.

———, *Die Gesammelten Schriften*, ed. Hans K. Roethel and Jelena Hahl-Koch, vol. 1, Berne: Benteli, 1980.

———, *Complete Writings on Art*, ed. Kenneth C. Lindsay and Peter Vergo, Boston, MA: Hall, 1982; New York: Da Capo, 1994.

———, *Über das Theater/Du théâtre/O teatre*, ed. Jessica Boissel and Jean-Claude Marcadé, Cologne: DuMont, 1998.

Kandinsky, Wassily and Franz Marc, eds., *Der Blaue Reiter*, Munich: Piper, 1912; 2nd edn, 1914; *Der Blaue Reiter: Dokumentarische Neuausgabe von Klaus Lankheit*, Munich: Piper, 1965; English edn *The "Blaue Reiter" Almanach*, London: Thames and Hudson, 1974.

Kandinsky, Wassily and Arnold Schönberg, *Letters, Pictures and Documents*, ed. Jelena Hahl-Koch, London: Faber and Faber, 1984.

Klussmann, Paul Gerhard, "Über Wassili Kandinskys Bühnenkomposition *Der gelbe Klang*," in Paul Gerhard Klussmann, Willy Berger, and Burkhard Dohm, eds., *Das Wagnis der Moderne: Festschrift für Marianne Kesting*, Frankfurt am Main: Lang, 1993, 279–297.

Moeller, Magdalena M., ed., *Der frühe Kandinsky, 1900–1910*, Exh. cat. Berlin: Brücke-Museum, 1994; Munich: Hirmer, 1994.

Pevitts, Robert R., *Wassily Kandinsky's "The Yellow Sound": A Synthesis of the Arts for the Stage*, Ann Arbor, MI: UMI, 1986.

Renaud, Lissa Tyler, *Kandinsky: Dramatist, Dramaturg, and Demiurge of the Theatre*, Ann Arbor, MI: UMI, 1990.

Ringbom, Sixten, *The Sounding Cosmos: A Study in the Spiritualism of Kandinsky and the Genesis of Abstract Painting*, Åbo: Åbo Akademi, 1970.

Selz, Peter, "The Aesthetic Theories of Wassily Kandinsky and Their Relationship to the Origin of Non-Objective Painting," *The Art Bulletin* 39:2 (June 1957), 127–136.

Sheppard, Richard W., "Kandinsky's Abstract Drama 'Der gelbe Klang': An Interpretation," *Forum for Modern Language Studies* 11 (1975), 165–176.

Stein, Susan Alyson, *The Ultimate Synthesis: An Interpretation of the Meaning and Significance of Wassily Kandinsky's "The Yellow Sound,"* M.A. Dissertation in Art History at SUNY Binghamton, 1980.

———, "Kandinsky and Abstract Stage Composition: Practice and Theory, 1909–1912," *Art Journal* 43 (1983), 61–66.

Towards a New Art: Essays on the Background to Abstract Art 1910–1920, Exh. cat. London: Tate Gallery, 1980.

Washton Long, Rose-Carol, *Kandinsky: The Development of an Abstract Style*, Oxford: Clarendon Press, 1980.

Weiss, Peg, *Kandinsky in Munich: The Formative Years*, Princeton, NJ: Princeton University Press, 1979.

———, "Kandinsky: Symbolist Poetics and Theater in Munich," *Pantheon* 35 (1977), 209–218.

Wham, Quincie Matalie, *Schoenberg/Kandinsky: The Genesis of a Tonality/Abstraction, 1908–1914*, Ph.D. Dissertation, Texas Technical University, 1987.

EXPRESSIONISM

Anz, Thomas and Michael Stark, eds., *Expressionismus: Manifeste und Dokumente zur deutschen Literatur 1910–1920*, Stuttgart: Metzler, 1981.

————, *Die Modernität des Expressionismus*, Stuttgart: Metzler, 1994.

Bablet, Denis and Jean Jacquot, eds., *L'Expressionisme dans le théâtre européen: Colloque Strasbourg 1968*, Paris: Centre National de la Recherche Scientifique, 1971.

Barron, Stephanie, ed.,*German Expressionism, 1915–1925: The Second Generation*, Exh. cat. Los Angeles: Los Angeles County Museum of Art, 1988; Munich: Prestel, 1988.

Barron, Stephanie and Wolf-Dieter Dube, eds., *German Expressionism: Art and Society*, Exh. cat. Venice: Palazzo Grassi, 1997–1998; London: Thames and Hudson, 1997.

Behr, Shulamith, *Women Expressionists*, Oxford: Phaidon, 1988.

Behr, Shulamith, David Fanning, and Douglas Jarman, eds., *Expressionism Reassessed*, Manchester: Manchester University Press, 1993.

Best, Otto F., ed., *Theorie des Expressionismus*, Stuttgart: Reclam, 1976; 2nd rev. edn, 1994.

Betthausen, Peter, ed., *Expressionisten: Die Avantgarde in Deutschland 1905–1920*, Exh. cat. Berlin: Staatliche Museen zu Berlin, Nationalgalerie, 1986; Berlin: Henschel, 1986.

Brand, Matthias, *Fritz Kortner in der Weimarer Republik: Annäherungsversuche an die Entwicklung eines jüdischen Schauspielers in Deutschland*, Rheinfelden: Schäuble, 1981.

Brandt, Regina, *Figurationen und Kompositionen in den Dramen Oskar Kokoschkas*, Munich: UNI-Druck, 1968.

Brinkmann, Richard, *Expressionismus: Forschungs-Probleme 1952–1960*, Stuttgart: Metzler,1961.

————, *Expressionismus: Internationale Forschung zu einem internationalen Phänomen*, Stuttgart: Metzler, 1980.

Bronner, Stephen Eric and Douglas Kellner, eds., *Passion and Rebellion: The Expressionist Heritage*, London: Croom Helm, 1983.

Brühl, Georg, *Herwarth Walden und "Der Sturm,"* Leipzig: Edition Leipzig, 1983.

Buchheim, Lothar Günther, *Die Künstlergemeinschaft Brücke: Gemälde, Zeichnungen, Graphik, Plastik, Dokumente*, Feldafing: Buchheim, 1956.

Calandra, Denis, "Georg Kaiser's 'From Mourn to Midnight': The Nature of Expressionist Performance," *Theatre Quarterly* 6:21 (Spring 1976), 45–54.

Carter, Huntly, *The New Spirit in Drama and Art*, London: Palmer, 1912.

————, *The New Spirit in the European Theatre 1914–1924: A Comparative Study of the Changes Effected by the Revolution*, London: Benn, 1925.

Chiarini, Paolo, *Il teatro tedesco espressionista*, Bologna: Cappelli, 1959.

————, *L'espressionismo: Storia e struttura*, Florence, La Nuova Italia, 1969; 2nd rev. edn, Bari: Laterza, 1985.

Chiarini, Paolo, Antonella Gargano, and Roman Vlad, eds., *Expressionismus: Una enciclopedia interdisciplinare*, Rome: Bulzoni, 1986.

Cossart, Axel von, *Kino-Theater des Expressionismus: Das literarische Resümee einer Besonderheit*, Essen: Die Blaue Eule, 1985.

Crawford John C. and Dorothy L. Crawford, *Expressionism in Twentieth-Century Music*, Bloomington, IN: Indiana University Press, 1993.

Denkler, Horst, *Drama des Expressionismus: Programm, Spieltext, Theater*, Munich: Fink, 1967; 2nd rev. edn, 1979.

Diebold, Bernhard, *Anarchie im Drama*, Frankfurt am Main: Frankfurter Verlags-Anstalt, 1921.

Diethe, Carol, *Aspects of Distorted Sexual Attitudes in German Expressionist Drama: With Particular Reference to Wedekind, Kokoschka and Kaiser*, New York: Lang, 1988.

Dube, Wolf-Dieter, *The Expressionists*, London: Thames and Hudson, 1972.

Durzak, Manfred, *Das expressionistische Drama*, 2 vols, Munich: Nymphenburger Verlagshandlung, 1978.

Edschmid, Kasimir, *Frühe Manifeste: Epochen des Expressionismus*, Hamburg: Wegner, 1957.

———, *Lebendiger Expressionismus: Auseinandersetzungen, Gestalten, Erinnerungen*, Vienna: Desch, 1961.

Elger, Dietmar, *Expressionism: A Revolution in German Art*, Cologne: Taschen, 1989.

Emmel, Felix, *Das ekstatische Theater*, Prien: Kampmann und Schnabel, 1924.

Expressionism: A German Intuition 1905–1920, Exh. cat. New York: Solomon R. Guggenheim Foundation, 1980.

Expressionisten: Die Avantgarde in Deutschland 1905–1920. 125 Jahre Sammlungen der Nationalgalerie, 1861–1986, Exh. cat. Berlin: Nationalgalerie 1986; Berlin: Henschel, 1986.

Furness, Raymond, *Expressionism*, London: Methuen, 1973.

Gabler, Karlheinz, ed., *Hein Heckroth 1901–1970*, Exh. cat. Kassel: Staatliche Kunstsammlungen, 1977.

Gordon, Donald E., *Expressionism: Art and Idea*, New Haven, CN: Yale University Press, 1987.

Gordon, Mel, "German Expressionist Acting," *The Drama Review* 19:3 (T67) (September 1975), 34–50.

———, "Lothar Schreyer and The Sturmbühne," *The Drama Review* 24:1 (T85) (March 1980), 85–102.

Gordon, Mel, ed., *Expressionist Texts*, New York: PAJ Publications, 1986.

Hain, Mathilde, *Studien über das Wesen des frühexpressionistischen Dramas*, Frankfurt am Main: Diesterweg, 1933.

Hamann, Richard and Jost Hermand, *Expressionismus*, Berlin: Akademie-Verlag, 1975.

Herbert, Barry, *German Expressionism: Die Brücke and Der Blaue Reiter*, London: Jupiter Books, 1983.

Hermand, Jost, "Expressionism and Music," in Gertrud Bauer Pickar and Karl Eugene Webb, eds., *Expessionism Reconsidered: Relationships and Affinities*, Munich: Fink, 1976, 58–73; reprinted as "Musikalischer Expressionismus," in J. Hermand, ed., *Beredte Töne: Musik im historischen Prozeß*, Frankfurt: Lang, 1991, 97–117.

Hodin, Josef Paul, *Oskar Kokoschka: The Artist and His Time. A Biographical Study*, Greenwich, CT: New York Graphic Society, 1966.

Hoffmann, Edith, *Kokoschka: Life and Work*, London: Faber and Faber, 1947.

Hüneke, Andreas, ed., *Der Blaue Reiter: Dokumente einer geistigen Bewegung*, Leipzig: Reclam, 1986; 2nd rev. edn, 1989.

Hüppauf, Bernd, ed., *Expressionismus und Kulturkrise*, Heidelberg: Winter, 1983.

Jones, M. S., *Der Sturm: A Focus of Expressionism*, Columbia, SC: Camden House, 1984.

Jäger, Georg, "Kokoschkas 'Mörder Hoffnung der Frauen': Die Geburt des Theaters der Grausamkeit aus dem Geist der Wiener Jahrhundertwende," *Germanisch-Romanische Monatsschrift* NF 32 (1982), 215–233.

Jähner, Horst, *Künstlergruppe Brücke: Geschichte, Leben und Werk ihrer Maler*, Stuttgart: Kohlhammer, 1984.

Keith-Smith, Brian, *Lothar Schreyer: Ein vergessener Expressionist*, Stuttgart: Heinz, 1990.

Knapp, Bettina, "Oskar Kokoschka's 'Murderer Hope of Womankind': An Apocalyptic Experience," *Theatre Journal* 35 (1983), 179–194.

Knapp, Gerhard Peter, *Die Literatur des deutschen Expressionismus: Einführung, Bestandsaufnahme, Kritik*, Munich: Beck, 1979.

Kokoschka, Oskar, *Schriften, 1907–1955*, ed. Hans Maria Wingler, Munich: Langen-Müller, 1956.

———, *Das schriftliche Werk*, 4 vols, ed. Heinz Spielmann, Hamburg: Christians, 1973–1976.

———, *My Life*, London: Thames and Hudson, 1974.

———, *Briefe*, 4 vols, ed. Olda Kokoschka and Heinz Spielmann, Düsseldorf: Claassen 1984.

———, *Letters, 1905–1976*, ed. Olda Kokoschka and Alfred Marnau, London: Thames and Hudson, 1992.

———, *Stories from My Life*, Riverside, CA: Ariadne, 1998.

———, *Plays and Poems*, Riverside, CA: Ariadne, 2001.

[Kokoschka, Oskar, catalogs] *Oskar Kokoschka: Die frühen Jahre. Zeichnungen und Aquarelle*, Exh. cat. ed. by Serge Sabarsky, Vienna: Historisches Museum der Stadt Wien, 1982–1983.

Oskar Kokoschka 1886–1980, Exh. cat. ed. Richard Calvocoressi and Katharina Schulz, London: Tate Gallery, 1986.

Oskar Kokoschka: Die frühen Jahre, 1906–1926. Aquarelle und Zeichnungen, Exh. cat. ed. by Serge Sabarsky, Hamburg: Kunsthalle, 1986; Munich: Jentsch, 1986.

Oskar Kokoschka, Exh. cat. ed. Klaus Albrecht Schröder and Johann Winkler, Vienna: Kunstforum Länderbank, 1991; Munich: Prestel, 1991.

Oskar Kokoschka: Das Frühwerk (1897/98–1917). Zeichnungen und Aquarelle, Exh. cat. ed. Alice Strobl and Alfred Weidinger, Vienna: Graphische Sammlung Albertina, 1994; English edn *Oskar Kokoschka: Works on Paper. The Early Years, 1897–1917*, Exh. cat. New York: Solomon R. Guggenheim Museum, 1994.

Oskar Kokoschka und die Musik, Exh. cat. ed. Heinz Spielmann, Gottorp: Schleswig-Holsteinisches Landesmuseum, 1996.

Kokoschka und Dresden, Exh. cat. ed. Birgit Dalbajewa and Werner Schmidt, Dresden: Staatliche Kunstsammlungen, 1996; Leipzig: Seemann, 1996.

Kronau, Trude, *Teatro e film nell' espressionismo tedesco*, Bologna: Leonardi, 1971.

Kruse, Joachim, ed., *Cesar Klein*, Exh. cat. Schleswig-Holsteinisches Landesmuseum, Schloß Gottorf, 1977; Schleswig: Schleswiger Druck- und Verlagshaus, 1977.

Kuhns, David F., *German Expressionist Theatre: The Actor and the Stage*, Cambridge: Cambridge University Press, 1997.

Lea, Henry A., "Expressionist Literature and Music," in Ulrich Weisstein, ed., *Expressionism as an International Literary Phenomenon*, Paris: Didier, 1973, 141–166.

Lemaître, Maurice, *Le Théâtre expressioniste allemand*, Paris: Centre de Créativité Lettriste, 1982.

Lischka, Gerhard Johann, *Oskar Kokoschka, Maler und Dichter: Eine literar-ästhetische Untersuchung zu seiner Doppelbegabung*, Berne: Lang, 1972.

Loyd, Jill, *German Expressionism: Primitivism and Modernity*, New Haven, CT: Yale University Press, 1991.

Ludwigg, Heinz, ed., *Fritz Kortner*, Berlin: Eigenbrödler-Verlag, 1928.

Mazurkiewicz-Wonn, Michaela, *Die Theaterzeichnungen Oskar Kokoschkas*, Hildesheim: Olms, 1994.

Miesel, Victor H., ed., *Voices of German Expressionism*, Englewood Cliffs, NJ: Prentice Hall, 1970.

Mülhaupt, Freya, ed., *Herwarth Walden 1878–1941: Wegbereiter der Moderne*, Exh. cat. Berlin: Berlinische Galerie, 1991.

Myers, Bernard Samuel, *The German Expressionists: A Generation in Revolt*, New York: Praeger, 1957.

Nölle, Eckehart, ed., *Expressionistisches Theater: Vom Kaiserreich zur Republik. Der "neue" Mensch auf der Bühne*, Exh. cat. Munich: Deutsches Theatermuseum, 1980.

Otten, Karl, ed., *Schrei und Bekenntnis: Expressionistisches Theater*, Neuwied: Luchterhand, 1959.

Overbeck, Alvin Henry, *The "Sturm-Kreis": Culmination of a Movement*, Ph.D. Dissertation, University of Nashville, Tennessee, 1971; Ann Arbor, MI: UMI, 1971.

Padmore, Elaine, "German Expressionist Opera," *Proceedings of the Royal Musical Association* 95 (1968–1969), 41–53.

Palmier, Jean-Michel, *L'Expressionnisme comme révolte: Contribution à l'étude de la vie artistique sous la République de Weimar*, Paris: Payot, 1978.

———, *L'Expressionnisme et les arts*, vol. 1: *Portrait d'une génération*, Paris: Payot, 1979.

———, *L'Expressionnisme et les arts*, vol. 2: *Peinture, théâtre, cinéma*, Paris: Payot, 1980.

Pam, Dorothy, "Kokoschka's 'Murderer, the Women's Hope'," *The Drama Review* 19:3 (T67) (September 1975), 5–12.

Pan, David, *Primitive Renaissance: Rethinking German Expressionism*, Lincoln, NE: University of Nebraska Press, 2001.

Patka, Erika, ed., *Oskar Kokoschka Symposion, abgehalten von der Hochschule für Angewandte Kunst in Wien vom 3. bis 7. März 1986 anläßlich des 100. Geburtstages des Künstlers*, Salzburg: Residenz Verlag, 1986.

Patterson, Michael, *The Revolution in German Theatre 1900–1933*, London: Routledge and Kegan Paul, 1981.

Perkins, Geoffrey, *Expressionimus: Eine Bibliographie zeitgenössischer Dokumente, 1910–1925*, Zurich: Verlag für Bibliographie, 1971.

———, *Contemporary Theory of Expressionism*, Frankfurt am Main: Lang, 1974.

Petzet, Wolfgang, ed., *800 Jahre München: Gedächtnisausstellung Otto Reigbert, Bühnenbildner*, Munich: Deutsches Theatermuseum, 1958.

Pfefferkorn, Rudolf, *Cesar Klein*, Berlin: Rembrandt, 1962.

Pickar, Gertrud Bauer and Karl Eugene Webb, eds., *Expressionism Reconsidered: Relationships and Affinities*, Munich: Fink, 1976.

Pirsich, Volker, *Der "Sturm" und seine Beziehungen zu Hamburg und zu Hamburger Künstlern*, Göttingen: Bautz, 1981.

———, *Der Sturm: Eine Monographie*, Herzberg: Bautz, 1985.

Poirier, Alain, *L' Expressionnisme et la musique*, Paris: Fayard, 1995.

Raabe, Paul, *Die Zeitschriften und Sammlungen des literarischen Expressionismus: Repertorium der Zeitschriften, Jahrbücher, Anthologien, Sammelwerke, Schriftenreihen und Almanache, 1910–1921*, Stuttgart: Metzler, 1964.

———, *Die Autoren und Bücher des literarischen Expressionismus: Ein bibliographisches Handbuch*, Stuttgart: Metzler, 1985; 2nd rev. edn, Stuttgart: Metzler, 1992.

Raabe, Paul, ed., *Expressionismus: Der Kampf um eine literarische Bewegung*, Munich: Deutscher Taschenbuch Verlag, 1965; 2nd edn, Zurich: Arche, 1987.

———, *Expressionismus: Aufzeichnungen und Erinnerungen der Zeitgenossen*, Olten: Walter, 1965; English edn *The Era of Expressionism*, London: Calder and Boyars, 1974.

———, *Index Expressionismus: Bibliographie der Beiträge in den Zeitschriften und Jahrbüchern des literarischen Expressionismus, 1910–1925*; 18 vols, Nendeln, Liechtenstein: Kraus-Thomson, 1972.

Reinking, Wilhelm, *Spiel und Form: Werkstattbericht eines Bühnenbildners zum Gestaltwandel der Szene in den zwanziger und dreißiger Jahren*, Hamburg: Christians, 1979.

Riedel, Walter E., *Der neue Mensch: Mythos und Wirklichkeit*, Bonn: Bouvier, 1970.

Ritchie, James McPherson, *German Expressionist Drama*, Boston, MA: Twayne, 1976.

Ritchie, James McPherson and Hans F. Garten, eds., *Seven Expressionist Plays*, London: Calder and Boyars, 1968.

Ritchie, James McPherson and J. D. Stowell, eds., *Vision and Aftermath; Four Expressionist War Plays*, London: Calder and Boyars, 1969.

Roethel, Hans Konrad, *The Blue Rider*, New York: Praeger, 1971.

Rothe, Wolfgang, *Tänzer und Täter: Gestalten des Expressionismus*, Frankfurt am Main: Klostermann, 1979.

Rothe, Wolfgang, ed., *Expressionismus als Literatur: Gesammelte Studien*, Berne: Francke, 1969.

Rötzer, Hans Gerd, ed., *Begriffsbestimmung des literarischen Expressionismus*, Darmstadt: Wissenschaftliche Buchgesellschaft, 1976.

Samuel, Richard and Hinton Thomas, *Expressionism in German Life, Literature and the Theatre, 1910–1924*, Cambridge: Heffer, 1939; 2nd edn, Philadelphia, PA: Saifer, 1971.

Schepelmann-Rieder, Erika, *Emil Pirchan und das expressionistische Bühnenbild,* Vienna: Bergland, 1964.

Schering, Arnold, "Die expressionistische Bewegung in der Musik," in Max Deri et al. *Einführung in die Kunst der Gegenwart*, Leipzig: Seemann, 1919, 139–161; reprinted in A. Schering, *Vom Wesen der Musik: Ausgewählte Aufsätze*, ed. Karl Michael Komma, Stuttgart: Koehler, 1974, 319–345.

Schreyer, Lothar, *Expressionistisches Theater: Aus meinen Erinnerungen*, Hamburg: Toth, 1948.

———, *Erinnerungen an Sturm und Bauhaus: Was ist des Menschen Bild?* Munich: Langen Müller, 1956.

———, *Zwischen Sturm und Bauhaus: Das expressionistische Werk von Lothar Schreyer. Texte 1916–1965*, ed. Brian Keith-Smith, Stuttgart: Akademischer Verlag Hans-Dieter Heinz, 1985.

———, *Dramen*, ed. Brian Keith-Smith, Lewiston, NY: Edwin Mellen Press, 1996.

———, *Theateraufsätze*, ed. Brian Keith-Smith, Lewiston, NY: Edwin Mellen Press, 2001.

Schultes, Paul, *Expressionistische Regie*, Ph.D. Dissertation, Universität Köln, 1961.

Schütze, Peter, *Fritz Kortner*, Reinbek: Rowohlt, 1994.

Schvey, Henry Ivan, *Oskar Kokoschka: The Painter as Playwright*, Detroit, MI: Wayne State University Press, 1982.

Schweiger, Werner J., *Der junge Kokoschka: Kunstgewerbeschule, Wiener Werkstätte, Cabaret Fledermaus, Kunstschau 1908*, Pöchlarn: Oskar Kokoschka-Dokumentation, 1983.

———, *Der junge Kokoschka: Leben und Werk, 1904–1914*, Vienna: Brandstätter, 1983.

———, *Oskar Kokoschka, der Sturm, die Berliner Jahre 1910–1916: Eine Dokumentation*, Vienna: Brandstätter, 1986.

Schwerte, Hans, "Anfang des expressionistischen Dramas: Oskar Kokoschka," *Zeitschrift für deutsche Philologie* 83 (1964), 174–191.

Selz, Peter Howard, *German Expressionist Painting*, Berkeley, CA: University of California Press, 1957.

Shearier, Stephen, *Das junge Deutschland, 1917–1920: Expressionist Theater in Berlin*, Berne: Lang, 1988.

Siebenhaar, Klaus, *Klänge aus Utopia: Zeitkritik, Wandlung und Utopie im expressionistischen Drama*, Berlin: Agora Verlag, 1982.

Sievert, Ludwig, *Lebendiges Theater: Drei Jahrzehnte deutscher Theaterkunst*, Munich: Bruckmann, 1944.

Sokel, Walter H., *The Writer in Extremis: Expressionism in Twentieth-Century German Literature*, Stanford, CA: Stanford University Press, 1959.

Sokel, Walter H., ed., *Anthology of German Expressionist Drama: A Prelude to the Absurd*, Garden City, NY: Anchor Books, 1963; 2nd edn, Ithaca, NY: Cornell University Press, 1984.

Spielmann, Heinz, ed., *Oskar Kokoschka 1886–1980: Welt-Theater, Bühnenbilder und Illustrationen 1907–1975. Ein Werkverzeichnis*, Hamburg: Museum für Kunst und Gewerbe, 1986.

Steffen, Hans, ed., *Der Deutsche Expressionismus: Formen und Gestalten*, Göttingen: Vandenhoeck und Ruprecht, 1965; 2nd rev. edn, 1970.

Steffens, Wilhelm, *Expressionistische Dramatik*, Velber: Friedrich, 1968.

Stuckenschmidt, Hans Heinz, "Arnold Schönbergs musikalischer Expressionismus," in Hans Steffen, ed., *Der Deutsche Expressionismus: Formen und Gestalten*, Göttingen: Vandenhoeck und Ruprecht, 1965, 250–268.

———, "Was ist musikalischer Expressionismus?" *Melos* 36:1 (January 1969), 1–5.

Taylor, Seth, *Left-Wing Nietzscheans: The Politics of German Expressionism 1910–1920*, Berlin and New York: De Gruyter, 1990.

Vietta, Silvio and Hans Georg Kemper, *Expressionismus*, Munich: Fink, 1975; 3rd edn, 1985.

Viviani, Annalisa, *Das Drama des Expressionismus: Kommentar zu einer Epoche*, Munich: Winkler, 1970; 2nd edn, 1981.

———, *Dramaturgische Elemente im expressionistischen Drama*, Bonn: Bouvier, 1970.

Völker, Klaus, *Fritz Kortner*, Berlin: Hentrich, 1987.

Von Troschke, Michael, *Der Begriff "Expressionismus" in der Musikliteratur des 20. Jahrhunderts*, Pfaffenweiler: Centaurus, 1988.

Wagner, Ludwig, *Der Szeniker Ludwig Sievert: Studie zur Entwicklungsgeschichte des Bühnenbildes im letzten Jahrzehnt*, Berlin: Bühnenvolksbund, 1926.

Wasserka, Ingo, *Die Sturm- und Kampfbühne: Kunsttheorie und szenische Wirklichkeit im expressionistischen Theater Lothar Schreyers*, Ph.D. Dissertation, Universität Wien, 1965.

Weidinger, Alfred, *Kokoschka and Alma Mahler*, Munich: Prestel, 1996.

Weisstein, Ulrich, ed., *Expressionism as an International Literary Phenomenon*, Paris: Didier, 1973.

Weller, Christian, "Abstraktion und Mystik: Lothar Schreyers 'Kampfbühne' zu Gast am Lerchenfeld," in Hartmut Frank, ed., *Nordlicht: 222 Jahre. Die Hamburger Hochschule für Bildende Künste am Lerchenfeld und ihre Vorgeschichte*, Exh. cat. Hamburg: Hamburger Kunsthaus and Hamburger Kunstverein 1989–1990; Hamburg: Junius, 1989, 164–172.

Werenskiold, Mari, *The Concept of Expressionism: Origin and Metamorphoses*, Oslo: Universitetsforlaget, 1984.

Whitford, Frank, *Expressionism*, London: Hamlyn, 1970.

———, *Oskar Kokoschka: A Life*, London: Weidenfeld and Nicolson, 1986.

Wingler, Hans Maria, *Oskar Kokoschka: The Work of the Painter*, Salzburg: Galerie Welz, 1958.

Wingler, Hans Maria, ed., *Oskar Kokoschka: Ein Lebensbild in zeitgenössischen Dokumenten*, Munich: Langen-Müller, 1956; 2nd edn, Frankfurt am Main: Ullstein, 1966.

GERMAN EXPRESSIONIST DANCE

Adamson, Andy and Clare Lidbury, *Kurt Jooss: 60 Years of the Green Table: Proceedings of the Conference Held at the University of Birmingham 17–19 October 1992*, Birmingham: University of Birmingham, 1994.

Aubel, Hermann and Marianne Aubel, *Der künstlerische Tanz unserer Zeit*, Königstein Ts.: Langewiesche, 1928.

Bach, Rudolf, *Das Mary Wigman-Werk*, Dresden: Reissner, 1933.

Blass, Ernst, *Das Wesen der neuen Tanzkunst*, Weimar: Lichtenstein, 1921.

Böhme, Fritz, *Rudolf von Laban und die Entstehung des modernen Tanzdramas*, Berlin: Hentrich, 1996.

Brandenburg, Hans, *Der moderne Tanz*, 3rd edn, Munich: Müller, 1921.

Brandstetter, Gabriele, *Tanz-Lektüren: Körperbilder und Raumfiguren der Avantgarde*, Frankfurt am Main: Fischer, 1995.

Cohen, Selma Jeanne, ed., *International Encyclopedia of Dance*, 6 vols, New York: Oxford University Press, 1998.

Coton, A. V., *The New Ballet: Kurt Jooss and His Work*, London: Dobson, 1946.

Curl, Gordon F. "Philosophical Foundations," *The Laban Art of Movement Guild Magazine* 37 (November 1966), 7–15; 38 (May 1967), 7–17; 39 (November 1967), 25–35; 40 (June 1968), 27–37; 41 (November 1968), 23–29; 43 (1969), 27–44.

Delius, Rudolf von, *Mary Wigman*, Dresden: Reissner, 1925.

Dove, Constance, "Kurt Jooss: An Appraisal of His Work," *Laban Art of Movement Guild Magazine* 55 (November 1975), 5–23.

Expressionist Dance. Special issue of *Ballet International* 5:4 (April 1982).

Franko, Mark, *Dancing Modernism/Performing Politics*, Bloomington, IN: Indiana University Press, 1995.

Fritsch-Vivie, Gabriele, *Mary Wigman*, Reinbek: Rowohlt, 1999.

[*German Ausdruckstanz*]. Special issue of *Ballet International* 4, 1982.

Gleisner, Martin M., "Conversations between Laban and Myself," *Laban Art of Movement Guild Magazine* 65 (November 1980), 16–19.

Hodgson, John, *Mastering Movement: The Life and Work of Rudolf Laban*, London: Methuen, 2001.

Hodgson, John and Valerie Preston-Dunlop, *Rudolf Laban: An Introduction to His Work and Influence*, Plymouth: Northcote, 1990.

Howe, Dianne Shelden, *Manifestations of the German Expressionist Aesthetics as Presented in Drama and Art: The Dances and Writings of Mary Wigman*, Ph.D. Dissertation, University of Wisconsin-Madison, 1985.

———, "Parallel Visions: Mary Wigman and the German Expressionists," *Dance: Current Selected Research*, vol. 1, New York: AMS Press, 1989, 77–88.

————, *Individuality and Expression: The Aesthetics of the New German Dance, 1908–1936*, New York: Lang, 1996.

Huxley, Michael, "Sylvia Bodmer Conversation," *Laban Art of Movement Guild Magazine* 68 (May 1982), 10–22.

Kurzdorf, Manfred, "The New German Dance Movement," in Stephen Eric Bronner and Douglas Kellner, eds., *Passion and Rebellion: The Expressionist Heritage*, South Hadley, MA: Bergin, 1983, 310–362.

Laban, Rudolf von, *Die Welt des Tänzers: Fünf Gedankenreigen*, Stuttgart: Seifert, 1920; 2nd edn, 1922.

————, *Ein Leben für den Tanz: Erinnerungen*, Dresden: Reissner, 1935; 2nd edn, ed. Claude Perrottet, Berne: Haupt, 1989; English edn *A Life for Dance: Reminiscences*, ed. Lisa Ullmann, London: Macdonald & Evans, 1975.

Lämmel, Rudolf, *Der moderne Tanz: Eine allgemeinverständliche Einführung in das Gebiet der rhythmischen Gymnastik und des Neuen Tanzes*, Berlin: Oestergaard, 1928.

Launay, Isabelle, *A la recherche d'une danse moderne: Rudolf Laban, Mary Wigman*, Paris: Chiron 1996.

Lidbury, Clare, ed., *Big City/Kurt Jooss*, London: Dance Books, 2000.

Maletic, Vera, *Body–Space–Expression: The Development of Rudolf Laban's Movement and Dance Concepts*, Berlin: Mouton De Gruyter, 1987.

Manning, Susan, *Ecstasy and the Demon: Feminism and Nationalism the Dances of Mary Wigman*, Berkeley, CA: University of California Press, 1993.

Markard, Anna, ed., *Kurt Jooss*, Exh. cat. Venice: Teatro La Fenice, Sale Apollinee, 1981; Venice: Marsilio, 1981.

Markard, Anna and Hermann Markard, eds., *Jooss*, Exh. cat. Essen: Museum Folkwang, 1985; Cologne: Ballett-Bühnen-Verlag, 1985.

Milloss, Aurel M., "Das Erbe des Expressionismus im Tanz," *Maske und Kothurn* 11 (1965), 329–343.

Müller, Hedwig, *Die Begründung des Ausdruckstanzes durch Mary Wigman*, Cologne: Hundt, 1986.

————, *Mary Wigman: Leben und Werk der großen Tänzerin*, Weinheim: Quadriga, 1986.

Müller, Hedwig and Patricia Stöckemann, "Der grüne Tisch: Eine Choreographie von Kurt Jooss," *Tanzdrama* 15 (1991), 22–28.

————, *". . . Jeder Mensch ist ein Tänzer": Ausdruckstanz in Deutschland zwischen 1900 und 1945*, Gießen: Anabas, 1993.

Nugent, Ann, "The Green Table and Café Müller," *Dance Now* 1:3 (Autumn 1992), 34–41.

Oberzaucher-Schüller, Gunhild, ed., *Ausdruckstanz: Eine mitteleuropäische Bewegung der ersten Hälfte des 20. Jahrhunderts*, Wilhelmshaven: Noetzel, 1992.

Odom, Maggie, "Mary Wigman: The Early Years 1913–1925," *The Drama Review* 24:4 (T88) (December 1980), 81–92.

Preston-Dunlop, Valerie, "Rudolf Laban: The Making of Modern Dance: The Seminal Years Munich 1910–1914," *Dance Theatre Journal* 7:3 (Winter 1989), 11–16; 7:4 (February 1990), 10–13.

Preston-Dunlop, "Rudolf Laban: The Nightmare Years in Zurich, 1914–1919," *Dance Theatre Journal* 10:3 (Spring/Summer 1993), 14–19; 10:4 (Autumn 1993), 33–35.

———, "Symbolism and the European Dance Revolution," *Dance Theatre Journal* 14:3 (1998), 40–45.

———, *Rudolf Laban: An Extraordinary Life*, London: Dance Books, 1998.

Preston-Dunlop, Valerie and Susanne Lahusen, *Schrifttanz: A View of German Dance in the Weimar Republic*, London: Dance Books, 1990.

Prevots, Naima, "Zurich Dada and Dance: Formative Ferment," *Dance Research Journal* 17:1 (Spring/Summer 1985), 3–8.

Scheyer, Ernst, *The Shapes of Space: The Art of Mary Wigman and Oskar Schlemmer*, New York: Dance Perspectives Foundation, 1970; also published in *Dance Perspectives* 41 (1970), 7–26.

Siegel, Marcia B., "The Green Table: Sources of a Classic," *Dance Research Journal* 21:1 (Spring 1989), 15–21.

Stefan, D. Paul, ed., *Tanz in dieser Zeit*, Vienna: Universal, 1926.

Stuber, Werner Jakob, *Geschichte des Modern Dance: Zur Selbsterfahrung und Körperaneignung im modernen Tanztheater*, Wilhelmshaven: Heinrichshofen, 1984.

Thiess, Frank, *Der Tanz als Kunstwerk: Studien zu einer neuen Ästhetik der Tanzkunst*, Munich: Delphin, 1920.

Thomas, Helen, *Dance, Modernity, and Culture: Explorations in the Sociology of Dance*, London: Routledge, 1995.

Ullman, Lisa, "My Apprenticeship with Laban," *Laban Art of Movement Guild Magazine* 63 (November 1979), 21–30.

Vaccarino, Elisa, ed., *La danza moderna: I fondatori. Seminario 1*, Milan: Skira, 1998.

Walther, Suzanne K., *The Dance of Death: Kurt Jooss and the Weimar Years*, Chur: Harwood 1994.

Wigman, Mary, "Rudolf von Labans Lehre vom Tanz," *Die Neue Schaubühne* 3:5/6 (September 1921), 99–106; 4:2 (February 1922), 30–35.

———, "The Dance and Modern Woman," *The Dancing Times*, November 1927, 162–163.

———, "My Teacher Laban," *Laban Art of Movement Guild Magazine*, December 1954, 5–12; reprinted in *Dance Magazine*, November 1956, 71–78.

———, *Die Sprache des Tanzes*, Stuttgart: Battenberg, 1963; 2nd edn, 1986; English edn *The Language of Dance*, ed. Walter Sorrell, Middletown, CN: Wesleyan University Press, 1966; 2nd edn, 1974.

———, *The Mary Wigman Book: Her Writings*, ed. Walter Sorell, Middletown, CN: Wesleyan University Press, 1973.

Wolfensberger, Giorgio J., ed., *Suzanne Perrottet: Ein bewegtes Leben*, Berne: Benteli, 1995.

Zivier, Georg, *Harmonie und Ekstase: Mary Wigman*, Berlin: Akademie der Künste, 1956.

FUTURISM

Agnese, Gino, *Marinetti: Una vita esplosiva*, Milan: Camunia, 1990.

Andreani, Stefano, *Marinetti e l'avanguardia della contestazione*, Rome: Edizioni Cremonese, 1974.

Antonucci, Giovanni, *Lo spettacolo futurista in Italia*, Rome: Studium, 1974.

Antonucci, Giovanni, ed., *Cronache del teatro futurista*, Rome: Abete, 1975.

———, *Il futurismo e Roma*, Rome: Istituto di Studi Romani, 1978.

Apollonio, Umbro, ed., *Futurismo*, Milan: Mazzotta, 1970; English edn *Futurist Manifestos*, London: Thames and Hudson, 1973.

Artioli, Umberto, *La scena e la dynamis: Immaginario e struttura nelle sintesi futuriste*, Bologna: Pàton, 1975.

Baldissone, Giusi, *Filippo Tommaso Marinetti*, Milan: Mursia, 1986.

[Balla, Giacomo], *Giacomo Balla*, Exh. cat. Turin: Galleria Civica d'Arte Moderna, 1963.

———, *Giacomo Balla* (1971–1958), ed. Giorgio de Marchis, Exh. cat. Rome: Galleria Nazionale d'Arte Moderna, 1971–1972; Rome: De Luca, 1972, French edn *Balla*, Paris: Musée d'Art Moderne de la Ville de Paris, 1972; Rome: De Luca, 1972.

———, *Futur-Balla*, Exh. cat. Vancouver: Art Gallery, 1986; Milan: Electa, 1986.

———, *Balla, the Futurist*, ed. Maurizio Fagiolo dell'Arco, Exh. cat. Edinburgh: Scottish National Gallery of Modern Art, 1987.

———, *Balla e i futuristi*, ed. Maurizio Fagiolo dell'Arco, Exh. cat. Paris: Galeries Nationales du Grand Palais, 1988; Milan: Electa, 1988; 2nd edn, 1989.

———, *Casa Balla e il futurismo a Roma*, ed. Enrico Crispolti, Exh. cat. Rome: Accademia di Francia, Villa Medici, 1989; Rome: Istituto Poligrafico e Zecca dello Stato, 1989.

Ballo, Guido, "Prampolini: Dalla scena illuminata alla scena illuminante," *Il dramma* 45:11 (August 1969), 91–100.

Barnes, Susan Elizabeth, *Giacomo Balla: His Life and Work, 1871 to 1912*, Ph.D. Dissertation, University of Michigan, 1977; 2nd edn, Susan Barnes Robinson, *Giacomo Balla: Divisionism and Futurism, 1871–1912*, Ann Arbor, MI: UMI, 1981.

Barsotti, Anna, *Futurismo e avanguardia nel teatro italiano fra le due guerre*, Rome: Bulzoni, 1990.

Bartolucci, Giuseppe, "La forma nuova del teatro di Marinetti," *Poesia e critica* 4:8–9 (May 1966), 142–164.

Baumgarth, Christa, *Geschichte des Futurismus*, Reinbek: Rowohlt, 1966.

Belli, Carlo, "Il teatro di Depero," *Teatro contemporaneo* 1:2 (October 1982–January 1983), 143–157.

Belloli, Carlo, "Giannina Censi negli anni Trenta danzava la poesia futurista," *La Martinella di Milan: Rassegna di vita italiana* 30:1–2 (January–February 1976), 3–18.

Bentivoglio, Leonetta, "Danza e futurismo in Italia, 1913–1933," *La danza italiana* 1:1 (Autumn 1984), 61–82.

Bentivoglio, Mirella and Franca Zoccoli, *Women Artists of Italian Futurism*. New York: Midmarch Arts Press, 1997.

Benton, Tim, ed., *Italian Futurism*, Milton Keynes: Open University, 1983.

Berghaus, Günter, "Danza futurista: Giannina Censi and the Futurist Thirties," *Dance Theatre Journal* 8:1 (Summer 1990), 4–7, 34–37.

———, "Dance and the Futurist Woman: The Work of Valentine de Saint-Point, 1875–1953," *Dance Research* 11:2 (1993), 27–42.

———, "Fulvia Giuliani, Portrait of a Futurist Actress," *New Theatre Quarterly* 10:38 (May 1994), 117–121.

———, *The Genesis of Futurism: Marinetti's Early Career and Writings 1899–1909*, Leeds: Society for Italian Studies, 1995.

———, *Futurism and Politics: Between Anarchist Rebellion and Fascist Reaction, 1909–1944*, Oxford: Berghahn, 1996.

———, *Italian Futurist Theatre, 1909–1944*. Oxford: Clarendon Press, 1998.

———, "The Futurist Banquet: Nouvelle Cuisine or Performance Art?" *New Theatre Quarterly* 17:1 (February 2001), 3–17.

Berghaus, Günter, ed., *International Futurism in Arts and Literature*, Berlin: De Gruyter, 2000.

Bianchi, Stefano, *La musica futurista: Ricerche e documenti*, Lucca: Libreria Musicale Italiana, 1995.

Blum, Cinzia Sartini, "The Futurist Re-Fashioning of the Universe," *South Central Review* 13:2–3 (Summer-Fall 1996), 82–104.

———, *The Other Modernism: F. T. Marinetti's Futurist Fiction of Power*, Berkeley, CA: University of California Press, 1996.

Blum, Cinzia Sartini, ed., *Futurism and the Avant-garde*. Special issue of *South Central Review* 13:2–3 (Summer-Fall 1996).

Boccioni, Umberto, *Gli scritti editi e inediti*, ed. Zeno Birolli, Milan: Feltrinelli, 1971; 2nd edn, 1979.

———, *Altri inediti e apparati critici*, ed. Zeno Birolli, Milan: Feltrinelli, 1972.

Bonfanti, Elvira, *Il corpo intelligente: Giannina Censi*, Turin: Il Segnalibro, 1995.

Brandstetter, Gabriele, "Flugtanz: Futuristischer Tanz und Aviatik," in G. Brandstetter, *Tanz-Lektüren: Körperbilder und Raumfiguren der Avantgarde*, Frankfurt am Main: Fischer, 1995, 386–421.

Brescia, Anna Maria, *The Aesthetic Theories of Futurism*, Ph.D. Dissertation, New York: Columbia University, 1971; Ann Arbor, MI: UMI, 1990.

Campanini, Paola, "Il 'mondo meccano' di Fortunato Depero: Storia e utopia dei Balli Plastici," *Ariel* 2–3 (1993), 295–321.

Cangiullo, Francesco, *Le serate futuriste: Romanzo storico vissuto*, Pozzuoli: Tirena [1930]; reprinted Milan: Ceschina, 1961.

Cangiullo, Francesco and F. T. Marinetti, *Teatro della sorpresa*, Livorno: Belforte, 1968.

Carrà, Carlo, *Tutti gli scritti*, ed. Massimo Carrà, Milan: Feltrinelli, 1978.

————, *La mia vita*, Rome: Longanesi, 1943; 2nd edn, Milan: Rizzoli, 1945; 3rd edn, Milan: Feltrinelli, 1981; 4th edn, Milan: SE, 1997.

Carrieri, Raffaele, *Il futurismo*, Milan: Il Milione, 1961; English edn *Futurism*, Milan: Il Milione, 1963.

Caruso, Luciano, ed., *Manifesti, proclami, interventi e documenti teorici del futurismo, 1909–1944*, 4 vols, Florence: S.P.E.S., 1980.

————, *Dossier futurista*, 2 vols., Florence: S.P.E.S., 1995.

Caruso, Luciano and Giuliani Longone, eds., *Il teatro futurista a sorpresa: Documenti*, Florence: Salimbeni, 1979.

Cheshire, David F., "Futurism, Marinetti and the Music Hall," *Theatre Quarterly* 1:3 (July–September 1971), 53–59.

Clough, Rosa Trillo, *Looking Back at Futurism*. New York: Cocce, 1942; 2nd edn, *Futurism: The Story of a Modern Art Movement. A New Appraisal*, New York: Philosophical Library, 1961; reprinted Westport, CT: Greenwood, 1969.

Crispolti, Enrico, ed., *Ricostruzione futurista dell'universo*, Exh. cat. Turin: Musei Civici Mole Antonelliana, 1980.

————, *La macchina mito futurista*, Exh. cat. Rome: Galleria Editalia, 1986.

————, *Futurismo e meridione*, Exh. cat. Naples: Palazzo Reale, 1996; Naples: Electa, 1996.

————, *Il futurismo attraverso la Toscana: Architettura, arti visive, letteratura, musica, cinema e teatro*, Exh. cat. Livorno: Museo Civico Giovanni Fattori, Villa Mimbeli, 2000; Cinisello Balsamo (Mi): Silvana; Livorno: Comune di Livorno, 2000.

Crispolti, Enrico and Albino Galvano, eds., *Aspetti del Secondo Futurismo Torinese. Cinque pittori ed uno scultore: Fillia—Mino Rosso—Diulgheroff—Oriani—Alimandi—Costa*, Exh. cat. Turin: Galleria Civica d'Arte Moderna, 1962.

Crispolti, Enrico and Franco Sborgi, eds., *Futurismo: I grandi temi 1909–1944*, Exh. cat. Genova: Palazzo Ducale, 1998; Milan: Mazzotta, 1998.

De Felice, Renzo, ed., *Futurismo, cultura e politica*, Turin: Edizioni della Fondazione Giovanni Agnelli, 1988.

De Maria, Luciano, *La nascita dell'avanguardia: Saggi sul futurismo italiano*, Venice: Marsilio, 1986.

Depero, Fortunato, *So I Think, So I Paint: Ideologies of an Italian Self-Made Painter*, trans. Raffaella Lotteri, Trento: Mutilati e Invalidi, 1947.

————, *Fortunato Depero: Opere 1911–1930*, ed. Bruno Passamani, Exh. cat. Turin: Galleria d'Arte Martano, 1969.

————, *Fortunato Depero 1892–1960*, ed. Bruno Passamani, Exh. cat. Bassano del Grappa: Museo Civico, 1970.

————, *Depero o del laboratorio teatrale*, ed. Bruno Passamani, Exh. cat. Modena: Galleria Fonte d'Abisso, 1982.

————, *Depero, Capri, il teatro*, Exh. cat. Capri: Certosa di S. Giacomo, 1988; Naples: Electa, 1988.

————, *Depero*, ed. Maurizio Fagiolo dell'Arco e Nicoletta Boschiero, Exh. cat. Rovereto: Museo d'Arte Moderna, 1988; Milan: Electa, 1989.

Depero, Fortunato, *Depero: Teatro mágico*, ed. Gabriella Belli, Nicoletta Boschiero, and Bruno Passamani, Exh. cat. São Paulo: Museu de Arte, 1989; Milan: Electa, 1989; Italian edn *Depero: Teatro magico*. Rovereto: Museo d'Arte Moderna e Contemporanea, Milan: Electa, 1989; English edn *Depero: Magic Theatre*, London: The Italian Institute, 1989; Milan: Electa, 1989.

————, *Pestavo anch'io sul palcoscenico dei ribelli: Antologia degli scritti letterari*, ed. Michele Ruele, Langhirano: Cucùlibri, and Trento: L'Editore, 1992.

————, *Scritti e documenti editi e inediti*, ed. Maurizio Scudiero, Trento: Il Castello, 1992.

D'Orsi, Angelo, *L'ideologia politica del futurismo*, Turin: Il Segnalibro, 1992.

Dotoli, Giovanni, "Valentine de Saint-Point e il futurismo," *Lectures* (Bari) 7–8 (August 1981), 233–237; reprinted in G. Dotoli: *Scrittore totale: Saggi su Ricciotto Canudo*, Fasano: Schena, 163–182.

Drudi Gambillo, Maria, ed., *Dopo Boccioni: Dipinti e documenti futuristi dal 1915 al 1919*, Rome: Edizioni Mediterranee "La Medusa," 1961; English edn *After Boccioni: Futurist Paintings and Documents from 1915 to 1919*, Rome: Edizioni Mediterranee "La Medusa," 1961.

Drudi Gambillo, Maria and Teresa Fiori, eds., *Archivi del futurismo*, 2 vols, Rome: De Luca, 1958–1962; 2nd edn, 1986.

Fagiolo dell'Arco, Maurizio, *Balla pre-Futurista; Compenetrazioni iridescenti; Balla: Ricostruzione futurista dell'universo*, 3 vols., Rome: Bulzoni, 1968; 2nd edn in one vol., *Futur Balla*, Rome: Bulzoni, 1970.

————, "The Futurist Construction of the Universe," in Emilio Ambasz, ed., *Italy: The New Domestic Landscape. Achievements and Problems of Italian Design*, Exh. cat. New York: Museum of Modern Art, 1972, 293–301.

————, *Futur-Balla: La vita e le opere*, Milan: Electa, 1992.

Fagiolo dell'Arco, Maurizio, ed., *Esposizione di pittura futurista*, Exh. cat. Venice: Studio d'Arte Barnabò, 1986; Venice: Marsilio, 1986.

Fossati, Paolo, *La realtà attrezzata: Scena e spettacolo dei futuristi*, Turin: Einaudi, 1977.

Futurismo 1909–1919: Exhibition of Italian Futurism, Exh. cat. Newcastle: Hatton Gallery, 1972.

Futurismo a Firenze, 1910–1920, Exh. cat. Florence: Palazzo Medici Riccardi, 1984; Florence: Sansoni, 1984.

Guatterini, Marinella, "La danza aerea del futurismo," *Balletto oggi* 35 (1986), 44–45.

————, "Come illustrare la velocità," *Alfabeta/La Quinzaine Littéraire* 8:84 (May 1986), 90–92.

Herbert-Muthesius, Angelika, *Bühne und bildende Kunst im Futurismus: Bühnengestaltungen von Balla, Depero und Prampolini, 1914–1929*, Ph.D. Dissertation, Universität Heidelberg, 1985.

Hultén, Pontus, ed., *Futurismo e futurismi*, Exh. cat. Venice: Palazzo Grassi, 1986, Milan: Bompiani, 1986; English edn *Futurism and Futurisms*, Milan: Bompiani, 1986.

Humphreys, Richard, *Futurism*, London: Tate Gallery, 1999.

Katz, M. Barry, "The Women of Futurism," *Woman's Art Journal* 2 (Fall 1986–Winter 1987), 3–13.

Kirby, Michael, *Futurist Performance*, New York: Dutton, 1971; 2nd edn, New York: PAJ, 1986.

Lambiase, Sergio and Gian Battista Nazzaro, eds., *F. T. Marinetti futurista: Inediti, pagine disperse, documenti e antologia critica*, Naples: Guida, 1977.

———, *Marinetti e i futuristi: Marinetti nei colloqui e nei ricordi dei futuristi italiani*, Milan: Garzanti, 1978.

Lapini, Lia, *Il teatro futurista italiano*, Milan: Mursia, 1977.

———, "Le Théâtre futuriste italien et la mise en scène," in Sando Briosi and Henk Hillenaar: *Vitalité et contradictions de l'avant-garde*, Mayenne: Corti, 1988, 171–183; "Il teatro futurista italiano dalla teoria alla pratica," in Alessandro Tinterri, ed., *Il teatro italiano dal naturalismo a Pirandello*, Bologna: Il Mulino, 1990, 249–264.

———, "Marinetti e il teatro: La vocazione alla scena," in Carlo Vanni Menichi, ed., *Marinetti il futurista*, Florence: Tellini, 1988, 69–116.

———, "Note sul teatro futurista," in Elvira Garbero Zorzi and Sergio Romagnoli, eds., *Scene e figure del teatro italiano*, Bologna: Il Mulino, 1985, 285–300.

Lawton, Anna, "Futurist Manifestoes As an Element of Performance," *Canadian American Slavic Studies* 19:4 (1985), 473–491.

Lista, Giovanni, "Esthétique du music-hall et mythologie urbaine chez Marinetti," *Du Cirque au théâtre*, Lausanne: L'Age d'Homme, 1983, 48–64.

———, *Giacomo Balla futuriste*, Lausanne: L'Age d'Homme, 1984.

———, *Le Futurisme*, Paris: Hazan, 1985; English edn *Futurism*, New York: Universe Books, 1986.

———, *Lo spettacolo futurista*, Florence: Cantini [1988].

———, *La Scène futuriste*, Paris: Centre National de la Recherche Scientifique, 1989.

———, *F. T. Marinetti: L'anarchiste du futurisme. Biographie*, Paris: Séguier, 1995.

Lista, Giovanni, ed., *Marinetti et le futurisme: Études, documents, iconographie*, Lausanne: L'Age d'Homme, 1977.

———, *Futurisme: Manifestes, proclamations, documents*, Lausanne: L'Age d'Homme, 1973.

———, *Théâtre futuriste italien: Anthologie critique*, 2 vols, Lausanne: L'Age d'Homme, 1976.

Lombardi, Daniele, *Il suono veloce: Futurismo e futurismi in musica*, Milan: Ricordi, and Lucca: LIM, 1996.

Lugaresi, Silvana and Maria Paola Patuelli, eds., *Omaggio a Francesco Balilla Pratella*, Ravenna: Patrocinio del Ministero dei Beni Culturali, 1980.

I luoghi del futurismo, 1909–1944: Atti del convegno nazionale di studio, Macerata, 30 Ottobre 1982, Rome: Multigrafica, 1986.

I manifesti del futurismo, Florence: Edizioni di "Lacerba," 1914.

I manifesti del futurismo, 4 vols, Milan: Istituto Editoriale Italiano [1918–1919].

Marinelli, Donald, *Origins of Futurist Theatricality: The Early Life and Career of F. T. Marinetti*, Ph.D. Dissertation, University of Pittsburgh, 1987.

Marinetti, Filippo Tommaso, *Opere di F. T. Marinetti*, vol. 1: *Scritti francesi*, ed. Pasquale A. Jannini, Milan: Mondadori, 1983; vol. 2: *Teoria e invenzione futurista*, ed. Luciano de Maria, Milan: Mondadori, 1968; 2nd edn, 1983; vol. 3: *La grande Milano tradizionale e futurista. Una sensibilità italiana nata in Egitto*, ed. L. de Maria, Milan: Mondadori, 1969.

———, *Teatro*, 3 vols, ed. Giovanni Calendoli, Rome: Bianco, 1960.

———, *Selected Writings*, ed. by R. W. Flint, London: Secker and Warburg, 1972; 2nd edn, *Let's Murder the Moonshine: Selected Writings*, Los Angeles: Sun & Moon Press, 1991.

———, *Taccuini, 1915–1921*, ed. Alberto Bertoni, Bologna: Il Mulino, 1987.

———, *Stung by Salt and Water: Creative Texts of the Italian Avant-gardist F. T. Marinetti*, ed. Richard J. Pioli, New York: Lang, 1987.

———, *Critical Writings*, ed. by Günter Berghaus, New York: Farrar, Straus and Giroux (forthcoming).

Marinetti domani: Convegno di studi nel primo centenario della nascita di FTM, Rome: Arte-Viva, 1977.

Martin, Marianne W., *Futurist Art and Theory 1909–1915*, Oxford, Clarendon Press, 1968; 2nd edn, New York: Hacker, 1978.

———, "The Ballet *Parade*: A Dialogue between Cubism and Futurism," *Art Quarterly* 1:2 (Spring 1978), 85–111.

———, "The Futurist Gesture: Futurism and the Dance," *Kunst Musik Schauspiel: Akten des XXV. Internationalen Kongresses für Kunstgeschichte, Wien 4.–9. September 1983*, vol. 2, Wien: Böhlau, 1985, 95–113.

Menichi, Carlo Vanni, ed., *Marinetti il futurista*, Exh. cat. Viareggio: Fondazione Carnevale, 1988; Florence: Tellini, 1988.

Menna, Filiberto, *Enrico Prampolini*, Rome: De Luca [1967].

Merwin, Ted, "Loïe Fuller's Influence on F. T. Marinetti's Futurist Dance," *Dance Chronicle* 21:1 (1998), 73–92.

Moliterni, Pierfranco, *Franco Casavola: Il futurismo e lo spettacolo della musica*, Bari: Adda, 2000.

Mosse, George L., "The Political Culture of Italian Futurism," *The Journal of Contemporary History* 24 (1989), 5–26.

———, "The Political Culture of Italian Futurism: A General Perspective," *Journal of Contemporary History* 25:2–3 (May–June 1990), 253–268.

Nazzaro, Gian Battista, *Introduzione al futurismo*, Naples: Guida, 1973; 2nd edn, 1984.

———, *Futurismo e politica*, Naples: JN Editore, 1987.

Nuzzaci, Antonella, *Il teatro futurista: Genesi, linguaggi, tecniche*, Rome: Edizioni Nuova Cultura, 1997.

Passamani, Bruno, *Fortunato Depero*, Rovereto: Comune di Rovereto, 1981.

————, "La vocazione teatrale di Depero," *I luoghi del futurismo, 1909–1944*, Rome: Multigrafica, 1986, 39–55.

Passamani, Bruno, ed., *Depero e la scena: Da "Colori" alla scena mobile, 1916–1930*, Turin: Martano, 1970.

————, *Depero o del laboratorio teatrale*, Exh. cat. Modena: Galleria Fonte d'Abisso, 1982.

Paton, Rodney J., "The Music of Futurism: Concerts and Polemics," *Musical Quarterly* 62:1 (January 1976), 25–45.

Perloff, Marjorie, *The Futurist Moment: Avant-garde, Avant Guerre, and the Language of Rupture*, Chicago: University of Chicago Press, 1986.

Plassard, Didier, "Le tecniche di disumanizzazione nel teatro futurista," *Teatro contemporaneo* 2:4 (June–September 1983), 35–64.

[Prampolini, Enrico], *Enrico Prampolini*, ed. Palma Bucarelli, Exh. cat. Rome: Galleria Nazionale d'Arte Moderna, 1961.

————, *Prampolini scenografo*, ed. Federico Brook and Vittorio Minardi, Exh. cat. Rome: Istituto Italo-Latino Americano, 1974.

————, *Enrico Prampolini: Pittura, disegno, scenografia*, Exh. cat. Todi: Palazzi Comunali, 1983.

————, *Carteggio 1916–1956*, ed. Rosella Siligato, Rome: Carte Segrete, 1992.

————, *Carteggio futurista*, ed. Giovanni Lista, Rome: Carte Segrete, 1992.

————, *Prampolini dal futurismo all'informale*, ed. Enrico Crispolti and Rosella Siligato, Exh. cat. Rome: Palazzo delle Esposizioni, 1992.

Pratella, Francesco Balilla, *Lettere ruggenti a F. Balilla Pratella*, ed. Giovanni Lugaresi, Milan: Quaderni dell'Osservatore, 1969.

————, *Autobiografia*, Milan: Pan, 1971.

————, *Caro Pratella: Lettere a Francesco Balilla Pratella*, ed. by Gianfranco Maffina, Ravenna: Edizioni del Girasole, 1980.

Radice, Mark A., "Futurismo: Its Origins, Context, Repertory, and Influence," *Musical Quarterly* 73:1 (January 1989), 1–17.

Rawson, Judy, "Italian Futurism," in Malcolm Bradbury and James Walter McFarlane, eds., *Modernism, 1890–1930*, Harmondsworth: Penguin, 1976, 243–258.

Rivolta, Lucia, "Musica futurista: Il contributo di Francesco Balilla Pratella e Luigi Russolo tra avanguardia europea e ambiente musicale italiano," in Romain H. Rainero, ed., *Futurismo: Aspetti e problemi*, Milan: Cisalpino—Istituto Editoriale Universitario, 1993, 175–199.

Roche-Pézard, Fanette, *L'Aventure futuriste 1909–1916*, Rome: École Française de Rome, 1983.

Russolo, Luigi, *L'arte dei rumori*, Milan: Edizioni futuriste di "Poesia," 1916; reprinted Rome: Carucci, 1976; French edn *L'Art des bruits*, ed. Giovanni Lista, Lausanne: L'Age d'Homme, 1973; English edn *The Art of Noises*, New York: Pendragon Press, 1986.

————, *The Art of Noise: Futurist Manifesto, 1913*, New York: Something Else Press, 1967.

Russolo, Luigi, *Luigi Russolo e l'arte dei rumori: Con tutti gli scritti musicali*, ed. Gianfranco Maffina, Turin: Martano, 1978.

———, *Russolo: L'arte dei rumori 1913–1931*, ed. Gianfranco Maffina, Exh. cat. Venice: Archivio Storico delle Arti Contemporanee, 1977; Milan: Regione Lombardia, Assessorato ai Beni e alle Attività Culturali, 1978.

———, *Russolo: Die Geräuschkunst 1913–1931*, ed. Gianfranco Maffina, Exh. cat. Bochum: Museum Bochum, 1985–1986.

Rye, Jane, *Futurism*, London: Studio Vista, 1972.

Salaris, Claudia, *Le futuriste: Donne e letteratura d'avanguardia in Italia, 1909–1944*, Milan: Edizioni delle Donne, 1982.

———, *Storia del futurismo: Libri, giornali, manifesti*, Rome: Editori Riuniti, 1985; 2nd rev. edn, 1992.

———, *Filippo Tommaso Marinetti*, Scandicci: La Nuova Italia, 1988.

———, *Bibliografia del futurismo, 1909–1944*, Rome: Biblioteca del Vascello, 1988.

———, *Artecrazia: L'avanguardia futurista negli anni del fascismo*, Scandicci: La Nuova Italia, 1992.

———, *Marinetti: Arte e vita futurista*, Rome: Editori Riuniti, 1997.

Satin, Leslie, "Valentine de Saint-Point," *Dance Research Journal* 22:1 (1990), 1–12.

Schafer, William Boulware, *The Turn of the Century: The First Futurists*, New York: Lang, 1995.

Schmidt-Bergmann, Hansgeorg, *Futurismus: Geschichte, Ästhetik, Dokumente*, Reinbek: Rowohlt, 1993.

Scrivo, Luigi, ed., *Sintesi del futurismo: Storia e documenti*, Rome: Bulzoni, 1968.

Segel, Harold B., "Italian Futurism, Teatro Grottesco, and the World of Artificial Man," in H. B. Segel *Pinocchio's Progeny: Puppets, Marionettes, Automatons, and Robots in Modernist and Avant-garde Drama*, Baltimore, MD: Johns Hopkins University Press, 1995, 260–296.

Shankey, Stephen Richard, *Art into Society: The Case of Italian Futurism*, Ann Arbor, MI: UMI, 1980.

Sinisi, Silvana, "Depero: Una vocazione allo spettacolo," *Marcatré* 50–55 (1969), 342–386.

Sinisi, Silvana, ed., *"Varieté": Prampolini e la scena*, Turin: Martano, 1974.

Taylor, Christina, *Futurism: Politics, Painting and Performance*, Ann Arbor, MI: UMI, 1979.

Taylor, Joshua C., ed., *Futurism*, Exh. cat. New York: Museum of Modern Art, 1961; New York: Doubleday, 1961.

Sipario 260 (December 1967). Special issue on Futurist Theatre.

Teatro: Rivista d'arte 5:3 (March–April 1927). Special issue on Futurist Synthetic Theatre.

Teatro futurista sintetico, vol. 1: *Supplemento al n° 114 de "Gli avvenimenti: Periodico illustrato della vita italiana,"* November 28– December 5, 1915; vol. 2: *Supplemento al n° 15 de "Gli avvenimenti,"* April 2–9, 1916.

Il teatro futurista sintetico creato da Marinetti, Settimelli, Bruno Corra, 2 vols, Milan: Istituto Editoriale Italiano, [1915–1916]; 2nd edn in 2 vols Piacenza: Ghelfi, 1921.

Il teatro futurista sintetico. Dinamico-alogico-autonomo-simultaneo-visionico. A sorpresa aeroradiotevisivo caffè concerto radiofonico, Naples: CLET, 1940.

Tisdall, Caroline and Angelo Bozzolla, *Futurism*, London: Thames and Hudson, 1977; 2nd edn, 1985.

Vaccari, Walter, *Vita e tumulti di F. T. Marinetti*, Milan: Omnia, 1959.

Vaccarino, Elisa, ed., *Giannina Censi: Danzare il futurismo*, Milan: Electa, 1997.

Verdone, Mario, "Drammi di macchine," *Palatino: Rivista romana di cultura*, fourth series, 12:3 (July–September 1968), 340–342.

———, *Il teatro del tempo futurista*, Rome: Lerici, 1969; 2nd edn, Rome: Bulzoni, 1988.

———, "Teatro pirandelliano e futurismo," *Teatro comtemporaneo* 2:4 (June–September 1983), 113–125.

———, *Manifesti futuristi e scritti teorici di Arnaldo Ginna e Bruno Corra*, Ravenna: Longo, 1984.

———, *Ginna e Corra: Cinema e letteratura del futurismo*, Rome: Bianco e Nero, 1968; 2nd edn, *Cinema e letteratura del futurismo*, Calliano: Manfrini, 1990.

———, "La sintesi teatrale futurista," in M. Verdone, ed., *Teatro contemporaneo*, vol. 1. *Teatro italiano*, Rome: Luciani, 1981, 141–173.

———, "Lo spettacolo futurista," *Teatro contemporaneo* 1:1 (May–September 1982), 1–18.

———, "Il teatro futurista a Firenze," in Gloria Manghetti, ed., *Futurismo a Firenze, 1910–1920*, Verona: Bi e Gi, 1984, 119–129.

———, "Balla e il teatro futurista a Roma," in Enrico Crispolti, ed., *Casa Balla e il futurismo a Roma*, Rome: Istituto Poligrafico e Zecca dello Stato, 1989, 73–82.

Verdone, Mario, ed., *Teatro italiano d'avanguardia: Drammi e sintesi futuriste*, Rome: Officina, 1970.

———, *Avanguardie teatrali: Da Marinetti a Joppolo*, Rome: Bulzoni, 1991.

Verdone, Mario and Geno Pampaloni, eds., *I futuristi italiani: Immagini, biografie, notizie*, Florence: Le Lettere, 1977.

Veroli, Patrizia, "Quello 'strafottentissimo' Depero: Giocondità ballerina futurista,' *Terzo occhio* 11:2 [#35] (June 1985), 21–23.

———, "Futurdanza," *Terzo occhio* 12:4 [#41] (December 1986), 35–37.

———, "Cangiullo e Diaghilev," *Terzo occhio* 18:4 [#65] (December 1992), 9–11.

Vicentini, Claudio, "Arte, politica e guerra nel futurismo di Marinetti," *Rivista di estetica* 2 (June 1979), 62–87.

———, "Azione politica e azione teatrale nel futurismo di Marinetti," in C. Vicentini, *La teoria del teatro politico*, Florence: Sansoni, 1981, 45–82.

Viola, Gianni Eugenio, *Gli anni del futurismo: La poesia italiana nell'età delle avanguardie*, Rome: Studium, 1990.

Zoccoli, Franca, "Futurist Women Painters in Italy," in Günter Berghaus, ed., *International Futurism in Arts and Literature*, Berlin: DeGruyter, 2000, 373–397.

———, *L'utopia futurista: Contributo alla storia delle avanguardie*, Ravenna: Longo, 1994.

Zornitzer, Amy, "Revolutionaries of the Theatrical Experience: Fuller and the Futurists," *Dance Chronicle* 21:1 (1998), 93–105.

DADA

Abastado, Claude, "Le 'Manifeste Dada 1918': Un tourniquet," *Littérature* 39 (October 1980), 39–46.

Aragon, Louis, *Projet d'histoire littéraire contemporaine*, ed. Marc Dachy, Paris: Gallimard, 1994.

———, *De Dada au surréalisme: Papiers inédits 1917–1931*, Paris: Gallimard, 2000.

Altshuler, Bruce, "Dada ist politisch: The First International Dada Fair, Berlin, June 30–August 25, 1920," in B. Altshuler, *The Avant-garde in Exhibition: New Art in the 20th Century*, New York: Abrams, 1994; reprinted Berkeley, CA: University of California Press, 1998, 98–115.

Arnaud, Noel and Pierre Prigioni, "Dada et surréalisme," in Ferdinand Alquié, ed., *Entretiens sur le surréalisme*, Paris and La Haye: Mouton, 1968, 350–393 .

Arp, Hans, *On My Way: Poetry and Essays, 1912–1947*, New York: Wittenborn, Schultz, 1948.

———, *Unsern täglichen Traum . . . : Erinnerungen, Dichtungen und Betrachtungen aus den Jahren 1914–1954*, Zurich: Arche, 1955; 2nd edn, 1995.

———, *Jours effeuillés: Poèmes, essais, souvenirs, 1920–1965*, Paris: Gallimard, 1966.

———, *Arp on Arp: Poems, Essays, Memories*, New York: Viking Press, 1972.

———, *Collected French Writings: Poems, Essays, Memories*, London: Calder and Boyars, 1974.

Association Internationale pour l'Étude de Dada et du Surréalisme, eds., *Revue de l'Association pour l'étude du mouvement Dada* 1 (1965); continued as *Cahiers de l'Association Internationale pour l'Étude de Dada et du Surréalisme* [Cover title: *Cahiers Dada surrealisme*], Paris: Lettres modernes, vols. 1–4, 1966–1970.

Baader, Johannes, *Oberdada: Schriften, Manifeste, Flugblätter, Billets, Werke und Taten*, ed. Hanne Bergius, Norbert Miller, and Karl Riha, Lahn: Anabas, 1977.

———, *Das Oberdada: Die Geschichte einer Bewegung von Zürich bis Zürich*, ed. Karl Riha, Siegen: Universität-Gesamthochschule, 1987.

———, *"Vierzehn Briefe Christi" und andere Druckschriften*, ed. Karl Riha, Berne: Lang, 1988.

———, *Trinken Sie die Milch der Milchstrasse: Texte und Taten des Oberdada*, ed. Karl Riha, Hamburg: Nautilus, 1990.

———, *Das Oberdada*, ed. by Karl Riha, Hofheim: Wolke, 1991.

Backes-Haase, Alfons, *Kunst und Wirklichkeit: Zur Typologie des DADA-Manifests*, Frankfurt am Main: Hain, 1992.

Bähr, Hans Joachim, "Hugo Ball und das Theater: Die Jahre 1910–14," *Hugo Ball Almanach*, 1982, 75–131.

———, *Die Funktion des Theaters im Leben Hugo Balls: Materialien zur Bestimmung der Jahre 1910–1914*, Frankfurt am Main: Lang, 1982.

Ball, Hugo, *Die Flucht aus der Zeit*, Munich: Duncker and Humblot, 1927; 2nd edn, Munich: Kösel and Pustet, 1931; 3rd edn, Lucerne: Stocker, 1946; 4th edn, Zurich: Limmat, 1992; English edn *Flight Out of Time: A Dada Diary*, ed. John

Elderfield, New York: Viking Press, 1974; reprinted Berkeley, CA: University of California Press, 1996.

——, *Briefe 1911–1927*, Einsiedeln: Benziger, 1957.

——, *Der Künstler und die Zeitkrankheit: Ausgewählte Schriften*, Frankfurt am Main: Suhrkamp, 1988.

Ball, Hugo and Emmy Hennings, *Damals in Zürich: Briefe aus den Jahren 1915–1917*, Zurich: Arche, 1978.

Hugo Ball (1886–1986): Leben und Werk, Exh. cat. ed. Ernst Teubner, Pirmasens: Wasgauhalle, 1986; Berlin: Publica, 1986.

Ball-Hennings, Emmy, *Hugo Ball: Sein Leben in Briefen und Gedichten*, Berlin: Fischer, 1930; reprinted Frankfurt am Main: Suhrkamp, 1991.

——, *"Ruf und Echo": Mein Leben mit Hugo Ball*, Einsiedeln: Benziger, 1953.

——, *Betrunken taumeln alle Litfaßsäulen: Frühe Texte und autobiographische Schriften 1913–1922*, Hanover: Postscriptum, 1990.

Bartsch, Kurt and Adelheid Koch, eds., *Raoul Hausmann*, Graz: Droschl, 1996.

Béhar, Henri, *Étude sur le théâtre dada et surréaliste*, Paris: Gallimard, 1967; 2nd rev. edn, *Le théâtre Dada et surréaliste*, Paris: Gallimard, 1979.

——, "Dada-Spectacle," in Sandro Briosi and Henk Hillenaar, eds., *Vitalité et contradiction de l'avant-garde: Italie-France 1909–1924*, Mayenne: Corti, 1988, 161–170.

Béhar, Henri and Michel Carassou, *Dada: Histoire d'une subversion*, Paris: Fayard, 1990.

Benson, Timothy O., *Raoul Hausmann and Berlin Dada*, Ann Arbor, MI: UMI Research Press, 1987.

Berghaus, Günter, "Dada Theatre, or The Genesis of Anti-bourgeois Performance Art," *German Life and Letters* 38 (1985), 293–312.

Bergius, Hanne, *Das Lachen Dadas: Die Berliner Dadaisten und ihre Aktionen*, Gießen: Anabas, 1989.

——, *Montage und Metamechanik: Dada Berlin—Artistik von Polaritäten*, Berlin: Mann, 2000.

Bergius, Hanne and Klaus Gallwitz, eds., *Dada: Dada in Europa. Werke und Dokumente*, Exh. cat. Frankfurt am Main: Städtische Galerie im Städelschen Kunstinstitut 1977–1978; Berlin: Reimer, 1977.

Bergius, Hanne and Eberhard Roters, eds., "Dada in Europa: Werke und Dokumente" *Tendenzen der zwanziger Jahre*, Exh. cat. Berlin: Neue Nationalgalerie, 1977; Berlin: Reimer, 1977, 3/1– 3/278.

Blago bung, blago bung, bosso fataka! First Texts of German Dada by Hugo Ball, Richard Huelsenbeck, Walter Serner, trans. and introduced by Malcolm Green, London: Atlas Press, 1995.

Bohle, Jürgen F. E., *Theatralische Lyrik und lyrisches Theater im Dadaismus: Eine Untersuchung der Wechselbeziehung zwischen lyrischen und theatralischen Elementen in dadaistischer Aktion*, Ph.D. Dissertation, Saarbrücken: Universität des Saarlandes, 1981.

Bohle, Jürgen F. E., "Moderne literarische Cabaret-Abende: Emmy Hennings und Hugo Ball," *Hugo-Ball-Almanach,* 1981, 97–116.

Bolliger, Hans, Guido Magnaguagno, and Raimund Meyer, eds., *Dada in Zürich,* Zurich: Arche, 1985.

Borràs, Maria Lluïsa, *Picabia,* London: Thames and Hudson, 1985.

Browning, Gordon Frederick, *Tristan Tzara: The Genesis of the Dada Poem, Or from Dada to Aa,* Stuttgart: Heinz, 1979.

Buffet-Picabia, Gabrielle, *Aires abstraites,* Geneva: Cailler, 1957.

———, *Rencontres avec Picabia, Apollinaire, Cravan, Duchamp, Arp, Calder,* Paris: Belfond, 1977.

Bürger, Peter, "Autonomie–Engagement–Aktion: Zur politischen Problematik dadaistischer Kunstpraxis," *Sprachkunst: Beiträge zur Literaturwissenschaft,* 15 (1984), 330–340.

Buschkühle, Carl-Peter, *Dada: Kunst in der Revolte. Eine existenzphilosophische Analyse des Dadaismus,* Essen: Die Blaue Eule, 1985.

Cabaret Voltaire, Der Zeltweg, Dada, Le Cœur à barbe: 1916 1922, ed. by Michel Giroud, Paris: Place, 1981.

Camfield, William A., *Francis Picabia, His Art, Life and Times,* Princeton, NJ: Princeton University Press, 1979.

Corvin, Michel, "Le Théâtre dada existe-t-il? Tzara et Ribemont-Dessaignes, ou la problematique d'un théâtre dada," *Revue d'histoire de théâtre* 23 (1971), 217–287.

Coutts-Smith, Kenneth, *Dada,* London: Studio Vista, 1970.

Dachy, Marc, *Journal du mouvement Dada: 1915–1923,* Geneva: Skira, 1989; English edn *The Dada Movement, 1915–1923,* New York: Rizzoli, 1990.

———, *Tristan Tzara, Dompteur des acrobates: Dada Zurich,* Paris: L'Echoppe, 1992.

———, *Dada & les dadaismes: Rapport sur l'anéantissement de l'ancienne beauté,* Paris: Gallimard, 1994.

Dada Reprint of nos. 1–8 (July 1917–September, 1921), Rome: Archivi d'arte del XX secolo, and Milan, Massotta, 1970.

Der Dada. Reprint of nos. 1 (1919), to 3 (1920), Nendeln: Kraus, 1977; Hamburg: Edition Nautilus, 1978 and 1980.

Dada: Réimpression intégrale et dossier critique de la revue publiée de 1916 à 1922 par Tristan Tzara, ed. Michel Sanouillet and Dominique Baudouin, 2 vols, Nice: Centre du XXe siècle, 1976–1983.

Dada 1916–1922: Réimpression de la collection des revues "Dada" publiées à Zurich et à Paris de 1916 à 1922, ed. Michel Giroud, Paris: Place, 1981.

Dada: Ausstellung zum 50-jährigen Jubiläum/Exposition commémorative du cinquante-naire, Exh. cat. Zurich: Kunsthaus Zürich, and Paris: Musée National d'Art Moderne, 1966/67; Zurich: Neue Zürcher Zeitung, 1966.

DADA Berlin 1916–1924: Documents d'art contemporain 1, Paris: A.R.C., 1974; 2nd rev. edn, Musée d'Art Moderne de la Ville de Paris, 1976.

Dada Conquers! The History, the Myth and the Legacy. International Conference Papers, ed. Fang-Wei Chang, Taipei: Taipei Fine Arts Museum, 1988.

DADA—Constructivism: The Janus Face of the Twenties, Exh. cat. London: Juda Fine Art, 1984.

Dada: Eine internationale Bewegung 1916–1925, Exh. cat. Munich: Kunsthalle der Hypo-Kulturstiftung, 1993.

Dada, l'arte della negazione, Exh. cat. ed. Maria E. Tittoni, Rome: Palazzo delle Esposizioni, 1994; Rome: De Luca, 1994.

Dada Zeitschriften. Reprint von 10 Zeitschriften: Prospekt des Verlags Freie Straße, Der Zeltweg, Cabaret Voltaire, Bulletin D, Der Dada, Dada Nr. 2, Dada 3, Dada Sinn der Welt, Dadameter, Calendrier 20, Hamburg: Nautilus, 1978; 2nd edn, 1980.

Doctorow, Erica, ed., *Dada in Berlin: An Exhibition Documenting the Artistic, Literary and Political Activities of the Dada Movement in Berlin at the time of the Weimar Republic*, Exh. cat. Garden City, NY: Swirbul Library Gallery, 1978; Garden City, NY: Adelphi University, 1978.

Drijkoningen, F., "Dada and Anarchism," *Avant Garde* 0 (1987): 69–82.

Erickson, John D., *Dada: Performance, Poetry, and Art*, Boston, MA: Twayne, 1984.

———, "The Apocalyptic Mind: The Dada Manifesto and Classic Anarchism," *French Literature Series*, vol. 7, Columbia, SC: Camden House, 1980, 98–109.

Erlhoff, Michael, *Raoul Hausmann, Dadasoph: Versuch einer Politisierung der Ästhetik*, Hanover: Zweitschrift, 1982.

Everling, Germaine, *L'Anneau de Saturne*, Paris: Fayard, 1970.

Fauchereau, Serge, "Expressionisme Dada: Vers une suppression des mots," *Apeïros* 6 (Spring 1974), 46–51.

Feidel-Mertz, Hildegard, ed., *Der junge Huelsenbeck: Entwicklungsjahre eines Dadaisten*, Gießen: Anabas, 1992.

Foster, Stephen C., ed., *Dada/Dimensions*, Ann Arbor, MI: UMI, 1985.

———, *The World According to Dada/Dada di shi jie*, Exh. cat. Taipei Fine Arts Museum, Taibei Shi: Taibei shi li mei shu guan, 1988.

———, *Crisis and the Arts: The History of Dada*, 9 vols, New York: Hall, 1996–1998; Detroit, MI: Gale, 2001–2001; New Haven, CN: Thomson, 2003f. The series includes: 1. *Dada, the Coordinates of Cultural Politics*, ed. Stephen C. Foster, New York: Hall, 1996; 2. *Dada Zurich, a Clown's Game from Nothing*, ed. Brigitte Pichon and Karl Riha, New York: Hall, 1996; 3. *Dada, Cologne, Hanover*, ed. Charlotte Stokes and Stephen C. Foster, New York: Hall, 1997; 4. *Eastern Dada Orbit: Russia, Georgia, Ukraine, Central Europe, and Japan*, ed. Gerald Janecek and Toshiharu Omuka, New York: Hall, 1998; 5. Hanne Bergius, *Dada Triumphs! Dada Berlin, 1917–1923: Artistry of Polarities: Montages, Metamechanics, Manifestations*, New Haven, CN: Thomson 2003; 6. *Paris Dada: The Barbarians Storm the Gates*, ed. Stephen C. Foster and Elmer Peterson, Detroit, MI: Gale, 2001; 7. Hubert F. van den Berg, *The Import of Nothing: How Dada Came, Saw and Vanished in the Low Countries (1915–1929)*, New Haven, CN: Thomson, 2003; 8. *Dada New York: New World for Old*, ed. Martin Ignatius Gaughan, New Haven, CN: Thomson, 2003; 9. *Dada and the Press*, ed. Harriett Watts, New Haven, CN: Thomson, 2004.

Foster, Stephen C. and Rudolf E. Kuenzli, eds., *Dada Spectrum: The Dialectics of Revolt*, Madison, WI: Coda, 1979.

Frenkel, Cornelia, *Raoul Hausmann: Künstler–Forscher–Philosoph*, St. Ingbert: Röhrig, 1996.

Füllner, Karin, *Richard Huelsenbeck: Texte und Aktionen einer Dadaisten*, Heidelberg: Winter, 1983.

Füllner, Karin, ed., *Dada Berlin in Zeitungen: Gedächtnisfeiern und Skandale*, Siegen: Universität-Gesamthochschule-Siegen, 1987.

Gallissaires, Pierre, ed., *Dada Paris: Manifeste, Aktionen, Turbulenzen*, Hamburg: Nautilus, 1989.

Glauser, Friedrich, *Dada, Ascona und andere Erinnerungen*, Zurich: Arche, 1976.

Goergen, Jeanpaul, *Urlaute dadaistischer Poesie: Der Berliner Dada-Abend am 12. April 1918*, Hanover: Postskriptum, 1994.

Gordon, Mel, "Dada Berlin: A History of Performance 1918–1920," *The Drama Review* 18:2 (T62) (June 1974), 114–133.

Gordon, Mel, ed., *Dada Performance*, New York: PAJ, 1987.

Grimm, Jürgen, *Das avantgardistische Theater Frankreichs 1895–1930*, Munich: Beck, 1982.

Grosz, George, *A Little Yes and a Big No: The Autobiography of George Grosz*, trans. Lola Sachs Dorin, New York: Dial Press, 1946; rev. German edn *Ein kleines Ja und ein Großes Nein. Sein Leben von Ihm selbst erzählt*, Reinbek: Rowohlt, 1955; 2nd edn, 1974.

———, *Briefe 1913–1956*, ed. Herbert Knust, Reinbek: Rowohlt, 1979.

———, *The Autobiography of George Grosz: A Small Yes and a Big No*, trans. Arnold J. Pomerans, London: Allison and Busby, 1982.

———, *George Grosz: An Autobiography*, trans. Nora Hodges, New York: Macmillan, 1983; 2nd edn, Berkeley, CA: University of California Press, 1998.

———, *Eintrittsbillett zu meinem Gehirnzirkus: Erinnerungen, Schriften, Briefe*, ed. Renate Hartleb, Leipzig: Kiepenheuer, 1988.

———, *So long mit Händedruck: Briefe und Dokumente*, ed. Karl Riha, Hamburg: Luchterhand, 1993.

Guggenheim, Kurt, *Alles in Allem. Roman*, vol. 2: *1914–1919*, Zurich: Artemis, 1953.

Hausmann, Raoul, *Courrier Dada*, Paris: Le Terrain Vague, 1958; 2nd edn, Paris: Allia, 1992.

———, *Raoul Hausmann et Dada à Berlin: Notes, documents et témoignages inédits, dossier critique*, ed. Roberto Altmann and Jean François Borg. Special issue of *Apeïros: Apériodique utopique communication marginal* 6 (Spring 1974).

———, *"Je suis pas un photographe": Raoul Hausmann. Textes et documents*, ed. by Michel Giroud, Paris: Chêne, 1976.

———, *Am Anfang war Dada*, ed. Karl Riha und Günter Kämpf, Gießen: Anabas, 1980, 3rd rev. edn, 1992.

———, *Texte bis 1933*, ed. Michael Erlhoff, 2 vols, Munich: Text + Kritik, 1982.

————, *Raoul Hausmann*, Exh. cat. Saint-Etienne: Musée d'Art Moderne, 1994.

————, *Der deutsche Spießer ärgert sich: Raoul Hausmann 1886–1971*, Exh. cat. ed. Eva Züchner, Anna-Carola Krausse, and Kathrin Hatesaul, Berlin: Berlinische Galerie, 1994; Ostfildern: Hatje, 1994.

————, *La sensorialité excentrique/Die exzentrische Empfindung*, ed. Adelheid Koch, Graz: Droschl, 1994.

————, *"Wir wünschen die Welt bewegt und beweglich": Raoul-Hausmann-Symposium der Berlinischen Galerie im Martin-Gropius-Bau Berlin, am 6. und 7. Oktober 1994*, ed. Eva Zücher, Berlin: Berlinische Galerie, 1995.

————, *Scharfrichter der bürgerlichen Seele: Raoul Hausmann in Berlin, 1900–1933: Unveröffentlichte Briefe, Texte, Dokumente aus den Künstler-Archiven der Berlinischen Galerie*, ed. Eva Züchner, Ostfildern: Hatje, 1998.

Hedges, Inez, *Languages of Revolt: Dada and Surrealist Literature and Film*, Durham, NC: Duke University Press, 1982.

Hering, Karl Heinz and Ewald Rathke, eds., *Dada: Dokumente einer Bewegung*, Exh. cat. Düsseldorf: Kunsthalle, 1958; reprinted New York: Arno Press, 1968.

Herzogenrath, Wulf, ed., *Vom Dadamax bis zum Grüngürtel: Köln in den 20er Jahren*, Exh. cat. Cologne: Kunstverein, 1975.

————, *Max Ernst in Köln: Die rheinische Kunstszene bis 1922*, Exh. cat. Cologne: Kunstverein, 1980.

Hille, Karoline, *Hannah Höch und Raoul Hausmann: Eine Berliner Dada-Geschichte*, Berlin: Rowohlt, 2000.

Hippen, Reinhard, *Erklügelte Nervenkultur: Kabarett der Neopathetiker und Dadaisten*, Zurich: Pendo, 1991.

Höch, Hannah, *Briefe und Texte: Dokumente 1920–1970*, Berlin: Galerie Nierendorf, 1970.

————, *Werke und Worte*, ed. H. Remmert und P. Barth, Berlin: Frölich und Kaufmann, 1982.

————, "Erinnerungen an DADA," in *Hanna Höch 1889–1978: Ihr Werk, ihr Leben, ihre Freunde*, Exh. cat. Berlin: Berlinische Gallerie, 1989–1990, 201–213.

————, *Hannah Höch: Eine Lebenscollage*, vol. I:1 (1889–1918); vol. I:2 (1919–1920), ed. Cornelia Thater-Schulz, Berlin: Argon, 1989; vol. II:1+2 (1921–1945), ed. Eva Zürcher, Ostfildern: Cantz, 1995.

Huelsenbeck, Richard, *Dada siegt: Eine Bilanz und Geschichte des Dadaismus*, Berlin: Malik, 1920.

————, *Deutschland muß untergehen: Erinnerungen eines alten Revolutionärs*, Berlin: Malik, 1920; reprinted in *En avant Dada*, Hamburg: Nautilus, 1984.

————, *En avant Dada: Eine Geschichte des Dadaismus*, Hanover: Steegemann, 1920; reprinted Hamburg: Nautilus, 1984.

————, *Mit Witz, Licht und Grütze: Auf den Spuren des Dadaismus*, Wiesbaden: Limes, 1957; reprinted Hamburg: Nautilus, 1991; English edn *Memoirs of a Dada Drummer*, ed. Hans J. Kleinschmidt, New York: Viking Press, 1974; reprinted Berkeley, CA: University of California Press, 1991.

Huelsenbeck, Richard, *Reise bis ans Ende der Freiheit: Autobiographische Fragmente*, ed. Ulrich Karthaus and Horst Krüger, Heidelberg: Schneider, 1984.

———, *Wozu Dada: Texte 1916–1936*, ed. Herbert Kapfer, Gießen: Anabas, 1994.

———, *Weltdada Huelsenbeck: Eine Biografie in Briefen und Bildern*, ed. Herbert Kapfer and Lisbeth Exner, Innsbruck: Haymon, 1996.

Huelsenbeck, Richard, ed., *Dada Almanach*, Berlin: Reiss, 1920; reprinted New York: Something Else Press, 1966; Hamburg: Nautilus, 1980; English edn *The Dada Almanac*, London: Atlas Press, 1993.

———, *DADA: Ein literarische Dokumentation*, Reinbek: Rowohlt, 1964.

Hugnet, Georges, "L'Esprit Dada dans la peinture," *Cahiers d'art*, vol. 7:1–2 (1932), 57–65, 7:6–7 (1932), 281–285, 7:8–10 (1932), 358–364, vol. 9:1–4 (1934), 109–114.

———, *L'Aventure dada, 1916–1922*, Paris: Galérie de l'Institut, 1957; 2nd rev. edn, Paris: Seghers, 1971.

Jürgs, Britta, ed., *Etwas Wasser in der Seife: Portraits dadaistischer Künstlerinnen und Schriftstellerinnen*, Berlin: AvivA, 1999.

Kessler, Erica, "Sophie tanzt," *Sophie Taeuber-Arp zum 100. Geburtstag/Nel centenario delle nascita*, Exh. cat. ed. Beat Wismer, Aarau: Kunsthaus, 1989, 76–85.

Knapp, Bettina, "Tzara's *Gas Heart*," in B. Knapp, *French Theatre 1918–1939*, London: Macmillan, 1985, 21–26.

Koch, Adelheid, *Ich bin immerhin der grösste Experimentator Österreichs: Raoul Hausmann, Dada und Neodada*, Innsbruck: Haymon, 1994.

Korte, Hermann, *Die Dadaisten*, Reinbek: Rowohlt, 1994.

Kühn, Joachim, "Ein deutscher Futurist: Die Futurismusrezeption Hugo Balls," *Hugo Ball Almanach* 1979, 86–103.

Kümmerle, Inge, *Tristan Tzara: Dramatische Experimente zwischen 1916 und 1940*, Rheinfelden: Schäuble, 1978.

Lach, Friedhelm, "Die Merzbühne von Kurt Schwitters oder Schwitters als Dramatiker," *Text und Kritik* 35–36 (1972), 69–72.

Leavens, Heana B., *From "291" to Zurich: The Birth of Dada*, Ann Arbor, MI: UMI, 1983.

Lemaître, Maurice, *Le Théâtre dadaïste et surréaliste*, Paris: Centre de Créativité, 1967.

———, *Sur Tristan Tzara, André Breton, Philippe Soupault, Georges Ribemont-Dessaignes*, Paris: Centre de Créativité, 1980.

Lemoine, Serge, *Dada*, Paris: Hazan, 1986; English edn *Dada*, New York: Universe Books, 1987.

Lewis, Helena, *Dada Turns Red: The Politics of Surrealism*, Edinburgh: Edinburgh University Press, 1990.

Lippard, Lucy R., "Dada in Berlin: Unfortunately Still Timely," *Art in America* 66:2 (March/April 1978), 107–111.

Lippard, Lucy R., ed., *Dadas on Art*, Englewood Cliffs, NJ: Prentice Hall, 1971.

Mann, Philip H., "Hugo Ball and the 'Magic Bishop Episode': A Reconsideration," *New German Studies* 4 (1976), 43–52.

————, *Hugo Ball: An Intellectual Biography*, London: Institute of Germanic Studies, University of London, 1987.

Matthews, John H., *Theatre in Dada and Surrealism*, Syracuse, NY: Syracuse University Press, 1974.

Mehring, Walter, *Berlin Dada: Eine Chronik mit Photos und Dokumenten*, Zurich: Arche, 1959.

————, *Verrufene Malerei; Berlin Dada: Erinnerungen eines Zeitgenossen und 14 Essais zur Kunst*, Düsseldorf: Claassen, 1983.

Melzer, Annabelle Henkin, "Dada Performance at the Cabart Voltaire," *Artforum* 12:3 (November 1973), 74–78.

————, "The Dada Actor and Performance Theory," *Artforum* 12:4 (December 1973), 51–57.

————, *Latest Rage the Big Drum: Dada and Surrealist Performance*, Ann Arbor, MI: UMI, 1980; 2nd edn, *Dada and Surrealist Performance*, New York: PAJ Books, and Baltimore, MD: Johns Hopkins Paperbacks, 1994.

Meyer, Raimund, *Dada in Zürich: Die Akteure, die Schauplätze*, Frankfurt am Main: Luchterhand, 1990.

Meyer, Raimund, Judith Hossli, Guido Magnagnagno, Juri Steiner, and Hans Bollinger, eds., *Dada global: Die Dada-Sammlung des Kunsthaus Zürich*, Exh. cat. Zurich: Kunsthaus, 1994; Zurich: Limmat, 1994.

Meyer, Raimund and Hans Bolliger, eds., *Dada: Eine internationale Bewegung 1916–1925*, Exh. cat. Munich: Kunsthalle der Hypo-Kulturstiftung, 1993.

Meyer, Reinhart, *Dada in Zürich und Berlin, 1916–1920: Literatur zwischen Revolution und Reaktion*, Kronberg, TS: Scriptor, 1973.

Middleton, Christopher, "Dada versus Expressionism, Or: The Red King's Dream," *German Life and Letters* 15 (1961/62), 37–52.

————, "Bolshevism in Art: Dada and Politics," in Christopher Middleton, *Bolshevism in Art and Other Expository Writings*, Manchester: Carcanet New Press, 1978, 38–61.

Motherwell, Robert, *The Dada Painters and Poets*, New York: Wittenborn, Schultz, 1951; 2nd edn, Boston, MA: Hall, 1981; 3rd edn, Cambridge, MA: Belknap Press of Harvard University Press, 1989.

Nenzel, Reinhard, *Kleinkarierte Avantgarde: Zur Neubewertung des deutschen Dadaismus. Der frühe Richard Huelsenbeck, sein Leben und sein Werk bis 1916 in Darstellung und Interpretation*, Bonn: Nenzel, 1994.

Paulsen, Wolfgang and Helmut G. Hermann, eds., *Sinn aus Unsinn: Dada International. Zwölftes Amherster Kolloquium zur Deutschen Literatur*, Berne: Francke, 1982.

Pegrum, Mark A., *Challenging Modernity: Dada between Modern and Postmodern*, Oxford: Berghahn, 2000.

Peterson, Elmer, *Tristan Tzara: Dada and Surrational Theorist*, New Brunswick, NJ: Rutgers University Press, 1971.

Philipp, Eckhard, *Dadaismus: Einführung in den literarischen Dadaismus und die Wortkunst des "Sturm"-Kreises*, Munich: Fink, 1980.

Picabia, Francis, *Écrites 1913–1953*, ed. Oliver Revault d'Allonnes et Dominique Bouissou, 2 vols, Paris: Belfond, 1975–1978.

Poupard-Lieussou, Yves, ed., *Dada en verve*, Paris: Horay, 1972.

Poupard-Lieussou, Yves and Michel Sanouillet, eds., *Documents Dada*, Bienne: Weber, 1974.

Prevots, Naima, "Zurich Dada and Dance: Formative Ferment," *Dance Research Journal* 17:1 (Spring/Summer 1985), 3–8.

Prosenc, Miklavž, *Die Dadaisten in Zürich*, Bonn: Bouvier, 1967.

La Rencontre Sonia Delaunay-Tristan Tzara, Exh. cat. Paris: Musée d'Art Moderne de la Ville de Paris, 1977.

Ribemont-Dessaignes, Georges, "Histoire de Dada," *La Nouvelle Revue française* 36:213 (June 1931), 867–879; 37:214 (July 1931), 39–52.

———, *Déjà jadis, ou Du mouvement Dada à l'espace abstrait*, Paris: Juillard, 1958; reprinted Paris: Union Parisienne d'Éditions, 1973.

———, *Théâtre*, Paris: Gallimard, 1966.

———, *Dada: Manifestes, poèmes, articles, projets, 1915–1930*, Paris: Champ Libre, 1974.

———, *Dada 2: Nouvelles, articles, théâtre, chroniques littéraires, 1919–1929*, Paris: Champ Libre, 1978.

———, *Dada: Manifestes, poèmes, nouvelles, articles, projets, théatre, cinéma, chroniques (1915–1929)*, ed. Jean-Pierre Begot; 2nd edn, Paris: Ivrea, 1994.

Richter, Hans, *Dada Profile*, Zurich: Arche, 1961.

———, *Dada, Kunst und Antikunst: Der Beitrag Dadas zur Kunst des 20. Jahrhunderts*, Cologne: DuMont Schauberg, 1964; 2nd rev. edn 1970; English edn *Dada, Art and Anti-art*, London: Thames and Hudson, 1965.

———, *Begegnungen von Dada bis heute: Briefe, Dokumente, Erinnerungen*, Cologne: DuMont Schauberg, 1973.

Riha, Karl, *Tatü Dada: Dada und nochmals Dada bis heute. Aufsätze und Dokumente*, Hofheim: Wolke, 1987.

———, "Dada im 'Cabarat Voltaire,' " *Die Horen* 40 (1995), 35–43.

———, "Dada (Dadaismus)," *Moderne Literatur in Grundbegriffen*, ed. Dieter Borchmeyer and Viktor Zmegac; 2nd edn, Tübingen: Niemeyer, 1994, 63–68.

Riha, Karl, ed., *Dada Berlin. Texte, Manifeste, Aktionen*, Stuttgart: Reclam, 1977.

———, *Da Dada da war, ist Dada da: Aufsätze und Dokumente*, Munich: Hanser, 1980.

———, *Dada Zürich: Texte, Manifeste, Dokumente*, Stuttgart: Reclam, 1992.

Riha, Karl and Jörgen Schäfer, eds., *DADA total: Manifeste, Aktionen, Texte, Bilder*, Stuttgart: Reclam, 1994.

———, *Fatagaga-Dada: Max Ernst, Hans Arp, Johannes Theodor Baargeld und der Kölner Dadaismus*, Gießen: Anabas, 1995.

Roditi, Edouard, "Interview with Hanna Hoech," *Arts* (New York) 34:3 (December 1959), 24–29.

Rugh, Thomas F., "Emmy Hennings and the Emergence of Zurich Dada," *Woman's Art Journal* 2:1 (Spring/Summer 1981), 1–6.

Sanouillet, Michel, *Picabia*, Paris: Éditions du Temps, 1964.

———, *Francis Picabia et "391,"* Paris: Losfeld, 1966.

———, *Histoire générale du mouvement Dada (1915–1923): Dada à Paris*, Paris: Pauvert, 1965; 2nd edn, Nice: Centre XXe siècle, 1980; 3rd edn, Paris: Flammarion, 1993.

Sawelson-Gorse, Naomi, ed., *Women in Dada: Essays on Sex, Gender, and Identity*, Cambridge, MA: MIT Press, 1998.

Schifferli, Peter, eds., *Die Geburt des Dada: Dichtung und Chronik der Gründer*, Zurich, Arche, 1957; partly reprinted as *Als Dada begann: Bildchronik und Erinnerungen der Gründer*, Zurich: Sanssouci, 1957.

———, *Das war Dada: Dichtungen und Dokumente*, Munich: Deutscher Taschenbuch Verlag, 1963.

Schmalenbach, Werner, *Kurt Schwitters*, Cologne: DuMont Schauberg, 1967; English edn London: Thames and Hudson, 1970.

Schmitt, Evamarie, *Abstrakte Dada-Kunst: Versuch einer Begriffserklärung und Untersuchung der Beziehungen zur künstlerischen Avantgarde*, Münster: LIT, 1992.

Schrott, Raoul, *Dada 15/25: Post Scriptum, oder: Die himmlischen Abenteuer des Hr.n Tristan Tzara*, Innsbruck: Haymon, 1992.

———, *Walter Serner (1889–1942) und Dada: Ein Forschungsbericht mit neuen Dokumenten*, Siegen: Universität-Gesamthochschule, 1989.

Schuhmann, Klaus, ed., *Sankt Ziegenzack springt aus dem Ei: Texte, Bilder und Dokumente zum Dadaismus in Zürich, Berlin, Hannover und Köln*, Leipzig: Kiepenheuer, 1991.

Schwab, Waltraut, "Emmy Ball-Hennings (1885–1948)," in Britta Jürgs, ed., *Wie eine Nilbraut, die man in die Wellen wirft: Portraits expressionistischer Künstlerinnen und Schriftstellerinnen*, Berlin: Aviva, 1998, 195–215.

Schwitters, Kurt: *Das literarische Werk*, 5 vols, ed. Friedhelm Lach, Cologne: DuMont, 1973–1981.

———, *Poems, Performance Pieces, Proses, Plays, Poetics*, ed. Jerome Rothenberg and Pierre Joris, Philadelphia, PA: Temple University Press, 1993.

Segel, Harold B., "Zurich: Dada & Cabaret Voltaire," in H.B. Segel, *Turn-of-the-Century Cabaret: Paris, Barcelona, Berlin, Munich, Vienna, Cracow, Moscow, St. Petersburg, Zürich*, New York: Columbia University Press, 1987, 321–361.

Serner, Walter, *Hirngeschwür: Walter Serner und Dada. Text und Materialien*, ed. Thomas Milch, Erlangen: Renner, 1977.

———, *Das Gesamte Werk*, vol. 2: *Das Hirngeschwür. Dada*, ed. Thomas Milch, Erlangen: Renner, 1977.

———, *Das Gesamte Werk*, vol. 8: *Der Abreiser. Materialien zu Leben und Werk*, Munich: Renner, 1984.

———, *Letzte Lockerung: Manifest Dada*, Hanover: Steegemann, 1920; reprinted Munich: Renner, 1989. Also in *Das Gesamte Werk*, vol. 2, 158–192.

———, *Dr. Walter Serner 1889–1942: Ein Ausstellungsbuch*, ed. Herbert Wiesner, Exh. cat. Berlin: Literaturhaus, 1989.

Sheppard, Richard, "Hugo Ball an Käthe Brodnitz: Bisher unveröffentlichte Briefe und Kurzmitteilungen aus den Dada-Jahren," *Jahrbuch der Deutschen Schiller Gesellschaft* 16 (1972), 37–70.

———, "Ferdinand Hardekopf und Dada," *Jahrbuch der Schillergesellschaft* 20 (1976), 132–161.

———, "What is Dada?" *Orbis Litterarum* 34 (1979), 175–207.

———, "Dada and Politics," *Journal of European Studies* 9 (1979), 39–74; rev. and expanded version in Richard Sheppard, *Modernism–Dada–Postmodernism*, Evanston, IL: Northwestern University Press, 2000, 304–350.

———, *Richard Huelsenbeck*, Hamburg: Christians, 1982.

———, *Modernism–Dada–Postmodernism*, Evanston, IL: Northwestern University Press, 2000.

Sheppard, Richard, ed., *Dada: Studies of a Movement*, Chalfont St. Giles: Alpha Academic, 1980.

———, *New Studies in Dada: Essays and Documents*, Driffield: Hutton Press, 1981.

———, *Zürich–"Dadaco"–"Dadaglobe": The Correspondence between Richard Huelsenbeck, Tristan Tzara and Kurt Wolff (1916–1924)*, Fife: Hutton Press, 1982.

———, *Dada Zürich in Zeitungen: Cabarets, Ausstellungen, Berichte und Bluffs*, Siegen: Universität—Gesamthochschule, 1992.

Soupault, Philippe, *Mémoires de l'oubli, 1914–1923*, Paris: Lachenal et Ritter, 1981.

———, *Vingt mille et un jours: Entretiens avec Serge Fauchereau*, Paris: Belfond, 1980.

Staber, Margit, *Sophie Taeuber-Arp*, Lausanne: Éditions Rencontre, 1970.

Steinbrenner, Manfred, *"Flucht aus der Zeit?": Anarchismus, Kulturkritik und christliche Mystik. Hugo Balls "Konversionen,"* Frankfurt am Main: Lang, 1985.

Steinke, Gerhardt Edward, *The Life and Work of Hugo Ball, Founder of Dadaism*, The Hague and Paris: Mouton, 1967.

Sullivan, Esther Beth, "Reading Dada Performance in Zurich through Nietzsche and Bergson," *Theater Studies* 15 (1990), 5–17.

Tison-Braun, Micheline, *Tristan Tzara, inventeur de l'homme nouveau*, Paris: Nizet, 1977.

Tzara, Tristan, *Sept manifestes Dada*, Paris: Budry, 1924; reprinted as *Lampisteries, précédées des sept manifestes Dada*, Paris: Pauvert, 1963; German edn *7 Dada Manifeste*, Hamburg: MaD Verlag, 1976; English edn *Seven Dada Manifestos and Lampisteries*, London: Calder, 1977; New York: Riverrun Press, 1981.

———, "Memoirs of Dadaism," in Edmund Wilson, *Axel's Castle*, New York: Scribner's, 1931, 304–312.

———, *Approximate Man, and Other Writings*, ed. Mary Ann Caws, Detroit, MI: Wayne State University Press, 1973.

———, *Tristan Tzara*. Special issue of *Europe: Revue littéraire mensuelle* 53:555–556 (July–August 1975).

———, *Œuvres complètes*, ed. Henri Béhar, 6 vols, Paris: Flammarion, 1975–1991.

———, *Dada est tatou, tout est Dada*, ed. Henri Béhar, Paris: Flammarion, 1996.

———, *Dada terminus: Tristan Tzara—E.L.T. Mesens: Correspondence choisie, 1923–1926*, ed. Stéphane Massonet, Brussels: Devillez, 1997.

Valeriani, Luisa, ed., *Dada Zurigo: Ball e il Cabaret Voltaire*, Turin: Martano, 1971.

Van den Berg, Hubert, "Dada Zürich, Anarchismus und Bohème," *Neophilologicus* 71 (1987), 575–585.

———, "Tristan Tzaras *Manifeste Dada 1918*," *Neophilologicus* 79 (1995), 353–376.

———, *Avantgarde und Anarchismus: Dada in Zürich und Berlin*, Heidelberg: Winter, 1999.

Verkauf, Willy, ed., *Dada: Monographie einer Bewegung*, Teufen: Niggli, 1957; 2nd edn, 1965; English edn *Dada: Monograph of a Movement*, New York: Wittenborn, 1957; 2nd edn, New York: Hastings-House 1961; 3rd edn, London: Academy Editions, 1975.

Vingt-trois manifestes du mouvement Dada. Special issue of *Littérature: Revue mensuelle* 2:13 (May 1920).

Wacker, Bernd, ed., *Dionysius DADA Areopagita: Hugo Ball und die Kritik der Moderne*. Paderborn: Schöningh, 1996.

Waldberg, Patrick, Michel Sanouillet, and Robert Lebel, *Dada, surréalisme*, Paris: Rive Gauche Productions, 1981.

Watts, Harriett, *Chance: A Perspective on Dada*, Ann Arbor, MI: UMI, 1980.

———, "The Dada Event: From Transsubstantiation to Bones and Barking," in Stephen C. Foster, ed., *"Event" Arts and Art Events*, Ann Arbor, MI: UMI, 1988, 119–131.

Webster, Gwendolen: *Kurt Merz Schwitters: A Biographical Study*, Cardiff: University of Wales Press, 1997.

White, Erdmute Wenzel, *The Magic Bishop: Hugo Ball, Dada Poet*, Columbia, SC: Camden House, 1998.

Whitton, David, "Tristan Tzara's *Mouchoir de nuages*," *Theatre Research International* 14 (1989), 271–287.

Wilson, Ruth, "The Plays of Tristan Tzara," *Yale Theater* 4 (1973), 129–151.

CONSTRUCTIVISM: GENERAL
AND RUSSIAN

Adaskina, Natalia Lvovna and Dimitri Vladimirovich Sarabianov, *Lioubov Popova*, Paris: Sers, 1989; English edn *Popova*, New York: Abrams, 1990.

Amiard-Chevrel, Claudine, "Entre peinture et architecture: Vesnine au Théâtre de Chambre," in Gérard Conio, ed., *L'Avant-garde russe et la synthèse des arts*, Lausanne: L'Age d'Homme, 1990, 181–188.

Amiard-Chevrel, Claudine, ed., *Théâtre et cinéma années vingt: Une quête de la modernité*, 2 vols, Lausanne: L'Age d'Homme, 1990.

Art into Life: Russian Constructivism 1914–1932, Exh. cat. Seattle/WA: The Henry Art Gallery, University of Washington, 1990; New York: Rizzoli, 1990.

Baer Nancy Van Norman, *Theatre in Revolution: Russian Avant-garde Stage Design, 1913–1935*, Exh. cat. San Francisco: Fine Arts Museums, 1991; London: Thames and Hudson, 1991.

Bann, Stephen, ed., *The Tradition of Constructivism*, New York: Viking Press, 1974, New York: Da Capo Press, 1990.

Bauer, Oswald Georg, ed., *Entfesselt: Die russische Bühne 1900–1930. Aus der Sammlung des Staatlichen Zentralen A. A. Bachruschin-Theatermuseums, Moskau*, Exh. cat. München: Bayrische Akademie der Schönen Künste, 1994.

Bochow, Jörg, *Das Theater Meyerholds und die Biomechanik*, Berlin: Alexander, 1997.

Bowlt, John E., "Constructivism and Russian Stage Design," *Performing Arts Journal* 1:3 (Winter 1977), 62–84.

Bowlt, John E., ed., *Twentieth Century Russian and Ukrainian Stage Design*. Special issue of *Russian History* 8:1–2 (1981).

———, *Russian Art of the Avant-garde: Theory and Criticism 1902–1934*, London: Thames and Hudson, 1988.

———, *Stage Designs and the Russian Avant-garde (1911–1929): A Loan Exhibition of Stage and Costume Designs from the Collection of Mr. and Mrs. Nikita D. Lobanov-Rostovsky*, Exh. cat. Washington, DC: International Exhibitions Foundation, 1976–1978.

———, *L'Avant-garde russe et la scène, 1910–1930: Une sélection de la collection N. D. Lobanov-Rostovsky*, Exh. cat. Brussels: Musée d'Ixelles, 1998; Wommelgem: Blondé Artprinting International, 1998.

Bowlt, John E. and Alexander Lavrentiev, *Stepanova: The Complete Work*, Cambridge, MA: MIT Press, 1988.

Bowlt, John E. and Olga Matich, eds., *Laboratory of Dreams: The Russian Avant-garde and Cultural Experiment*, Stanford, CA: Stanford University Press, 1996.

Rickey, George, *Constructivism: Origins and Evolution*, New York: Braziller, 1967.

Braun, Edward, "Constructivism in the Theatre," in *Art in Revolution*, Exh. cat. London: Hayward Gallery, 1971, 59–81.

———, *The Theatre of Meyerhold: Revolution on the Modern Stage*, London: Eyre Methuen, 1979.

———, *Meyerhold: A Revolution in Theatre*, London: Methuen, 1995.

Carter, Huntly, *The New Spirit in the Russian Theatre, 1917–28, and a Sketch of the Russian Kinema and Radio 1919–28, Showing the New Communal Relationship between the Three*, New York: Brentano, 1929.

Caton, Joseph Harris, *The Utopian Vision of Moholy-Nagy*, Ann Arbor, MI: UMI, 1984.

Ciofi degli Atti, Fabio and Daniela Ferretti, eds., *Russia 1900–1930: L'arte della scena*, Exh. cat. Venice: Museo d'Arte Moderna Ca' Pesaro, 1990; Milan: Electa, 1990.

Cohen, Ronny H., "Alexandra Exter's Designs for the Theatre," *Artforum* 19:10 (June 1981), 56–49.

Conio, Gérard, ed., *Le Constructivisme russe: Textes théoriques, manifestes, documents*, 2 vols, Lausanne: L'Age d'Homme, 1987.

———, *L'Avant-garde russe et la synthèse des arts*, Lausanne: L'Age d'Homme, 1990.

Curjel, Hans, "Moholy-Nagy und das Theater," *du/atlantis* 24 (November 1964), 11–14.

Dada-Constructivism: The Janus Face of the Twenties, Exh. cat. London: Annely Juda Fine Art, 1984.

De Stijl; Cercle et Carré: Entwicklungen des Konstruktivismus in Europa ab 1917, Exh. cat. Cologne: Galerie Gmurzynska, 1974.

Deutsche Avantgarde 1915–1936 (Konstruktivisten), Exh. cat. Cologne: Galerie Gmurzynska-Bargera, 1971–1972.

[Exter, Alexandra] *Alexandra Exter*, Exh. cat. ed. Andrei B. Nakov, Paris: Galerie Jean Chauvelin, 1972.

————, *Alexandra Exter: Artist of the Theatre. Four Essays with an Illustrated Check-List of Scenic and Costume Designs*, Exh. cat. New York: Vincent Astor Gallery and the New York Public Library at Lincoln Centre, 1974, New York: New York Public Library, 1974.

————, *Alexandra Exter e il Teatro da Camera/Aleksandra Ekster i Kamernyi teatr*, Exh. cat. ed. Fabio Ciofi degli Atti and Mikhail M. Kolesnikov, Rovereto: Museo d' Arte Moderna e Contemporanea di Trento e Rovereto, 1991; Milan: Electa, 1991.

Finkeldey, Bernd, ed., *Konstruktivistische Internationale: Schöpferische Arbeitsgemeinschaft 1922–1927: Utopien für eine europäische Kultur*, Exh. cat. Düsseldorf: Kunstsammlung Nordrhein-Westfalen, 1992; Stuttgart: Hatje, 1992.

The First Russian Show: A Commemoration of the Van Diemen Exhibition Berlin 1922, Exh. cat. London: Juda Fine Art, 1983.

From Painting to Design: Russian Constructivist Art of the Twenties/Von der Malerei zum Design: Russische konstruktivistische Kunst der Zwanziger Jahre, Exh. cat. Cologne: Galerie Gmurzynska, 1981.

Fülöp-Miller, René and Joseph Gregor, *The Russian Theatre: Its Character and History with Especial Reference to the Revolutionary Period*, London: Harrap, 1930.

Gassner, Hubertus, ed., *Wechsel Wirkungen: Ungarische Avant-garde in der Weimarer Republik*, Exh. cat. Kassel: Neue Galerie, 1986–1987.

Gassner, Hubertus and Eckhart Gillen, eds., *Zwischen Revolutionskunst und Sozialistischem Realismus: Dokumente und Kommentare. Kunstdebatten in der Sowjetunion von 1917 bis 1934*, Cologne: DuMont, 1979.

Gladkov, Aleksandr Konstantinovich, *Meyerhold Speaks, Meyerhold Rehearses*, Amsterdam: Harwood, 1997.

Gordon, Mel, "Meyerhold's Biomechanics," *The Drama Review* 18:3 [T63] (September 1974), 73–88.

The Great Utopia: The Russian and Soviet Avant-garde, 1915–1932, Exh. cat. New York: Solomon R. Guggenheim Museum, 1992.

Grübel, Rainer Georg, *Russischer Konstruktivismus: Künstlerische Konzeptionen, literarische Theorie und kultureller Kontext*, Wiesbaden: Harrassowitz, 1981.

Hammer, Martin, *Constructing Modernity: The Art and Career of Naum Gabo*, New Haven, CT: Yale University Press, 2000.

Hamon-Siréjols, Christine, " 'La Terre Cabrée' de Martinet: Adaption de Tretiakov, mise en scène de Meyerhold au TIM," in Denis Bablet, ed., *Les Voies de la création théâtrale*, vol. 7: *Mises en scène années 20 et 30*, Paris: Centre National de la Recherche Scientifique, 1979, 45–60.

Hamon-Siréjols, *Le Constructivisme au théâtre*, Paris: Centre National de la Recherche Scientifique, 1992.

Harten, Jürgen, ed., *Vladimir Tatlin: Leben, Werk, Wirkung. Ein internationales Symposium*, Cologne: DuMont, 1993.

Heidt, Renate, ed., *Alexander Rodtschenko und Warwara Stepanowa: Werke aus sowjetischen Museen*, Exh. cat. Duisburg: Wilhelm-Lehmbruck-Museum, 1982–1983.

Hight, Eleanor M., ed., *Moholy-Nagy: Photography and Film in Weimar Germany*, Exh. cat. Wellesley, MA: Wellesley College Museum, 1985.

Hirdina, Karin, *Pathos der Sachlichkeit: Tendenzen materialistischer Ästhetik in den zwanziger Jahren*, Berlin: Dietz, 1981.

Hoover, Marjorie L., *Meyerhold: The Art of Conscious Theater*, Amherst, MA: University of Massachusetts Press, 1974.

——, *Meyerhold and His Set Designers*, New York: Lang, 1988.

Poling, Clark V., ed., *Kandinsky: Russian and Bauhaus Years 1915–1933*, Exh. cat. New York: Solomon R. Guggenheim Museum, 1983.

Khan-Magomedov, Selim Omarovich, *Rodchenko: The Complete Work*, London: Thames and Hudson, 1986.

——, *Alexandr Vesnin and Russian Constructivism*, New York: Rizzoli, 1986.

——, *VHUTEMAS, Moscou 1920–1930*, 2 vols, Paris: Éditions du Regard, 1990.

Kleberg, Lars, *Theatre as Action*, Houndsmill: Macmillan, 1993.

Konstruktive Kunst: Elemente und Prinzipien, Exh. cat. Nuremberg: Kunsthalle and Institut für Moderne Kunst, 1969.

Korvacs, Istvan, "Totality through Light: The Work of Laszlo Moholy-Nagy," *Form* (Girton, Cambridge) 6 (December 1967), 14–19.

Kovtun, Yevgenij F., *Sangesi: Chlebnikow und seine Maler*, Zurich: Stemmle, 1993.

——, *The Russian Avant-garde in the 1920s and 30s*, Bournemouth: Parkstone, 1996.

Kunst und Technik in den 20er Jahren: Neue Sachlichkeit und gegenständlicher Konstruktivismus, Exh. cat. Munich: Städtische Galerie im Lenbachhaus, 1980.

Lavrentiev, Alexander, *Varvara Stepanova: A Constructivist Life*, London: Thames and Hudson, 1988.

Law, Alma, "The Revolution in Russian Theater," in Stephanie Barron and Maurice Tuchman, eds., *The Avant-garde in Russia, 1910–1930: New Perspectives*, Exh. cat. Los Angeles: Los Angeles County Museum of Art, 1980, 64–71.

——, "The Death of Tarelkin: A Constructivist Vision of Tsarist Russia," *Russian History* 8:1–2 (1982), 145–198.

——, "Meyerhold's *The Magnanimous Cuckold*," *The Drama Review* 26:1 (T93) (Spring 1982), 61–86.

——, " 'Le Cocu magnifique' de Crommelynck," in Denis Bablet, ed., *Les Voies de la création théâtrale*, vol. 7: *Mises en scène années 20 et 30*, Paris: Centre National de la Recherche Scientifique, 1979, 13–43.

Law, Alma H. and Mel Gordon, *Meyerhold, Eisenstein, and Biomechanics: Actor Training in Revolutionary Russia*, Jefferson, NC: McFarland, 1996.

Leach, Robert, *Vsevolod Meyerhold*, Cambridge: Cambridge University Press, 1989.

———, *Revolutionary Theatre*, London: Routledge, 1994.

Leger et l'esprit moderne: Une alternative d'avant-garde à l'art non-objectif (1918–1931), Exh. cat. Paris: Musee d'Art Moderne de la Ville de Paris, 1982; English edn *Leger and the Modern Spirit: An Avant-garde Alternative to Non Objective Art (1918–1931)* Houston, TX: Museum of Fine Arts, 1982; Stuttgart: Metzler, 1982.

Lodder, Christina, *Russian Constructivism*, New Haven, CT: Yale University Press, 1983.

Lissitzky, El, "The Electrical-Mechanical Spectacle," *Form* (Girton, Cambridge) 3 (December 1966), 12–14.

———, *El Lissitzky: Maler, Architekt, Typograf, Fotograf. Erinnerungen, Briefe, Schriften*, ed. Sophie Lissitzky-Küppers, Dresden: VEB Verlag der Kunst, 1967; 2nd edn, *Proun und Wolkenbügel: Schriften, Briefe, Dokumente*, ed. Sophie Lissitzky-Küppers and Jen Lissitzky, Dresden: Verlag der Kunst, 1977; English edn *El Lissitzky: Life, Letters, Texts*, Greenwich, CN, New York Graphic Society [1968].

Mansbach, Steven A., *Visions of Totality: Laszlo Moholy-Nagy, Theo Van Doesburg, and El Lissitzky*, Ann Arbor, MI: UMI, 1979.

Marcadé, Jean-Claude and Valentine Marcadé, *L'Avant-garde au féminin: Moscou, Saint-Petersbourg, Paris (1907–1930)*, Paris: Artcurial, 1983.

Martin, Leslie, Ben Nicholson, and Naum Gabo, *Circle: International Survey of Constructive Art*, London: Faber, 1937; reprinted Faber and Faber, 1971.

Merkert, Jörn, *Naum Gabo: Ein russischer Konstruktivist in Berlin 1922–1932*, Berlin: Nishen, 1989.

Meyerhold, Vsevolod, *Meyerhold on Theatre*, ed. Edward Braun, London: Methuen, 1969.

Milner John, *Russian Revolutionary Art*, London: Oresko Books, 1979; 2nd edn, London: Bloomsbury Books, 1987.

———, *The Exhibition 5 ×5 = 25: Its Background and Significance*, Budapest: Helikon Artists Bookworks, 1992.

———, *Vladimir Tatlin and the Russian Avant-garde*, New Haven, CT: Yale University Press, 1983.

Moholy-Nagy, László, *Vom Material zur Architektur*, Munich: Langen, 1924; reprinted Mainz: Kupferberg, 1968; English edn *The New Vision: From Material to Architecture*, New York: Brewer, Warren and Putnam, 1930; 2nd rev. edn, *The New Vision: Fundamentals of Design*, New York: Norton, 1938; 3rd rev. edn, *The New Vision and Abstract of an Artist*, New York: Wittenborn 1946; 4th rev. edn, 1947.

———, *Malerei, Photographie, Film*, Munich: Langen, 1925; 2nd edn, 1927; reprinted Mainz: Kupferberg 1967; English edn *Painting, Photography, Film*, London: Lund Humphries, 1969; Cambridge, MA: MIT Press, 1987.

Moholy-Nagy, "Lichtrequisit einer elektrischen Bühne," *Die Form: Zeitschrift für gestaltende Arbeit* 5:11–12 (July 7, 1930), 297–299.

————, *Laszlo Moholy-Nagy, Laszlo Peri: Zwei Künstler der ungarischen Avantgarde in Berlin 1920–1925*, Exh. cat. Bremen: Graphisches Kabinett Kunsthandel Wolfgang Werner, 1987.

————, *Moholy Nagy*, ed. Richard Kostelanetz, New York: Praeger, 1970; 2nd edn *Moholy-Nagy: An Anthology*, New York: Da Capo Press, 1991.

Moholy-Nagy, Sibyl, *Moholy-Nagy: Experiment in Totality*, New York: Harper, 1950; 2nd edn, Cambridge, MA: M.I.T. 1969.

The Moscow Kamerny Theatre, Moscow: Intourist [1934?].

Nakov, Andrei B., ed., *Tatlin's Dream: Russian Suprematist and Constructivist Art 1910–1923*, Exh. cat. London: Fischer Fine Art, 1973–1974.

————, *Russian Constructivism: "Laboratory Period": Ermilov, Exter, Klucis, Lissitzky, Popova, Rodchenko, Tatlin, Vesnin*, Exh. cat. London: Annely Juda Fine Art, 1975.

Nash, Steven A. and Jörn Merkert, eds., *Naum Gabo: Sixty Years of Constructivism*, Exh. cat. Dallas, TX: Dallas Museum of Art, 1985, Munich: Prestel, 1985.

Noever, Peter, ed., *Aleksandr M. Rodchenko, Varvara F. Stepanova: The Future Is Our Only Goal*, Exh. cat. Vienna: Österreichisches Museum für Angewandte Kunst, 1991; Munich: Prestel, 1991.

Passuth, Krisztina, *Moholy-Nagy*, London: Thames and Hudson, 1985.

Picon-Vallin, Béatrice, *Meyerhold*, Paris: Centre National de la Recherche Scientifique, 1990.

————, " 'Octobre Theâtrale et la transformation de l'espace scénique et du jeu de l'acteur," in Gérard Conio, ed., *L'Avant-garde russe et la synthèse des arts*, Lausanne: L'Age d'Homme, 1990, 189–196.

Popova, Liubov, "From Her Manuscripts and Notes," in Krystyna Rubinger, ed., *Künstlerinnen der russischen Avantgarde/Women-Artists of the Russian Avantgarde 1910–1930*, Exh. cat. Cologne: Galerie Gmurzynska, 1979–1980, 211–214.

————, *Liubov Popova*, Exh. cat. ed. Magdalena Dabrowski, New York: Museum of Modern Art, 1991; New York: Abrams, 1991; rev. and enlarged edn, Cologne: Museum Ludwig, 1991; Munich: Prestel, 1991.

Quilici, Vieri, ed., *Rodcenko e Stepanova: Alle origini del costruttivismo*, Milan: Electa, 1984.

Raumkonzepte: Konstruktivistische Tendenzen in Bühnen- und Bildkunst, 1910–1930, Exh. cat. Frankfurt am Main: Städtische Galerie im Städelschen Kunstinstitut, 1986.

Rave, Horst, ed., *Die Explosion des Schwarzen Quadrats: Realität und Utopie der rationalen Kunst. Symposion 6. bis 8. Oktober 1989*, Bonn: Gesellschaft für Kunst und Gestaltung, 1990.

Richter, Horst, ed., *El Lissitzky: Sieg über die Sonne. Zur Kunst des Konstruktivismus*, Exh. cat. Cologne: Galerie Christoph Czwiklitzer, 1958.

Rickey, George, *Constructivism: Origins and Evolution*, London: Studio Vista, 1968.

Rodchenko, Alexandr, *Écrits complets sur l'art, l'architecture et la révolution*, ed. Alexandre N. Lavrentiev, Paris: Sers, 1988.

————, *Aufsätze, Autobiographische Notizen, Briefe, Erinnerungen*, Dresden: Verlag der Kunst, 1993.

Rotzler, Willy, *Konstruktive Konzepte: Eine Geschichte der konstruktiven Kunst vom Kubismus bis heute*, Zurich: ABC, 1977; 3rd rev. edn, Zurich: ABC, 1995; English edn *Constructive Concepts: A History of Constructive Art from Cubism to the Present*, New York: Rizzoli, 1989.

Rubinger, Krystyna, ed., *Künstlerinnen der russischen Avantgarde/Women-Artists of the Russian Avantgarde 1910–1930*, Exh. cat. Cologne: Galerie Gmurzynska, 1979–1980.

Rudnitsky, Konstantin Lazarevich, *Meyerhold the Director*, Ann Arbor, MI: Ardis, 1981.

————, *Russian and Soviet Theatre*, London: Thames and Hudson, 1988.

Roman, Gail Harrison, ed., *When All the World Was a Stage: Russian Constructivist Theatre Design*, Exh. cat. Louisville, KY: J.B. Speed Art Museum, 1989.

Russian Constructivism and Suprematism, 1914–1930, Exh. cat. London: Annely Juda Fine Art, 1991.

Russian Constructivism Revisited, Exh. cat. Newcastle upon Tyne: Hatton Gallery, 1973.

Schmidt, Siegfried J., *Der Kopf, die Welt, die Kunst: Konstruktivismus als Theorie und Praxis*, Vienna: Böhlau, 1992.

Souritz, Elizabeth, "Soviet Ballet of the 1920s and the Influence of Constructivism," *Soviet Union/Union Soviétique* 7:1–2 (1980), 112–137.

————, *Soviet Choreographers in the 1920s*, Durham, NC: Duke University Press, 1990.

————, "Constructivism and Dance," in Nancy van Norman Beer, ed., *Theatre in Revolution*, London: Thames and Hudson, 1991, 129–143.

Spielmann, Heinz, ed., *Die russische Avantgarde und die Bühne 1890–1930*, Exh. cat. Schleswig: Schleswig-Holsteinisches Landesmuseum Schloss Gottorf, 1991.

Stepanova, Varvara, "Occasional Notes," in *From Painting to Design: Russian Constructivist Art of the Twenties*, Exh. cat. Cologne: Galerie Gmurzynska, 1981, 122–144.

[Stenberg, Georgi, and Vladimir], "Conversation with Vladimir Stenberg," *Art Journal* 41:3 (Fall 1981), 222–233.

————, *2 Stenberg 2: La period "laboratoire" (1919–1921) du constructivisme russe/The "Laboratory" Period (1919–1921) of Russian Constructivism*, Exh. cat. ed. Andrei B. Nakov, London: Annely Juda Fine Art, 1975; London: Idea-Books, 1975.

————, *Stenberg Brothers: Constructing a Revolution in Soviet Design*, Exh. cat. ed. Christopher Mount, New York: Museum of Modern Art, 1997; New York: Abrams, 1997.

Steneberg, Eberhard, *Russische Kunst, Berlin 1919–1932*, Berlin: Gebrüder Mann, 1969.

Symons, James M., *Meyerhold's Theatre of the Grotesque: The Post-Revolutionary Productions, 1920–1932*, Coral Gables, FL: University of Miami Press, 1971.

Tairov, Aleksandr Yakovlevich, *Das entfesselte Theater*, Potsdam: Kiepenheuer, 1923; 2nd edn, 1927; Cologne: Kiepenheuer und Witsch, 1964; English edn *Notes of a*

Director, Coral Gables, FA: University of Miami Press, 1969; French edn *Taïrov: Le Théâtre libéré*, ed. Claudine Amiard-Chevrel, Lausanne: L'Age d'Homme, 1974.

Vladimir Tatlin: Retrospektive/Vladimir Tatlin: Retrospektiva, Exh. cat. ed. Jürgen Harten, Düsseldorf: Städtische Kunsthalle 1993; Cologne: DuMont, 1993.

Watzlawick, Paul, *The Invented Reality: Essays on Constructivism*, New York: Norton, 1985.

Weitemeier, Hannah, *Licht-Visionen: Ein Experiment von Moholy-Nagy*, Berlin: Bauhaus-Archiv, 1972.

Williams, Robert Chadwell, *Artists in Revolution: Portrait of the Russian Avant-garde, 1905–1925*, Bloomington, IN: Indiana University Press, 1977.

Worrall, Nick, "Meyerhold's 'The Magnificent Cuckold,' " *The Drama Review* 17:1 (T57) (March 1973), 14–34.

———, *Modernism to Realism on the Soviet Stage: Tairov–Vakhtangov–Okhlopkov*, Cambridge: Cambridge University Press, 1989.

Yablonskaya, Myuda Naumovna, *Women Artists of Russia's New Age, 1900–1935*, London: Thames and Hudson, 1990.

Zelikson, Michael, ed., *The Artists of the Kamerni Theater, 1914–1934*, Moscow: Ogiz, 1935.

Zhadova, Larissa Alekseevna, ed., *Tatlin*, London: Thames and Hudson, 1988.

BAUHAUS AND GERMAN CONSTRUCTIVISM

Bajkay-Rosch, Eva, "A Hungarian Stage Designer of the Bauhaus," *The Hungarian Quarterly* 92 (1983), 199–202.

Bauhaus. Special issue of *ICSAC-Cahier* 6/7. Brussels: Internationaal Centrum voor Structuuranalyse en Constructivisme, 1987.

Bauhaus, Exh. cat. Dublin: Douglas Hyde Gallery, Trinity College, 1979; Stuttgart: Institut für Auslandsbeziehungen, 1979.

Bauhaus: Fifty Years. German Exhibition, London: Royal Academy of Arts, 1968; German edn *Bauhaus: 50 Jahre*, Stuttgart: Württembergischer Kunstverein, 1968.

Bauhaus Dessau Dimensionen 1925–1932, Exh. cat. Dessau: Bauhaus, 1993.

Bauhaus: Dessau, 1926–1931. Faksimile Reprint, Nendeln/Liechtenstein: Kraus Reprint, 1976.

Bauhaus 1919–1933: Meister- und Schülerarbeiten Weimar, Dessau, Berlin, Exh. cat. Zurich: Museum für Gestaltung, 1988; Berne: Benteli, 1988.

Bauhaus Weimar: Werkstattarbeiten 1919–1925, Exh. cat. Weimar: Kunsthalle am Theaterplatz, 1989.

Bauhaus: Zeitschrift für Gestaltung 1–3 (1926–1931), Nendeln: Kraus Reprint, 1977.

Bayer, Herbert, Walter Gropius, and Ilse Gropius, eds., *Bauhaus, 1919–1928*, New York: Museum of Modern Art, 1938; London: George Allen and Unwin, 1939; Boston, MA: Branford, 1952; 1959; New York: Museum of Modern Art, 1972; German edn, Stuttgart: Hatje, 1952, 1955, 1959, 1972, 1975.

Bortoluzzi, Alfredo, "Meine Erinnerungen an die Bauhaus-Bühne," *Das Kunstwerk* 8:12 (February 1959), 37–38.

Bothe, Rolf, Peter Hahn, and Hans Christoph von Tavel, eds, *Das frühe Bauhaus und Johannes Itten: Katalogbuch anläßlich des 75. Gründungsjubiläums des Staatlichen Bauhauses in Weimar*, Exh. cat. Weimar: Kunstsammlungen zu Weimar, 1994; Ostfildern-Ruit: Hatje, 1994.

Clemens, Roman, *Bühnenbilder*, Zurich: Orell Füssli, 1941.

———, *Bühne und Raum: Roman Clemens. Bühnenbildner. Architekt. Gestalter*, Exh. cat. Munich: Theatermuseum, 1970.

Draffin, Nicholas, ed., *Two Masters of the Weimar Bauhaus: Lyonel Feininger, Ludwig Hirschfeld-Mack*, Exh. cat. Sydney: Art Gallery of New South Wales, 1974.

Droste, Magdalena, *Bauhaus 1919–1933*, Cologne: Taschen, 1998.

Droste, Magdalena, ed., *Experiment Bauhaus: Das Bauhaus-Archiv, Berlin (West) zu Gast im Bauhaus Dessau*, Exh. cat. Dessau: Bauhaus, 1988; Berlin: Kupfergraben Verlagsgesellschaft, 1988.

Farmer, John David and Geraldine Weiss, eds., *Concepts of the Bauhaus: The Busch-Reisinger Museum Collection*, Exh. cat. Cambridge, MA: Busch-Reisinger Museum, 1971.

Fiedler, Jeannine and Peter Feierabend, *Bauhaus*, Cologne: Könemann, 2000.

Flocon, Albert, *Scénographies au Bauhaus: Dessau 1927–1930. Hommage à Oskar Schlemmer en plusieurs tableaux*, Paris: Séguier, 1987.

Forgacs, Eva, *The Bauhaus Idea and Bauhaus Politics*, Budapest and New York: Central European University Press, 1995.

Franciscono, Marcel, *Walter Gropius and the Creation of the Bauhaus in Weimar: The Ideals and Artistic Theories of its Founding Years*, Urbana, IL: University of Illinois Press, 1971.

Gilbert, Basil, "The Reflected Light Compositions of Ludwig Hirschfeld-Mack," *Form* (Girton, Cambridge) 2 (September 1, 1966), 10–14.

Greenberg, Allan Carl, *Artists and Revolution: Dada and the Bauhaus, 1917–1925*, Ann Arbor, MI: UMI, 1979.

Hahn, Peter, ed., *Kandinsky: The Russian and Bauhaus Years*, Exh. cat. New York: Solomon R. Guggenheim Museum, 1983; German edn *Kandinsky: Russische Zeit und Bauhausjahre 1915–1933*, Berlin: Bauhaus-Archiv, 1984; Berlin: Publica, 1984.

Herold, Marianne, *Roman Clemens*, Zurich: ABC Verlag, 1991.

Herzogenrath, Wulf, "Die Bühne am Bauhaus," in *Bauhaus Utopien: Arbeiten auf Papier*, Exh. cat. Cologne: Kölnischer Kunstverein, 1988; Stuttgart: Cantz, 1988, 295–313.

Hirschfeld-Mack, Ludwig, *Farbenlicht-Spiele: Wesen–Ziele–Kritiken*, Weimar: Private Edition, 1925.

———, *The Bauhaus: An Introductory Survey*, Croydon, Victoria, Australia: Longmans, 1963.

———, *Ludwig Hirschfeld-Mack, Bauhäusler und Visionär*, Exh. cat. ed. Andreas Hapkemeyer and Peter Stasny, Bozen: Museion—Museum für Moderne Kunst, 2000; Ostfildern: Hatje Cantz, 2000.

Hochman, Elaine S., *Bauhaus: Crucible of Modernism*, New York: Fromm International, 1997.

Holz, Hans Heinz, *Xanti Schawinsky: Bewegung im Raum, Bewegung des Raums*, Zurich: ABC-Verlag, 1981.

Hühneke, Andreas, "Oskar Schlemmer und die Bauhausbühne," *Bauhaus* 5: 97. *Verkaufsausstellung 21.11.–20.12. 1981. Katalog 21*, Berlin: Staatlicher Kunsthandel der DDR, 1981, 34–36.

Isaacs, Reginald R., *Walter Gropius: Der Mensch und sein Werk*, 2 vols, Berlin: Mann, 1983; English edn *Gropius: An Illustrated Biography of the Creator of the Bauhaus*, Boston, MA: Little, Brown, and Company, 1991.

"Kathedrale der Zukunft": Zur Gründung des Bauhauses vor 80 Jahren, Weimar: Bauhaus-Universität Weimar, 1999.

Keith-Smith, Brian, *Zwischen Sturm und Bauhaus: Das expressionistische Werk von Lothar Schreyer. Texte 1916–1965*, Stuttgart: Akademischer Verlag Hans-Dieter Heinz, 1985.

Költzsch, Georg-Wilhelm. and Margarita Tupitsyn, eds., *Bauhaus Dessau–Chicago–New York*, Exh. cat. Dessau: Bauhaus, 2000; Cologne: DuMont, 2000.

Krüger, Jochen, "Die Bühne als Laboratorium: Bemerkungen zu Oskar Schlemmer's Bauhaustänzen," *Tanzdrama* 4 (1988), 4–7.

Kuspit, Donald, "Oskar Schlemmer's Bauhaus Dances," *Artforum* 21:8 (April 1983), 70–71.

Lahusen, Susanne, "Oskar Schlemmer: Mechanical Ballets?" *Dance Research* 4:2 (Autumn 1986), 65–77.

Lang, Lothar, *Das Bauhaus 1919–1933: Idee und Wirklichkeit*, Berlin: Zentralinstitut für Formgestaltung, 1966.

Lazarowicz, Klaus, "Dilettantismus und 'strenge Regularität': Über Oskar Schlemmers Bühnentheorie und seine szenischen Experimente," *Maske und Kothurn* 17 (1971), 339–356.

Mauldon, Elizabeth, "Oskar Schlemmer: Bauhaus Dancer and Choreographer," *The Laban Art of Movement Guild Magazine* 53 (November 1974), 5–18.

Maur, Karin von, "Der Bühnengestalter," *Oskar Schlemmer*, Exh. cat. Stuttgart: Württembergischer Kunstverein, 1977, 197–212.

———, "Oskar Schlemmer: Künstlertraum vom Ballett," *art: Das Kunstmagazin* 6 (June 1980), 20–33.

———, *Oskar Schlemmer: Monographie*, Munich: Prestel, 1979.

———, *Oskar Schlemmer: Œuvrekatalog*, Munich: Prestel, 1979.

Michaud, Eric, *Théâtre au Bauhaus (1919–1929)*, Lausanne: L'Age d'Homme, 1978.

Moynihan, D. S., "Oskar Schlemmer's Bauhaus Dances: Debra McCall's Reconstructions," *The Drama Review* 28:3 (T103) (Fall 1984), 46–58.

Neumann, Eckhard, ed., *Bauhaus und Bauhäusler: Bekenntnisse und Erinnerungen*, Berne: Hallwag, 1971; 2nd edn, Cologne: DuMont, 1985; English edn *Bauhaus and Bauhaus People: Personal Opinions and Recollections of Former Bauhaus Members and their Contemporaries*, New York: Van Nostrand Reinhold, 1970; 2nd rev. edn, 1993.

Naylor, Gillian, *The Bauhaus*, London: Studio Vista/Dutton, 1968.

Plassard, Didier, "Ni Théâtre, ni cinéma: Les jeux de lumière colorée au Bauhaus," in Claudine Amiard-Chevrel, ed., *Théâtre et cinéma années vingt: Une quête de la modernité*, vol. 2, Lausanne: L'Age d'Homme, 1990, 25–38.

Poling, Clark V., ed., *Kandinsky: Russian and Bauhaus Years 1915–1933*, Exh. cat. New York: Solomon R. Guggenheim Museum, 1983.

Schädlich, Christian, *Bauhaus Weimar 1919–1925*, Weimar: Ständige Kommission für Kultur der Stadtverordnetenversammlung der Stadt Weimar und des Kreistages Weimar-Land, 1980; 2nd edn, 1989.

Schawinsky, Xanti [Alexander], "Vom Bauhaus-Happening zum Spectrodrama, " *das kunstwerk* 7 (January 1966), 24–28.

———, "Spectrodrama: Play, Life, Illusion (1924–37),"*Form* (Girton, Cambridge) 8 (September 1968), 16–20.

———, "From the Bauhaus to Black Mountain," *The Drama Review* 15:3 (Summer 1971), 31–59.

———, *Xanti Schawinsky: Malerei, Bühne, Grafikdesign, Fotografie*, Exh. cat. Berlin: Bauhaus Archiv, 1986.

Scheper, Dirk, *Oskar Schlemmer: The Triadic Ballett*, Berlin: Akademie der Künste, 1985.

———, *Oskar Schlemmer: Das Triadische Ballett und die Bauhausbühne*, Berlin: Akademie der Künste, 1988.

Schlee, Alfred, "The Stage of the Bauhaus," *Theatre Arts Monthly* 4 (1931), 343–350.

Schlemmer, Oskar, *Briefe und Tagebücher*, ed. Tut Schlemmer, Munich: Langen Müller, 1958; Stuttgart: Hatje, 1977; English edn *The Letters and Diaries*, Middletown, CN: Wesleyan University Press, 1992.

———, *Oskar Schlemmer und die abstrakte Bühne*, Exh. cat. Zurich: Kunst-ge-wer-be-mu-seum, 1961.

———, *Bild und Bühne: Bühenbilder der Gegenwart und Retrospektive "Bühnenelemente" von Oskar Schlemmer*, Exh. cat. Baden Baden: Staatliche Kunsthalle, 1965.

———, *Mostra arte e scena: Mostra di studi teatrali di Oskar Schlemmer*, Exh. cat. Venice: La Biennale di Venezia,1965.

———, *Man: Teaching Notes from the Bauhaus*, ed. Heimo Kuchling and Janet Seligman, London: Lund Humphries, 1971; Cambridge, MA: M.I.T., 1971.

———, *Oskar Schlemmer*, Exh. cat. ed. Arnold L. Lehman and Brenda Richardson, Baltimore, MD: Museum of Art, 1986.

———, *Idealist der Form: Briefe, Tagebücher, Schriften 1912–1943*, ed. Andreas Hüneke, Leipzig: Reclam, 1990.

———, *Oskar Schlemmer: Tanz, Theater, Bühne*, Exh. cat. Düsseldorf: Kunstsammlung Nordrhein-Westfalen, 1994; Stuttgart: Hatje, 1994.

Schlemmer, Oskar and Laszlo Moholy-Nagy, eds., *Die Bühne im Bauhaus*, Munich: Langen, 1925; reprinted edn ed. Hans M. Wingler, Mainz: Kupferberg, 1965; English edn *The Theater of the Bauhaus*, ed. Walter Gropius, Middletown, CN: Wesleyan University Press, 1961; 2nd edn, 1967; London: Eyre Methuen, 1979; Middletown, CN: Johns Hopkins University Press, 1996.

Schlemmer, Tut, *Oskar Schlemmer und die Bauhausbühne: Vortrag*, Zurich: Kunstgewerbeschule, 1961.

———, "Das Datum: 22.9.1923. Tut Schlemmer erinnert sich an das Bauhausfest und das Bauhaustheater," *Theater Heute* 6:5 (May 1965), 37–39.

Schmidt, Dieter, *Bauhaus: Weimar, 1919 bis 1925; Dessau, 1925 bis 1932; Berlin, 1932 bis 1933*, Dresden: VEB Verlag der Kunst, 1966.

Schmidt, Joost, *Lehre und Arbeit am Bauhaus 1919–32*, Düsseldorf: Marzona, 1984.

Schmidt, Kurt, *Bauhaus*, Exh. cat. Gera: Kunstgalerie, 1981.

———, *Kurt Schmidt*, Exh. cat. ed. Ulrike Rüdiger, Gera: Kunstgalerie, 1990.

Schreyer, Lothar, *Erinnerungen an Sturm und Bauhaus: Was ist des Menschen Bild?* Munich: Langen Müller, 1956.

Schöne, Günter, "Oskar Schlemmer and the Theatre of Abstraction," *Theatre Research* 10 (1965), 103–109.

Siebenbrodt, Michael, *Bauhaus Weimar: Entwürfe für die Zukunft*, Ostfildern-Ruit: Hatje Cantz, 2000; English edn *Bauhaus Weimar: Designs for the Future*, Ostfildern-Ruit: Hatje Cantz, 2000.

Staatliches Bauhaus in Weimar 1919–1923, Munich: Langen, and Cologne: Nierendorf, 1923; reprinted Nendeln/Liechtenstein: Kraus Reprint, 1980.

Stuckenschmidt, Hans Heinz, *Musik am Bauhaus*, Berlin: Bauhaus Archiv, 1978.

Tower, Beeke Sell, *Klee and Kandinsky in Munich and at the Bauhaus*, Ann Arbor, MI: UMI, 1981.

Weininger, Andor, "Bauhaus und Stijl," *Form: Internationale Revue* 6 (1959), 7–8.

———, *Andor Weininger: Vom Bauhaus zur konzeptuellen Kunst*, Exh. cat. ed. Jiri Svestka and Katherine Jánszky Michaelsen, Düsseldorf: Kunstverein für die Rheinlande und Westfalen, 1990; English edn *Andor Weininger: From Bauhaus to Conceptual Art*, Düsseldorf: Kunstverein für die Rheinlande und Westfalen, 1991.

———, *Andor Weininger: Weimar 1921, Dessau 1925, Berlin 1928, Amsterdam 1938, Toronto 1951, New York 1958*, Exh. cat. Cologne: Erzbischöfliches Diozesanmuseum, 1999.

———, *Andor Weininger: Zum 100. Geburtstag/100th Birthday Centennial. Schenkung an das Ulmer Museum/Donation to Ulmer Museum*, Exh. cat. ed. Brigitte Reinhardt, Ulm: Ulmer Museum, 1999.

———, *Weininger in Wahn: Arbeiten fürs Bauhaus*, Exh. cat. Cologne: Theatermuseum Wahn, 1999.

———, *Andor Weininger: Works in the Busch-Reisinger Museum*, Exh. cat. ed. by Peter Nisbet, Cambridge, MA: Busch-Reisinger Museum, 2000.

Whitford, Frank, *Bauhaus*, London: Thames and Hudson 1984.

———, *The Bauhaus: Masters and Students by Themselves*, London: Conran Octopus, 1992.

Wick, Rainer K., *Bauhaus-Pädagogik*, Cologne: DuMont, 1982; 2nd edn, 1994.

———, *Bauhaus: Die frühen Jahre*, Wuppertal: Bergische Universität Gesamthochschule Fachbereich 5, 1996.

————, "Kurt Schwerdtfegr (1897–1966): Künstler und Kunstpädagoge," in Johannes Busmann, eds., *Kunst und Architektur: Festschrift für Hermann J. Mahlberg zum 60. Geburtstag*, Wuppertal: Müller und Busmann, 1998, 198–208.

————, *Bauhaus: Kunstschule der Moderne*, Ostfildern-Ruit: Hatje Cantz, 2000; English edn *Teaching at the Bauhaus*, Ostfildern-Ruit: Hatje Cantz, 2000.

Wingler, Hans Maria, ed., *Das Bauhaus, 1919–1933*, Bramsche: Rasch, 1962; 2nd rev. edn, 1968; 3rd rev. edn, 1975; English edn *The Bauhaus: Weimar, Dessau, Berlin, Chicago*, Cambridge, MA: MIT Press, 1969; 2nd edn, 1976.

About the Author ❧

Günter Berghaus was formerly a Reader in Theatre History and Performance Studies, has been Guest Professor at the State University of Rio de Janeiro and at Brown University, Providence/RI, and is now a Senior Research Fellow at the University of Bristol. He has published over a dozen books and a large number of articles on theatre anthropology, avant-garde performance, Renaissance and Baroque theatre, and dance history. He has directed numerous plays from the classical and modern repertoire and devised many productions of an experimental nature. He was principal organizer of several international conferences and held research awards from the Polish Academy of Sciences, the German Research Foundation, the Italian Ministry of Culture, the British Academy, and the Brazilian Ministry of Education.

Other titles by the author include

J. N. Nestroy's Revolutionspossen (1978)
A. Gryphius' "Carolus Stuardus" (1984)
The Reception of the English Revolution, 1640–1669 (1989)
Theatre and Film in Exile (1989)
The Genesis of Futurism (1995)
Fascism and Theatre (1996)
Futurism and Politics (1996)
Italian Futurist Theatre (1998)
On Ritual (1998)
International Futurism in the Arts and Literature (1999)
Theatre Studies and Performance Analysis: New Trends and Methodologies (2001)
New Perspectives on Prehistoric Art (2004)
Avant-garde Performance: Live Events and Electronic Technologies (2005)
F. T. Marinetti: Critical Writings (forthcoming)

Name Index ❦

Subject Index ❧

18528026R00219

Printed in Great Britain
by Amazon